D0948210

BAG OF TOYS

BAG OF TOYS

SEX, SCANDAL, AND THE DEATH MASK MURDER

DAVID FRANCE

WARNER BOOKS

A Time Warner Company

Warner Books, Inc., 1271 Avenue of the Americas, New York, NY 10020

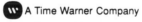 A Time Warner Company

Printed in the United States of America
First printing: June 1992
10 9 8 7 6 5 4 3 2 1

Library of Congress Cataloging-in-Publication Data

France, David.
    Bag of toys : sex, scandal, and the death mask murder
/ by David France.
        p.   cm.
    ISBN 0-446-51606-6
    1. Murder—New York Metropolitan Area—Case studies.   2. Gay men—
New York (N.Y.)—Social conditions—Case studies.
3. Sadomasochism—New York (N.Y.)—Case studies.   4. Crispo, Andrew.
5. LeGeros, Bernard.   6. Vesti, Eigil Dag.   I. Title.
HV6534.N52F73   1992
364.1′523′0974728—dc20   91-50075
                                                                   CIP

Book design by Giorgetta Bell McRee

ACKNOWLEDGMENTS

I am indebted to the hundreds of people I met during the six years spent researching this book. Many of them are named in these pages, many are not; all willingly shared their candid, unlaundered, and generous insights. It is their story I have written. Too many of the people whose lives comprise this account have since succumbed to AIDS, a horror as real and ugly as any detailed herein, and to their memories I offer special recognition.

Specific gratitude is owed Chief Stephen Scurti and Det. Sgt. William Franks of the Stony Point Police Department, and Linda Fairstein of the Manhattan District Attorney's office, as well as their staffs and detectives and investigators, who were kind enough to make room in their schedules for repeated interviews.

For their research assistance, fact checking, and encouragement, my appreciation and thanks to Frances Chapman and Vaughan Scully, two individuals who devoted a mysterious amount of time to this project. Additional help from Michele Andreoli, Margaret Cordi, Sarah John Francis Manges, and Faigi Rosenthal (of the *New York Daily News* library) proved invaluable.

ACKNOWLEDGMENTS

Lawyers Mitchell Benson, Ed Hayes, and Henry Kaufman found time to help me understand evidence and how it can be presented, and Mark Eissman energetically helped give my Freedom of Information Act request some teeth. My editors along the way—Dan Bischoff, Tina Brown, Sharon DeLano, Patrick Merla, and Robert Walsh—found space in their publications for the articles that preceded this book. The lessons they taught me about journalism and writing, and bravery and integrity, will serve me throughout my life.

A posse of friends and colleagues sustained me throughout this project by offering inspiration, information, patience, criticism, and humor—or simply by taking my calls. They include: Cindy Adams, Kate Butler, Bill Elverman, Michael Evans, Steven Gaines, Ian Daniels-Horst, Jim Hubbard, Richard Israel, Leslie Kossoff, Hilton Kramer, Jerry Nachman, Maury Terry, Katrina Van Valkenburgh, Tony Whitfield, Barry Yeoman, and Linda Zalkauskas. In particular, Ellen Fleysher, Sheryl Fragin, and Doug Ireland provided faith beyond any expectation.

Anthony Haden-Guest lent even more: He allowed me access to his reporting on the Crispo case, his talent and expertise, and his intellect. Without him, this volume might never have materialized.

Finally, there is a group of people whom I feel I can never adequately repay for their confidence and dedication. Nancy Love, my agent, found a manuscript lurking somewhere in my pile of notes; Charlie Conrad and Tracy Bernstein, my editors, found a book hiding out in my very bulky manuscript (Tracy had the harder job, keeping me sane during the endless rewrites that brought it to the surface). More than anyone else, I owe Betsy Carter, Gary Hoenig, and especially Sally Chew in ways I'll never fully grasp for things I couldn't completely detail. Their wisdom, intelligence, compassion, and friendship are all reflected in this book, as it is in my life. I have been exceptionally fortunate to know them.

AUTHOR'S NOTE

Andrew Crispo, still technically a suspect in the death of Eigil Dag Vesti, declined to cooperate with this account of his life and times. All dialogue attributed to Crispo, therefore, has been reconstructed from court transcripts, police notes, depositions, published accounts, and other documents, as well as from the recollections of scores of sources.

Throughout the course of my interviewing, subjects were pressed to recall exact bits of conversation with my irritating and clumsy demands: "What did you say?" and "What did *he* say?" Where opposite versions of a single event surfaced, I generally did not include those incidents at all; sometimes, if it seemed important enough, I've presented all credible versions. Dialogue throughout the book has been similarly reconstructed. It is my belief that the words, actions, transgressions, motivations, histories, and crimes which are ascribed to the characters herein are wholly and reliably accurate.

Several other standard journalistic devices were used in compiling this account, including blind quotes and pseudonyms, all done in the interest of encouraging people to say what they knew at minimal risk or inconvenience to themselves. Some sources required such cloaking as a precondition to cooperation, citing their involvement in crimes, or their careers or families, or fear. Of those who were afraid to speak for the record, many cited a vague belief that retaliation might follow (a claim I felt somewhat founded once an anonymous death threat was forwarded to me). Children have been disguised universally.

All pseudonyms are listed in italics in the index (any similarity with the names of living persons is, of course, accidental). Otherwise, all biographical and physical descriptions throughout the book are true and accurate.

Additionally, thoughts and beliefs are sometimes ascribed to individuals in an effort to explain motivation. These are based on their comments to me, or comments voiced contemporaneously to friends who repeated them to me. Sometimes, as with the law enforcement officials from New York City and Rockland County, they represent my informed speculation as to state of mind. The Stony Point police department, and Det. Sgt. William Franks in particular, were exceptionally helpful in the research that constitutes this book, but code did not allow them to speak directly to Andrew Crispo's involvements. Their files on Crispo are available only as they relate to Bernard LeGeros's conviction, making them public record. It is my opinion, though, that the detectives who worked on the murder investigation are profoundly disappointed that Crispo has so far evaded prosecution.

And as time goes by, less can be expected from this "open" investigation. Memories grow dim and evidence vanishes. And witnesses move on. Already, several key players in this drama have died. They took with them testimony that, except for this record, will never be aired again.

—David France
New York City
March 12, 1992

For My Mother and My Father
And for Doug

It is up to man now to belong to himself completely, that is to say to maintain in an anarchic state the band, every day more powerful, of his desires.

—André Breton,
Manifeste de Surréalism

PROLOGUE

Manhattan, 1984

Andrew Crispo and Hal Burroughs, an oddly paired couple, sat at the horseshoe bar smack in the center of the Hellfire Club, drawing cocaine through a short plastic straw. From time to time, they declined (always graciously) the advances of a near-naked man who crawled up to them on the cement floor and asked—begged, whimpered—for the pleasure of sucking on their toes. A polite no caused him to slither away temporarily, groveling among the flats and pumps and military boots that milled around the dark room at his eye level. But he always returned, a dog coming back to the dinner table.

Once, Hal leaned down from his stool to engage this man in conversation. Hal's straightforward, inquisitive manner was out of place here—it broke the aura, broke the spell, disregarded the rules. At that moment, the man had in his mouth the length of a toe belonging to a Connecticut-bred woman who absentmindedly allowed this while sipping a drink at the bar. "Why do you do this?" Hal inquired, his smooth, round Irish face suspended over the scene. "What's in this for you?"

The man, perhaps in his late forties, seemed surprisingly willing to explain, given the timing and the setting. It was a penance, a rich self-denigration, an unflagging worship, a service to himself and to others, male or female, shod or no. It was his duty to perform this service. His punishment and his reward. The bridle of discipline *and* a wanton ventilation of his private passion; Sisyphean *and* Dionysian.

Unplugging his mouth, the man said, "I completely get off on it," and Hal nodded.

In Hellfire's main room, the room with the bar in it, a small plywood stage crowded one wall, itself crowned with exhibitionists, or lovers of bondage and discipline, masters and slaves. A wrinkled man with a marked absence of hair below the knees and a smattering of gray on his chest had maintained an erection there for several hours, defying age and gravity and deserving (it was muttered somewhere else in the room) applause for such a feat. He accomplished it without hands! An imposed reality. Mind over matter. Apparently, recognition of this talent is what the gentleman wished for. Only at Hellfire could he expect to receive it.

Near the edge of the stage, a black leather sling hung down from the ceiling, into which would occasionally be strapped—spread-eagle—a man or woman whose now-accessible cavity freely accepted intrusions the size of a fist. Nearby, a prison cell with metal and leather shackles awaited half-naked detainees. A shaft of light struck the stone wall behind the gate and made the bars orange rust and cold.

Perhaps three hundred people roamed through this cramped, windowless dungeon located in the basement of a two-story building at East Fourteenth Street and Ninth Avenue. Some of them were dressed in fashionable black trousers and shirts, having stopped by on their way to somewhere else. Some wore leather harnesses and thigh-high riding boots. Many were naked and marched zombielike around the place, while others—the younger men in blue jeans and chinos, particularly—wore their flies open, their penises and testicles exposed.

In waves, this unlikely mass paced slow circles around the club, into the back room and the wooden stalls there, around the Hugh Hefner jungle gym, ducking past the leather sling upon reentering the main room. A sound track blasted from exposed stereo speakers, mixing acid-funk rhythms with songs from the S&M hit parade like Nancy Sinatra's "These Boots Are Made for Walkin'," guaranteed to elicit a smile from participants and tourists alike.

Andrew Crispo opened a black compact container and spooned some coke out on the bar. "Here you go, Father Hal," he said, presenting the straw. Crispo liked making people here think Hal was a priest. It seemed to pique sexual interest in his friend—his youth (mid-twenties) and mus-cled appearance were not enough at Hellfire, where kinks were valued over such common attributes. "Go to it," Crispo said, and headed for the bathroom.

This involved ascending a very short flight of stairs into a low-ceilinged room that was located, quite literally, beneath the sporadic traffic on Ninth Avenue. A tiny stall with a toilet was closed and latched; the noises of sloppy embraces spilled out. That left the two bathtubs, which were used as urinals in this place. Instead of the expected ice blue hockey pucks commonly found in public latrines, each tub had a naked man nestled inside.

A score of men and women were inching toward the tubs, waiting to relieve themselves on the men's bodies. In this line, Andrew Crispo seemed slightly out of place. Dressed in suit pants, a white unpressed shirt, and lace-up leather shoes, he fitted in neither among the casual nor among the seriously sadomasochistic. His newly acquired belly pushed a shirttail out from his belt. He had come directly from the art gallery he owned uptown.

Having developed a full bladder of his own, Hal Burroughs cued up several feet behind his friend. It was not Hal's pleasure to participate. Watching—that was his fascination. Watching and inquiring. And Crispo's cocaine, which allowed him to engage in the first two preoccupations for hours on end, night after night, all summer long and into the fall.

All of which, of course, added up to trouble at home for Hal. He had tried to explain to his wife his intense infatuation with observing the "Naked Lunch" served up in this basement emporium, to no avail. He even brought her along once to witness it. What he found to be mysterious and "totally under control," she saw as "disgusting," nothing more. The fact that Hellfire was unarguably a sex den—when stripped of all the metaphysical intrigues it clearly held—played no role in her objections. This was 1984; sex dens were on the cutting edge of New York's cultural consciousness. She was more disturbed by the long evenings spent away from her, and away from the studio where he practiced his art. But even on this score, she only politely, and infrequently, scolded him.

Crispo, though, did not escape her more immediate, unchecked judgments. She harbored a particularly sharp distaste for him—"one of those creepy little spidery conniving creeps," in her words—and she frequently voiced it to her husband. Many women who met him felt the same way. Hal considered the impression unfounded, and unperceptive. To him, Crispo represented the "nutty" mind of an avant-garde talent. "The stakes are higher and the losses are greater," he had said once. "Creative people, and all the fruitcakes I've known—there've been a lot—they're interesting to know, and they can be shocking, with different intriguing things about them. But all together, it's not unusual that they come across as strange."

Nonetheless, Hal Burroughs had noticed that Crispo's reaction to the Hellfire Club was different from his own. "He was always disappearing and reappearing," he explained, "and he would at times leave and go back to his apartment for a while and come back." Crispo lived only a few blocks away in the same desolate corner of Greenwich Village. "But he was real shady about what he was really doing or what was going on. I sort of felt I didn't want to know that much about his sexual appetites, so I didn't push it." Burroughs knew that Crispo was gay; just about everybody in the art world knew this. So he assumed Crispo was leaving the club with guys—there was a little bit of everything available at this ambisexual bazaar—although he never actually witnessed a meeting, or a departure, or a scene involving his friend. Not in the dozens of times they'd attended this club, not even in their few visits to the Mineshaft, the all-male, all-gay equivalent located two blocks south.

Except for this night in Hellfire's bathroom. Believing that Hal was still leaning on the bar outside, believing he was alone in the privacy of this crowded room, Crispo threw down a gauntlet. Standing beside him were two big men dressed in heavy motorcycle attire: chains, unfashionable leather suits, imposing caps with stiff brims. "One of these guys seemed very violent," Burroughs said later, "and crazy. I thought it wasn't mock violence but a really bad situation. And Andrew actually pushed this guy, pushed him against the other guy, and maybe even hit somebody. He was inciting this, fanning this. Purely violent, not sexual or teasing or anything. There was something really strange going on, and it seemed to me that he was pushing it forward. And enjoying it."

The room was packed bladder-to-bladder, and people were being tossed about in the melee. Those who could, including Hal Burroughs, fled down the steps into the club proper, while others pressed against walls and tubs and one another, hoping to outlive the conflict. There was a brief flood of fear in the place, a flurry of mumbles and grunts, but no words were spoken.

When Crispo emerged from the rest room, he sported a pronounced flush on his normally pasty face. "Another line?" he asked, slapping the black plastic container on the bar.

Hal Burroughs glanced over to where a crowd had formed at the stone archway leading to the club's back room. Clothing was dropping beneath a riot of naked elbows and shiny hands. Against an opposing wall, the wooden old flesh of a gentleman's buttocks was turned pink by a dominatrix in a tightly laced bodice. Following each swing of her crop, she adjusted her position, reaching for fatty terrain, allowing hot spots to cool off. A thin muscle in the victim's neck twitched reflexively at each swipe; his wrists, roped to a metal ring well above his head, did not strain or twist or yank. The arms dangled there, a testament to his will and endurance. From the surrounding stones and concrete, a musky, moldy odor rose up in fits.

The scene Burroughs witnessed in the bathroom was separate from this. What happened in the bathroom had no place among this differentiated civility, this stupor mundi, this dark world beneath Manhattan's meat-packing district. Briefly, Hal Burroughs was worried about his friend's apparent breach of protocol. But maybe he was wrong. Maybe "getting off" was a category of sensation without visible or permanent boundaries.

Didn't matter, really. He turned back toward the bar and chased all doubt up his nose with the powder.

Rockland County, New York, 1985

"Don't forget jackets," Robert Billet's mother must have shouted as he and his little brother, Michael, and three young chums tore out of the house.

A high sun beat through the lifeless trees that lined Buckberg Mountain Road, but there was still a damp chill in the air. All winter, record-high temperatures had lured the neighborhood's children from their dens, kitchens, basements, only to send them home with sniffles and aches and dry mouths. This was the winter that saw *global warming* enter the suburban lexicon.

"Robert!" The door slammed. Five small frames scampered across sodded lawns, out of the sun, into the woods. It was March 17, St. Patrick's Day, although that was of no particular importance in this hamlet. This was a Sunday-afternoon adventure.

Tomkins Cove. Just across the Hudson River from the more affluent refugees of urban living in Westchester, just high enough on certain rolling knobs to make out New York City's towers and its golden haze, just undeveloped enough to entertain the possibility of an afternoon discovery—large woodland animals? Historic ruins? Native American relics? The Billets' home, sitting like a prop on a miniature golf landscape, was ideally located for such an outing, just across the street from the bluff high above the Hudson River. Far off, beyond the freighters and speedboats on the river, stretched park preserves and brick mansions and a valley of civilized outposts. But on the west side—the Tomkins Cove side—in this stretch of Rockland County, the cluttered woods sheltered the remains of algae-and-stone houses, caves, fossils, artifacts.

The boys chattered about earlier expeditions, perhaps including some talk about the Indian Point nuclear power plant, whose bulbous structures pointed out from the Westchester County bank of the Hudson like radioactive breasts. Everybody had heard the same story about that place. In the mid-seventies, there were repeated alien sightings near there, beacons of cold light that were frequently spotted coming to rest just a few feet above the cones, growing brighter, and then floating upward and retreating into the night. Some neighbors (and one or two local cops, privately) came to believe the power plant was being used as a refueling stop for intergalactic visitors.

But that would have been before Robert Billet, a redheaded fifteen-year-old, or any of the younger members of this mission could remember. Besides, only Robert and his little brother, Michael, were natives; the other three kids, relatives from Queens, were on a weekend visit.

Robert had certainly explored, or at least heard about, the old Rockland dynamite shack, a blocky concrete edifice once used to store the explosives that had blasted out the Palisades Interstate Parkway and thus linked Tomkins Cove the hamlet—and Stony Point the township, and all of Rockland County—with New York City to the south. The bunker stood hiking distance ahead of them, in the deepest part of the woods, the foot-thick steel door now removed, the two-foot walls now pocked with the evidence of three generations of target shooters. It was a "must see" on any forage through these parts.

In the years since the tomblike thing was first abandoned, newer and grander homes had been sprouting up in ever-narrowing circles around it. Indeed, the entire area surrounding Tomkins Cove was bustling with newcomers, young families with flashy ideas of rural life who were erecting palaces of glass and wood right in the middle of the woods. And legions of planned communities, spreading like rust, were replacing acres of red maples, locusts, and dogwoods with lime green aluminum homes. All this in an attempt to accommodate the droves of New Yorkers who, in a fire drill of panic, were fleeing the big city as quickly as the shelter could be erected; between 1970 and 1980, New York City's head count had dropped by nearly 2 million, and the locals were convinced they were all settling here.

Stony Point, once a loose cluster of shops where Central Highway tees into Route 9W, was now home to endless strip malls, arranged in a DNA structure of twists and overlaps that stretched along 9W right into West Haverstraw, two miles to the south. Any distinction that once existed between those two towns had been reduced to one small green sign on the shoulder of the wide thoroughfare (ENTERING WEST HAVERSTRAW) and a few words lettered on plastic over commercial establishments. On this side was the Stony Point Diner; on that side was the Haverstraw Senior Apartments, spitting distance apart.

Although it was just two miles in the other direction, only Tomkins Cove remained defiantly unaltered—even unpainted—during the boom. Where Buckberg Mountain Road swooped up off of 9W, there stood four dusty stores in four whitewashed clapboard buildings, each with a dipping porch: The Cove Deli, half home and half market; The Tomkins Cove Garage and Gas (a neon sign proclaiming this); the Post Office, with a hanging ivy in the small square window; and a tiny boarded-up shed. THE DOG HOUSE, read a peeling hot dog–shaped sign over the door.

The northwest corner of this intersection was vacant except for a small white rock and a state historical marker on a post. BUCKBERG MOUNTAIN ROAD, it said. "In 1776–83, this was an important military route over the Dunderberg to Doodletown, Fort Clinton and Montgomery and West Point."

A dreary nontown, Tomkins Cove had none of the commercial prospects of the neighboring burgs. This, despite the fact that heavy building equipment had turned past the corner so frequently, chugging up the steep embankment of Buckberg Mountain Road and toward the Billets' home with such bouncing weight that dangerous crowns and valleys formed in the sinking blacktop at the corner. Up on the hill, each lot was parceled and parceled again, sprouting up stone foundations like fungus.

For Robert and his entourage, this progress made it more difficult to conjure up frontier fantasies in the undergrowth of Rockland County, the rural parts of which were becoming little more than a thin strip of meticulously preserved backyard. It would have been impossible to ignore the rock chimneys that towered over the bushes, or the imposing white-shingled homes that threw sunlight through the naked trees. But such is the power of a child's mind. They kept their eyes trained studiously on Rockland soil, digging their way into the overgrowth along the steep riverbank, steering themselves away from any hint of civilization and into the wild.

Being the senior member of the crew, Robert led the way south, paralleling the Hudson. Michael, the youngest (at six), began complaining instantly: He needed a bathroom. His older brother, after attempting unsuccessfully to explain that such amenities were not essential in the forest, announced that he knew just the place. Out on his own a week earlier, he'd discovered three rectangular pillars, rocks fixed by cement, that rose above fallen trees and rotting leaves and hibernating grapevines and the brown and gray and snow-covered lower limbs of oaks and locust trees. He led his brother there.

The posts were fifteen feet high, standing all in a line, evenly paced along the hillside. Crumbled pieces of foundation were scattered nearby, beneath debris. And a few paces away, the mouth of a well—a five-foot-square opening, a fathom-deep shaft—was completely covered by broken boughs and uprooted trees. They climbed the ruins; they kicked over the logs. "Hey." The mouth of a cave appeared, just three or four yards from the well and obscured with debris. A man-made cave, obviously. Stones rimmed its entrance, cemented in place, and a shallow tunnel burrowed into the hill. Inside was evidence of a newer civilization—a faded green screen door and shards of broken glass; two fish tanks, blown apart and scattered in adjoining mounds.

There had been a fire in this tiny cave. Carbon coated the entrance, and ashes covered the stone floor. "C'mon." Robert considered it a perfect makeshift outhouse for his kid brother, and fought his way past the felled trees to lift the screen door aside.

Bones! Robert's heart pounded terror rhythms to his ears. Black, dirty, fleshless bones. A rib cage, a pelvis, braided legs tucked under a body fetally, all balanced on a pillow of soot. Did he see the grizzly leather hood that encompassed the head? Or the gold ring still anchored to a crooked fleshless finger? The screen door fell. Did someone shriek? Five small frames bounded through the woods, into the sun, across sodded lawns. Robert, in the lead, headed for the second house over; he knew people there. They arrived in moments. Out of breath and charged with fear, Robert rang the bell. A middle-aged man answered the door.

For some reason, the teenager chose not to address the subject directly. "I live about a half mile down the road," he stammered. The man smiled socially, and nodded. "I was wondering . . . if you ever need any yard work done."

The man, scanning the faces of the kids, instantly realized something was the matter. He asked, "What is it?"

"We, we . . ." Robert's face was as red as his hair. "We just found a body down there."

"With a hat on," one of the other boys said.

"There was a fire."

"In a cave."

It was just after 3:00.

Within five days, the news account—black on gray, commanding full covers on the *New York Post* and the *Daily News*—hung from kiosks on corners around Manhattan, shivering in warm breezes of a premature spring. It carried the same face that had appeared on posters around the city nearly a month before: Handsome Eigil Dag Vesti was missing, those posters had proclaimed from lampposts, mailboxes, bus stops, and brick walls. FOUL PLAY SUSPECTED. They had captured the city's attention in an unusually direct way. People chatted casually about this stranger, about what might have happened to him.

The newspapers of late March 1985 carried the answer: He was slaughtered during a bizarre torturous sadomasochistic ritual. He was drenched in gasoline and set afire. He was left in an old smokehouse in rural Tomkins Cove to be fed upon by wild animals. Foul play confirmed.

A vague, unspoken wave of remorse rolled in over the city. It grabbed the city's gay community hardest—by all appearances, this young man was one of them. Were the rest in danger?

Shortly, another handsome man landed in the news—twenty-two-year-old Bernard LeGeros was arrested, charged with the murder. Then the spotlight landed on a third—the older, prominent art dealer Andrew Crispo. LeGeros, his friend and employee, had implicated him as an accomplice. Everybody in the gay community, it seemed, had a story to tell about Andrew Crispo.

Then came the stories of what they had done to Eigil Dag Vesti in the hours leading up to his death. A rush of grotesque accusations followed, with a parade of other "victims" running to counselors, reporters, police. Some of them moved away. In apartments, houses, mansions throughout the country—and in South America and in Europe—people canceled vacation plans, quit jobs, went to stay with friends. Some employed bodyguards. Some begged for police protection, and some of them got it.

Thirty miles north of Manhattan, a pounding terror struck the Billet family; an innocent Sunday outing had placed them in the center of a murder that would change the social makeup of New York City, that would dramatically—and finally—close a window on a wild, unmitigated era. They had their phone number unlisted and ultimately refused to cooperate with prosecutors. "Our boys have been through too much already," the soft, shaky voice of their mother scolded callers.

Manhattan, 1985

Winter made a few halfhearted bids to return: A flurry in early April never reached the city streets; a few icy rains splashed the skyline like astringent. Spring, such as it was, quickly gave way to a hazy and uncomfortable summer before May was half over.

Andrew Crispo spent those weeks in a sort of unofficial exile. He never returned to his uptown gallery following the discovery of the body, except to gather up essential belongings. He rarely slept in his Village apartment, and only infrequently retreated to his luxurious country home in Southampton, Long Island. Yet every time he did appear, his picture would show up in one of the many daily editions of the *New York Daily News*, which seemed to make tracking him a priority. Frequently, a photographer captured him at a pay phone—wearing dark glasses and a dark shin-length trench coat—placing the personal calls he felt he couldn't make from any of his homes. "I'm tapped," he told a friend. "They're watching me."

Each photo was accompanied by a story repeating the same legend: Andrew Crispo, the key suspect still outstanding in the Vesti murder— the "Death Mask murder"—may be arrested soon. Bernard LeGeros, his gallery employee and personal associate, had confessed and fingered him.

Once, the story stood without a picture. The headline read, CRISPO PLAYS ARTFUL DODGER, and insinuated he had fled the country altogether. It was a furious drumbeat that seemed to assure readers that no matter where he might run, he was unable to escape prosecution—or the papers. But by June, after three full months of this, the headlines began focusing more on the city's pending drought and less on Andrew Crispo.

And one hot, sunny Sunday afternoon, Andrew roamed out of his hiding place to gauge the city's sentiment. He wore no coat. He pushed his dark glasses up on his forehead. He made his presence known. He strolled down Christopher Street, the heart of Manhattan's gay ghetto in Greenwich Village.

Kirk Green saw him coming from half a block away, and he stood still in anticipation of greeting him. Green was one of scores of young graffiti artists—street kids, mostly, with unpolished artistic skills—who had been invited into Crispo's universe the summer before. At seventeen, he had sold Crispo coke, had listened to his wild stories about sex, and torture, and necrophilia, and death. Once, he even raped a man for Crispo. At his mentor's bidding, Kirk Green had rummaged through the duffel bag that Crispo called his bag of toys and pulled out the death mask, then pulled it over his head. Crispo had helped lace it up the back. Green then entered a room, pushed a young man down on a bed, and held a long knife to his throat.

Now, though he was eighteen, the import of that incident had not yet sunk in. He was pleased to see his old friend, even giddy to be able to talk with the man who had so publicly been linked to a murder and so mysteriously sidestepped arrest. Green tugged a little tank top down toward his navel; it ended several inches above his tight spandex bicycle shorts, which left no doubt about his assets.

He was also anxious to show Andrew Crispo that he had begun the process of coming out. As one of Crispo's "boys," he had acted straight, had participated in antigay jokes, had talked about "killing that faggot" whenever it seemed that was expected of him. As a very tall, very muscular teen, he could pass as heterosexual easily, given the proper attire. But exposing his belly on Christopher Street could mean just one thing.

"I still have one of your paintings," Crispo said to him, extending his hand like a guest on a talk show.

"Oh really," said Green, smiling.

"Oh, yeah. I keep it in the bathroom. I look at it every time I piss." He smiled.

A stream of gay men milled around them disinterestedly, peering in windows, peering at one another or at the literature on a card table set up several feet away. Gay Men's Health Crisis was distributing safe-sex brochures and collecting donations to fight the new AIDS crisis.

"You should come up sometime," Crispo said, "like before."

"Sure," Green said. "Maybe I'll come by and have a cup of blood with you and chat." Both men pushed out little bursts of laughter.

Then somebody from the card table figured out who this was; he froze. A man next to him whispered into another man's ear. A group of friends who had been watching from the corner began walking toward Crispo and Green. Fingers pointed their way from across the street.

"Look," said Crispo, pulling his glasses onto his nose, "I've got to go."

Kirk Green put on his own dark glasses, turned away, and walked back toward Sheridan Square. He couldn't understand why he had made that joke. He couldn't understand why it was so exciting to talk to Andrew Crispo. He couldn't understand why he never thought, Poor Eigil, when he first learned about the killing.

He had met Eigil Vesti the previous fall, at the Andrew Crispo Gallery, and found him attractive, if a little bit too precious. Vesti was wearing a designer leather jacket and a small black leather skullcap. Crispo, at that time, had tried to fix them up. "The blond gentleman out front thinks you're really sexy," he told Green. "And he'd like to blow you." It was Crispo's way of pressing the "gay question," belittling the obvious homosexual in the eyes of the apparent heterosexual. Fags exist to give service, to entertain, and relieve, according to this ethos. Crispo was an exception. He was "a good gay" who served as an official interpreter of other gays. Green responded predictably: "Fuck it, Andrew," he said in the street-tough, in-your-face attitude of a teenage graffiti writer. "Do some more coke."

When Eigil Vesti died, Kirk Green felt nothing. But running into Andrew Crispo changed that. Together, they were not remorseful. Together, they were making jokes! It made Green suddenly nauseous, and he descended into the subway station and left the Village.

Crispo didn't follow. He would not be exiled from gay society so easily.

PART
I

Simple Passions

If thou, O Art, couldst represent also character and virtue, there would be no more beautiful image on earth.

—Martial's *Epigrams*,
A.D. first century

CHAPTER
1

Andy Crispo was too young to enter any of the gay bars along Philadelphia's Spruce Street near Broad when he first made the scene in 1962—at least not legally. The drinking age was twenty-one, and the homosexual hangouts—Allegro, Maxine's, Penrose, Westbury—were having enough trouble with the law in those days to risk a charge that they were corrupting minors. Homosexuality was, of course, outlawed. Even taking a drink at a gay establishment—because they weren't legal establishments—was risky. Police officers paid frequent visits and allowed their palms to be greased openly. If the money dried up, they'd start arresting. Sometimes, because the owners and employees refused to make themselves known, each and every patron would be pressed into a paddy wagon and rushed off to Central Booking, all charged as owners of an unlicensed tavern.

Security was understandably tight. Windows were covered with wood planks to keep away gawking cops or thugs and to deflect hurled projectiles. Large, generally tattooed men were stationed on a stool at the door like gargoyles, there to keep out unsavories and to signal a warning when the police appeared less than happy. Bare light bulbs, placed in key locations around the bar, were a universal symbol of impending trouble: When lit, customers fled out the back doors. As imposing and chain gang–like as these doormen seemed, they served a gentle purpose. Body-guards for a community, gatekeepers to Oz. They tended to look the other way when younger men walked through the door.

Teenagers, though, were another story, and Andy Crispo was frequently "flagged" at the entrance and turned back. Nevertheless, he slipped through regularly, sometimes twice a night, to spin through the crowded dance floor and shop for a john who might take care of him for the night—sometimes with the bartender or the bouncer literally chasing him out of the place. Crispo learned to work very fast. And, according to one old friend, "he had about a twenty percent success rate"—not bad, considering that he rarely got more than a couple of minutes to troll about. On those occasions when he was unable to score inside, he sat himself down on a hydrant known to some as "Andy's Fireplug," on the corner where Spruce met a small alley that wrapped behind the Allegro, and he went to work under the evening skies.

On lucky nights, he and his date would go off to the older man's home, and Andy would leave refreshed—and sometimes a bit richer. If there was no place for them to go, the two would walk four blocks over to Rittenhouse Square, the meticulously tended, and at night quite private, garden smack in the center of Philadelphia. There, a shrub or a rhododendron or a gnarled thicket would become their honeymoon suite. In Philadelphia in the early sixties, such action was commonplace among gay men, who were leading the charge in the sexual liberation movement.

Wednesdays were reserved for major new offensives. "If you didn't go out on Wednesdays," said one gay man, "you were just nobody, you were out of it, you were lost. Forget about showing up at the bars on Saturday if nobody saw you on Wednesday! It just wasn't done."

Tommy Martin, a third-generation ironworker from Trenton, New Jersey, first "honeymooned" with Andy Crispo in Rittenhouse Square one Wednesday that spring. He was twenty; Andy was eighteen. They exchanged names and numbers afterward—well, Tommy gave his number to Crispo, who said he had no phone, no *home*, where he could be reached. As they strolled back toward the bars, Andy Crispo—dark-haired, thick-lipped, Italian/French—said he was an orphan, and talked about being raised by nuns at St. John's Orphanage. Recently, he had been placed in a foster family, but that hadn't worked out. "I'm still looking for a place," he said.

Tommy Martin—Irish-red hair bouncing above a freckled face and blue eyes—said he couldn't remember having better sex. Indeed, Martin was smitten, and when Crispo called him a week later and suggested they meet again on the southwest corner of the square, he sneaked out of his family's house in Trenton, borrowed his sleeping brother's car, turned onto crowded Route 1, and floored it—hoping to make the hour-long trip to Philadelphia in half the time. He was that hungry.

When the cops caught up to him, he was doing well over a hundred miles an hour. They threw him in jail. It was the first—and last—time Tommy Martin was ever in trouble with the law. "That Andy is dangerous," he told a friend. "It's exciting as all getout!"

Over the summer, Martin and Crispo became best of friends—part of a handsome young street gang of Catholic, sexually ambitious, high school–educated gay men. Their weeks began on Wednesdays. Always, they chose the same green bench on the quietest corner of Rittenhouse Square. Theirs was the first seat on the brick path. Five or six benches up, just on the other side of a large oak tree, was home turf for the "caddy girls"—Rittenhouse parlance for younger gays who were less attractive, less well dressed, less Catholic but only a slight bit more rambunctious. Around the concrete water fountain, the older crowd held sway and, despite the strict stratification, they all shared time in the same patch of bushy cover whenever a willing partner made himself known.

On colder, less populous evenings, Martin would invite Andy Crispo for a drive in his brother's sedan, and invariably they'd pull high up into the dark parking lot behind Philadelphia's Museum of Art, letting the car idle beneath a statue of *Stephen Girard, Mariner*. This was their romantic getaway, and through the windshield, before it steamed over, they could look down upon the skyline of cool, orderly Philadelphia.

It was on one of those occasions that Andy Crispo first broke the rules of sex, as they were followed on this bluff. He stripped naked in the car, when the more logical thing to do (given the frequent police rousings there) was just to slide one's pants down around one's ankles like leg cuffs. Naked, Crispo flung open the car door and shouted "C'mon" to Martin, who watched his date begin to scale the short rock wall to the museum's cropped lawns. Unwilling, but incapable of refusing, Tommy Martin followed. The two embraced under the shivering moon, their clothing scattered across the front seat of the sedan fifty feet away.

Martin filed away savory memories of every aspect of that encounter, from his own unrelenting passion to Crispo's apparently unequaled stamina, displayed once Martin was pressed facedown in the damp grass. Two dense, muscular boy bodies, one freckled and fresh as snow, one the color of olive oil, thrashed about, called out each other's names, professed love and admiration. And when it was all over, they hid in the bushes behind the museum until they could sprint back to safety.

Nobody was there with Crispo to verify his tale of his first encounter with the finer arts, but friends who heard him tell it said it must have happened this way: Andy Crispo signed in at the Philadelphia Art Alliance as an assistant buyer for Sotheby's, the British auctioneers of top-of-the-line arts and collectibles. He went virtually undetected dressed in what he called his confirmation outfit—the uniform of gray slacks and white striped shirt, suspenders, and a deep blue blazer and plain Catholic tie. The occasion was a gallery opening featuring the oil paintings of Vincent Price, the actor who was little known for his dabbling. Before the evening had begun to wind down, Crispo headed toward the door with one of the canvases tucked under his arm—unpurchased, unwrapped, unnoticed.

"Sure," exclaimed an excited Tony Capucci some days later as Crispo told him the story. "I read about it in the paper! They said someone robbed the place!" And then, with deep-throated admiration, he added, "That was *you?*"

Tony Capucci had replaced Tommy Martin as Crispo's lover in 1963, and retained the title for only a matter of months. Like Andy, Tony was a South Philly boy—Italian, very Catholic, he was a good boy who had slipped through the cracks. Just fantasizing about gay sex did that to a person. Being an outsider in this particular aspect of life—especially during the post-McCarthy years of the early sixties, and especially in working-class South Philadelphia—made one an outsider in all other aspects. Capucci reacted by doing the unspeakable: He left the tight neighborhood of squat clapboard row houses where his ancestors had been born, had procreated, and died, and moved into a "balcony bedroom" apartment in a converted warehouse on Lombard Street, in Center City. Foot-tall letters over the entrance to the building proclaimed it the AMERICAN BAPTIST PUBLISHING CO., a name he viewed as a poignant commentary on his own defection.

He was living the heretical life of a Protestant, too. Years earlier, a friend of the family had helped him land a job waiting tables at DaVinci's, a fancy Italian restaurant downtown, which paid him adequately though not handsomely. There, another waiter showed him how the wages could be supplemented. "I have this friend," he said, "who gets lonely. He's a doctor, a married man, and he'll pay a hundred dollars if you're discreet." This rather unromantic beginning introduced Tony Capucci to the larger gay world, and provided him with enough money (the dalliances were frequent, lasting from 1961 to 1963) to pay his rent.

All of which, of course, made him quite a coveted bachelor. Handsome in a very delicate way (people frequently commented on his resemblance to Sal Mineo, which he encouraged by combing a fob of shiny black hair over his forehead), he had a boyish figure, though he was twenty-five, and was always studiously well dressed and polite. Only his voice—

unusually deep, with a sloppy irreverence for the last syllables of words—seemed to link him to the generations of construction workers that had preceded him in the Capucci clan.

But there was one other residual South Philly trait he couldn't shake, and that was a steadfast streak of Italian monogamy. He had specifically broken off all relations with his john, the married doctor, when things started getting serious between him and Andy Crispo, who had, quite shortly after their first fling together, moved into Tony's downtown flat.

But it soon became clear to Capucci that his new boyfriend had replaced him as the doctor's escort, taking over the task of assuaging the gentleman's loneliness. Plus, Andy was still getting it on with Tommy Martin, and was frequently surprised inside Capucci's apartment with one date or another, freshly picked from Rittenhouse Square. "Get out!" Tony would holler, too frequently (it sounded like *geh ough*). "And take ya' numba wichew!"

Tony Capucci never saw the Vincent Price painting, but he was convinced it existed, in part because other artworks appeared in their apartment over the months. "Andy's a fine-art collector," he would tell his friends, all of whom had an idea of Crispo's acquisitive technique. Nobody believed the salary he drew as a guy Friday at family court was propping up his fast lifestyle. There was the Halloween party he and Tony threw for what seemed like every gay person in the city. And there were the infamous weekends when Crispo would call up from one hotel or another and announce, "I've checked into room five fourteen for the weekend. C'mon over."

"We'd send flowers to all our friends and charge the room," Capucci recalled later. "We'd order up food for everybody and have a party. And on Sunday afternoon, I'd leave first, and Andy would take a small bag with our stuff—leaving the empty suitcase in the room—and go up to the counter and say, 'I'm goin' out for supper. There been any calls?' And then he'd just leave." In the days before credit cards, the only way he could get caught was if he forgot, and pulled the same scam at the same hotel later, which he never did.

Though they had a great deal of fun together, things deteriorated between the lovers nonetheless, finally coming to a head when their landlord announced they would both be evicted unless Andy Crispo left on his own accord.

"I don't know what kinda trouble he was gettin' in with the neighbors," Tony told Tommy Martin, "but people say things are disappearing."

"And those same things seem to appear in your apartment," Martin commented. "It's just a miracle, that's all."

Homelessness, however, didn't suit Andy Crispo, who soon managed to trade up to a wealthier john, an older executive in a prominent stereo and piano shop who invited the teenager to live with him in Society Hill Towers, the newly erected luxury apartment building located on the Delaware River and designed by I. M. Pei. Tony (like Tommy before him) bounced back quickly, too, and the three young, Catholic gay men retained an uninterrupted friendship. Indeed, Crispo occasionally slipped into the dark alleyway between Tony's apartment and the abandoned warehouse next door, teetered on a garbage can, grabbed the fire escape ladder, and heaved himself into his ex-boyfriend's second-floor window. As angry as Tony had gotten over Andy's infidelities, his troublemaking, and his brutishness, he always kept the window slightly cracked. It was impossible to extinguish desire when it came to Andy Crispo, such were his charms, charisma, and skills.

So it wasn't surprising when Crispo called DaVinci's restaurant one spring evening in 1964—almost a year after they had broken up—and invited his friend to a Liberace concert at the Latin Casino, a short drive from Philadelphia in Cherry Hill, New Jersey. Because Crispo had signed up for night classes at St. Joseph's University, a Roman Catholic college downtown, their visits had grown less frequent since January. But since he had taken up with the fellow from the hi-fi shop, they were also more lavish. The two young men sat at a private table, dead center stage, right on the other side of the footlights, sipping cocktails before the show opened.

Crispo scribbled a note on a napkin, and called over a waiter. "Give this to Liberace," he said with absurd confidence.

Tony Capucci was puzzled. "What are you doin'?"

"Don't worry about it," was all Crispo said, and through the first set, Liberace seemed to be directing his act toward the two handsome youths. Crispo wore dark slacks with a white pinstriped shirt and suspenders. His tie was dark blue, like his jacket. Capucci had on a solid white shirt and a dark suit and tie. Their haircuts were alike, cropped short on the side with a little extra on the top that swung down like hammocks over their sparkling eyes. During intermission, the waiter brought word: "Liberace will see you both later, after the show."

Tony Capucci leaned forward and rasped, "Backstage?" And when the waiter concurred, he turned to his friend. "I don't believe you! You're nuts!"

Having pulled off the impossible once more, Crispo said only, "Don't worry about it; it'll be fine."

Backstage later, they sipped a drink politely with "Lee," as they were instructed to call him, in his dressing room. Mickey Hargitay, the bodybuilder who later married Jayne Mansfield, was currently working as

Lee's bodyguard. He stood watch inside the door; another large man waited outside.

And when the small talk had run its course, Andy Crispo said, "I'm staying at Society Hill Towers. Why don't you come over; we'll have cocktails. I want you to meet a couple friends of mine."

Liberace didn't hesitate. "Okay, fine." He sent a twinkling glance to Mickey Hargitay.

"Then we'll leave now," Crispo said, "to go get things ready."

On the way out the door, Tony reiterated his incredulity: "You're nuts, Andy! What's your john gonna say?"

But that base was covered. The older gentleman would be away—out of town on business—and was not expected for days. "He'll never know," Crispo said. "And what he doesn't know . . ."

Perhaps surprising everyone, the star actually showed up at the illicit gay party in the borrowed digs, and the cocktails poured into the early morning. The kids, including Tony Capucci's current steady, Michael (who brought along Spot, their dog), and Billy Marino, another South Philly boy in his early twenties, tried on Liberace's diamond rings—one shaped like a candelabra and the other like a piano. One of them asked him about life at the top, and Lee complained that nobody treated him like an ordinary person, that he didn't have any real friends. He made oblique references to antigay treatment he continually suffered. "I don't care what they say about me," he said finally. "I'm still the one walking to the bank with the money."

Tony Capucci said, "Look, if ya don't have no friends, come and see me and Michael." He scribbled down the address of the American Baptist Publishing building and handed it to Liberace, who, in turn, wrote his California address on a piece of paper. "I'm staying at the Warwick Hotel now," he told the young couple. "Come see me! And whenever you guys are out in California, just give me a call. We'll get together."

Before he left, a Polaroid camera was produced for the obligatory pictures. There were a few shots of the group sitting on the sofa in front of a picture window, and a few more of them on antique chairs lined up around a table with a white linen tablecloth. It was scattered with half-empty glasses and overflowing ashtrays. For the last portrait, Andy Crispo moved off his chair and ground his buttocks onto Liberace's lap. Mr. Showmanship, in his forties, offered a glittering, satisfied smile for the camera; he tilted his head to one side and rested a hand in a relaxed curl over Andy's shoulder. The teenager tightened his parted lips into a sensual half kiss. He lingered in that pose with his hands cupping his knees, and leveled dark, close eyes square into the lens. If it weren't for those eyes, he might have seemed to be mugging for the camera. But the picture captured a hurt, cocky Andy Crispo at one end of a table overflowing with other people's joy.

Perhaps it was because Lee hadn't pointedly included him in his California invitations—it was to Tony, without question, that he had handed the slip of paper—or it may have been because Crispo, the one who had sent the note backstage, the one who had suggested the cocktail party and then pulled it off so flawlessly and secretively in the borrowed apartment, felt insufficiently central to the revelry. He began to smolder. The party ended shortly thereafter, and the following days and weeks— moving right through the summer of 1964—brought a tumult of troubles from Andy Crispo.

First, a Wednesday or two later, Crispo came galloping through Ritten-house Square, past Tommy and Tony, who were sitting on their usual bench, and grabbed young Richard Figliolo by his small shoulder. Known by just about everyone in the park as "Harlow" because of his platinum dyed hair and long, mascaraed lashes—and universally referred to as "she"—Richard was already a Wednesday-night regular. There was no question about his identity, which was unyieldingly gay.

Back in his South Philly neighborhood, he was notorious for, among other things, being the first person on the block to wear bell-bottoms. There, he was the lightning rod for a level of bigotry that other South Philadelphia gays might duck. He was "Faggot," and he was "Queer." Though he was the youngest in the Rittenhouse gang, he was also among the most resilient—the kind who, some Wednesday evenings, might sit away from the lamppost, afraid a heavy pancake mask wasn't covering up the welts that queer-bashers had left on his fine cheeks.

"Hold this for me, hold this for me," Andy Crispo barked breathlessly as he thrust a large, framed oil painting into Richard's arms.

"What is it?" The boy's voice was high, yogurty.

"Just take it! I'll get it from you later." Crispo pushed Richard toward the far corner of the park, and the young boy stashed the painting in a remote bush so densely overgrown that not even an excessively shy couple of homosexuals would find themselves there.

Andy Crispo kept walking, along the park, down Spruce toward Broad. Tommy Martin ran after him.

"What's going on, Andy?"

Proudly, he started from the beginning, and there was a crisp magical aura about him as he spoke. He had heard about a party at Henry McIlhenny's mansion, decided to crash it, and, finding it was a showcase for a young artist McIlhenny was introducing, couldn't help himself. "I just took it, that's all."

Around town, at least those parts of town familiar to young, rambunctious homosexuals, McIlhenny was known as the most flamboyant of older queens, a man whose taste for late-night intrigue was said to include the Rittenhouse Square crowd. Indeed, his home—two connecting brownstones, actually—held down one corner of the park, at 1914–1916 Locust Street. The front door, twenty feet tall, with an exaggerated large brass doorknob right in the middle, stood just yards from the gang's regular bench on the southwest corner.

In more legitimate circles, he was considered Main Line Philadelphia's scholarly plutocrat: chairman of the board of the Philadelphia Museum of Art, director of the Philadelphia Orchestra Association, consummate entertainer at his adjoining town houses, or in his Irish castle, which overlooked thirty thousand acres of McIlhenny's own land. Among his frequent guests—and there were *always* guests—were Brooke Astor, Stephen Spender, and John Huston, whom the boys in the park would ogle through flung-open doors. His money was inherited (his father invented the gas meter), and his hobbies included art collecting. Inside his town houses, he had what was often called the best private collection of French paintings in the country: Degas's haunting *Interior*, Toulouse-Lautrec's *La Danse au Moulin Rouge*, Renoir's exquisite painting of a little girl titled *Mlle. Legrand*, works by van Gogh, Matisse, Cézanne.

Andy Crispo had donned his finest clothing, and had just walked through that grand doorway, down a marble foyer, past Dali's famous sketch of Harpo Marx, and into the cool green drawing room (the walls were draped in silk), where the assemblage of Philadelphia's hautiest society mavens, perched uncomfortably on Charles X chairs, paid him no attention. "I stayed for ten minutes," Crispo told his friend with a nervous giggle. "Nobody even saw me."

On the street in the following days, word had it that McIlhenny had reported the incident to the authorities, and a team of heterosexual men (believed to be FBI agents) had inquired several times about Andy Crispo at the Spruce Street bars. But if Henry McIlhenny (in his fifties at the time and a dead ringer for George McGovern) *had* fingered Crispo to the police, he soon revoked the grudge, for the two were caught in an intimate moment in the middle of the summer. "I ran into Andy at the old Centerbridge Inn," said Jack Buckley, an acquaintance, "where he was being, how can I put this, *sponsored* for the weekend by Mother McIlhenny." The Centerbridge, a rickety hotel overlooking the Delaware River from the New Jersey side, was a popular gay retreat just beyond Philly's suburbs. "McIlhenny was propped up in a four-poster bed," Buckley said, "stroking Andy's hair." Crispo's friends all believed the account; he was that irresistible, after all. Besides, Henry McIlhenny was a forgiving and generous man. Over the years, he frequently recited the dictum by which he lived his life: "Wealth must be used for the enjoyment of others."

The tailspin in the wake of the Liberace snub didn't end with McIlhenny. Word surfaced that Crispo's keeper, who had suffered a financial nosedive, was to be evicted from the Society Hill Towers (his sprawling Church Street showroom had already been shuttered). Andy himself helped to spread this word, and enlisted the aid of a few people, including Tony Capucci, to enter the apartment one last time. The goal was to pick it clean of valuables before the marshals got there. (Nobody really knew where the executive had been that night, but everybody accepted that, as one said, "a john without a job is not a john worth keeping.") There was no shortage of helping hands that night. Some took furniture—short pedestals, chairs; others took clothing, stereo equipment, art, and cash.

Most of Crispo's friends gleefully took part in the antics, but Tommy Martin was growing concerned that his precious bad-boy routine was going a bit too far. He confronted his friend during their last nocturnal visit to the parking lot behind the museum in the summer of 1964. That night, as they stood on the bluff up above their car, Crispo stripped himself naked—this was now standard—and reached into a small travel bag he was carrying.

"He pulled out this crazy black leotard outfit," Martin told his friends later, "and he put it on and handed me a rope and said, 'There's something in there I need.' He was going to break into the museum! Just like that!

"I said, 'You know I'm Catholic. I can't do anything like that,' and he said, 'There's nothing to it; I've done it before.' So he showed me this window, a basement window, that he was going to kick open, and I was supposed to hold the rope while he went in there and got some statue, or something like that. I just kept refusing, you know? And finally I said I was going to leave, just leave him there, if he wouldn't come with me, which he did. He said he'd get somebody else to help him, and all the way back, I kept saying I was a good Catholic boy. I told him he was trying to collect things that belonged to *God.*"

The story didn't surprise those who knew Andy Crispo. Jack Buckley put it this way: "You know, he always wore a full coat."

But it didn't stop at that. A week or more later, Tony Capucci and Crispo were enjoying a soda at Dewey's, the hangout on Seventeenth and Locust, when Andy decided to go across the street to the Warwick Hotel and pay a call on Liberace. It was more than an hour before he returned, flashing a wad of cash.

"Where the hell you been?" Capucci demanded.

"We were getting it on," Crispo said very matter-of-factly. "She's got *so much money*," he said, referring to Liberace, and then, in a soft voice, added, "I think I can get a lot of money from her. A lot." He narrowed his eyes, looking solidly at his friend with a mischievous intensity. "A lot of money."

"What are you talkin' about?" Tony Capucci asked suddenly. "Like that great plan of yours with the bartenders?" In the weeks since they had last seen each other, Capucci heard that Crispo had hatched a get-rich-quick scheme that involved threatening to publicize the names of gay bartenders, or expose the gay-bar owners, or the doorkeepers, or some related group of people. Blackmail. Antigay blackmail. With an underaged gay man behind it all. While it wasn't clear that the plan had ever gotten off the ground, the backlash certainly did. Crispo found himself eighty-sixed from all of the community watering holes, and the sidewalks in front of them, the alleys around back.

When Crispo didn't answer, Tony Capucci emphatically instructed, "Leave that guy alone! He's a nice guy." Capucci may have found the gay-bar scam amusing, but this was getting too close to home. Since that first party, Lee had arrived several times unannounced at the Lombard Street apartment for coffee with Capucci, his boyfriend, and Spot. Tony felt they had become close friends. "Don't even think about it," he said, forever closing the conversation.

And although the matter was never raised again, Tony Capucci immediately found himself "cut off" by Liberace, "off limits, out of the loop."

"Something," he later concluded, "must have happened."

Liberace was not a man to be called names, true or not. Eight years earlier, in 1956, British columnist "Cassandra" had written a scathing review of his London tour, poking fun at the nasal mamma's boy. "This deadly, winking, sniggering, snuggling, chromium-plated, scent-impregnated, luminous, quivering, giggling, fruit-flavored, mincing, ice-covered heap of mother-love," the columnist fumed. "He is the summit of sex—the pinnacle of Masculine, Feminine, and Neuter. Everything that He, She, or It can ever want."

Liberace sued for libel, declaring that "this article has attacked me below the belt on a moral issue. On my word of God, on my mother's health, which is so dear to me, this article only means one thing, that I am a homosexual and that is why I am in this court." He also seemed to be particularly defensive about the comments on his colognes. "I always smell clean and fresh," he said more than once. "I have noticed the smell of the press many times."

When pushed to deny his homosexuality while testifying on his own behalf, Liberace said only, "I am against the practice because it offends convention and offends society." It was no act of gay pride, but no flat denial, either.

Three hours and twelve minutes into jury deliberations, according to *Time* magazine, "the jurors were back with their verdict, eleven of them wearing the traditional stolid stare. But the twelfth, Mrs. Jean Friend, a gray-haired, forty-nine-year-old widow, could not keep the delicious secret. She winked at Liberace. All over the courtroom the middle-aged motherly doves twitted: 'He's won!' " The court awarded him $22,400 in damages for the scurrilous remarks which (though accurate) nobody would believe, anyway. Crispo hadn't done his homework.

All summer long, he flirted with the law, picking his adversaries ineptly. The rumors in Rittenhouse Square had several different police forces besides the FBI gunning for him.

Not only for his sake, but for their own peace of mind, Tony Capucci and Tommy Martin convinced their friend that it was time for him to leave town. "Philadelphia's too small for you," Martin said in his breathy voice. "It's all catching up, all coming to a head. New York is calling." Crispo dropped out of St. Joseph's College after the summer semester, and the three of them, under an early fall sun, walked quickly toward the train station together, each clutching the several paper bags that held Crispo's worldly goods. Capucci pressed three dollars into his hand for the train, and he was gone.

As they walked back toward Spruce Street, Martin said to Capucci, "He got out just in time."

"Not a minute too soon," Capucci said.

"He outgrew this place."

"Or it outgrew him."

"Had to leave without proper luggage," Martin said. "How scandalous."

Tony Capucci laughed. "If he only had half the suitcases he left in those hotels over the years!"

They spent the afternoon piecing together what they knew of the hectic few months that had mandated this dramatic exit, with alarm and admiration.

"Paces ahead of the law," Tommy Martin said.

"Paces."

"What's he going to do for money?"

"Well, he's got some money from that trick he turned with Lee," Capucci said, "and he's been tricking regular with that old john of mine, the married doctor, who, matter of fact, I just saw, and he said he bought some art from Andy."

"That hot art!"

Capucci smiled. "Guess so," he said, and then his voice got uncharacteristically high. "Then why did he take that three dollars from me?"

Martin, the good Catholic boy, guffawed. "He's fucking crazy!"

"Yeah."

In the dark embrace of the Allegro, Tommy Martin asked, "What about that orphan stuff. You ever believe that?"

"Not for a minute! Are you kidding? Orphan Andy!"

When Andrew John Crispo "first blossomed," as a chum from those teenage years once said, he moved from the wide, clean sidewalks of South Philadelphia into the city proper, and immediately commanded the attention and admiration of a new circle of worldly friends—other staunchly Catholic kids of Irish and Italian families who, like himself, swapped their St. Christopher medals for neckties, and their parochial training for other, less holy endeavors. When he "blossomed again," said that same friend, he packed his things and went on to New York City, where he managed to harness a new crowd of admirers, including exceptionally wealthy and powerful ones, the same people he had once derided for having "book-smarts—streetwise, they don't know *what's* going on."

It was the end of 1964, and on that two-hour train trip north, Crispo—young, warmly handsome, a man who could already make things happen magically and with an apparent sense of entitlement that amazed his friends—changed his name from Andy to Andrew. Appropriate that it should happen then, for he was dressed in the confirmation outfit, his trademark since his first Holy Communion. That was at St. John's, the orphanage where his unwed mother had deposited him twenty years earlier, as a newborn. He remained a ward of the state into his teens.

Just weeks before heading north, he had learned a few details about his mother: She was of Italian origin, and had chosen the name Crispo from her mother's maiden name; she was just sixteen when Andrew was born; her lover was French. The judge for whom Crispo had been working at family court—short, white-haired Adrian Bonnelley, known for standing on soda crates and delivering fiery lectures over his bench—revealed this. And he gave Crispo the opportunity to meet her. "I told him I wanted to think about it," Crispo said, and the next day he declined. "I didn't feel like knocking on my mother's door," he told friends, adding that he had learned to enjoy his independence. "I have this wonderful feeling of being *me*." That's another reason that donning "that gray-and-blue number," as Tommy Martin called it, was particularly appropriate at this point in Andrew's life.

This was, indeed, one of his greatest undertakings since baptism, as the train plunged him beneath the Hudson River and dropped him out on the other side of the tunnel. He had no prospects, but he brought with him a righteous confidence—and the address of his newest lover, Arthur Smith. That Crispo had somebody to stay with in New York was kept a secret from his Philadelphia friends. They knew nothing about Arthur's existence.

A southern gentleman just three years older than Crispo, Smith was nonetheless well established in New York. He had a studio apartment in Manhattan and a job as assistant to Edward Garrett, the noted purveyor of antique furniture, with a sprawling showroom on the Upper East Side. Smith had met Crispo five months earlier in Philadelphia, and extended a casual invitation for him to come to New York. When Philadelphia withdrew its welcome mat, Crispo fished out his number, packed it into his shopping bags, made a brief stopover to the draft board (he told them he was gay and was handed his waiver), and headed off to call in the chit.

"I got a job in Georg Jensen the very first day," he told writer Anthony Haden-Guest years later, referring to Fifth Avenue's august silversmith and jeweler. He started as a stock boy, but quickly rose to window dresser and table setter. It was an unimportant job—except for a single memorable flirtation. An elderly gentleman imposed upon the clerk for help reaching a blue and white cup and saucer in one of the windows, and there was a lingering moment between them. Several weeks later, Crispo left Jensen's for the evening, and headed from Fifty-third Street and Fifth on his way to Fifty-seventh and Lexington, where he was to fetch Arthur Smith at the antique shop. He was sidetracked by a second-floor art gallery. Particularly amusing was a painting of a clown in a top hat that hung in the window. He walked up the stairs and found the same white-haired man who had visited Jensen's, art dealer Maynard Walker, who that day committed himself—out of an apparently romantic affection for the young man—to providing Andrew Crispo with formal instruction in art.

"The clown? It's by Walt Kuhn, an American painter," the art dealer said.

"Walter Kuhn," mused Crispo, lengthening the artist's name—a true faux pas.

"Out! Out!" In the somber, self-possessing world of art, naïveté is grounds for fury. Of course, the point was lost on Andrew. "It's *Walt*! Out!"

Andrew, who responded to all loud voices in the way he'd learned in the orphanage, sheepishly lowered his head and immediately sought to comply. Walker, somewhat apologetically (though showing no signs of retreat from his indignation), added, "But come back tomorrow."

He did return, often, and soon he made his first *legitimate* acquisition. For some weeks, he had been admiring a drawing that Walker had displayed on a mantel. "Who did that?" he asked finally.

"Robert Henri. Do you like it?"

"Yes," said Crispo.

"Its price is three hundred and fifty dollars, but I will let you have it for half."

Crispo smiled, sadly, boyishly, and said he simply could not afford it. It melted Maynard Walker's heart. The kindly gentleman, a former *Kansas City Star* art critic who considered himself a good judge of character, the grand man who had made his own way in New York, let Andrew take the piece on layaway.

Soon, he made an outright gift of another Henri, an oil painting called *Trees*, and the next day Andrew returned to the second-floor shop with some shockingly ungracious news. He had sold it, for fifteen hundred dollars, well above its market price. In an effort to redeem himself, Andrew reinvested the money in other paintings from the Walker gallery, many of which he also turned around profitably.

By the early seventies, Walker had retired to Wayne County, in eastern Pennsylvania, where he lived with the artist Joe Stegner, both of whom died shortly thereafter. Twice, Crispo and Smith visited him there, and both times, after they had left, Walker turned to his groundskeeper and said, "He was supposed to be learning art; I was trying to teach him. But he's a fake. A complete fake."

Fortunately for Crispo, few people made such quick judgments, and he continued dabbling in the art world on this bottom rung, as a "schlepper" or runner of works he would buy from one gallery and sell, at a markup, to another. That's how he first met Irma Rudin, an assistant at ACA Galleries, one of the flagship dealers on Fifty-seventh Street, who was absolutely taken by this adorable young man. "I sold him his first painting," she would vaunt over the years—apparently Andrew had used the same lines on her that had helped him win over his first art-world mentor, for Crispo and Rudin met in late 1965, twelve months into his budding career as a collector.

But she didn't find the novice status hard to swallow, either. He was, after all, very young. "Looked like a rich kid," she said later, "very well dressed—*extremely* well dressed—well groomed, very polite. And bouncy. And energetic." Yet she knew he was not well off, for he would frequently speak frankly to her about his years of abandonment, and life in South Philadelphia.

They developed what seemed to her an immediate intimacy. In one of their first conversations, he shared with her the sad story of his childhood in an orphanage. "It was a horrible place," he told her. "But they would take us to museums a lot. That's where I developed my interest in art."

Irma Rudin sold him a drawing—a Robert Henri drawing—at a "good price." Over the months that followed, she sold him several solid Henri pieces, at a few hundred apiece.

She also introduced him to George Perret, her coworker at ACA, and the three of them (George at over forty-five, Irma at nearly forty, and Andrew, who was twenty-one but said he was younger) struck up a close friendship. Close enough, anyway, for the two to take Andrew into their confidence about an unethical coworker.

"He's very dishonest," Irma complained. "Wicked. In every way! He doesn't care what he does." They contemplated confronting him, or his clients, or his boss. But the muttered allegations remained just that, and the individual remained entrenched in his job. Irma Rudin eventually left, in disgust, to go into business for herself.

Her departure as gallery assistant left an opening that Crispo—with some persistent advocacy on George Perret's part—filled in 1967 despite his tender age and slim experience. Besides the schlepping, he had taken over Arthur Smith's job at the antique shop, when Arthur was hired on by Billy Baldwin, the venerable decorator to the stars (Braniff chairman Harding Lawrence and his wife, Mary Wells Lawrence; Cole Porter; Slim Keith; bankers Joe Allbritton and Paul Mellon; fashion doyenne and *Vogue* editor Diana Vreeland). Although Crispo was known as a consummate salesman at the antique shop and had made some handsome commissions in his sideline, he had no formal experience in the art world. That didn't matter much to Sidney Bergen, ACA's founder and owner. "He was charming," he said later, "and he knew how to sell." His job title was gallery assistant, and for five years, he worked under the tutelage of the scalawag who had so offended Irma Rudin.

While Maynard Walker and Irma Rudin were equally responsible for launching Crispo's career, neither could lay claim for having shaped it. That honor goes to the fiftyish part owner of a strange emporium who went by many names, including "Darracova."

Andrew wandered north to 959 Madison only months after his arrival in the city, just a short time after Darracova's Wickersham Gallery was profiled in *Screw* magazine (although it's unknown whether he had read the story). From the street, the place seemed conventional enough, tucked behind a sapling tree on an immaculate sidewalk, with a curtained show window bannering certain tasteful oils. Inside, even, it appeared an ordinary gallery with very ordinary artists counted among its stable.

But the *Screw* profile suggested what other simple reviews of the Wickersham Gallery had all missed, or omitted—that the place was as much a cutting-edge temple of the burgeoning sexual liberation movement as it was a showroom for the higher arts.

A typical opening would go like this. Upstairs, in the main gallery area, hundreds of invited guests would browse among the paintings and photographs that lined the off-white walls—some landscapes, some still lifes, all by contemporary artists. All the while, they'd steer wide paths around the life-sized statues of naked men and women, painted metallic colors and balanced on pedestals scattered about the room. Perhaps there were some revelers who hadn't noticed that the statues were living, breathing artworks. If so, Alice Neel, the famed portraitist, wasn't one of them. She allowed herself to be photographed standing underneath a scandalously well-proportioned male figure.

And perhaps a smaller minority was able to ignore Darracova's attire—sheer jumpsuits he'd fashioned himself, which revealed every wrinkle and fold on his sagging body except for the very small patch covered by a G-string of sequins, velveteen, or suede. Regardless, some of the city's most daring celebrities were unfailingly on hand, including Joan Crawford and Pia Lindstrom, Ingrid Bergman's daughter. Society journalists like Chauncey Howell stopped by and hobnobbed with Ethel Merman and her son, and the Duchess of Windsor.

If pictures are to be believed, the celebrities stayed only for the cocktails, and a smaller, more intimate (and exclusively male) gathering formed downstairs later on, where the statues came to life, Darracova said later. There are pictures of that, too, many of which focused on primary organs (flesh-colored or metallic, youthful or geriatric) in various stages of attention.

Andrew Crispo "never missed an opening" at Wickersham in those early years, according to Darracova, and remained a devotee of the Wickersham world into the seventies, when neighborhood protests grew to such a hue that the place was shut down. By his own admission, Darracova began displaying more provocative paintings in his curtained windows as time went on. At a 1970 exhibition called "The Love Pictures of Betty Dodson," he poked fun at the protests by hiring his own picketer to parade in front of the gala opening. The placard read, DOES DODSON'S MOTHER KNOW?

After a decade in business, the Wickersham Gallery was shuttered in the summer of 1971. Arguably, the Wickersham's unique service was no longer required. Many of Darracova's serious artists went on to enjoy serious careers in established galleries. Also soaring was gay sex, long celebrated in the funky privacy of secret back rooms, isolated park thickets, and the furtive enclosures of toilets and flophouses and Lower East Side walk-ups. After the fifties backlash, it needed the coddling and cultivating that the Wickersham could offer; in the seventies, homosexuality was uncontainable.

And Crispo, similarly incubated in that basement society, took a place in line for the celebration.

CHAPTER

2

Nineteen eighty-four. The humid September sky stretched right down to the highway, a hazy yellow scrim washing away the horizon. Weekday traffic moved along at a respectable clip, nearly thirty miles an hour, though still not fast enough for Elana Martos. The hired car had arrived later than it should have, and the driver was slow to load her things in the trunk. Elana had planned this trip back to Rumania almost from the minute she and her parents escaped that country when she was seven. Now, her anticipation was greatly outpacing the rest of the universe.

Bernard John LeGeros had been of no help, moping around as he was, and dwelling on the topic she'd rather not address until she was unpacked and alone, on the other end of her flight. A cousin's wedding there would take up some of her thoughts and most of her time; the rest of the month away would allow her to consider her future with this man.

Recently, their relationship had been more strained than ever. Almost nightly, they had argued—about his parents' disapproval of her, which was marked; about Bernard's paternal claim on her child, which was fantastical; about the amount of time he had begun spending with cocaine and Andrew Crispo, which she collectively dubbed "your wives" and he called "The Two Cs." She didn't know that he'd taken up with another woman, Lisa, or that he sometimes made it with any one of the prostitutes who caught his eye on the walk between her apartment on the West Side and his on the East.

Nor was she fully aware of the long, romantic evenings spent with Peter Sande, the boyish forty-three-year-old owner of the Paris Commune restaurant, who lived in a small duplex in the East Village. Bernard had helped him renovate his apartment, and used it as a hideaway from everyone else in his life. When he spent the night there, he would tell nobody close to him where he had been.

Those nights, which were frequent, Peter and he shared the same covers. "There was a genuine closeness between us," Sande said later, "a trust, a romantic friendship. Not fucking—but there was definitely a physicalness there, and a kind of emotional attachment. I think the invitation was always there, but I just wasn't interested. When someone has sex with me, I want them to be gay and glad they're having it. I want someone to be in it wholeheartedly, not lying back and letting it happen.

"He was always very macho, a he-man—liked to talk about guns and wear military clothing and stuff, which I was never into, and so I kind of ignored that stuff. But at the same time, Bernard was needing a lot of love. He needed to be close to someone, more than the physical act of sex. Instantaneously people think all kinds of things. But the truth was, maybe he was lonely.

"He spent the night a lot, and we could get into bed together and—cuddle, kind of—have some contact. Brothers and sisters sleep together. One night, he drew maps on my back, that kind of thing. Sometimes you have a relationship with a person that you can't label," Sande said, "it's not in one place or another."

Elana Martos knew Peter—they'd met a few times at his restaurant—and knew that he was gay. She also knew that Andrew Crispo was gay, and felt that Bernard obsessed on their sexuality, and on gay sex in general. Bernard had even told her a few stories about Crispo's involvement in strange S&M games—stories of male victims, involuntary sex slaves, blows that left marks—which she discounted as his fantasy. Or, she thought, Andrew had actually "handcuffed and beaten a guy," told Bernard about it, and Bernard had merely inserted himself in the story. "Bernard could daydream like that," she said.

Once, she'd openly encouraged him to explore male love, but he had angrily quashed the conversation. "He could be gay or bisexual," she told a friend. "There is a very erotic side to Bernard. That's why he's so obsessed with homosexuality. Because it was so erotic. Because it might mean sex on a stairway, you know? I understand that in Bernard. I *like* that in him.

"But that's nothing in his family that could be tolerated. I was the one that told him that his Uncle Sonny was gay. I could tell from meeting him. And Bernard said, 'Don't say that. Don't say that to my mother.' Angry. His parents, I think they worry about this in him, too. Nothing he ever did was right. He could have been a great actor. He could have probably been a model, anything. And I think the mother, everybody, because he was so talented, they probably thought he was gay!"

Bernard's crisp, delicate good looks encouraged this perception. There was an element about him that defied his age (at the time he was twenty-two) and his experience. His voice, on the one hand, was that of a man's, studiously masculine and resonantly tenor. Consonants crackled against his teeth and cheeks. But the words his voice carried—often melodramatic, sometimes death-obsessive—seemed childish and naïve. Favored expressions, such as "I walk into the room like death itself," proved no cause for alarm. "I'll stick a fork in your retina," another frequent utterance, came out as threatening as "I'll be a great artist one day." His soft beauty undermined those stark utterances, allowed them to be forgiven. And in part, it fed that propensity.

The son of a midwestern father of French descent and a mother from the Philippines, Bernard had a face that favored his exotic feminine heritage. Golden flesh, penciled lips, black-rimmed black and white eyes, and the two circumflex brows were all pleasingly arranged on his face, shaped like a heart. Sable-thick hair, swept back and cropped high on the ears, cut his forehead with a sharp, black widow's peak. His nose was finely sculpted, a bonus from his father's side, and turned up at its end. Sorrow or humor or fright showed in each of these elements equally and readily; the hostile emotions, though, seemed so out of place as to be rendered virtually unbelievable.

Although he was slightly built, he was physically imposing nonetheless. Broad, square shoulders narrowed toward a firm waist. Regular workouts had built gristly muscles on his legs and biceps. Onto this scaffolding, he draped fine clothing: Italian leather jackets, double-breasted suits, a gold band beneath the knot in his ties. The evidence of a dandy overwhelmed the vernacular of a thug.

Racquel LeGeros, his mother, may indeed have harbored suspicions regarding her eldest child's affectional preferences, though her harsh treatment of his successive girlfriends offered no clue to this. Elana was exceptional in that Racquel had a particularly candid, straightforward distaste for her. Between courses at a Thanksgiving table once, she flatly told the young woman that she was "not good enough" for Bernard. She lacked a college education and had a bastard child. Making matters worse, Bernard had taken to calling Julius Martos his son, and had spoken of his desire to adopt him. Together with John—Bernard's father, who thought of Elana as a Middle European gold digger (which inflated, to a great degree, the amount of LeGeros gold)—Racquel forced the two young adults to sign affidavits saying the baby would have no claim on the family fortunes.

These having constituted the more noteworthy elements of their summer together, Elana was heading toward Rumania with quite a sour taste in her mouth. Furthermore, it had been some time since she and Bernard had made love. For several weeks, she had contemplated leaving him, but each time she declared this, Bernard would holler, then whimper, then cry powerless tears. One evening, he pulled a pistol out of his glove compartment and pushed it into her hand. "Go ahead and shoot me," he said. "You might as well put a bullet through me, because you're killing me with this talk." The episode frightened Elana a great deal, but it became one of the evenings that she would look back on with rich emotion.

In the car to the airport, and at the terminal, Bernard was crying again. Before she boarded, Elana whispered false words of promise and hope.

Bernard hired another car for the trip home, and sat deep in the back contemplating suicide. I came into the world by a woman, he thought, and I'm leaving because of one. He smiled at the poetry of the phrase.

This car, a stretch limo with a bar and a cellular telephone, was much nicer than the one he and Elana had taken to the airport. Bernard dialed Andrew Crispo at the Andrew Crispo Gallery, though there were other friends—friends his own age—who knew him better, and spoke of his feelings of abandonment. Then, rather forwardly, he said, "I'd like to come work for you. I'm ready to work for you."

The Andrew Crispo Gallery, located (Andrew liked to say) at "the crossroads of the art world," took up two huge floors in the Fuller Building, on the corner of East Fifty-seventh Street and Madison Avenue. With nearly ten thousand square feet of flattering, bright rooms, it was considered (at least by the agent who rented it) the "largest nonmuseum art space in the country." More practically, it was also one of the most flush enterprises in the building and in the neighborhood, both of which were stacked with competing galleries. As specialists in nineteenth- and twentieth-century American art, Crispo and his employees had chosen the most explosively desirable period of works long before other dealers entered the fray, and had capitalized on it handsomely—and diligently.

Through his efforts, and those of Ronnie Caran, the gallery director, Crispo had captured some of the world's wealthiest and most prolific collectors as clients. Joe Allbritton, chairman of the blue-blooded Riggs

National Bank in Washington, D.C., was a regular client. So were the millionaire Hunt brothers of Texas, and the Johnson D'Arcs of New Jersey (and the Johnson & Johnson fortunes). Hollywood mavens, along with tycoons such as Gianni Agnelli, chairman of Italy's Fiat automobile company, showed up with their friends regularly. But the crowning glory in Crispo's Rolodex file was the Baron Hans Heinrich von Thyssen-Bornemisza, the world's leading collector of fine art. When Crispo landed "Heini," as he was called, he guaranteed a place in the history books for himself. And he had become a rich man almost overnight.

That was a decade earlier. Now, in 1984, at just forty years old and with an estimated $50 million in the bank, Andrew Crispo had allowed himself to become focused on other things. Chief among them was a web of legal entanglements that seemed to amuse him at the moment more than art, and an investigation into his finances by the Internal Revenue Service.

New York's sexual underground was right up there on Andrew's entertainment list. Hal Burroughs, in his mid-twenties, became one of Crispo's closest confidants early in the summer, and frequently escorted him to the clubs. A struggling artist with a New England education, he worked variously as an artist's assistant and as a free-lance carpenter to make ends meet. He was full-bodied and enormously handsome, with blue Irish eyes and a head of bobbing blond curls. Indeed, he looked a lot like Tommy Martin had twenty years before, when Tommy and Andrew were inseparable partners in the demimonde of Philadelphia's Rittenhouse Square.

Burroughs originally teamed up with the older man in the hope it would further his career. Instead, he found himself spending more time in the various downtown sex clubs, his nose full of coke.

"Andrew had what he called his good weeks and his bad weeks," Hal said later, "and on his bad weeks he'd have baskets of coke and we'd go over to Hellfire. He gave it out to just about anybody. On his good weeks, he would not do anything for a couple of weeks, or days or whatever, and then he would go back on. He didn't think he had a problem. And he resented anybody saying anything about it. He once said, 'You know the only reason I do this is because it amuses me.' "

Andrew said the same thing about the Hellfire Club, the city's flagship emporium for sadomasochists and their amused witnesses. "It was a fascinating place," Hal Burroughs said later. "It was packed, really full of everybody, and not all whips and chains, either. It was diverse sexually. A little something for everybody. A multisexual situation. We'd go for a couple of drinks and, of course, the coke. He did once say, 'Do you know what would happen if anybody knew that I went to a place like this, what it would do to me?' I was into it from a curiosity point of view. I thought he was looking at it in much the same way, although I knew he was a little more involved in it than I was."

Hal maintained that he was faithful to his wife through these months, which stretched right past the summer. Although Andrew told a mutual friend that they had been lovers ("I fucked his brains out, all night long," was how he had put it), this was not the case. According to Burroughs, there was only one invitation, and it came indirectly—from Bernard LeGeros, with whom Andrew had taken up toward the end of the summer. "Bernard asked me if I would ever beat Andrew," he remembered, "and I said of course not. My impression was that he was asking *for* Andrew. I don't think Andrew would have ever asked me directly to do that, because I think he knew that I would say no, and that would be embarrassing."

On one occasion in August or early September, Burroughs was called to participate in a scene at the gallery, and—as he recalled it—his presence seemed to defuse the ritual. "Here was a guy, dressed in leathers—skimpy black leather S&M clothing, like a jockstrap and something else. This was upstairs, in the gallery room upstairs, where some Abdell sculptures were set up. This kid, probably my age or late twenties, was loosely bound to something with, like, leather straps. He was there completely consensually. If he wasn't, I wouldn't have . . . I mean, I was freaked out as it was.

"Okay. I was invited to whip him. And my curiosity is pretty broad. And at first, I said, 'No, I don't—no.' And I think I was sort of induced to at least attempt. I was very curious. I had seen it a million times.

"I did pick up the whip, and I said, 'Why do you want to do this? I think it's real strange, I don't really understand it, and I've seen a lot of strange things.' He wasn't too conversant, because I think he didn't want to talk about it, just wanted to do it. But I couldn't; I'm not into it.

"And Andrew heard the whole thing and I think he realized, you know, Hal may be fun and curious and all that, but he's not into whipping somebody. Whether or not . . . I mean . . . the guy wanted it . . . to be whipped . . . bad . . . but I don't take any pleasure in it myself. I said, 'What's the point?' And I still don't get it."

Bernard LeGeros was there observing the scene, and he clearly *did* get it. "Just hit the faggot," Bernard commanded. "Fucking whip the shit out of him, man! What are you waiting for?"

Andrew hired Bernard over the telephone the September afternoon that Elana left, and Bernard instructed the limo driver to drop him at the gallery. There, Crispo told LeGeros that his unofficial titles would be "my bodyguard" and "my executioner." His job description included helping with a highly secret mission against the IRS investigators, and his hours, initially, were five to midnight.

The "command center" in this battle was a two-room apartment Crispo had recently taken in the Galleria, a luxury building down the street from the art gallery on East Fifty-seventh Street. "Nobody knows about this place," Andrew explained, "not even people in the gallery. It's completely top secret."

Bernard accepted the job on these mysterious terms. Soon, he also became Crispo's partner in other, even more nefarious matters. His first official act was to repossess Ronnie Caran's keys. He just walked up to the older man, the gallery's director for the past decade, and demanded them.

This made his discovery during his second official act no less alarming. Andrew had asked Bernard to house-sit his spacious penthouse apartment on West Twelfth Street over the long Labor Day weekend. One afternoon, Crispo called from Europe and asked Bernard to deliver a message to the gallery. He agreed, and rifled through a desk drawer for a pencil. There, Bernard found the set of keys that he had lost two full years before, the night he first visited Andrew at his apartment.

Bernard's gay uncle, whom he called Tito Sonny, using the Tagalog word for uncle, was an acquaintance of Crispo's and a friend of Ronnie Caran's. In 1982, Sonny had encouraged Bernard to approach them for employment opportunities. Andrew Crispo was helpful then, and sent Bernard away with the assignment to write a resume. Months passed before Bernard called again, to thank him for the advice. The resume had finally materialized, but was unimpressive, he said. He had to add a list of places visited and a sentence on which languages he expected to study someday in order to make it fill a page. Crispo seemed extraordinarily delighted to hear from him nonetheless, and asked how the job search had gone. "Actually," Bernard said then, "I got a good job, working for a relative. I'm building scaled-down models." There was little conviction in his voice.

"What about photography? You were going to look for a job at a magazine, I thought."

"Well, heh-heh. That sort of got put on hold."

"Tell you what," offered Andrew, "you pick up some magazines—go to a newsstand and find some magazines you'd like to work for and let me look at them. Maybe I know somebody there who you could go talk to." Bernard agreed. "Good. I'll send a car over for you," Andrew said on the phone, "and you'll come over to my apartment."

From the balcony atop Crispo's building, headlights on the West Side

Highway seemed like a racing forest fire, burning uptown and downtown in separate gales. Cross sections of this chaos were visible between boxy factory buildings down below. Facing north, Bernard identified every major building in the midtown skyline: Chrysler, Empire State, Citicorp. Behind him, Woolworth, Chase Manhattan, World Trade glimmered before a yellow-green sky. On West Twelfth Street, directly below the terraced gardens—at just eight stories, the building was one of the tallest around—the shiny heads of men meandered purposefully along the dark streets, sometimes turning around and following another shiny head that had just passed; sometimes they'd walk off together, energetically, sometimes alone, in a saunter.

Inside, Andrew Crispo's apartment was a single large room, although it took some time to notice this. The door entered onto a spacious living room, with delicate furniture and colorful Art Deco appointments all around. Behind the sofa, a corklike screen rose up like a wall, dividing off the bedroom, which was also divided in two by an elaborate partition. A kitchen and bathroom grew off either side of the living area like ears. All around, dark, warm, comforting colors played on the walls, the paintings, the priceless objets d'art scattered deliberately about.

"My friend Arthur Smith decorated it," said Andrew after Bernard complimented the decor. "Let me show you *his* place." They walked out to a terrace and crossed to the building's other penthouse, which was two stories tall, with a tremendous greenhouse garden. Crispo and Smith— friends for twenty years and lovers for just the first two or three—owned the roof of this building and moved freely between the two apartments. Arthur, Crispo said, was out of town on business, but wouldn't mind. "We share everything," he explained. "Mostly we eat over here, though."

Back at the smaller place, cocaine was spooned out of the black container. There was a matching straw. Conversation wandered, and was pleasant; magazines were opened, discussed, tossed aside. The resume passed hands, and Andrew admired it, perhaps a little too ebulliently. It listed two jobs, the courses Bernard had completed at NYU, and his hobbies: painting, photography, writing, hunting. Andrew said he'd make copies and show them around to friends at *House & Garden* and *Architectural Digest*. Bernard polished off a glass of white wine, and stood to leave. With his right hand, he shook a grateful farewell to Andrew, and with his left, he patted his pocket in a reflexive inventory of his belongings.

"Uh-oh"—an embarrassed laugh—"my keys," and he pushed his fingers into the sofa cushions as Andrew watched curiously. Nothing. He walked little circles around the apartment, retracing his steps. "This is just great," he muttered, "nobody's at home, either. You didn't see them, did you? Little black leather loop at the top? About six keys?" Andrew hadn't, he said. "Great. My parents are away at some science conference, and my brother's upstate. Great." He seemed oddly inconsolable. Too loud for the apartment.

They marched around the terraces, around Arthur's, around the living area once more before Crispo made a sensible suggestion: "You could stay here, I guess," he said.

"Thanks, but I'll just call up some friends," Bernard said, looking at his watch. It was after midnight, a weeknight. Only Billy Mayer would be up, he thought, but when he called there, he got no answer.

"Really," his new friend said, tapping more coke onto the coffee table, "I've got that other bed. It would be no problem. Really."

Bernard leaned into the table, leaned into his disappointment, and inhaled deeply, adapting begrudgingly.

In the bedroom, they undressed to their underpants on respective sides of the dividing screen, and chatted idly. Crispo was in exceptionally fine physical condition. His youthful hollowness had filled in appropriately, though not excessively. He hardly looked twice Bernard's age. Both men mounded their clothing at the side of the beds.

Andrew said, laughing, "I feel like Claudette Colbert in that movie, *It Happened One Night.*"

"I seen that movie," Bernard said, "the one where the couple put the blanket up between the beds! Yeah. But that was a guy and a broad."

Andrew said, "I didn't tell you something"—no hesitation, no coy, flirtatious clues—"about myself. I'm gay."

Suddenly, the screen between them seemed half its size, and Bernard's head was prickly with cocaine. "Now's a fine. Fuckin'. Time. To tell me this shit," he snorted.

Andrew laughed a loud hoot. "Don't worry about it," he said kindly, "I'm not going to do anything—but if you feel like coming over to this side, that's another story."

"You come over here," Bernard said, "and I'm gonna kill you."

"That's what I like about you. You're so *butch!*" Andrew rolled over, a smile on his face, and fell asleep.

Nothing happened that night to cause Bernard to be suspicious, but when he found his keys tucked in his boss's desk two years later, suspicion was his first impulse. He used unmeasured words. "These *are* my keys, Andrew! What the fuck are you doing with them?"

"Oh yes," came the response over the phone. "They were under the cushions somewhere."

"I *looked* under the cushions. I looked everywhere under the cushions that night, remember? You took 'em, didn't you?"

Andrew grew silent for a moment on the overseas line—perhaps he was weighing Bernard's anger, measuring the circumference of its righteousness, the viscosity of its innocence. Maybe he was making plans for Bernard even then, thinking about nurturing this immediate and fearless wrath and making it an extension of himself. There's a chance he was frightened. Finally, he said, "Don't be silly," and left it at that.

On several shopping sprees during their first weeks as coworkers, Andrew Crispo and Bernard LeGeros dropped several thousand dollars on surveillance equipment from Spectra Audio Research, located on the ground floor of the Fuller Building: directional microphones, Nixon-type telephone taps, dozens of pocket-sized microcassette recorders for scattering in drawers, garbage pails, and bathroom stalls throughout the gallery. Bernard kept one inside his black leather jacket at all times. "Every place you turned," said a frequent visitor, "there were little tape recorders. Andrew would open a drawer, there was one; he'd open a cabinet, there was another. There must have been hundreds."

It was one of Bernard's duties to maintain the exploding tape library, produced through his own covert techniques, or through the taps on the office lines. As many as a dozen tapes were made a day; hundreds piled up around the gallery.

"Sometimes," Bernard said later, "I'd listen in during a call before deciding whether or not to put on the machine. I'd say, 'Ronnie, line one,' and then make a noise—click—by tapping the phone, like I hung up. And I'd listen a while, see if it was kosher. See if it was on the up-and-up. If it wasn't, I flicked on one of the machines." At night, after the other employees had left work, the bugs were disarmed and hidden. Another nightly ritual was to remove the film cartridges from the typewriters around the gallery and hold the spent Mylar up to a light. "Just to see what kind of communications they were making," Bernard said. Letters would be re-created, retyped, and turned over to his boss. Crispo, his cocaine use causing great paranoia, suspected everybody of anything. And he took every transgression to be an act of treason.

"I got Ronnie saying how upset he was about Andrew, calling him a drug addict," Bernard said; this justified repossessing Caron's keys.

"Susan Slack, she was a ditzbag on the phone, with her boyfriend all the time talking about cartoons of 'Mighty Andy,' this and that. 'How's the adventures of Mighty Andy,' like that. And she'd laugh. Yeah. 'Today's episode, about the love of Andy for René Arlington,' you know, 'a passionate comic.' Shit like that. So there I got another one, another so-called loyal person to Andrew being unloyal." Her tenure as the gallery's receptionist would not be long.

"He appreciated that I did this stuff for him. There were a lot of people who were just using him, or just feeding off him without giving anything back. Everyone was scared to death of me because I was like Andrew's KGB, you know? Do the reconnaissance, compile the information. Keep the employees in control."

Bernard's findings were logged into files and placed in a cabinet marked S&S, for Snoop and Scoop. The cabinet was kept in a "secret location"— Manhattan Mini-Storage, a commercial warehouse located a dozen blocks north of Crispo's Village apartment. Some of the dossiers were for employees, some for former associates and lawyers and lawyers of those lawyers. Some, like the S&S file for Joe LaPlaca, were opened for unfortunate strangers.

LaPlaca owned a downtown gallery that specialized in graffiti art, and counted among his biggest stars Rammellzee and Delta, at the zenith of their careers. This was street art's heyday, the first year graffiti "writers" were invited to the exclusive beau monde Basel Art Fair in Switzerland. That year, Keith Haring and Jean-Michel Basquiat were pulling in five, sometimes six, figures for their works.

Aside from his few graffiti-world friends, Andrew's gallery never bowed to that movement. There was no competition or crossover of any kind between the small, bohemian Joe LaPlaca Gallery and the glimmering Andrew Crispo Gallery uptown.

Until Bernard became an uninvited guest at one of Joe's parties on Delancey Street—Lisa, Bernard's "other woman," knew someone there and dragged him along. LaPlaca found Bernard to be "brooding, completely paranoid" that night. "He was just sitting on a chair not really talking or fitting in. But he got involved in a conversation with Delta, this tough street-kid graffiti artist from the Bronx, about guns. And he was really keeping up."

More than keeping up, Bernard appeared itching for an altercation. "What about an Uzi with a carbine bit," Bernard challenged. "You want one of those?"

"Want one? Man, you're crazy!"

"Well, any asshole can *talk* about it."

Delta seemed as if he was about to pounce. Joe LaPlaca—a very small and soft man no older than twenty-four—stepped in to play host. "I hear you work for Andrew Crispo," he said, changing the subject. "What do you do for him?"

"Security," Bernard said, reaching into his leather coat.

"What do you mean security? He needs to be protected?"

Bernard's response was something like, "That's none of your business."

Joe LaPlaca parried. "How is Andrew doing, by the way?"

"Doing?"

"Well, the coke and things. Everybody hears about his gallery troubles."

"What makes you think he does coke?"

"Well"—he laughed—"I've been at a good number of his openings, in the back room, where there's dishes of it! Everybody associates him with coke!"

Bernard wasn't laughing along, so Joe left it alone and the party wound down without incident. But the next morning at work, as Joe was recounting the conversation, a phone call came in. "Is this Joe LaPlaca?"

"Yes it is. Who is this?"

"What do you think you're doing, spreading rumors about me? Do you want to end up dead?"

"We all end up dead," Joe said easily. "Who is this?"

"Andrew Crispo, of the Crispo Gallery. And I don't mean dead eventually. You know what I mean."

"Frankly, I don't. Do you even know who I am?" They had met just once, years earlier—not at one of those openings. Joe had been consigned the sale of a painting by George Inness, from his pseudo-Impressionist period, and had carried it up to Andrew, where he found that the legendary art dealer would rather talk dirty than talk business. In the middle of the day, in a room full of people, he remembered Crispo chirping, "We'll look at your paintings, but we'd rather see something else of yours." Joe later described him to a friend as "a Petronius."

"Of course I know who you are. My security agent has you on tape."

"Tape?"

"I'm not going to allow people, you or anybody, spreading rumors about me. I'm going to be coming to see you. I'm going to be down there, *in person*! You'll be seeing me."

Due east from LaPlaca's gallery, in the more offbeat East Village, Ronnie Caran was thrashing through his own escalating nightmare with Crispo. Ronnie was no mere stranger who misspoke at a party. For a decade, he had been the linchpin of the gallery's business, the experience behind Andrew's quick eye, the sandwich board for his social and economic successes.

The payoff for these services had once been dramatic. While his salary was just three hundred dollars a week, the bulk of Caran's earnings came from commissions: 10 percent for bringing a piece into the gallery and 10 percent for moving it out, all duly charted in the ledgers. Only rarely were those figures paid outright. Instead, Crispo took care of his employees' bills—cars to the airport, hotels, dry-cleaning tabs, rent. "Everything is taken care of," Andrew told Ronnie. "Everything is taken care of," Ronnie told his friends, landlords, tailors.

But in the early fall of 1984, Caran considered Beulahland, a Caribbean bar and social club on a partially lit corner of Avenue A, the only safe haven left in his life. After falling more than five months behind in his uptown rent, he moved into a cheap, dark apartment with eye-level windows on East Tenth Street. Crispo, to his credit, had tried to halt the eviction at the very last moment. He called the landlord on the day Caran was to have his things out of the apartment and hollered, "It's not his fault; you shouldn't do this to him! It's all my fault, so let him back in." When that didn't work, he tried the soft touch. "Come over to the gallery, and maybe we can work something out." When that failed, Crispo sent one of his young cronies uptown with Caran to help with the move.

There was no question the eviction was, at root, Crispo's fault. He had just stopped paying. At one point before things had gotten so bad, Caran had sat down with another gallery employee and calculated that he was owed nearly $6 million in unpaid commissions and bonuses. Crispo disputed the sum, and showed him ledgers reflecting a much smaller debt, but a debt nonetheless. Brancusi's famous sculpture *The Muse* wasn't on those books—Caran should have earned a finder's fee for bringing it into the gallery. That commission alone would be nearly one hundred thousand, and several recent buys and sales were entered at a fraction of the value Caran remembered for the transactions. They fought bitterly about the money.

And they fought about Crispo's drug use. Back in March 1984, on the evening of one of the last major gallery exhibitions—sculpture by Bruno Amata—Andrew had summoned Ronnie to wish him a happy birthday. It was his eleventh birthday since first teaming up with Crispo. "I'd like to get you something nice," he said, pulling out the corporate checkbook.

Ronnie Caran spoke in a voice loud enough for others to hear. "If you want to do something for me, you can take that checkbook and bring it over to the Betty Ford clinic. You need help, Andrew. You're ruining your life and everybody's life around you."

Crispo exploded. "Don't you fucking ever tell me what to do, or how to fucking run my business. That's my fucking name over the door out there—*my FUCKING name*." The leather-bound checkbook went back in a drawer. Even those commissions that Crispo's ledgers acknowledged had stopped flowing, and the forty-thousand-dollar loan Caran had made to the gallery years before—at a time when cash flow was poor and Crispo feared losing his lease—had apparently become uncollectable. Caran felt he had been designated as much an enemy as the countless characters who now appeared in the playbills of Andrew's fiscal dramas—most of which had spawned suits, countersuits, specious claims, affronts, and allegations and whispers of vengeance. Crispo's fallings-out, mostly over money, were never about money alone. The difference was that, for more than a decade, Ronnie and Andrew had been best friends, partners, coconspirators—the *we* in expressions such as *when we're rich*, and *when we're old and gray.*

Then came Bernard LeGeros. Instructing this kid to confiscate his keys was one thing. To Caran, that came as a relief. It meant that when the alarms at the gallery went off in the middle of the night—a frequent event of late—he no longer had to answer the call from the police, no longer had to leave his bed to reset the security system, no longer had to clean up the empty wine bottles and full ashtrays that had somehow mysteriously appeared there since closing time the night before.

But there was more. Ronnie Caran had the distinct impression that Bernard was tailing him. He was, he said often, "scared for my life."

Sometimes, it was obvious: As he was leaving the gallery, Bernard would say to him, "I'm going downtown, too. Wait for me."

Sometimes, it was intended to be covert. On the subway south, he'd spot Bernard ducking clumsily behind a newspaper at the end of the platform or eyeing him through the glass panels separating the subway cars. More than once, he saw Bernard through the curtains in his dark East Village tenement, standing across the street or sitting on the curb.

"There's never been a direct statement, a direct threat," Caran told Susan, the Beulahland co-owner, "but I'm sure it's a possibility. Andrew's been getting blacker and blacker and blacker and blacker. He's more than capable of having Bernard bump me off, I'm convinced. I know this sounds foolish, but I'd rather let everybody know how scared I am than just turn up dead, too dumb and embarrassed to have said anything."

Susan and her husband, Dominick, probably disbelieved Ronnie in the beginning, although they never said so. Then Susan got a small taste of what it must have been like up on Fifty-seventh Street: She called Ronnie at work. Crispo answered the phone.

"What do you want him for? What are you calling about?"

"Well, it's personal, actually."

Crispo jumped on her. "Nothing is personal here. You're calling him at *my* gallery, on *my* telephone. You have to go through me. I demand to know what's going on. You tell me what this is all about!"

Pouring Caran a vodka-rocks later that day, Susan said, "I had absolutely no idea it was so bad."

"The only salvation is that he barely comes into the office anymore," Ronnie said. "He set up some headquarters in the Galleria. Which is supposed to be a big secret. Furniture was being moved out, paintings were being moved out, cushions were being moved out, the pillows that match the sofa. A coffee table. It was all disappearing from the gallery. And we're, of course, not supposed to even *notice* this. But the moving men, while Ellery, Susan, and I were sitting at the front desk, had no idea we were supposedly in the dark: 'What else goes over to the Galleria?'

" 'Galleria?'

" 'Mr. Crispo's new apartment there.'

"So this is going on for weeks—I'm figuring that he just can't face me, or something, because I would say that about the drugs or about my money. Nights, I'd leave the gallery and sometimes go to the IBM building next door, and about ten minutes after I left the gallery, which is just about as much time as it takes to leave the Galleria and walk down the street, Andrew would enter the Fuller Building and go up to the office. It seems clear he's avoiding me."

In recent weeks, since Caran's move downtown, two fellow employees had been fired. One of them was Ann Marie Scully. Crispo charged her with writing checks off the gallery accounts, "but when we pressed him for evidence—anything!—he couldn't come up with anything," said a witness.

"Today at work," Caran continued, "somebody finally said something about it. Somebody said to Bernard, 'We know Andrew has a new apartment at the Galleria.' Bernard: 'No, he doesn't.' Like that!" Caran imitated a mobster's voice. " 'I don't know where you got that idea; he doesn't have an apartment there.' "

Susan refilled the drink.

"No one has access to the downstairs back rooms anymore. They're all locked. Upstairs storage rooms, same thing. Bernard let it slip the phones are all tapped, or so he says."

Ice cubes dropped to the bottom of Ronnie's glass. "And it's not just Bernard," he nearly whispered nervously. "There's dozens of tough young kids in and out of that place every day. Drug dealers, hoodlums. Day and night."

Ronnie Caran's blue eyes grew comically large. "And get this! Bernard, the other day, came to me and said that Andrew had him beat up a guy. That friend of Andrew's who helped me move—it turns out that I paid him, and then Andrew paid him again. So he was double-paid. 'Andrew let me beat the guy,' Bernard said. Smiling!"

PART
II

Complex Passions

By plane, car, horse, camel, elephant, tractor, bicycle and steam roller, on foot, skis, sled, crutch and pogostick the tourists storm the frontiers, demanding with inflexible authority asylum from the "unspeakable conditions obtaining in Freeland," the Chamber of Commerce striving in vain to stem the debacle: "Please to be restful. It is only a few crazies who have from the crazy place outbroken."

—WILLIAM BURROUGHS,
Naked Lunch

CHAPTER

3

The gay society that Andrew Crispo entered, during his first years in New York, was a fast and dangerous one.

Fast, because the sex marketplace of the sixties, speaking generally, was experiencing clearance-sale foot traffic. Zippers were meant to be opened; there were few prevailing norms to regulate what happened thereafter. Crispo was young enough, and handsome enough, and sexually aggressive enough to thrive here. Immediately, that meant that his romantic ties with Arthur Smith, who took him in in 1964, began to represent an artificial boundary to his lovemaking, a wall against his curiosities. By 1967, Andrew was telling close art-world friends that he and Smith were no longer intimate, though they remained roommates in the nine-hundred-square-foot one-bedroom apartment on East Seventy-ninth Street they had taken together.

And dangerous, because the counterculture—with its forbearance—wasn't in charge. The cops and their laws were. And they hated gays.

Nearly a century earlier, the painter John Sloan had stood atop the arch in Washington Square and declared Greenwich Village an independent nation. While this was never formally disputed, and the territory never officially reclaimed, the neighborhood on Manhattan's lower West Side deviated only slightly from the norms of the rest of the United States, never really rewriting its fundamental constitution. Certainly, there rose up pockets of bohemia, of avant-garde writers and painters and sculptors and poets, experimental filmmakers and performers; there were jazz and Beat and abstract riots over the years, and socialists and communists and Yippies. And drugs. Then came the Stonewall Riots of June 26, 1969. For three days and three nights, Irish cops massed on one side of the skirmishes, raising protective shields against women in motorcycle boots and young men in bell-bottoms and halter tops, their painted fingernails putting a wicked spin on bottles and bricks and stones.

It was all touched off by a seemingly innocent—or at least undeniably common—event: a police shakedown of the gay establishment, which apparently had failed to make timely "security" payments to precinct officials. Innocent, because the beat cops had been in the gay shakedown business since the beginning of time, pocketing public laurels along with the cash at each rousting. These, after all, were homosexual meeting places! The city's tabloids led the praise parade, underscoring the predictable tongue-in-cheek humor behind the police activities, as a 1969 *New York Daily News* story about "Twilight Types" illustrated. Reporting on a raid at The Sewer, a club apparently operating without a liquor license, the paper noted that, after netting the bartenders, the police task force "then spent the next three hours checking the 'pedigree' of each customer. In all, police said they found 15 men impersonating women, and one woman dressed as a man. They were charged with dressing in the clothes of the opposite sex in public without an apparent masquerade party in progress."

A subsequent story in the *News*, dated just three weeks before the riots at the Stonewall Inn, led with the headline COP IN WIG PLAYS TROJAN HORSE IN RAIDS.

> A detective wearing a shoulder length black wig and hippie garb played Trojan horse for police yesterday who raided three Greenwich Village private clubs suspected of selling liquor without a license.
>
> The raiders arrested 26 persons in the clubs. At about the same time 26 other persons were arrested in a coordinated sweep against loiterers along the Village waterfront.
>
> Prior to the club raids, the cops said, Detective Frank Dailey donned his disguise and entered each of the clubs, staying only until police were ready to make arrests.
>
> Then Dailey would slip outside, signal to a waiting detail of detectives and lead them back inside. All those arrested were

given summons on charges of selling liquor without a license, because police could not determine who owned the places.

The raided clubs were the Telestar, 146 W. 4th St.; the 17 Barrow St. Club at that address, and El Barrio, 507 West St.

Those persons picked up along the West Village waterfront were summoned on charges of loitering within 500 feet of a pier, a rarely used charge.

In this raid, staged on June 8, 1969, the wig was more of a beard, the "Trojan Horse" more a red herring serving no particular purpose other than, perhaps, to land the escapade, giggling, on page three; if the bust humiliated fifty-two people, the story slapped all homosexuals in the face. There must have been similar raids between then and June 26. But they went unrecorded by the media.

And there were certainly raids afterward, but the Stonewall Riots became a touchstone for a community and the impetus for a movement that, by the seventies, made sure antigay bigotry could not be meted out without having to face down the "purple column," as the *Village Voice* dubbed the early liberationists. The *New York Post*, under the liberal stewardship of owner-publisher Dorothy Schiff, began to offer affirmative coverage of the community, and the rabid *New York Daily News*, which in 1972 editorialized against "fairies, nances, swishes, fags, lezzes—call 'em what you please," did its own quiet about-face over the years.

With the political landscape thus transformed, so went the Village, which dropped its "bell-bottoms like the rest of you" attire and pulled on (when the situation demanded pants) outfits that set the community apart as gay gay gay—the myriad "clone" motifs suggesting construction worker, biker, bodybuilder, cowboy. A community identity was born (and the Village People, too); Greenwich Village, indeed, had reinvigorated—and redefined—the John Sloan legacy. Now it meant nihilism as political dogma, sex as sedition, the new nation's pastime. It meant role-playing, costuming, adorning, fucking in a way that differentiated gays as a community *proudly* set apart, not merely shunted aside.

With the sun still high, men crowded the abandoned roofless piers thrusting into the Hudson off West Street—naked and sated. "The Piers" became a geographical reference point, like Chelsea or SoHo. So did "The Cars," which came to mean that deeply shadowed area beneath the elevated West Side Highway, where actual cars fogged up and rocked out a passion rhythm on squeaking shocks; "The Trucks" was a small parking lot south of Fourteenth Street offering quasiprivate accommodations amid (and atop and behind and beneath) the cold, camp masculinity of eighteen-wheel rigs.

These weren't hidden locales, either, but highly populated and well-publicized gathering spots where the police rarely rustled and bat-wielding teens (a clear and present danger) only rarely ventured. A menu of indoor, though equally public sex spots—backroom bars and bathhouses such as St. Marks Baths, Eberhardt Baths, Broadway Arms, Man's Country—was also available, guaranteeing that the hands-on field research in the area of positive and unbashful and disembodied sexuality would remain undisturbed by the elements. Most were located within a few short, dark blocks from one another, the nocturnal streets connecting them crowded with sucking noises and the clatter of belt buckles dropped. These were the few, short years preceding the AIDS epidemic, which nobody anticipated in any form, the glory-hole celebration of a sexuality untethered by shame and uninhibited by love.

It was this last part that Crispo truly embraced, though he never joined the political movements that marshaled in the changes. His growing sexual appetite consumed a burlesque of lovers, some not lasting long enough to exchange a name, some not lasting long enough to make it back to the apartment. (Eventually, enough tricks did make it uptown to cause a problem in the small flat. But instead of dissolving their partnership, Andrew Crispo and Arthur Smith took the apartment just upstairs and cut a stairway between them—creating two separate dwellings with a single entrance.) Crispo was attractive, young, energetic—the emblem of the frantic, playful subculture to which he now belonged.

But even this world within a world had rules.

When asked to write down her memories of Bernard John LeGeros's milestones in the years 1970 through 1974, his mother, Racquel, could recall little. Bernard and his brother, David, a year and three days younger, "were swimming in a lake located a good walk from the house down the hill," was how she began the entry. "David cut his foot on a broken glass, B.J. took care of him and practically carried him uphill until a good neighbor gave them a ride to our house.

"David and B.J. had a bicycle accident, it was a bloody incident which made both boys sick.

"Bernard was intensely involved with aggressive fish. The Oscars held special fascination for him. At age ten he had a significant collection of books on fish and reptiles. He also had a pet grass snake."

When pressed later, she added one more item: "He came home from first grade or second grade, and announced we couldn't call him B.J. anymore. 'B.J.'s for babies,' he said. I don't know what happened. 'My name is Bernardo,' which was his grandfather's name."

That was it, every word. Racquel could more lucidly have explained her own activities during that time, mostly spent finishing up her dissertation on artificial bone research—which she interrupted with two bursts of maternal revelry (Katherine, called Kara, was born in 1970, and Alessandra, called Sasha, arrived in 1974) before breaking into the demanding field she had chosen for herself. Her husband's attentions in the early seventies were equally self-directed. Anxiously, John was trying to keep his own career from remaining adrift. After marrying Racquel, he made a thwarted attempt to change his scientific interests from physics to dental research, her field, before leaving the laboratories behind for an early computer software company.

Within two years, however, he concluded that private enterprise was "too stressful and taking too much time, and not making me any money," and he joined the United Nations as a director of international development projects. "What I thought would be an easy bureaucratic life turned into a difficult life where I was frequently sent on missions. In fact, in one case, in 1971—no, it was 1970—I was to go to Jordan for a week. I promised my wife I would be home by Friday, and I came home six weeks later."

To the other things that happened in those difficult years, Bernardo seemed to be paying closer attention than his parents. Rhodesia declared itself a white-ruled republic; antibusing protests puffed new life into the Klan; eleven Israeli Olympic athletes were killed in Munich by eight Arabs. Racial tensions were at an all-time high, and the local reverberations, which were all over the television in the metropolitan area, commanded great concern from Bernardo, the darkest-skinned adolescent on Buckberg Mountain Road.

"Mom," he began, after watching one such newscast, "are you black or white?"

"I'm brown," she said gently.

"Why don't you be white," Bernardo asked earnestly, "like me and Dad?"

With a soft palm, she pushed back his coarse black hair. "Your father is white," she said. "And you are half white. The other half comes from me—some British, some German, some Chinese, a little bit of everything."

Later that summer, Bernardo came home with a stubbed toe, saying, "I hope it's my Chinese blood coming out. I hate my Chinese blood."

So, apparently, did the neighbor kids, who saw him as "nigger" and "blackie," presumably not only because of his deep, sallow coloration and pan-black hair but because of the black woman who stayed home with the kids while Racquel taught, studied, wrote, advanced. She must have appeared to all concerned to be related to these dark kids, and when she stood in the door calling them for meals or baths, the epithets rose like pigeons.

The strife metastasized into the muscle of Bernardo's family life in a very personal way. John's aging mother, Catherine, a white-haired woman of physical substance, had very publicly and furiously disinherited her son because of his repeated refusals to divorce his "alien" wife and abandon his "foreign" children. Over the years since his marriage to Racquel—an impromptu ceremony—John had paid repeated visits back home alone to help out with family affairs: his father's death, his mother's investments, his uncle's estate. Only once did he take one of his "colored" family members. He was refused entry into the South Dakota house. "My mother wouldn't see me," John told Murray Sprung, his friend and lifelong attorney, "until I left Bernardo, baby Bernardo, with a baby-sitter. In a town sixty miles away! In Sioux Falls!"

But then, for reasons that no one could recall, Catherine LeGeros came to New York in the spring of 1972. Her evident purpose was to size up Racquel and the boys—a test of their character and coloration that took a lot out of Bernardo, especially. Before her arrival, he had been told of her "extreme, irrational" prejudices against the family, but he was also acutely aware of his father's unimpugned love for her.

For several weeks, she sat stubbornly in the living room at 100 Buckberg Mountain Road, making unremarkable efforts at civility, and she left with a position that was virtually unchanged. "I will not come back again," Bernardo heard her say. She didn't come back, either, and might have maintained the banishment of her grandchildren even if she hadn't dropped dead that fall.

Bernardo, just ten years old, took the death hard. It left him as the unabsolved grandchild of the woman his father adored. He was different, other, hated, renounced. By virtue of something he could do nothing to change. By virtue of his very being.

After the funeral, in the small country home where Grandma Catherine had lived, Bernardo stayed in the kitchen, away from the rest of the pale family, away from his pale father, who was crying openly. Away from the humiliation of being different. Bernardo cried, too, for himself and his siblings.

Quite by accident, Ronnie Caran ran into Andrew Crispo—a man he barely knew—as the two were walking south on Madison Avenue. Andrew was twenty-eight and Ronnie was twenty-six, and it was the summer of 1972, months after Bette Midler had entertained the gyrating, towel-wrapped throngs in the Continental Baths, and months before Catherine

LeGeros's funeral. It was a promising time for the two young men on the avenue.

Caran was no longer the "token Gentile" curator at the Jewish Museum, an important cultural institution on Fifth Avenue that had given him his start in the art business. Instead, he was piecing together a living by brokering, here and there, the sale of major works for the commission money—a couple thousand dollars a pop. It meant months of schmoozing with potential clients, all big collectors, in Paris and London and St. Tropez. Then, after a nibble, he'd fly back to New York to locate the perfect acquisition for their collections. A few more flights with transparencies in hand and the money would be his. In his opinion, it was a charmed life: certainly not a standard job, and not really a career, yet it was an undeniable source of cash, and of that it produced enough to keep his peripatetic life aloft. He was a second-generation jet-setter. His Long Island family was "comfortable—there was always a BMW or a Jag in the driveway," he recalled, but he was not clear how their money came in (or so he liked to say). As a young adult, he was a bon vivant traversing the same circuit as Egon von Furstenberg and the others with whom he had shared boys' school insignia jackets. "I don't even have an apartment here anymore!" he told Crispo. "And you?"

"I'm opening my own gallery," Crispo announced with a boyish grin. He said he was leaving ACA Galleries, the blue-chip art dealership where, for five years, he had practiced the trade. "Come on, I'm going to look at the space now."

Together they entered the Fuller Building on the corner of Madison and Fifty-seventh, which was just inking its mark on the map as *the* apex of the art world.

A doorman stopped them in the lobby.

"We're here to see the space for rent," said Crispo.

"Which one?"

"Both of them," Caran jumped in, and then whispered to Crispo, "Never accept limitations."

The first office, in the back on a high floor, was the one Crispo had already seen, and the one he had intended to take. But the second one they saw, just a flight above street level, with huge windows overlooking all those potential clients, seemed to Caran to be infinitely more promising—although at twice the size, it also proved infinitely more expensive, renting at over six thousand dollars a month. The New York Jets had just vacated it, and a massage parlor and an Off-Track Betting branch were interested, they were told.

After a brief discussion, the two made the only appropriate decision, and Andrew Crispo laid down money for the larger space.

Caran applauded all the way. "Andrew, you're insane to open a space now, anyway—they're closing galleries all over the city. If you're going to go down, make sure there's lots of smoke and flames. Otherwise, nobody will notice that you were here at all."

Crispo, apparently quite pleased upon hearing such a sensible maxim, offered Caran a job that day. "Come on," was how he put it, "this is going to be real fun."

"Frankly," Caran said, "the last thing in the world I want is a job." Instead, he agreed to help out from time to time—putting together shows, helping lure artists away from more prominent galleries, and chipping in on the sales side, where he would collect his precious commissions.

But plans for the new space didn't develop exactly according to blueprint. Crispo had received a promise of a quarter of a million dollars from Josephine Gershman, the wife of a New York real estate mogul and an avid collector in her own right. Gershman had met Andrew only recently, at the ACA, and had bought several paintings from him. "I admired his eye," she told friends later, "and his business sense, where it came to art." When he approached her, she enthusiastically offered the loan.

Almost immediately after Crispo signed the Fuller Building lease, though, Gershman's husband died suddenly, and she found her wealth tangled up in the labyrinthine halls of probate court. Andrew Crispo would have to make due on the sixty-thousand-dollar check she had advanced him, much of which went toward his deposits. (Gershman later said he paid back every cent: "It was a purely business arrangement," she said.) So he tendered his resignation to ACA founder Sidney Bergen, an older gentleman, and took with him one of Bergen's best and brightest, George Perret, along with a handful of clients and artists. As a team, with Caran pitching in, they pinched and scraped along.

Arthur Smith, of course, was a principal player. Shortly after he went to work for Billy Baldwin (often called the most sought-after decorator in America), Baldwin—reportedly quite taken by Arthur's aristocratic taste and his southern style—packed his riches off to a Nantucket retirement, willing his cash-rich and redecoration-crazy clientele to his young associate.

Smith stepped in immediately to spearhead a shoestring renovation of the Crispo Gallery. It was he who chose the placements of the gallery walls, the colors of the rooms, the fabric on the furniture. He had special-ordered the towering front doors ("We saw some just like them in Italy," he explained) and studiously selected the brass fixtures that adorned them. And it was a graceful, magnificent space. Each room had a name, inspired by the colors that decorated it: The Brown Room was for viewing paintings from a select period; the Green Room had a green sofa facing a blank wall, where prospective buyers—the high rollers—could study select works in hushed, dramatic environs; the Main Gallery, painted white and carpeted gray, was gently and seductively lit so as to bathe the displayed works in compliments.

Crispo's office, the Red Room, was dark and curtained. The deep, rich walls and ink red rug gave a wicked sense of power to this place; they seemed to close in from all sides, more half nelson than caress. This is where the deals would be hammered out, where the checks would be signed. The room held one of Andrew's first treasures: a Louis XVI desk, "signed by Avril," that he bought from Edward Garrett, the antique dealer, for nine thousand dollars.

The end product was glorious, thanks to Arthur Smith. Said an acquaintance from back then, "Andrew was a creation, from top to bottom, of Arthur's. He gave him the class, the decorum, the taste, and the style to pull this whole thing off."

Artists found the place intoxicating, and drooled at the thought of exhibiting there. Some, like the contemporary painter David Ligare, followed Crispo over from Sidney Bergen's ACA Galleries without hesitation. "We're the same age," said the twenty-eight-year-old artist to his friends, "but he seems so well connected, he's got some kind of a clout I can't explain." And when challenged by the staff at ACA, Ligare said he didn't care to know anything about where Crispo's seed money was coming from. "I thought it had something to do with the Florsheim Shoes that was downstairs in the building," he said later, "but that didn't matter. He was an extremely energetic guy, had a very good eye. It was a great pleasure to be around him. To feel that energy of his."

Soon, some of the art world's powerhouses signed up. Richard Pousette-Dart, considered among the first members of the "first generation" of American Abstract Expressionism, staged some of his most important shows there. Arman, the collage maker whose work—the random accumulation of objects (gloves, paintbrushes, sneakers) affixed to a board—placed him in the forefront of the European neo-Dadaist movement, joined the gallery early on. So did Charles Seliger and Robert Courtright. And Richard Anuszkiewicz, the Op Art maverick, and Lowell Nesbitt, the popular still-life painter best known for his mural-sized depictions of bright flower blossoms. Andrew Crispo was on the ground running.

Fred Eversley, a young sculptor in plastics, swelled at his inclusion in this stable. "I first laid eyes on Andrew Crispo at ACA Galleries, back in 1973," explained Eversley, a black artist who later became the first artist-in-residence at the Smithsonian.

"Later, when he was opening his gallery, an acquaintance of mine named Ronnie Caran talked me into going over. I had had some fair amount of exposure already: My first showing was at the Jewish Museum, and the Whitney had given me a one-man show. And so I felt that that kind of showcase was for me. A good space. And he was obviously putting together a good gallery, with good people. And so I said I was proud of the company I was in."

Such a mix of talented young artists lent prestige and credibility to a gallery, but did not make it successful automatically. Arman's work was selling for the relatively affordable price of a couple thousand dollars each, and Eversley's going prices ran no higher than four thousand dollars, half of which was split between the gallery and the employee responsible for closing the sale. The big money was in back-room sales—the merchandising of established paintings done by established artists, living and dead. Successful galleries owned a sizable inventory of these coveted works, or took in masterpieces on consignment from other dealers or owners to draw serious collectors with serious checkbooks.

Crispo built up his back room just as quickly (and mysteriously, and enviably) as he amassed his stable. He chose nineteenth- and twentieth-century works, and developed a reputation for his ability to ferret them out of attics and estates and other galleries like no one else.

His particular love was for that group of American and European modern artists who belonged to an elite circle around the late photographer Alfred Stieglitz. 291 Madison, Stieglitz's first gallery, showcased Rodin, Matisse, Picasso, and Brancusi; at The American Place, his last gallery, he promoted contemporaries such as Ansel Adams, Arthur Dove, Marsden Hartley, and Georgia O'Keeffe, his wife. Among them, Crispo preferred the Americans, especially O'Keeffe, renowned for her sensual southwestern landscapes and superdetailed floral paintings. From the start, he collected O'Keeffes whenever cash flow permitted it (once, noticing there were seventeen of her canvases in the gallery, Andrew staged a one-day Georgia O'Keeffe show, using inventory alone).

Perhaps he granted O'Keeffe—known as a recluse who was particularly unfriendly to strangers—a special admiration because she had agreed, a few years before, to receive Crispo and Arthur Smith at her home in New Mexico. The meeting was brief and sweet, and on the way out, Crispo gave her his denim jacket—the one she later wore in the famous photograph of herself. She gave him a small objet trouvé sculpture, fashioned from two small white pieces of driftwood that she had scavenged herself. Crispo called it "the first sculpture she ever made."

At least that's the way he told the story, time after time. People loved to hear it, even in repetition, and no one he told ever seriously doubted it—although there was reason to. O'Keeffe already had a "first sculpture," called *Weeping Lady*. She had given it to Stieglitz and he placed it in her first one-woman show. The contradiction, though, did not matter. The story presented Crispo as a man who knew no obstacles, who saw what he wanted and went about grabbing it—and people ate it up.

"Andrew had such a sense of confidence about himself," said David Ligare, "that would make you feel that this was an absolutely ordinary thing that he would get in to see Georgia. He took great pleasure in presenting it that way—very matter-of-fact." When it came to showing off the growing collection of O'Keeffe paintings, and other works from the Stieglitz circle, his excitement shone through in white flashes.

"He was just like a child," one of his artists said. "He had an unrestrained delight in the whole art world. But when it came to certain paintings—O'Keeffe's, Arthur Dove's, John Marin's—he would absolutely spill over! 'I got this in a coup,' or 'I can't believe this is actually *mine!*' It was love, it was fun; this wasn't just business."

With the paint on the gallery walls still drying, Crispo, George Perret, and Ronnie Caran, who was still just pitching in, began laying the groundwork for the first large-scale show at the Andrew Crispo Gallery, which they called "Pioneers of American Abstraction."

"We're not doing this for the money," Crispo explained, "but for the quality. I don't care if we don't sell a thing." The three of them rounded up a catalogue of nineteenth- and twentieth-century paintings that was "a surprise," according to one *New York Times* reviewer. Crispo's prized O'Keeffes were on display, and many of the offbeat collages by Joseph Stella that he'd been collecting long before that area of his work was prized. He mixed in loaners representing some of the best, and most familiar, works of the masters: Stuart Davis, Arthur Dove, John Marin, Charles Demuth, Oscar Bluemner, Charles Sheeler, and Max Weber. Some were borrowed from private collections; most were on consignment from the leading galleries around town: ACA and Hirschl & Adler, Marlborough and André Emmerich.

When the show opened in early 1973 and good notices poured in ("Whether it means to or not, the show puts a familiar band of painters in a changed and very appealing light," said the *Times*), Andrew Crispo met a man who would change his destiny.

"You have misspelled the name of the owner of this one," a middle-aged man with a Teutonic accent said to Crispo. He was pointing at a Charles Demuth watercolor on the wall, called *Rooftop and Steeples*. A caption beneath it announced it was on loan from the Baron Hans Heinrich von Thyssen-Bornemisza and the name was incorrectly spelled.

"I don't think so," Crispo replied politely. "What makes you say that?"

"Because I am Baron Thyssen-Bornemisza," he said, slowly enunciating *TEES-an-born-a-MEES-ah.*

He was a jovial, kindly man of great wealth and slight pretensions. Everyone called him "Heini." The baron's German grandfather (the Andrew Carnegie of Europe) built up one of the continent's largest steel and iron fortunes ("My mother irons and my father steals," Heini enjoyed saying). His father and uncle, by virtue of a split decision on the Hitler question, did business with Germany and the Allies, making the family empire one of the world's largest private corporations, which eventually encompassed countless unglamorous concerns such as auto parts, packaging, farm machinery (and farms), and electrical products. Gross yearly receipts, spread over several Thyssen-related conglomerates on three continents, were in the billions.

Heini inherited the whole thing—giving him an estimated annual income near $50 million—along with his father's coveted collection of old master paintings, which interested Heini much more than the myriad businesses in his empire. From his castle on Lake Lugano in Switzerland ("La Villa Favorita," the Thyssens called it), Heini began adding to the collection, and had already built it up to the point where it was considered the largest in the world by private standards—second only to that of England's Queen Elizabeth II, which is considered a public collection. (He saw another difference between the two holdings. He was only the third generation building this cache, and personally handpicked each of the new additions; the queen merely inherited hers from the centuries of royalty before her. "Her Majesty is no collector," he used to snipe, "she is interested in horses!") About his acquisitiveness, the *Washington Post* once wrote, "The Baron single-handedly competes with wealthy nations and with great museums. His eye is sharp, his fortune large, his ambition even larger. He buys and buys and buys."

Andrew Crispo was mortified by his typographical gaff. There were apologies, and hands were clasped in brisk forgiveness. Though Crispo was half the baron's age, and a fraction of his social stature, and infinitely more embarrassed, he did not cower. Nor did he pretend that his beautiful, humble gallery in midtown was anything more than that. They joked, held out wine to one another, and struck up a relaxing rapport. Baron Thyssen left the gallery that evening with four new paintings to add to his Lugano stocks.

More importantly, he also strengthened his resolve to bulk up his collection with American works, particularly the early modernists that Crispo loved so much. And he left New York with an admiration for the young man whose "Pioneers" show had helped him to understand the importance of that creative movement.

* * *

A gusty night in May 1974. Searchlights scratched the sky in moth-flight patterns, occasionally flashing on the bellies of three flagpoles jutting out from the Fuller Building and casting aloft huge shadows like rips in the heavy black facade. A two-deep stream of taxis and limousines inched toward the building's shiny doors, barely stopping as they deposited the city's leading figures on the curb to nod to photographers and step into the cool marble and brass lobby. There, a fair man in a tuxedo ushered them into the elevator, and pushed 2, for the Andrew Crispo Gallery. Here came Liza Minnelli, direct from a Broadway show; there was Joel Grey, and Carol Channing, and Sammy Davis, Jr., and Leonard Bernstein, arriving to salute Geraldo Rivera, the newcomer to this society and (all of a sudden) the one man everybody wanted to meet.

As a general-assignment reporter for the local ABC station, Rivera was not accustomed to being a celebrity. But an exposé two years earlier had begun his ascent. He had used a stolen passkey to enter the Willowbrook State School, which he termed a "leper colony" for unwanted and severely retarded youth. His cameras captured some of the most disturbing pictures ever aired of American children—some smeared with their own feces, many naked and sitting on hard floors, most roaring a monosyllabic wail that had since echoed relentlessly in the national conscience. "This is what it looked like," Rivera's narration went, "this is what it sounded like. But how can I tell you about the way it smelled? It smelled of filth, it smelled of disease, and it smelled of death."

Not the kind of calling card that would ordinarily land one in the middle of the season's glitziest Café Society soiree. But the reporter was able to parlay the whole affair into a major career curtain raiser. To pay his dues, or to keep the flames fanned, he had recently helped found the One-to-One Foundation, a charity aimed at finding workable solutions to the problems he had helped expose. And that night's black-tie crowd plunked down between $125 and $1,000 apiece to sip strong drinks and be part of it all.

Young Andrew Crispo, an even newer parvenu, was bobbing along on the same wave—and with motives as mixed as Geraldo Rivera's, ambitions just as grand.

In the eighteen months since opening his space, his resolve to make the Andrew Crispo Gallery one of the most important art spaces in the city, "the next Marlborough Gallery," had been cemented. The earlier "Pioneers of American Abstraction" had put him on the map virtually overnight. For his encore, he planned a major retrospective, "Ten Americans: Masters of Watercolor," and in anticipation he'd hired Patricia Hamilton, a rising star (though just twenty-four) in the art-curating world, to pull the thing together. Her first discovery was that no museum would loan masterpieces to this fledgling gallery show unless it affiliated with a charity benefit. One-to-One was suggested to Crispo, and he gave the nod; the rules of the game were acknowledged.

Plus—and he truly enjoyed telling this part—Andrew Crispo really understood what life must be like in the Willowbrooks of the world, for he, too, had been committed to an institution. St. John's Orphanage, a Roman Catholic holding center for unwanted children in southwest Philadelphia, had been his first home. At least once after that (he was never clear on this point), promising foster parents returned him to the home for some unstated reason. Brute determination alone did not enable him to have come so far; for his reentry into society, he credited the elderly, eccentric Judge Bonnelley from family court, "my white-haired angel," who had entrusted him with a job, told him about his family, and planted in him a bulb of confidence that had grown larger and flashier every year since he had arrived in New York. One-to-one, the judge had changed Crispo's life.

Andrew Crispo gave temporary office space to the foundation, and helped organize one of the grandest affairs of 1974, all the while mounting the most ambitious private exhibition of the season. There were original watercolors by Milton Avery, Charles Burchfield, Charles Demuth, Arthur Dove, Edward Hopper, Maurice Prendergast, and Andrew Wyeth; masterworks by John Marin, Winslow Homer, and John Singer Sargent. One hundred fifty-eight pieces in all, each worth a tidy sum, even in the days before artworks began fetching millions. It was a museum-quality show, the buzz of the Fuller Building and the rest of the art community. Jackie Kennedy Onassis had lent from her private collection.

The opening-night gala benefit for Geraldo's cause was more lavish still, perhaps disproportionately grand. Following the cocktail hour (and a socially acceptable amount of time musing on the works displayed in the gallery), the celebrants were escorted back into the brass elevator, back through the lobby, and out to the sidewalk. From there, a twelve-foot-wide red carpet drew them across East Fifty-seventh Street's four lanes and into the Jaguar showroom (cleared of cars for the evening), where an orchestra played into the morning hours. For more than an hour, though, Carol Channing, Joel Grey, and Liza Minnelli sang along to the music of Fats Waller, Jr., who jammed away wildly. It was after 4:00 A.M. when police lifted their barricades and allowed crosstown traffic to resume.

Crispo showed giddy pleasure with the magical world he had created, and after the masses had glided across the street, he called a meeting of the troops. The gallery looked beautiful, he told Patricia Hamilton and

Ronnie Caran; the paintings were expertly hung; the drinks were just strong enough. *The New York Times* agreed, in the days to come, and twice raved about the show. "Thank you," Crispo said in a pouring voice.

The genuflection done with, those present recalled, he began dishing dirt. "Nice ass on that boy," he said of someone's tuxedoed date. "And *him*," he said of another young man, "he must have a dick like a fireplug!" It was vintage Crispo, on a hormone roll. "Control yourself, Andrew," came the always candid—and booming—response from Patricia Hamilton, the show's curator and the only woman employee at the gallery then. "He looked too expensive for you, anyway!"

Despite her protestations, Hamilton seemed to enjoy Crispo's postpubescent impertinences, and when she entertained her boyfriend with the tales of "boys' world," he enjoyed it, too. "Sometimes he gets downright disgusting," she would say, not altogether disturbed, "but that's just *him*." Patricia was not a delicate woman herself—standing just under five feet six, she had the young, robust, forceful presence of a golf pro. Her blond hair was lopped across the front in unattended bangs. Sitting, she tended to plant her feet wide and press her square palms into each knee. Sometimes, to make a point, a hand would rise quickly and rocket back down into place.

Macho sparring, in their first few months together, was one of her worktime pleasures, one of the things that made her happier at "boys' world" than she had been as a senior editor at the prestigious magazine *Art in America*, her last job and a position she felt both unqualified for and uninspired by. Here, it was her against the wily wits of Andrew and Ronnie, and she held her own handsomely.

Except for once, in their early days together. She had already boarded a plane for Europe and had fastened her seat belt when a stewardess called her off the plane. There, a stammering airline official whispered, "Miss Hamilton? Your doctor has left an urgent message. You have a serious case of syphilis, and will not be allowed into France." It took several phone calls before she was able to convince the ground crew that it was her priapic boss (calling from her own still-bubbling going-away party), and not a doctor, who had made the diagnosis.

When she returned from her trip, Caran and Crispo giggled like toddlers. "*Not* funny," she said, scooping the air around her ear with a cupped hand. The matter was laid to rest.

Andrew and Ronnie, after the black-tie crowd had cleared out of the gallery and the staff had been dismissed, pressed their foreheads against the window in the reception area that overlooked East Fifth-seventh Street and gazed down into the showroom dance hall.

"Why don't you go over? *Every*body's asking for you," Caran ventured.

Despite his sexual gregariousness, Crispo was a painfully shy man in social situations; he wanted fame but not the society fracas that went along with it. If he could have made his name famous without putting in a single appearance—the Andy Warhol method—he would have been quite pleased.

"For a little while, maybe," Andrew said.

Ronnie ribbed him gently about staying so distant at the opening, and Andrew smiled, acknowledging it, and pointed down to a woman dancing wildly in a red sequined dress behind the Jaguar windows. "Is that Liza?" He had missed seeing her at the gallery. Indeed, Crispo spoke only to the people he *had* to speak to and he avoided, or was missed by, the many cameras on hand.

To anyone strolling below the Andrew Crispo Gallery that night, the men posed in that window wouldn't have seemed particularly remarkable. Ronnie Caran looked like the older of the two (although he was twenty-seven, two years Andrew's junior) and infinitely more at ease with the type of clientele to which a successful art gallery must tenderly cater. His elastic face already sported lines and balloons of flesh that, on his slight (five seven) figure, gave him a cuddly, pixyish look; there was a temptation always to pat his curly head, and too often that urge was aggressively vented.

Crispo was more traditionally handsome, 1974-style. His floppy brown hair parted in the middle and dangled in strands on his tux jacket, making him seem entirely too young to be the man behind the gold lettering— ANDREW CRISPO GALLERY—that floated on the window above his head like a thought bubble in a comic strip. His tuxedo swam like a sack suit on his lithe body. When he smiled, which was often that night, arching dimples drew upward on his hollow cheeks and formed a wicked downturn at the far corners of his chestnut eyes, and those always seemed to sparkle. He was having too much fun to be an entrepreneur; indeed, he looked more like one of the actor-waiters who had just left his gallery, and most of the visitors undoubtedly mistook him for just that.

Not that he had done anything to stop the confusion. Peter Brown, who had been the Beatles' manager and was a social acquaintance, had taken to calling Crispo "Funny Money," in the absence of any reliable explanation of how he managed to open the gallery and sustain its staff, however meager. Each time Crispo heard the name, the corners of his eyes curled down and his thick Italian lips parted in a whoop of amusement. He said nothing. Brown found this evasiveness refreshingly enigmatic: "When he learned about the Funny-Money appellation," he said later, "he certainly wasn't embarrassed by it, and he obviously was amused. And it amused me that it amused him that people were so curious; and he wasn't going to let them know. An explanation could have been quite simple, of course, but that wouldn't have been good enough."

Everyone seemed to enjoy the mystery surrounding Crispo. Even those few tidbits of information Andrew made available about his background seemed suspicious: He said he was orphaned as an infant, which seemed hard to believe, so charming and well spoken was he; he said he had received no formal art training, despite his keen eye for rare and exciting works. It was widely known that he was gay—professionally, he never tried to hide that—but it was viewed as his private business. Yet he regularly told potential partners he met in gay bars—people for whom his private business would normally matter more—that he was straight! A favored story had his wife and child perishing recently in a terrible car accident, leaving him still in shock, seeking comfort where he could find it.

Andrew Crispo saw in the world a Procrustean conspiracy—immutably rigid rules of expected conduct that required a rote response. Wherever possible, he rebelled. In any new situation, he studied the boundaries, the strictures and regulations, and then, in a choreographed flurry, he would carefully and surely ignore them.

Faced with the vague suggestion that underworld types had financed his gallery, for example, he would jauntily hint that he entered and left via a back stairway on Fifty-eighth Street, "in case I'm being followed." He never suggested who might be so interested in his activities. That was left up to the imagination of others.

On the night of the Geraldo Rivera benefit, though, he took the traditional route out to the street, joining the crush of stars across the way. Later, he and Caran mopped the floors themselves before heading to their separate homes.

Three months before the benefit, on Valentine's Day, 1974, eleven-year-old Bernardo LeGeros and his father walked around their property on Buckberg Mountain Road (or "Buckberg," family shorthand for the weekend home), kicking branches out of the deer paths below the house and not talking much. It had become their ritual, this swing through the woods, and as always they doted tenderly on their two dogs in a way they did not share with one another.

Each straightaway in the paths had been given a name, each bend another, just as Andrew Crispo had named each of his gallery rooms: Three Snake Way, Turtle Turn, Revolutionary Road. It was John's idea. He had decided that, with small children and several acres of land, it was a good idea to name major geographical cross points. "In case something was lost," he would proudly explain, "at least we would have an idea where to look." It was that kind of near-military forethought that characterized his every action, informed his every plan.

It was just one small symbol of the kind of chilly, strategic way he handled fatherhood—not *harsh* as much as it was textbook-inspired; not *authoritarian* as much as instructive. Bernardo couldn't remember the last time he had kissed, or hugged, or spoken intimately with his father, a tall white-haired gentleman with a lumpy face. But it didn't necessarily seem wrong to him. It seemed particularly natural to John, who had grown up in Watertown, South Dakota, with a rugged farmer's perspective on maturity, masculinity, and family management. He was a man for whom tradition held the weight of science. Each of his sons, for example, bore the middle name John, just as he had inherited his middle name from his father.

Nonetheless, he was also a man of some dark mystery. Months after Bernardo was conceived, some trouble erupted back in his hometown. When Racquel pressed him for information, he was forced to admit, for the first time, that he had been married before, and had fathered several children. The circumstances of that marriage, and why it dissolved, were never fully revealed.

To Bernardo, though, one fact about his older half brothers seemed extremely significant: Their middle names were all John, too. The tradition extended in all directions.

"Do you think Major and Gypsy will be okay with us gone, Dad?" Bernardo was asking.

"They'll be fine."

"Hope so," the young boy said. He grabbed a dog's tail for a little help ascending one of the steep hills back behind the house. "Hear that, Major?"

The mammoth St. Bernard had been Bernardo's closest companion since they had moved into this house years before, and the young LeGeros was only now approaching the dog's size, while still not three-quarters the weight. Gypsy, a golden retriever, had been around just as long, but she was more independent—less of a friend—and Bernardo's allegiance was no secret. Once, when Gypsy returned home after a days-long outing, Bernardo scolded her: "See what you've done to Major? He was so *worried* about you!"

This afternoon, Bernardo and David would be sitting next to their father on a plane headed for Yemen, where John was about to begin a three-year foreign posting. Racquel would stay behind with their two daughters, whom she considered too young for such an experience.

She had her own reasons for remaining in New York. Having been awarded her long-sought Ph.D., Racquel was not about to give up the opportunity to take her first teaching assignment, at NYU in Manhattan. Her career had been delayed long enough, what with this litter of four and a husband who couldn't seem to stay in any single field long enough to bring the family comfort or give her time to focus on herself. Despite her religious upbringing (her father was a Methodist minister of the evangelical sort), Racquel Zapanta-LeGeros was not a traditional Filipina by any measure. She was ambitious, brilliant, and impatient. She had left for America to study as soon as she turned eighteen. So determined was she to make the trip, and so convinced that there'd be objections, she waited until just before her flight to break the news to her parents. Now in her late thirties, she would finally have her turn.

John helped her find a small apartment in a well-kept tenement on East Fourteenth Street in the city. This would put her within walking distance of work, and would allow the family to rent out Buckberg, the four-bedroom Tomkins Cove home that they really couldn't afford, anyway. "We fell in love with it and mortgaged everything, long before we were ready," she had said. Her mother had already flown over from the Philippines and set up the new apartment, in anticipation of helping with the girls—Kara was just four and Sasha was a newborn.

On Valentine's Day, they were saying good-bye to the country house. The females would be dropped off on Fourteenth Street, and the males would continue on to the airport; the boxes and suitcases were already in the trunk. The dogs—and Bernardo didn't know this—would be cared for by neighbors until they could be given away, or otherwise disposed of.

John returned to the house after the short hike, and organized the crowds into their various vehicles. It seemed every time something of even the most marginal import happened to the LeGeros family, a swarm of Racquel's relatives (most of whom had since followed her to this country) would arrive to take part in it. A dozen car doors slammed, and there they all sat.

When Bernardo finally appeared in the driveway, Racquel was livid. "Where *were* you? Everybody was looking for you," she snapped.

"Well, I had to—I was talking to Major."

"It was a half an hour, *really*," she said. Her voice could leap octaves; remnants of a Tagalog inflection surfaced in heated moments. "What did you tell him?"

Bernardo said, "I told him to take care of you, to take care of the house, this and that."

"My God, it's a *dog* only," she said, and dug around impatiently in her purse for something. "And don't start about wanting to bring him along with you again. There's not enough food in Yemen for the people there, and to bring a two-hundred-pound animal! It would be almost a *sin*."

The cultural transition was very difficult for Bernardo, in particular. Except for a brief visit the boys paid to New York later that summer, it wasn't until Christmas, when his mother and sisters came to Yemen, that the family was united again. Life over those long months had been fascinating in the most unpredictable—if not perilous—ways.

On their first weekend in a windowless house in San'a, the Yemeni capital, David and Bernardo had walked to the nearby souk, an open-air marketplace where food and supplies are sold, just in time to witness a double beheading. It was unclear to them whether this was a governmental act or some renegade event; the heads fell to the ground with an momentous thud, nonetheless. They were immediately retrieved and displayed on tall wooden poles that pierced their windpipes and forced their lifeless mouths open in a quiet scream.

Some weeks later, by most accounts, Bernardo was kidnapped. He had been back to the souk with some other boys from the "international community" and a man draped in cloth sashes had "lured him away with snakeskins," John later told Racquel. "I'm convinced it was for some white-slavery ring, or something like that. I looked for him for hours and so did the authorities before he was able to escape and get back to the house." The white-slavery part seemed a dubious assessment, though; the low sun over Yemen bronzed Bernardo's skin and he appeared more Filipino than ever.

The effects of these strange events were immediately evident in Bernardo's schoolwork. He was having a difficult time keeping up at the American school, and had raised some concern with the creepy, apparently death-obsessed drawings he was submitting to his art instructor. The school's director, Dr. James Gilson, was so concerned that he called John in to discuss what might be souring the boy's mind. John examined the creations—mostly warlike scenes of bombings, or executions, or gunfire, or plane crashes—and dismissed Dr. Gilson's preoccupations. "Boys do this," he said.

Bernardo's written expression, however, was not as easily ignored. In response to an essay question, he once wrote: "One of these days I will rob the cold store of all its goods. I really want to kill but I don't know of anybody to kill."

"Perhaps," Dr. Gilson suggested to the elder LeGeros, "the changes here have just been too great for him. We've seen this happen to other children." And he suggested that a private school, perhaps in Britain, might better serve Bernardo's needs.

So when Racquel (with Kara and Sasha) arrived in Yemen for their Christmas break, she came in part to help explain to the boys that they'd be going to England. Bernardo would study at the Pierrepont Military School in Surrey, and David had been registered at Lindesfarne College, hours away in North Wales. "We have thought about it, and think it would be good for the two of you to be apart for a while," Racquel explained. "That way, you'll be able to develop independently."

Bernardo appealed to his father, who said, "This has already been decided. There will be no discussion."

The visit—and it was just ten days long—was off to a pretty shaky start.

For one thing, Racquel often cried during the days and frequently argued into the night with John. Bernardo drew his own conclusions: She must fear that John was having an affair with one of his coworkers, although she never confessed such a thing to him. But then, Bernardo had developed a similar suspicion. "Dad's friendly with everybody," Bernardo explained to David one night, "maybe extremely *beyond* friendly. To the point where some women get this little thing in their heads that he's in love with them." Privately, he suspected his father's friendship with one woman in particular, but he did not tell his mother about this. Instead, he hugged her regularly, and tried to spend as much time as possible at her side.

But it wasn't a pure sympathy he was offering, either. "I think she's weak," he'd tell David, confidentially, after they were sent to bed. "And he's fucking indecisive."

"We'll write letters, right?" asked David tentatively. "We'll still be brothers?"

"Aw, 'course," said Bernardo. And he held up the palm of one hand and curled over his knuckles into their secret wave, inspired by Major, the St. Bernard. "Big Bear Paws," he said.

"Big Bear Paws."

CHAPTER

4

By mid-September of 1984, the key functional task Crispo set for his new employee, besides the "bodyguard" and "executioner" services, was to rebuild the gallery's dispersed sales records. When word of the IRS investigation had first reached Crispo more than a year before, he had bundled up his sales receipts, tax filings, and provenance charts and shipped them to various locations around the city. Hal Burroughs took a few boxes and stashed them in his small studio. So did his friend Hank and a handful of other acquaintances, not absolutely sure why they were doing it (but neither did they ask too many questions). A few boxes were squirreled away in the Manhattan Mini-Storage bin where Crispo kept the Snoop and Scoop records on his untrustworthy employees, or in Crispo's downtown apartment.

When Crispo took the secretive new headquarters in the Galleria apartment near the Fuller Building, on a sublease ("no formal lease, no paper trails," he told a friend), he felt sufficiently safe to reunite them. A gallery's files are essential to its successes. They represent years of research and study into each artist's works—their origins and their current locations—and hundreds of thousands of dollars in invested time, materials, and art-world intelligence. That they were scattered, Crispo was convinced, was the main reason business had slacked off so dramatically over the past year.

Bernard set about retrieving the boxes and taking them back to the two-room apartment, outfitted with a large bed, a typewriter, a Xerox machine, and a marble shower so spacious that a waist-high male figurine stood in one corner. With the office equipment, Crispo undertook the enormous task of changing his receipts to mirror his tax filings, packing new boxes page by page with the erroneous records for Bernard to carry down to the U.S. Attorney's office. He had absolute confidence that the doctoring would go undetected.

At the same time, though, he felt that he couldn't trust the junior attorney from the law firm handling the case—Saxe, Bacon & Bolan, legal home to Roy Cohn. "Andrew feels that he's going against him," Bernard told a friend about the associate working with them. "That he's trying to make a deal, sell him out. So I go downtown with him every time, and take a microcassette, a bug. I make recordings of everything he says, and I read all the papers he has, everything he's turning over, and memorize it all. All of those boxes, I just absorb the information and give an intelligence report to Andrew later in the day."

Only Bernard seemed immune to suspicion on the tax front. In fact, while working late one evening, Bernard offered to take the heat for Crispo.

"How much would you want?" Crispo wondered.

"Well, how much time would I get?"

"A misdemeanor? About a year, year and a half."

"I think two hundred a year would work. Two hundred plus a million dollars up front."

"A million up front! You're crazy. You'd be going to Allentown—Club Fed. That's not worth a million."

"Okay, how much then?"

"Flat fee. Two hundred a year. You sign an affidavit, you go before the grand jury, and you say that I had no knowledge of this. That you were doing this to protect me, to save me some money. That I knew nothing about this. And spell it out: A, B, C, D."

"Two hundred for twelve months."

"Probably less. Good time, you get out in seven."

"Fuck it, Andrew," said Bernard, smiling. "You got a deal."

He never filled out that affidavit, in part because Crispo's attention to the tax matters waned quickly, and his intrigue with Bernard's rougher skills grew proportionately.

With each mission of terror, espionage, and counterespionage successfully completed, Bernard was rewarded with friendship, and with most-trusted status. He was quickly anointed the unchallenged gallery director. Not that he knew a thing about art: With just two years of continuing education behind him—he had dropped out of political science courses at NYU to take the gallery job—Bernard was an art-world neophyte. "He was always asking what you were doing, what official business you were tending to," said one gallery worker. "And if, on those rare occasions when Andrew came in, you walked back to the Red Room, he would stand in front of you and demand, 'What do you want? Nobody goes in there but me!' " If he caught an employee studying something they shouldn't study, he would bark, "You want to lose those eyes?"

Susan Slack, the receptionist, and Ronnie Caran were both square in the young man's cross hairs. The two other gallery employees were deemed apparently trustworthy, especially George Perret, the elderly gentleman whom Andrew had hired away from ACA a decade back. Ellery Kurtz was something of a question mark, until he tattled on Susan. Then his tenure was cemented.

In late September, Andrew Crispo sat in an easy chair in the Red Room and summoned Susan to see him. He pointed to a folder that was resting on the coffee table. In pen across the top was written: "Susan Slack, S&S." Snoop and Scoop.

Crispo accused her of stealing prints from the gallery, which he said she had attempted to sell at several hundred apiece. He pointed to the dossier and called it "irrefutable evidence." She stayed in his office for nearly an hour, the door tightly closed.

Bernard, meanwhile, approached Caran and Ellery Kurtz, demanding to know where Susan kept her purse. "In the back, I guess," one of the men said, and they both followed Bernard and watched him rifle through it. He removed papers (which he later said were examples of the gallery's tax records) and grabbed her keys. Then he left the gallery.

Later, he confessed, "I made copies of her keys. I gave 'em to Andrew, and he gave 'em to somebody to go through the apartment later. We found out where she was keeping the prints. All kinds of shit."

Bernard had no way of knowing how significant it was for Crispo to be turning on Susan Slack. He knew nothing of their longtime friendship, nor of the alliance between them, and against Victor Ruggiero, a former gallery employee whom he never met. But even if he had known, it's not clear it would have mattered. Bernard was eager to please his new boss's most illogical whim.

Bernard knew Andrew Crispo on a level much more profound than any of the older man's former confidants. Of that, Bernard was convinced.

With him, Andrew acted more naturally, said things directly and honestly. Theirs was a playful relationship, filled with play words and play realities. Alone, they had code names for people and places: The Command Vehicle was Bernard's Vista Cruiser; the Crystal Palace was Andrew's secret Galleria apartment. Bernard was called Raven, and Andrew was Condor. Susan, before she was fired, was Pigeon 1, and Ronnie was Pigeon 2. "Stool pigeons," they would say, chuckling between endless lines of cocaine. "Pigeons under glass!"

And alone, they discussed other, very important similarities, which Bernard found completely beyond comprehension. At first. Andrew— like Bernard and his brother, David, and his father, John—was born in April. And Andrew's middle name was John, the same as Bernard and David. When he pointed out the coincidence to Andrew, his new boss acted as though he'd already discerned it. "You know, I was an orphan," Crispo said, "abandoned by a father of French descent to live alone in the orphanage. Maybe I'm your half brother."

"Well," Bernard said, flustered, "that couldn't have been *my* dad. He never lived in Philadelphia. And he wouldn't do that."

"Didn't you tell me he did it to his other family? Just abandoned them?"

Bernard, of course, didn't reject the story entirely; he filed it away as a topic that he must consider further.

Their intimacies were not limited to personal chatter over family matters. Indeed, they included sexuality, if not sex itself. They were regulars at the Hellfire, and in the coke-rushed hours before dawn, they were frequently seen walking through the sticky streets of the meat-packing district shopping for young men for Andrew. The coke and wine and sleepless nights—weeks, sometimes—had begun to spoil Andrew's looks; he was bloated and pale, his arms had broken through the seams in his expensive jackets, and although his trousers no longer met in the front, it didn't stop him from wearing them. Bernard was an especially attractive piece of bait, an invaluable asset on such outings.

When they scored, Bernard would disappear into the streets. "I give him a few hours," he would tell a friend, "and then go and make sure everything was all right." What could go wrong? "Coupla things," he'd say. "Number one, he likes grabbing a few of them a little young, corruption of the morals of a minor and shit like that.

"For another, sometimes he worries things might get out of hand."

At first, he wasn't exactly sure what Andrew favored in his sexual outings. Bernard had perused the bag of toys, had slapped that giant dildo into his palm like a billy club, and had once tried on the leather hood. The world of sexual dominance and submission was not entirely alien to him: Twice, he had let a prostitute tie him to her bedposts and hold a handgun to his head. He found that it enhanced his "load." Yet he showed little interest in Crispo's involvements. What gay men did together, he said, did not interest him in the slightest.

He was not destined, though, to maintain this distance. One night, still in his first month in Crispo's employ, Bernard returned to the gallery after dinner and found Andrew and a guest in the Red Room. Andrew was wearing dark brown running shorts, a black T-shirt, and a baseball-style police cap. The guest, a dentist in his late twenties, was naked on the floor, in a dog's cower. For a long time, Bernard watched from the doorway as Andrew used a horse whip on the man's backside.

Then Andrew reached for the dildo, fourteen inches and eight pounds of latex, and ordered it inserted, which the dentist did, slowly but willingly, an impressive feat.

Bernard left the room as Crispo was forcing his captive to pray for his safety to a large African fetish, which ordinarily stood on a pedestal behind the sofa. "It's made of blood and mud," Bernard heard Crispo saying. "Pray that your blood doesn't become part of it." Then the strapping started up again.

In the late fall of 1984, Lowell Nesbitt was the only notable artist remaining in the Crispo Gallery stable, which had once been so prestigious. But he hadn't seen a sale in months, and it had been even longer since he'd received a check. With some hesitation and sadness, Nesbitt sent his studio assistant up to Andrew's gallery with a letter of resignation. "I was told to just get back as many of his paintings as I possibly could," said Tim, the assistant. "There was no doubt that some of them would not be retrieved. 'Just get what you can,' Lowell told me. It was like pulling teeth."

Back in the old days, the Crispo Gallery was among the first on that hallowed stretch of Fifty-seventh Street to begin selling the experimental works of contemporary modern artists. And it was among the first to back away from them, too. There were fewer of those lavish one-man shows that had set Crispo apart from the other dealers, though he was still giving catalogues ("Every show gets a catalogue," he promised his artists, luring them to his camp, "not the flyers you're used to. A catalogue!"). But he was seeing quite clearly what others knew well, that the money— *the money*—was generated out of the back room. A Robert Rauschenberg that had changed hands three times already had a market. In a week's time, Crispo could bank tens of thousands. But it took years of dedicated energy, for instance, to shape the reputation of Douglas Abdell, who first came to Crispo as a very young man. It took dozens of catalogues, countless exhibitions, tender cajoling, and careful planning to raise a similar amount of money.

Not that Crispo was ready to cut anybody loose. Instead, he cut corners. "Andrew was always very straightforward with us," said Evelyn Pousette-Dart, wife of the artist and mother to the rock group. "But he never took us out to lunch, like you might have expected. We knew nothing about him socially." Robert Courtright saw the same trend, likewise David Ligare. "It seemed odd, in a way," Ligare said, "but he finally explained that that was something he wanted to keep separate, his social life from his artists. So while I felt very close to Andrew, in a working sense, there was never any kind of a personal relationship whatsoever. Never."

There were other cost-saving measures, too. He never threw a party for an artist following an opening. Per custom, ten or fifteen people— friends and guests of the artist—would be invited for dinner after such an event. This was how it was done; these were the rules of the game. Fred Eversley didn't know, until his first opening night was almost through, that there was nothing scheduled afterward. "I ended up inviting these people down to Max's Kansas City myself," Eversley said. "This was very weird."

Eversley remained in the gallery's stable for many years, although Crispo was quite furious with him for not sharing the limelight of his Smithsonian appointment. Further—although this was a kosher arrangement, given the contract they had—Eversley didn't cut Crispo in on his large commissioned work for display in the entrance of the Miami airport, two large cylindrical towers. So there was already some bad blood when Andrew suggested to Fred that he contribute money toward advertising for one of his shows. "It's for your career," he remembered Crispo saying then, "to build your sales." Eversley refused.

From there, he said, it snowballed. "He said he could get me a story, a story about me in an art magazine, if I paid for a certain size ad for the gallery. Split the ad costs with him. I said no again. And then, when I went over later to see how my sales were doing, he offered me this: Said there was a major museum that was willing to add one of my pieces to its collection, but there would have to be a payoff, a kickback, to the museum's buyer.

"It never came out of my pocket, and I never heard any more about it—except that the museum bought the piece. For all I know, he wanted to pocket the money himself! I wouldn't even speculate on whether the museum ever got a dime, or the director got a dime—I'm not even saying the name of the museum. I'm saying that this didn't happen to me since, or before. But he said that that's what was supposed to happen."

Nonetheless, the stories about Andrew Crispo's gallery made their rounds, right on up to the clubby Art Dealers Association, which never allowed him to join. Membership might have allowed his gallery to be listed in a roster every week in *The New York Times*, among other perks. "We always found him a bit . . . *off*," an Establishment figure told a reporter. "Everybody had heard the stories," said another.

Privately, they were apparently upset about something very central to the way this gentleman's business was done. He broke the most sacred rule of honor among dealers in fine arts. Andrew Crispo burned paintings.

Not with a torch, but with a greedy marketing strategy. Every gallery in the city was freely releasing major works to Crispo on consignment, under the unspoken assumption that they were "being shown to the baron." Some would attempt to confirm the assumption directly, saying, "It's my understanding you'll be showing this to Thyssen, right?"

Says a former gallery employee, "We never actually *lied*, but we never came clean. If they wanted to think it was going to Heini, that was fine by us."

Most, of course, were indeed passed on to the baron, for a first crack. If he rejected one, Crispo would put it in play on a larger arena—for the same inflated price he had hoped to get from Thyssen. While Knoedler had asked seventy-five hundred, for example, Crispo was asking twenty thousand dollars. And he was showing it to every major collector—from Los Angeles, to Dallas, to Düsseldorf—who were likely to find it a tad expensive. Next, he'd put the piece on the auction block. "I want twenty net," he'd say, "net." Sotheby's would list it for twenty-five thousand dollars, minimum, where it would get no takers—being worth just seventy-five hundred.

The piece would go back to Knoedler, at no profit and no loss to Andrew Crispo. But Knoedler staffers would soon find themselves showing the piece to the same people that Andrew had hit up. Only now, the piece was listed for seventy-five hundred dollars. The reply was universal: "That's a *fraction* of the price I was originally quoted! What's wrong with it?" The item was burned. Nobody wanted it. *It's public knowledge that nobody wanted it!* Perhaps it was a fake, or damaged, or the subject of legal proceedings.

No longer worth even seventy-five hundred, only a decade or more in a closet could mend its reputation. And that wasn't even guaranteed.

Crispo played a similar trick on the very artists his gallery represented. "There was a double price list," said Patricia Hamilton. "During a Charles Seliger show, he gave me this piece of paper and said, 'Never, never, *never* show this to Charles.' It was a parallel price list. One piece that Charles thought he was going to sell for fifty-five hundred, Andrew had priced at eighty-five hundred. So if the piece sold, the artist would get fifty percent of fifty-five hundred, and have no idea! Cynthia Polsky, same thing."

Only two artists, over the years, seemed immune to Crispo's shenanigans. One of them was Douglas Abdell, the sculptor. "He had a screaming case of the hots for Douglas," said one gallery employee. "Andrew was not quiet about his screaming cases of the hots." And not very discreet, either. Victor Ruggiero, the gallery's former registrar, found a black and white photograph of Abdell in one of Crispo's desk drawers, in the same file folder as his gallery leases. Dark, with a bushy mustache and a gorgeous chiseled twenty-year-old face, he had the pectorals and large hands of a man who hoisted giant pieces of steel into monuments. Douglas was naked in the picture, climbing out of a shower, water playing brightly on his full scrotum.

Lowell Nesbitt was the other sacred cow, because he was Crispo's best friend in the art world. For years, it had been Crispo's ritualized practice to call him each morning and, over coffee and morning cigarettes, discuss the artist's work schedule, his inspirations, his business. "They were real close," said Tim, Nesbitt's assistant, "every morning on the phone, from seven-thirty to eight. I think he felt that Andrew was probably smarter than he was, and he liked having smart, attractive people around him— Andrew was a good person to have around. Because Andrew was powerful. And he was his provider." When Lowell's bills outpaced his sales, Andrew would send money on account—a thousand for Con Ed, two thousand for rent. When debits overwhelmed credits on the Crispo ledgers, there'd be a show, grand and successful.

Crispo even formed a separate corporation for Nesbitt, which sold limited, numbered editions of Nesbitt prints. His work was everywhere, his name well known, a downtown artist with an uptown career-maker spinning his brushstrokes to gold.

Crispo freaked out when Nesbitt resigned, of course, and vowed to make it difficult—perhaps impossible—for the artist to disengage the gallery. When Tim returned from delivering the resignation letter to Crispo, he brought very few of Lowell's works. Nesbitt told him to keep going back until they were able to get more.

"I told Andrew, 'Look, it looks like you're having some very serious difficulties that you're not paying any attention to,' " Tim recalled later. " 'There's been a great decline here; everybody's noticed. I don't know if you are, but you should be doing something about your tax problems.' He was very relaxed about it, and I said, 'I don't know how you can laugh about it. You can go to jail.'

"He said, 'I'm not going to go to jail, and besides, I wouldn't mind if

I did.' Which I thought was pretty weird. Like he's just completely bored out of his mind and looking for some new challenge."

Nesbitt, who had relied so heavily on his friendship with Crispo, clung to Tim's story, passionately concerned about his friend. "Look at his upbringing," Tim said, "his orphanage days and all. Nothing very normal or regular happened throughout his childhood, so it seems like he had a behavior pattern in his life that excluded normal, routine things. I think he got adjusted to it, and once the gallery was doing so well, once it got to that point, what was next? And when he said, 'I wouldn't mind going to jail,' that makes you think here's somebody that's got to be truly bored to entertain the possibility of there being fun in that. And it wasn't boys; it wasn't sex at all. I think it was an adventure."

Perhaps because it seemed too off-the-wall, Tim didn't repeat the other part of their conversation, which took place in a private meeting that also included Bernard. "We've got to break into Lowell's," Crispo had said to him. "Take his paintings, take his papers, take any cash we find lying around."

Crispo would not drop the preposterous subject despite Tim's protestations. Several times during those follow-up trips to reclaim Nesbitt's works (eight or ten of which were never returned), either Bernard or Crispo would bring it up, showing particular interest in details about the location of Nesbitt's sales records. Apparently, they feared those records might contain information that they wouldn't want the IRS to discover.

Sometimes, Crispo called Tim at home with the request. At a large New Year's Eve party he and his wife threw, Tim was overheard shouting into a telephone, "Andrew, you're absolutely insane! Lowell's sitting right here! I'm having a party! You think I'm going to leave here and rob his *house?*"

Crispo had apparently belabored the point, citing the "perfect" timing.

"Now is *not* a perfect time for this," Tim insisted. "I'm at my own party!"

By late September, Crispo was showing visible frustration that Bernard had not placed anything significant into Ronnie Caran's S&S file, and announced it was time to turn up the heat. "He besmirched me," Crispo said over and over. He never offered specifics and Bernard never asked. "He's got to pay." Through Bernard, Andrew contracted members of an East Village gang called The Midtown Crew to carry out the mission. They were paid in cash and cocaine.

In phase one, according to the plan, the goal was to gaslight Caran. "The best time to do something to a person is when you have him as disoriented as possible," Crispo explained to Bernard, who explained it to the gang members. "Just keep calling him and calling him and calling him on the phone. Especially in the middle of the night—it fucks up his REM sleep. Calling and calling and calling. Maybe have a couple of people bumping into him on the street, knocking him over, knock over all his groceries or something."

The Midtown Crew made records of his visits to Beulahland, the East Village bar: who sat with him, what they ordered, what times he frequented the place. After a short time, they found it possible to predict Ronnie's movements. One of them placed a call to Bernard.

"About your *ciabotto*, your fucking snitch," he began. "Why don't we take him out? We'll take care of him right away."

Bernard took the suggestion to his boss, who gave this steely reply: "Now is not the time."

"These people are posed for the tango delta," Bernard argued, not altogether surprised at the stakes about which they were talking. It was just a game, like the games he had played with his brother years ago in Rockland County. "Victor's in the house, the fish is red, the sky is blue, the fish is red," Bernard said, loosely quoting the famous Bay of Pigs alert. "Victor's in the house. Go and visit him."

Ordinarily, Crispo enjoyed Bernard's self-styled code-speak, but now he was not playing along.

"That's not part of my plan," Crispo said, outlining phase two. "We've got to be out of the state when this happens. We've got to be in California or something. We gotta have somebody take him to someplace, and then we can sneak back and watch it being done."

"Watch this?" Bernard had never heard of phase two. "Andrew, you're crazy; you can't just do that."

"I want to be the one to take him out," Crispo continued. "We'll both go fly to another state; we'll rent a car and drive back. That'll do the job. Then we'll go back to the place and take the plane back like we're supposed to."

Bernard and his Midtown Crew contacts weren't the only people over whom Crispo lorded authority in the days since his powers in the art business had begun to fail him. Crispo was exercising almost complete domination over a cadre of young followers—dozens of them—who went to his gallery at night, after Bernard LeGeros had sent the other employees home. With them, he was wielding a power that was never his before, not during his apogee, not in the dining rooms of ambassadors, or barons, or Mafia lawyers where he had casually, even sheepishly, sipped cocktails and shared inconsequential observations.

And the young dentist was not the only testing ground for this mastery.

Sexual power, or some variation thereof, had become Crispo's prime focus, his weapon, his quest, and these kids were his soldiers. He didn't allow them to mix with Hal Burroughs, his good friend and fellow traveler to the S&M clubs. Hal wouldn't approve of them; *they* never quizzed the men they found bound and hooded at the gallery, or at the Galleria apartment nearby, or the penthouse in the Village. The intellectual concepts of consent and pleasure were of no palpable interest. They had other concerns.

The boys, most of them young street toughs, would go into the spacious lobby of the Fuller Building, take the elevator to the second floor, and be admitted to Crispo's suite by Bernard, with his neat double-breasted suits and soft face. They were usually heterosexual, sometimes drug dealers, and almost always willing to "party" with someone who must have seemed to them awesomely powerful and wealthy. The boys were either too poor or too dumb, or too ambitious, to resist Andrew Crispo's blandishments, and for enough money or enough drugs, they would perform some decidedly strange services.

They believed what they were told: that the beatings and the rapes would never be reported to the authorities, because the victims—a parade of young gay men who, at least at some point in the evening's activities, had assented to a liaison with Crispo—were too humiliated or too scared to recount what had happened.

Kirk Green and his friend John Parker were part of this sinister world through the summer of 1984 (they called it their "Crispo summer") and into the fall. "It's still a huge mystery to me," recalled Green later, after becoming an art student, "how I got involved. Or how I ever managed to escape."

At seventeen, he was a muscular, attractive boy with a close relationship to his parents, a middle-class couple from Manhattan's Upper West Side. But he fell in with a rough crowd, and by the time he met Crispo, he had already made a name for himself in certain circles as a graffiti artist—scrawling his "tag" in subways, on buildings, or any flat surface he could find. One day, Parker, a part-time drug dealer, took him to meet Andrew Crispo. "You're going to like him," Parker said. "He can do a lot for you."

The two began selling cocaine to Crispo, who would pay them top dollar for two and a half grams at a pop, several times a week. He spent more than other clients would because, Green figured, Crispo liked having them around. Further, he would offer to share his drugs with them, and the three would snort all the coke in one sitting in the back room of the gallery. They'd get high and take home one hundred dollars apiece. "I remember thinking this was a dream connection," Kirk Green said. "I hadn't even started studying art yet, and already I had a gallery owner as a friend. I never questioned his motives once."

Meanwhile, John Parker, had been performing other private services for the art dealer. On at least one occasion, for a hundred-dollar bill, he put on the mask and whipped a nineteen- or twenty-year-old kid named Timmy. He was blond and six feet tall, Parker recalled. It was a strange world, to be sure, but according to Crispo's instructions, there were some rules. "To have the other person be the slave, you have to find out a vulnerability about them, something that you can use to make them feel like they should be punished," Parker explained of the lessons Crispo taught him. About the mask: "He said, 'I wear this or I can make the person wear it,' and he said, 'It'll let me know something of that person, their vulnerability. You should know your people and have control of them, even psychologically.' "

In his own experience, Parker felt the control firsthand. After he had agreed to the terms of the scenario Crispo had spelled out, after he had begun whipping the young man called Timmy, Crispo grew agitated. "Harder," he barked. "Hit him harder or I'll spit on that painting you made for me. I'm telling you!"

Parker threw full force into the lashing, which went on for ten minutes.

Sometimes, Crispo would pose as the victim's "long-lost father" or orphaned brother: blood ties severed, a family blown apart. "To make that person feel, psychologically feel bad and want to be punished," Parker said. "That's what he explained to me."

He had other techniques, as well. Once, Crispo took the leather jacket of one tough-talking twenty-one-year-old and dangled it out a twelfth-floor window, threatening to drop it in traffic; another time, he accused a kid of walking "like a homo." Often, he'd pit one against the other, saying, "He called you a fag" or "He could beat the shit out a weakling like you," and a fight would typically ensue. These, Andrew Crispo watched from the sideline, slightly hunching his shoulders, his eyelids heavy.

One early fall afternoon, Kirk Green went alone to the gallery and was shooting the bull with Bernard when Crispo offered him membership in the "club."

"You're a big, handsome guy," Crispo began. "Bernard and I have this club you really should join."

Bernard smiled quietly—he hardly spoke when his boss was entertaining other boys.

Green asked what it would entail. "We go out and find victims, bring them back here, and . . . have some fun," he was told. Kirk brushed off the idea. "Fuck you guys; just do some more lines." While the concept of torturing someone did not appeal to Green, sex with other men had its secret allure. But this was not something he was going to come clean about, especially not with Crispo, whose antigay hostilities bordered on the violent—even toward himself, it seemed to Green. Once, when he was visiting Crispo at the downtown apartment, the older man reached into a black bag and handed a huge dildo to him. "It was a mammoth thing," he recalled later, "a soft rubber dong with two huge, unbelievable balls hanging off the end." Andrew said he knew of "fags who could take the whole thing."

Then without warning, Crispo pulled a small pistol from the bag and knocked the barrel against the side of Kirk Green's head. For a reason Kirk never tried to figure out, he was not at all afraid, which seemed to frustrate Andrew. But when Kirk grabbed the gun and said, "How's it feel to have it pointed at you?" Andrew seemed sodden with excitement. "Oh, no. Don't do that," he said, "please don't hurt me." Kirk put down the gun and noticed—he thought—that Andrew was disappointed.

Nonetheless, it was impossible to hold out against Crispo, and a month or so later, Kirk Green took one hundred dollars from Andrew Crispo to rape a young man. "I genuinely believed the kid wanted it, that he knew about what was going to happen. At least I think I did."

Early one fall evening, Green went to the gallery and Crispo explained that a young Frenchman was going to show up, a man who wanted to have sex with Green. There would be money in it for him, Crispo said. When the young man arrived, the three took a cab down to the Greenwich Village penthouse, and in the bedroom Crispo ordered the Frenchman to undress, which he did, Green said, "willingly—he seemed to like me." Andrew took Kirk across the terrace to another room and instructed him to put on a black leather hood, which was fetched from the black nylon bag. He told him to take off his shirt and handed him a long butcher knife, then headed him back to the bedroom.

"It was weird," Green recalled, "because in my mind it was a rape *scene*, not an actual rape, you know. It was supposed to be kinky, not a crime, if you can see the difference."

The Frenchman was lying on his back, naked. Kirk Green held the butcher knife over his head with one hand and unbuttoned his pants with another. Then, with the free hand, he forced the man's legs up and apart. He penetrated quickly, with a rabid aggression forcing himself. He put the butcher knife near the man's throat. He was causing pain. He did not speak.

"The guy got real tense, because of the mask, I think, and said, 'Stop, you're hurting me.' He was hurting. And I didn't stop, and I didn't say anything." Instead, he looked at the man blankly, two brown eyes peering through leather cutouts in the hood, a silver zipper covering his mouth and making cold skeleton teeth. The headgear covered everything above his neck.

He crashed his belly against the back of the man's legs with escalating power. Finally, the man screamed. "I tried to quit, when I didn't like the way things were going down at all, but Andrew got real angry and shouted, 'You're not supposed to stop, don't you dare stop.' He was just standing there in this fab Armani suit giving these orders. 'You don't stop just because he says stop! You're supposed to keep going!' "

Ronnie Caran and Ellery Kurtz spoke often about quitting, in the days that followed the dramatic firing of receptionist Susan Slack, but Kurtz was encouraged to stay on. A fledgling artist himself, Kurtz had convinced Crispo to hang some of his paintings in a group show that was opening in October. "Just hold your breath," Caran had told him, "and it will all be over soon."

Ronnie Caran had nothing at stake. He was just an unpaid gallery director working for a gallery with very little future, being bullied daily by a twenty-two-year-old thug. He was a former friend of a man who, before the coke, was warm and funny and generous. Now, Caran could only guess why Crispo had turned on him: "Because I was brazen enough to tell him to get help," he told a friend, "because I wouldn't ignore it like everybody else."

Many times over the years, other gallery owners had offered him jobs. "Name your price," went the frequent invitation. But he had stayed put since 1973, believing (as he often said) that "my time, my money, my friendship was working for me."

In October 1984, he penned his letter of resignation. It was just a few lines long. One afternoon, he left the note on the coffee table in the Red Room.

A week later, returning to his dark East Village apartment, he found a message on his answering machine. It was a man's voice, although not Crispo's or Bernard's. But the directive seemed to come from both of them.

"This is a message for Ronnie Caran," it said. "Keep your big, fat, *fucking* mouth shut."

CHAPTER

5

Despite the critical successes of his "Ten Americans" show of water-color masters, Andrew Crispo chugged into the mid-seventies without gaining a strong financial foothold for his gallery or the artists he was representing. Except for an anemic parade of casual art buyers wandering in off the street, there was not a great deal of business. Sometimes, Arthur Smith would refer one of his decorating clients to the gallery, and there were some tenuous business ties with an art dealer in Detroit and another in Florida that generated some cash. But Crispo's costs were far outpacing his earnings. And his friendly foot-in-the-door with Baron Heini Thyssen-Bornemisza never went anywhere.

Not that Crispo didn't try. Each day, he would pull aside one or the other of his staff and dictate letters to Heini, offering this painting or that. He also sent daily entreaties to "Madame Something-or-other in Paris, and the D'Arcs," a former staffer recalled, referring to Mary Lea Johnson of the pharmaceutical family, and her husband, Victor D'Arc. (Because of the frantic correspondence, the couple eventually dubbed him "Duddy Kravitz.")

So Crispo staged yet another attention-getter: a show of oils by Edward Hicks, the American primitivist—and fallen minister—best known for his folk-art interpretations of biblical texts. There was something about Hicks that spoke to Crispo: The artist had been orphaned at three. Back at ACA, Crispo had curated a group show that included Hicks paintings, which proved very successful and profitable. He hoped to repeat the coup in a one-man show.

The risks involved were substantial: Not only did Crispo lack capital for a major offering but he also lacked Hicks paintings. He didn't own a single one, said a person who knew him then: "He thought the publicity around the show would scare up some Hickses from attics around the country. He thought he was bigger than a museum, so things would just fall in his lap."

Patricia Hamilton was in charge of curating the show, called "Edward Hicks, A Gentle Spirit." The Juvenile Diabetes Foundation was lined up as the charity front, but Hamilton immediately discovered that no one would loan any more paintings to the gallery, because of unpaid bills from the watercolor show the year before. A Worcester museum, proud owner of a Hicks, told her they'd love to lend, except that they had wound up paying shipping costs on the Hopper they'd contributed earlier. She blew up. "Andrew, how the *hell* could you send me up to Worcester, Massachusetts, to beg this person for a Hicks when you knew you stiffed them on the Hopper? How could you embarrass me like that?"

Andrew gazed up at her silently.

"Obviously you knew! Because the shippers were dunning you for the money and they *stopped* dunning you for the money. How did they get the money? The museum paid! That's how."

"So? What did you do?" His voice was still, his question full of curiosity.

"I gave the museum a check—a personal check."

"And did you get the Hicks?"

"Of course I didn't get the Hicks! They're never going to lend a thing to you again. They may never lend *me* anything ever again, either."

She pounded circles in the red carpet in front of Andrew Crispo's desk as her boss slowly grew red-faced himself. Finally, he spoke: "And you expect me to reimburse you?"

"I absolutely do," she said firmly, and, when nothing else was said, turned and marched into the accountant's office to requisition a check— a check that eventually cleared in her account four weeks later.

Soon, as though nothing had happened, Crispo approached Patricia with an idea for how to fill out his upcoming show. "I want you to call up Dorothy Miller—she's got a Hicks—and ask her to reduce her insurance value on the painting so that we don't have to pay so much." Hamilton was dumbfounded; she agreed, but later announced that

Miller, the founding curator of the Museum of Modern Art and a power-house figure in the arts world, was unreachable by phone. "There were certain things I just fucking wouldn't do," she declared to friends.

Things were simply not right after that—Patricia felt her relations with the gallery had been in decline since the previous fall, when Andrew had assigned her to help Mary Lea Johnson D'Arc erect a private sculpture show on the lawns behind her Far Hills, New Jersey, mansion. Andrew seemed to feel she was just too independent, building her own career from his gallery without passing her credits up to him.

In the wake of the newest blowup, inneroffice tensions escalated. Andrew unleashed a round of apparently retaliatory measures against her and the rest of the staff, which at that point had grown to five, including Ronnie Caran, now the full-time gallery director. New office rules were propagated: The air conditioner and the lights were to be kept off unless potential clients wandered into the office; lunch hours were to be staggered so that no two employees would share a sandwich—and a gripe—out of the office; sick days were docked from paychecks; personal calls were banned outright. Petty affronts also reigned. "You'd type up a letter and it would take you a long time to type it up, then he'd take his coffee cup and put it down. Right on top of the freshly typed letter—that he'd stood there and watched you type," said an assistant who did a lot of typing.

One day, Jay Gourney, a slight, lilting employee, showed up at work wearing contacts instead of his thick glasses. "Ooooooh," said Crispo, dogging the young man around the gallery. "Miss Thing! You're just *sooo* beautiful, aren't you? Isn't she? Aren't you?"

The enmity even extended to Ronnie Caran, a fact that the rest of the staff found to be a true sign, one said, of "the bloom coming off the rose." The two had left for Nashville, a bundle of masterworks under their arms, in an effort to raise some cash from a collector there. As was their generally successful custom, Crispo stayed just long enough to pitch the pieces, and left Caran behind to close the deal. But three days later, on a hot June afternoon, Caran returned empty-handed, and Andrew hit the roof. "Do you think this is a game?" he demanded. "How the hell do you think we're going to get by now? What the hell did you *do* down there, anyway?" He waved around just a few of the lawsuits that had landed on his desk in recent months: H. O. Gerngross, the unpaid advertising agency, was suing for six figures; the catalogue printers wanted five.

Even worse, Crispo found himself deeply in debt going into a Hicks show for which he didn't have a single Hicks of his own for sale! That meant there was no possibility of recouping costs. Hirschl & Adler had a Hicks, but the gallery down the street wouldn't put it in the show on commission (which is often done); they wanted cash, and were driving a hard bargain.

In the weeks that followed, according to gallery artists and staffers alike, a parade of unusually ill-mannered middle-aged men made near daily excursions past the front desk to Andrew's red offices in the back. "I remember shiny suits, lots of them. And cigarette-stained fingers," said Patricia Hamilton. Fred Eversley, the sculptor, was similarly struck (he spent several weeks in the gallery building bases for displaying his sculptures, having been told there was no money to have carpenters do the job). A sleazy financier who chain-smoked cigars had regular, private meetings in the Red Room, with his stretch-pantsed wife in tow.

However, by most accounts it was Marty Ackerman who ponied up the bridge money to keep the gallery afloat through the Malaise Years, beginning with some up-front cash in 1975.

A self-made millionaire, Ackerman was best known as the brash thirty-six-year-old Philadelphia attorney who had bought the venerable *Saturday Evening Post* in 1968 and killed it in 1969, a move that reportedly allowed him to pocket a good deal of assets earned, and squirreled away, over 148 years of publishing. But along with the move came a blitz of hostile press that didn't abate even after Ackerman sold off all his holdings (LIN Broadcasting, Perfect Film and Chemical Corporation, Curtis Publishing Company, a string of cemeteries in the Midwest) and, tail between legs, fled the limelight. Burying *The Saturday Evening Post*, after all, was nearly an exilable offense.

It got worse. Practicing law quietly in 1972, Ackerman found himself representing the novelist Clifford Irving. Called "a minor writer" by *Life* magazine, Irving landed the coup of the decade: access to Howard Hughes, the billionaire recluse, and permission to pen his autobiography. Or so the novelist said, and so Ackerman repeatedly confirmed to the press. Hughes denied any knowledge of the book, making McGraw-Hill immediately curious about the checks they had issued, totaling $650,000 and cut in the order of "H. R. Hughes," which were deposited (then withdrawn) at a Swiss bank. *The New York Times* published a highly confusing account of events, per Ackerman: "The attorney for Clifford Irving, the novelist who asserts that he compiled an autobiography of Howard R. Hughes, said yesterday that he and his client were 'leaning' to the theory that the novelist had been a victim of a hoax by a 'gang of six to eight people.' However, several hours later, after Mr. Irving had left for Spain, Martin S. Ackerman denied that he really favored this theory and said instead that he leaned to what he called 'the loyal servant' theory."

News accounts in the following days were equally complex until the *Times* headlined a lead story: IRVING DISCLOSES HIS WIFE IS 'HELGA HUGHES' WHO TRANSFERRED $650,000 TO SWISS BANK. It had become, in one newspaper's term, "the most sensational scandal in recent publishing history," outplaying even the death of *The Saturday Evening Post*. Although it was accepted that he had played no role in the hoax, Ackerman and his wife, Diane, were called before grand juries, impugned again. They moved to London.

Ackerman, now in his forties, and Diane made a cautious reentry stateside in 1974 by reinvigorating a company they quite reverently called Sovereign American Arts. Their specialty was acting as dealers, investors, and factors of contemporary paintings—a term meaning they engaged in the risky task of accepting artworks as collateral against sizable loans. As corporate secretary, Diane brought the requisite artistic knowledge to the endeavor (in filing papers, she described her various occupations as "free-lance publicist, interior decorator, and art and antiques dealer," although she would later become better known as a best-selling author and frequent *Parade* contributor); Marty lent his unromantic—even mischievous—love for the bottom line. The loans were so tightly written that only a desperate dealer or collector would apply.

Andrew Crispo was that desperate. He called on Irma Rudin, his friend from the ACA Galleries, and asked her to arrange an introduction.

"I'd be happy to," she said. "He's a personal friend of mine, a very good friend. But if you borrow money from Martin, you're going to have to pay a very high interest rate."

Crispo said, "It's either that or I lose the gallery."

"Well, then you have no choice," Rudin replied, and helped set up the deal.

In exchange for fifty thousand dollars in cash—enough to cover the Hicks painting Andrew needed to salvage the show—the gallery "sold" a Morris Louis painting worth twice that figure to the Ackermans. It was agreed that, in exchange for a fixed monthly sum, Crispo retained an option to buy the painting back for the same fifty thousand dollars. The cleverly worded scheme allowed those regular payments to exceed the usurious interest-rate boundaries set by federal law—it was a "purchase," not a "loan"; the payments were "options," not "interest."

It was not a perfect solution, but it was the only one available to Crispo. Banks were not loaning against artwork, because of its intangible value, especially in this period of elastic price tags. Crispo's only remaining option was to sell some of the paintings he, or the gallery, had collected over the years, but that was out of the question. Crispo had developed a singular revulsion to relinquishing anything, perhaps a quality rooted in those meager days in the orphanage.

He turned the "borrowed" cash over to Hirschl & Adler in exchange for the Hicks work, called *The Peaceable Kingdom*—one of the artist's most famous paintings.

Late in 1975, the Edward Hicks show opened amid a lavish party— including the customary stiff drinks (which Crispo didn't touch). When John Russell, the *New York Times* reviewer, arrived to chronicle the show, Andrew found Patricia in the back room. "Man, I'd like some doughnuts," he said, and when she concurred, he added, "Why don't you get us some?" While she was out, Andrew Crispo showed the critic through the gallery, and took credit for its magnificence. Patricia Hamilton, who had personally chosen each piece, was not mentioned at all in the review.

She resigned a week later, and on her way out the door (she said later), Crispo grabbed a few envelopes out of her hand, barking, "What have you got there? *My* mail?" He ripped them open.

"Andrew, they're my bank statements."

"Oh, they're your bank statements," he said, handing them over with no apology.

Later, Patricia said, "I felt like saying, 'Honey, if you're worried about your catalogues, I got them out two weeks ago.' I mean, I took a box of Hicks catalogues and a box of 'Watercolor' catalogues, and I don't think that was more than I was entitled to, for God's sake." Other galleries would have understood this; Hamilton assumed the worst of Crispo. "I know he would have made me pay," she said later.

The truth was, Andrew had already figured out that she'd slipped out with the show catalogues. And he had already decided that she would, indeed, be made to pay.

In the meantime, Jay Gourney, the registrar, was fired two weeks after Patricia's exit, following a nasty set-to that had him racing to a Bergdorf's telephone booth for consolation from friends. Only Ronnie Caran and one other full-timer—the elderly George Perret—were left.

And a week later, mysteriously, a work crew arrived to begin renovations on the floor above the Crispo Gallery, which would be connected to the existing space. According to a self-congratulatory full-back-page ad in *Interview* magazine, it would make Andrew Crispo's East Fifty-seventh Street gallery the largest nonmuseum art space in the country.

Renovation was finished by January 1976, and the grand opening was accompanied by a lavish exhibit of Lowell Nesbitt works, called his "autobiography," and an after-the-opening party at Rockefeller Center, where Crispo had rented out the entire skating rink and reserved a rinkside restaurant. Guests were transported south by a waiting fleet of charter buses. David Hockney was there, wrapped in a bow tie and a hirsute date; Asha Puthli Goldschmidt, the offbeat singer, came alone and shared a bottle of white wine with Mick Jagger and Jerry Hall. (Robert Reed, the "Brady Bunch" dad, left early, perhaps overwhelmed by the joints his curvaceous young date reportedly kept rolling for him.) Bushy-headed Paul Getty III (the one missing an ear) made the bus ride south and traded sneakers for blades, as did actresses Maria Smith and Renee Paris. Even Egon von Furstenberg, the prince, tried his hand, spinning and bobbing to Donna Summers's insistent "Love to Love You Baby"—the song of the season, according to writer Bob Colacello, which one reviewer called "a single line stretched out over twenty-two orgasms."

Casually dressed in jeans and a blue and white short-sleeved polo shirt, with two small silver chains on his left wrist, Andrew Crispo meandered graciously, quietly, among the guests, beaming and proud. Occasionally, he lifted his small hands like puppy-dog paws and did an awkward jig under the cool, dark January sky.

In the summer of 1975, Bernardo and David LeGeros spent an unremarkable few months in their mother's apartment on East Fourteenth Street, biding their time anxiously before their British separation in the fall. There was only one hitch that anyone remembers: It was then that Bernardo learned about the disposition of his dogs, Major and Gypsy—they had run away and were lost. At least, that's the story Racquel told. In truth, she had arranged for a family with an expansive yard somewhere north of Tomkins Cove to adopt them both. Certainly telling that story would have traumatized Bernardo less, but it would have implicated Racquel, and she didn't want the blame.

When fall came, Racquel's brother Salvador—Tito Sonny—accompanied the two boys on a plane to England and deposited them one at a time at their boarding schools. No one remembered, as time passed, why Racquel was unavailable to make the trip.

David appeared to adjust nicely, even flourished without his older brother's "smothering," as Racquel had termed their relationship. He excelled in classes, made friends, and had only one regret—that he was not at a military school like Bernardo's, or like the one his father had attended a generation before. As a sixth grader, David had already set sights on a career in the army. It wasn't the killing and the battles that attracted him, though he did enjoy war games with his older sibling. It was the discipline, and the wholesome patriotism, that he fancied.

It's something he shared with Bernardo—actually, he shared everything with Bernardo; they finished each other's sentences, ate each other's food, cried at each other's pain. In the woods, back behind Buckberg, they'd become the Avengers—just like in the TV show—out to eliminate communists from the Hudson Valley. Politically, they were throwbacks, untouched by the sixties (having been born in 1962 and 1963) and uninspired by the rock-and-roll anthems that had suckled their neighborhood peers.

John LeGeros, a political amalgam of opinions, was nonetheless just as patriotic, and harbored his own fetish for things military. He encouraged his boys' interest in military history by taking them to every movie ever made about General Douglas MacArthur, a particular hero of his (and Racquel's, and many middle-class Filipinos'). Sending Bernardo to a military school, then, seemed like a perfect fit—to everyone but Bernardo.

"Me and my brother started growing apart," he complained later, "and I was locked in this bizarre environment." By bizarre, he meant regimented, structured, continually monitored, unprivate. He called his mother's New York office collect almost daily, and wrote panicked letters to David and his father. Each one contained the message "I hate it here, I really hate it." Twice, he tried unsuccessfully to run away.

Christmas break didn't come too soon, and when Bernardo's plane landed at the San'a airport to meet his entire family for a Yemeni holiday, he brought every suitcase, every carton and book and article of clothing that had surrounded his bed in the barracks-style English dormitory, among them an American flag that had hung over his bed.

"Bernardo!" Racquel was scolding in her highest pitches. "This is only a couple of weeks! You shouldn't have brought with you everything you *own*." (That last word crossed nearly an octave during the drawn-out consonant alone.)

"I'm not going back," he said. Period.

"We'll see about *that*," she said.

Eventually, though, she gave in, after a crying jag in which Bernardo related to her, in his untidy conversational way, that he had been abused at the school—abused unspeakably by a group of prefects from Waterloo House. "They held me down," he said. "They were trying to do something, because they did something to somebody else before."

Racquel was confused, impatient. "Something!"

"Something. Of a major scale. Well, first they ripped off my uniform and gave me a scrub-brush treatment—take a scrub brush and rub it all over your back till your back is all raw and bleeding. They did stuff to this guy over there; they didn't do it to me."

More bewildered, his mother's voice rose higher. "What are you talking about?"

"They bungholed a kid, this and that," Bernardo said. "Yeah, they had done that to a kid; he was Iranian. For the hell of it. They just didn't like him, I guess. It's a military school, so what do you expect! And then once I was getting ready to go outside, it was the next day, and they said, 'A friend of yours is upstairs, wants to talk to you. Needs something from you.' One of the friends of mine from school. So I went up to the dorm and I was waiting for him there. And I went in the dorm, and there was nobody there, and I was sitting on my bed waiting for him."

He backtracked. "See, I sold cigarettes, because I used to go get cigarettes and bring them back, and keep them under the floorboards. I was operating a friggin' business! Like porno magazines, this and that. So I sold them that and I sold them cigarettes. All kinds of crazy things. Food and stuff, because you can't have a lot of food there, either. I had all these things, like loaning money and collecting twenty percent interest on it, too. And I wasn't giving them a piece of the action."

"Porno! What goes on up there?" Racquel was shocked.

John interrupted testily. "You were loan-sharking? A confidence man!"

"That's why they came after me," Bernardo continued, not allowing the complications to be stripped from his story. "A bunch of them, and they took the handle of this shower brush . . . Not that they *had*. They attacked me, but they didn't get to the point. If that person didn't intercede—end of the ball game."

"*What* did they try to do?" insisted Racquel.

Bernardo had trouble saying it. "Tried to—but I kept—they were holding me down! Tried to—insert it. Had my pants down, and they started, but they didn't! And you can have a doctor check it out."

On his floor at Trafalgar House, although he did not say this, Bernardo was not particularly well liked. At first, the other boys whose beds surrounded his called him "Israeli," by mistake; later, after Bernardo pinned the American flag behind his bed, they called him "Yank," with remarkable disdain. In his few months there, he made just one friend, and then lost her.

She was the school nurse, and one of the few young (mid-twenties) women on the school grounds. Bernardo had taken refuge in her office frequently, having fallen victim to a string of virulent phantom illnesses. She may have misunderstood his pilgrimages, and when he went to her after the scrub-brushing incident, mostly for comfort, though he complained of a cold, she had him lie on his back on a cot and opened his shirt. Her fingers danced over his chest, down his belly, over his gray wool fly, which rose up to fill her palm. Embarrassed by his own involuntary gesture, Bernardo said nothing, prayed it would be ignored. Until she reached for his zipper.

"What are you doing?" the thirteen-year-old demanded, bolting upright while pleading to stop the woman in a pleated skirt. But she already had a handful of Bernardo, and he was seconds away from splashing his virginity over his chest. "No! No, no, no, no!" he shouted, and it was done. Smiling simply, she finger-painted her name on his belly.

Though he visited the woman three times thereafter, behind closed doors, he eventually broke it off. The relationship didn't comfort him; he found it disturbing. "It wasn't right," he told a friend. "She's the friggin' matron!" But he considered it less stigmatizing than the more hazardous practices of the older boys. He chose to edit it out of his list of protestations delivered to his parents.

"I'm not going back to a place where they do that," he stated absolutely, and began to cry angrily now. "Military schools are full of faggots."

The story unnerved Racquel, while John had trouble believing it—struggled even to follow the tale's periphrastic themes. A rape story! He must have seen it in a movie and adopted it as his own life story, John figured.

It was agreed, nevertheless, that the British environment was apparently no less distressing for Bernardo than the Yemeni school. His wishes were granted. But instead of taking Bernardo home to New York, Racquel left him behind once again, to live with his father in a simple primitive home in a country on the verge of war. He stayed through 1976 and into 1977, returning just a few weeks before meeting Andrew Crispo for the first time.

Opening the expanded gallery, and throwing the lavish skating party afterward, put Crispo and the Crispo Gallery on the map more than anything before it. Socialite Slim Keith became a client, as did the Texas Hunt brothers (oil, banking, and eventually silver), and others. Paintings flowed out the gallery's tall doors to midwestern brokers, Florida brokers, European brokers. Corporate buyers, such as Johnson & Johnson and the Riggs National Bank in Washington, D.C., outfitted executive suites with Crispo purchases.

The beautiful two-floor gallery became an important stopover for celebrities, a place to be seen. Baroness Minda de Rothschild dropped in regularly, and Tony Randall began making repeat visits, though he never bought anything. "On his way in, he'd make a joke," a gallery worker said of Randall, "and on his way out, he'd make another."

Julie Andrews, in a black leather miniskirt, bought a Milton Avery canvas that her husband, Blake Edwards, admired. Mary Tyler Moore shopped a few times, and brought along friends. Steve Martin strolled in one afternoon, during a break in shooting *Dead Men Don't Wear Plaid*, and made one of several purchases.

"Maybe Mr. Martin would like to see that Franz Kline," Crispo suggested to Victor Ruggiero. "Go bring that from the storage room, would you?"

Ruggiero and Crispo had seen the piece just that morning. It was in the showroom of Marisa DelRe, another dealer, who was located several flights up in the Fuller Building. Ruggiero went out the back door, took the elevator up, and "borrowed" the piece on consignment. Steve Martin bought the painting, a floor-to-ceiling abstract work of huge white-on-black brushstrokes. Crispo's markup was in the neighborhood of fifty thousand dollars, just for Ruggiero's legwork. But Martin was delighted, and several weeks later he mugged in front of it for the cover of *Rolling Stone* magazine in a suit that was painted to match.

The young man who vowed to build a gallery as important as the Marlborough Gallery had at last found the golden path to take him there. He was in full stride, and his bank accounts were exploding.

There was just one thing missing. By the mid-seventies, he hadn't been able to draw any of the world's serious collectors—such as Babe Paley, or Saul and Gayfryd Steinberg, or Daniel Terra, or the baron— to launch him into the stratosphere. This is the stuff of a Marlborough, a Hirshl & Adler, a Leo Castelli. Sheer traffic and volume, even with a quality product—that was plain mercantilism. In the art world, one also needed quality clientele.

Sure, Baron Thyssen-Bornemisza had been back to the gallery a few times since their first meeting, and in 1975 he took a fancy to a seascape by the nineteenth-century American painter Martin Johnson Heade. ("Tell me about this," he had said in his casual window-shopping manner. Ronnie Caran put the piece in perspective by mentioning Heade's European counterparts—whom he knew Heini collected—and the baron declared, "That's the root of Surrealism! I'd like to have that." He didn't even ask the price.) But after a subsequent trip, when he had chosen two other pieces from the same period, two more influential individuals paid a hostile visit to the gallery, laying down the law.

Denise, the baron's fourth wife, walked in unannounced. The icy, beautiful daughter of a Brazilian doctor (a blond Jackie O.), Denise spoke up—forcefully, in a thick accent—when things weren't going her way. This was just such a time. She strode disdainfully among the oils her husband had ordered, fingering them like carpet samples. She pointed her toe at one, a 1960s Willem de Kooning portrait of a woman, and said, "That's hideous. Cancel that one. Cancel them all."

With her was Franco Rappetti, a tall, blond Roman socialite who was known throughout the art world as the baron's exclusive dealer, the turnstile through which all purchases, and commissions, passed. He had another reputation, too: as a frequent "walker" for Denise, when the baron was unavailable at board meetings or corporate functions. Franco Rappetti was also her very public lover. Thyssen himself was reportedly aware of the arrangement—it was said he kept the younger man on staff anyway, in part to avoid another messy divorce. Together, the lovers had worked out a business arrangement that allowed them to share in the excitement and lucre of Heini's buying sprees, barnacles on the baron's belly.

Rappetti took Crispo aside. "It is the practice," he began, sotto voce, "that the baroness be consulted on all acquisitions. This means that if you want to sell pictures to the baron, you pay me a commission." A straightforward business proposition in which, apparently, Franco and Denise pulled steely strings.

"Franco," Crispo said without hesitation, "forget it!" And that, for the next three years, was that.

But into 1978, the bonds in this Lugano triangle began to decay, marked by escalating tensions between Denise and the baron on one side, and Denise and Rappetti on the other. In June of that year, the baroness took a break from the whole mess and fled to Manhattan to clear her head. Rappetti soon followed, according to one account, but she rebuffed him in a terse exchange in her rooms at the Waldorf, and he went instead to stay with a friend in the Meurice, an apartment building on West Fifty-eighth Street favored by Italian society mavens.

Another account had Franco showing up unannounced and checking into the Waldorf, and then checking out again in favor of an invitation at the Meurice. Those details weren't important.

Several hours later, his crumpled body was found in a deep groove in the roof of a Volkswagen bus, clad only in underpants and several large gold medallions. Eleven flights up, the small window he had exited was stuck open, such was the force with which it had been lifted. The police listed the case as a possible suicide, but Rappetti left behind no note— just a small valise, his folded T-shirt, and the admission, made several times that night, that he was depressed over Denise, and troubled by a "heart condition."

Diane von Furstenberg, the fashion designer and Denise's longtime friend, was the one who ventured into the sticky predawn morning to identify the body. "Denise was destroyed by this," von Furstenberg said later, explaining why the lover couldn't enter the morgue. "She truly loved Franco, and having to see him like that . . . You can't imagine how horrible it was."

Diane von Furstenberg notified Heini, who grabbed the next Concorde to New York to make arrangements. But it was Andrew Crispo, not one of the Thyssen corporation flunkies, who dealt with Frank E. Campbell's, the famous Upper East Side funeral home, and Andrew Crispo who chartered the jet that would return the corpse to Italy. In an interview about the incident with writer Anthony Haden-Guest, Crispo said that a large conveyance was required by the size of the casket that the baron had picked out for Rappetti, and the cheapest jet with such a berth came to $150,000. "Isn't that a bit expensive?" he recalled asking the baron. Thyssen (who Crispo said contemplated the spiraling commissions paid out over the years) reportedly replied, "Believe me, it's a bargain."

Dark, teasing rumors swirled around the death, of course. One of them suggested that Rappetti was a casualty of his efforts to blackmail Denise, having warned her that an intimate letter bearing her signature would be made public. Still others thought the butler did it: Reached in Italy with the bad news, the servant "just didn't react," said the person who had called, adding that everything of value had been looted from the dead man's home by the following day.

Another apparently baseless story had Andrew Crispo doing the dirty work, at the baron's bidding. For whatever reason, Crispo himself fueled these tales. Seated next to Hebe Dorsey, the powerful *International Herald Tribune* editor, at a 1981 dinner party in Paris, Crispo jokingly confessed that he had never been able to shake the scuttlebutt. Ronnie Caran's stage whispers were overheard: "Andrew! You fucking idiot! Don't you know who that is?"

His response: "Hebe Dorsey. So?"

"Don't you have a *clue* what she does for a living?" Another guest, attorney Roy Cohn, spent some time convincing her not to print Crispo's comments, according to a man seated at the same table.

In the gallery, the scuttlebutt was lore: Rappetti's Rolodex card, for example, wasn't removed following his defenestration; instead, the word *murdered* was scratched over it in thick red marker, and there it remained for nearly a decade.

The more likely truth to the matter was that Franco Rappetti hurled himself through that window under his own steam. There was a woman in the apartment at the time, though in another room, with whom he had discussed his waning will to live. According to her, Rappetti arrived at the apartment clearly in emotional turmoil; he was given a guest room and, at nearly 3:00 A.M. on June 8, he excused himself and headed to sleep. After closing the door, he removed his T-shirt and folded it carefully. Then he climbed to the windowsill, still wearing his underpants and the gold medallions around his neck, and plunged. Among the first building residents to spot his body down below was Franco Rossellini, the famous film director's nephew. "I thought it was my butler!" he told police.

"He jumped," Rappetti's hostess said definitively, "but he was pushed, too; pushed by sharp, emotional weapons."

As vague and mysterious as the death was, one thing became abundantly clear. "All of a sudden," said one art-world observer, "if you wanted to sell something to Thyssen, you had to go through Crispo."

In one week, Baron Thyssen-Bornemisza made electronic transfers totaling $3 million to the Crispo Gallery; another week, more money was transferred. "Landscapes, landscapes, landscapes," said one gallery worker. "He snapped up Westerns," said another, "saying, 'I'll take that, and that, and that, and that, and that.'" He purchased Picassos, Frederick Edwin Churches, Frederick Friesekes, Hans Hofmanns, and Franz Klines, paintings by de Kooning and Pollock and O'Keeffe.

Between visits from the baron, Crispo and Caran and their minions scoured galleries in New York for works to offer Heini. And the galleries Andrew Crispo had hoped to emulate were now pushing paintings into his hands, hoping to get a piece of the action.

And a bit of the prestige. In serious art collections, the kinds that went on tour, the provenance of each item is meticulously catalogued, listing each owner since the paint was finished, a genealogy of fine taste, an advertisement of access. For instance, Andrew Wyeth made an ink sketch of a dead crow, a study for the oil entitled *Winter Fields*. He gave it to a family friend, who passed it on to Mrs. Josiah Marvel, of Greenville, Delaware, where Hirschl & Adler Galleries found it; they took it to Nicholas Wyeth, the artist's son, who verified the signature; it next sold to Andrew Crispo for ten thousand dollars. All this is duly noted on the back of the piece, with little cards affixed to the frame offering all the significant dates. In this instance, it gave witness to the untiring skills of the Hirschl & Adler staff.

This was art-world tradition. These were the rules of the game.

But at the Crispo Gallery, the registrars were ordered to "clean up the provenances" of the paintings. They stripped those tags off the backs (and

placed them in a secret envelope, in case the painting had to be returned
to the gallery of origin). In their place, the registrars attached phony
documentation. The policy had two purposes. It made Andrew Crispo's
operation seem capable of staging one major art discovery after another.
And because many pieces were on commission, it kept the savvy collector
from peering behind the frame, jotting down the information, then calling
the gallery of origin and asking, oh so innocently, "Have you got a
Remington?" A substantial savings could be realized by sidestepping the
consignment markup.

Not that Crispo really needed to take the credit in order to keep the
baron on board. It was simply a fail-safe plan: Andrew didn't want to give
Heini that temptation.

The practice proved undeniably successful. Within a few years, Baron
Thyssen had bought an estimated four hundred nineteenth-century
American paintings from the Crispo Gallery, totaling more than
$90 million in gross receipts. Andrew, in his early thirties, was a very
rich man.

Some of his growing wealth went into his pocket, but the majority
went toward building his private art collection, with plenty left over to
continue staging glittery openings at the Fuller Building.

As SoHo, the formerly abandoned neighborhood of iron buildings and
low rent, began to establish itself as the focus of hot avant-garde artists,
Andrew Crispo had the resources to place his uptown gallery square in
the movement. He promoted the outrageous sculptor Arman, who had
hit mid-career. In the fifties, Arman drenched springs, cam wheels,
bicycle chains, and nails with ink, hurled them at canvases, and called
the results "tracings"; in the sixties, he smashed to smithereens an assortment of imitation Henri II furniture in a performance he called "conscious
vandalism"; in the seventies, he began a "random accumulation of garbage," and Crispo gave him walls to hang it on. "The work was not
fantastic," said an art lover who frequented an exhibit of his work at the
Crispo Gallery "but the installation sang. The installation was absolutely
gorgeous." Some of Arthur Smith's technique, Arthur Smith's gentle-
manly style, had been rubbing off on Andrew.

When photographer Christopher Makos was preparing for the publication of his first book, his friend and mentor Andy Warhol encouraged
him to coordinate it with a gallery show. "You should try to show uptown," Warhol said, "you know, to bring some air of something to the
book." Makos was not much of a self-starter, and Warhol stayed on his
case, finally suggesting, "Well, why don't you try Andrew Crispo?"

Makos and Warhol considered Crispo the "Upper East Side Art Mafia"
by this time, while Makos was a relative unknown, despite his photo

column in *Interview* magazine. Besides, he thought, his pictures were probably a bit racy for East Fifty-seventh Street. Andy Warhol made him dial the gallery, nonetheless, with Chris Makos—in his mid-twenties and no more gregarious than his mentor—protesting: "I just don't like asking people for things."

But he knew a little something about Crispo: For one thing, he knew Crispo's boyfriend, the actor Dennis Erdman (whom Chris had met through Tony Perkins), and that made the man seem a little more accessible. So he called, and he asked, and Andrew Crispo invited him up with the proofs for the book *White Trash*. The first print, which would become the book's cover photograph, was a close-up of the thigh of Debbie Harry, of Blondie fame, with a razor blade safety-pinned to her hem. The second picture was called *Christopher Makos and Friend, New York*. Clearfaced and glassy-eyed and ultra-blond, Makos was teetering on the far edge of an apparent drug stupor, staring sullenly into the camera. His unnamed friend gripped his shoulder, taut and dangerous. The focal point of the picture was crotch. The two photos set a tone for the entire book.

"I think he was bored up there, sitting around all that art," Makos said after his meeting with Crispo. "I'm sure he thought maybe I was coming on by this book—some guy comes in and shows you all these racy, sexy pictures." Just the kind of story Andy Warhol hoped he'd be able to get out of the episode; Andy's twice-removed sexuality piqued, and sated.

The Makos show opened, the party was grand (Sylvia Miles, Paul Morrissey, and the rest of the Factory crowd), and the book hit the stores. It carried an introduction, Chris Makos was a little surprised to learn, written by Andrew Crispo. "Christopher Makos lives a secret life in art," it said. "Mixing memory and desire, he has created a fertile cosmos in which nothing remains sacred and yet everything becomes alive, containing images of sophistication and naïveté, innocence and corruption. By his imaginative probing and fierce recollections, Makos documents and—in an act of intense identification—*becomes* the culture he defines; an unruly *mise-en-scène* of punkish posturing and ambisexual allure."

"What does that mean?" Chris asked repeatedly after reading it. "What does that *mean*?" His friends were baffled, too. "I don't live a secret life, 'cause it's all here, you know what I mean? It's pretty up-front. I don't know. But it says a lot about him, doesn't it? It says a lot about Crispo. More than it does about me."

Perhaps because of the young art dealer's impertinences, Baron Thyssen-Bornemisza found him extremely amusing. The two men had become friends, an "unruly mise-en-scène" of culture and class. They spoke on the phone several times a week, about art, politics, people; they socialized in person at least twice monthly, in New York or London or Rome or Switzerland.

Once, even though they supplied nothing to a show of the baron's old masters that was touring the world, Thyssen invited Crispo and Caran to accompany him to an opening exhibit in Kansas City. Peopled with the good, moral denizens of that city, the party was predictably dull and the dinner afterward did little to spice up the evening. The baron distracted himself by flirting with a nineteen-year-old waitress, who, having no apparent idea who this man was, invited him and his two friends to a local disco that evening.

"Put on turtlenecks," Thyssen commanded his New York friends, "we're going out." Then, checking himself, he leaned forward and added, "Don't tell my bodyguards."

Thyssen was a choice target for kidnappers, but he had only recently hired a private SWAT team—apparently upon the insistence of his friend Gianni Agnelli, who had told several people he feared for Heini's life. "Gianni came into the gallery one afternoon," said Vinny Marcus, a gallery worker, "and said he'd just spoken to Denise, the baron's wife, and she said she was so worried about Heini. She said he was drinking a lot and she was very, very worried that he might fall down a flight of stairs or something.

"So I said, 'This, from a woman who didn't care if Thyssen has holes in his socks,' and he said, 'That's the point. Perhaps she's laying a groundwork, so nobody will be surprised if he *does* fall. Things are not going well between them.' "

Sometime after that conversation, Denise flew to New York in an airplane weighed down by dozens of the baron's old master paintings, and filed for divorce. He hired bodyguards, and posted armed Pinkertons around his various residences (of which there were nine), especially at his castle in Lugano, where the majority of his works were housed. Despite this last precaution, she was able to swoop onto the rolling lawns in a helicopter, pinching even more of his collection. He pressed charges in several countries—seeking return of the art, of her jewelry, and cash in excess of $1.5 million—and Denise was jailed, briefly, in Liechtenstein, for embezzlement. The divorce remained down and dirty until the end.

The bodyguards were all American—ex-cops, ex–court officers, ex–prison guards. Heini Thyssen was not quite accustomed to them, and this evening, for once, he would give them the slip.

The three men reconnoitered in the parking lot and climbed into the waitress's Volkswagen, already packed with her buddies. Across town, in a very loud corner of Kansas City, they partied, drank, and danced into the morning with a pack of kids a fraction of their ages. Until they were interrupted by a tall, corn-fed man in a uniform. "Are you Baron Thyssen?"

"Why, yes," he said thickly.

"Sir," said the officer, "half the officials in the city are awake, worried sick about you! The mayor, the chief of police, the—"

"Ah," said the baron, quite chagrined. "I suppose we must return to the hotel."

Turning to Crispo, he said, "At least we got to play for a while, right?"

He was no longer the handsome, sharp-nosed baron he had been, say, in the forties, when he married Teresa, a German princess of Lippe, or in the fifties, when two models, Britain's Nina Dyer and Scotland's Fiona Campbell-Walter, were his back-to-back baronesses. Then, his skin was very tight, his cellophane lips strong and wan and regal. Before his black hair turned gray and thin, it swept back confidently over his rather long head.

Teresa divorced him, one society friend said, because of his dalliances; she later became Princess Teresa von Fürstenberg. Nina Dyer, the second baroness, walked, too. Described by writer Dominick Dunne as "indifferent to gender when it came to love partners," Nina left Heini for a succession of people, including an internationally acclaimed film actress (who called her "Oliver"). She eventually settled down with Prince Sadruddin Aga Kahn, the uncle of the Aga Kahn, whose son married Rita Hayworth, who was the mother of Princess Yasmin Aga Kahn, who was the person who comforted Denise Shorto, the baron's fourth wife, in the days and weeks following the mysterious death of Franco Rappetti. In those stratospheres, the world is a small place indeed.

Baron Hans Heinrich von Thyssen-Bornemisza was considered one of the world's richest men. So was his father, who moved the German industrial empire to Hungary when he married into Bornemisza nobility there, earning himself the royal title and the hyphenation. But the Thyssen-Bornemiszas were forced into Holland when communist leader Béla Kun sentenced all Hungarian landowners to death. Heini was born there, and moved to Switzerland nineteen years later to study the art collections that two earlier generations of Thyssens had amassed. His grandfather's contribution was minor but significant: August Thyssen had befriended, and became patron to, the young sculptor Auguste Rodin, and had gathered a sizable collection of his early works. He left them, and his shipbuilding and stevedoring concerns, to his youngest son (his eldest, an

early Hitler fan and later a defector, got the iron and steel businesses).
Heini's father, more enamored of art than commerce, added six hundred
masterworks by Cézanne, van Gogh, Goya, Rembrandt, and Chagall.

The elder Thyssen-Bornemisza passed them down to his children,
especially Heini, who—though he also received stewardship of his father's business affairs—inherited his father's love of art.

Now in his late fifties, Heini's face showed the strain of a life increasingly hemmed in by corporate responsibility, alimony, security, the
press. By the time Lucian Freud painted his portrait, he looked
haunted and lost (he protested, "Maybe that's how I will look someday,
but it's not how I look now"). Already, he was lightening his load.
Georg-Heinrich, his son by Nina, was named to lead the labyrinthine
Thyssen empire and its nineteen thousand employees, though he was
just in his twenties. This left Heini free to spend "eighty percent of my
time" building the art collection. What was left of his energies, as the
seventies became the eighties, was expended on the disentanglement
from Denise.

With increasing regularity, he needed to escape the whole mess, and
he went to Andrew and Ronnie, his new friends, his commoner allies,
outsiders to the asperity of castle living.

In Andrew Crispo, he saw something of himself, a man whose craving
for art was infinitely more secure, more profound, than a hunger for
flesh. In Crispo, he felt he'd isolated the most earthly embodiment of
the Thyssen-Bornemisza family motto emblazoned on its crest: "*Vertu
surpasse richesse.*" This friendship led to speculation that he and Crispo,
or his young son and Crispo, had conducted other, more physical transactions, but the baron seemed not to care. He once told a visitor to his
Daylesford estate in Gloucestershire, England, that he knew Crispo used
his name to open doors and pry loose paintings and raise eyebrows. "He
is convenient," Thyssen said then, "he is very helpful." He saved the
baron from having to rake the world's galleries and estate sales and
garages for the acquisitions he wanted.

If Andrew Crispo used Baron Hans Heinrich Thyssen-Bornemisza as
a pole vault into a different society, it didn't bother him. Sometimes, as
with the Roy Cohn connection, it even paid off for the baron.

When Cohn was representing a commericial development in Perth,
Australia, he complained to Crispo about his difficulties pulling together
an opening gala. Crispo called Heini. "Do you have any business interests
in Australia?"

Baron Thyssen, always mysteriously vague about his holdings, mulled
it over. "Well, some sheep farming, I guess. Shipbuilding. Some businesses."

Crispo said, "Why don't you lend some paintings, Heini?" and the show, "One Hundred Years of American and European Art," was launched. It helped place the Australian complex in the shoppers' guides, which advanced Cohn's clients. And it put Cohn in contact, if indirectly, with Thyssen. "Cohn liked barons around," said biographer Sidney Zion in the starkest terms. "He collected them."

But it did something much grander. It was the first time that the baron had allowed a cross section of his works to be exhibited publicly. His father had been immensely private about the collection, and kept it sequestered in a gallery he erected alongside the Lugano castle. By convincing the baron to stage the show, Andrew Crispo had pried the famed collection loose. What followed was a flurry of important exhibitions, all launched by the Andrew Crispo Gallery—or with the gallery's help—that toured the world.

Roy Cohn reciprocated Crispo's kindnesses with off-the-cuff legal advice, and eventually took him on as a full-blown client, although it was suspected that Crispo was never billed for these services. (Many of Cohn's accounts were handled that way, much to the dissatisfaction of his partners at Saxe, Bacon & Bolan.)

Their formal relationship began during a little legal battle Crispo was having—somebody had actually demanded prompt payment for services rendered, and he had refused. He dictated a letter to Cohn, beginning with the words, "I think you could have some fun with this," and Crispo became thereafter a client of the firm that represented Park Avenue divorcées and notorious gangsters, tax cheats and gamblers and politicians such as Donald Manes, Mario Biaggi, and Stanley Friedman, all on a path toward eventual indictment (or, in Manes's case, suicide). Cohn, of course, never appeared for Crispo in that case, or for any of the others that were soon to pile up. That work was left to hapless associates. Cohn wasn't in this to service Crispo, he wanted a piece of the baron, as acquaintance more than as client, as celebrity more than as human being, as cachet more than as friend.

And he got it. Cohn became Heini's confidant on the Denise Shorto divorce proceedings, the secret, behind-the-scenes counselor who helped (through his connections) find matrimony attorneys in France, England, Brazil, and Spain. With his help and encouragement, Heini and his attorneys had Denise arrested in the tiny principality of Liechtenstein on charges she had stolen millions in art and jewels from Lugano. Again with Cohn's covert help, Denise was extradited to Switzerland and brought up on the charges.

Roy Cohn made several clandestine trips to Lugano to instruct the baron's lawyers in this brand of postmatrimonial assault. "They were on the phone cooking and scheming," said a mutual friend, "bouncing around names and what-ifs and possible outcomes." Cohn, of course, was kicking in his time gratis, and bubbling over at being a part of it.

Bernard and his father had been back in the country since the spring of 1977. He had dropped the *o* from his name the day he got off the plane, as far as his mother knew. It was the first thing he told her, reunited after more than half a year: "Bernardo isn't an American name." She recalled the words distinctly, and was somewhat taken aback by his display of frank seriousness about himself. "And I'm an American. My name is Bernard." He tucked his long bangs behind his ears with shaky aggression.

"Of course you are, honey," she said, trying to hug him as he twisted away. "Honey?"

Bernard was fourteen, and Racquel LeGeros was now the ill-equipped mother of a teenager. She hardly felt old enough to be confronting teenage problems. And she hated changes. As a physicist, she was accustomed to things mutating in very measured steps in highly controlled environments. Bernard John LeGeros was her eldest, and most beautiful, child. He was also the eldest child in her wing of the family, giving him an honored Filipino position. He was *kuya*, the senior member of his generation. His Filipino relations looked up to him, and honored him unquestioningly, by code and tradition.

As an infant, from what she could remember of those first few months before Bernard was shipped off to Manila to live with Racquel's mother for a year, he was a smiling, giggling, cherubic boy. Much more like a B.J. than like a Bernardo, but she had readily accepted his earlier moniker ultimatum. This time it was more difficult, yet she agreed. "The name change thing I could handle," she said later. "But that he wouldn't let me hug him!"

"But honey, I missed you." She whispered this; other people waiting at the gate at JFK were beginning to stare.

Yeah, right, he thought.

Life in Yemen had clearly traumatized Bernard in some way his parents couldn't identify. He was icy to them now, and spent most of that summer telling wild stories about his adventures in the Middle East and in England. There was the time he allegedly stole his father's jeep, mounted an M-60 on its turret, and fired into local Yemeni marketplaces. Or when he and the family cook butchered a pet monkey for dinner. He told similarly unbelievable stories about life in New York, which his new buddies at the United Nations International School, a private institution on the East Side, tended to ignore. "He told me that for three thousand dollars, he'd shoot somebody," said Anil Singh, who was assigned to show the new kid around. "Or if I said I was pissed off at somebody, he'd want to know who, and where they lived, and stuff like that. Said he'd take care of it."

Bernard's father, who tended to ignore the stories himself, had no explanation. "Most of these things never happened, of course," he said. "But something in his mind makes him think that they are very true."

Bernard had shown signs of having a "fantastical mind" from early on, and had been unruly and incorrigible for years. Still, his disturbed fascinations after the Middle East experience were of a more serious sort, and in the summer of 1977, his parents decided to do something about it.

Racquel called her younger brother Salvador Zapanta and asked him to take Bernard under his wing.

In part because of his age—Salvador was in his late twenties—and in part because he was very Americanized and because Bernard looked up to Tito Sonny, the teenager enjoyed spending time with him in the apartment he shared with his "friend," Jack Kelly. As a measure of this trust, Salvador could sometimes call the teenager B.J. without too much of an uproar.

Throughout the summer, Bernard spent every day with Salvador, going to the Manhattan travel agency his uncle owned with Kelly, an older man whom others in Salvador's family thought, mistakenly, was a kindly father figure for the youngest Zapanta. Occasionally, Bernard returned with them to their apartment and helped with dinner, before walking the few blocks south to his apartment at Waterside Plaza, where his folks saw little of him.

The LeGeros family now visited their home on Buckberg Mountain Road, in Rockland County, only on weekends and holidays. The rest of the time, they lived in two two-bedroom apartments in the Waterside complex, a four-tower structure overlooking the East River, where many UN executives lived. In one of the thirty-seven-story buildings, Racquel and John lived with their two young daughters. In another, Bernard lived in a room he shared with David. Their apartment nominally belonged to their maternal grandparents, who came to the city infrequently.

The arrangement was necessitated, John LeGeros said later, by the arrival of "a group of Afghan refugees, who we took into our home," thus displacing their sons. Why the boys, and not the strangers, were exiled to building 40 from building 10 was never explained.

David and Bernard were only several hundred feet away from their parents, but the trip between apartments took fifteen minutes or more, involving several elevators and a brief walk past a dry cleaner, a grocery store, and a restaurant, all along an outdoor plaza that made Waterside an integrated community. The two boys might as well have lived across town.

As summer became winter (a rapid event in the city), Bernard was telling fewer shocking tales. In school, he became known as a natty, if inappropriate, dresser: Suits of two and three pieces, hats, and canes were his trademark. Most of the other students steered a wide path, but he had a girlfriend, Anya, and Anil Singh remained a close friend.

Meanwhile, he kept up with his errands at the travel agency, which included running airline tickets to Tito Sonny's clients. One of the clients was Ronnie Caran, who had been a friend of Salvador's from summers in Long Island. Through him, Bernard met Andrew Crispo in late December. It was after business hours, and Andrew was alone in the gallery.

"Here's the tickets from KelTour Travel," Bernard told the older man. "For Rio de Janeiro, right?"

"Thank you, young man," Andrew said. "Come in. Please."

Crispo was in his early thirties, more than twice Bernard's age. His hair was long and dark and his chocolaty brown eyes twitched with enthusiasm. He had been setting up a show of modern sculptures by Douglas Abdell—mostly large zigzagging public monuments of the kind that appeared in malls around the country in the seventies. He walked the boy into the central gallery, telling him about each piece. The attention struck Bernard as odd, coming from an adult, and he ate it up. Crispo plied the youngster with questions: "Where are you from? What nationality are you?" Finally putting it together, he said, "Oh! You're Manila Bean's nephew!"

"What?" Bernard had never heard the pet name used for his uncle.

"Salvador's nephew, I mean," corrected Crispo. He and Salvador had met occasionally, but they were not close; Ronnie Caran had popularized the nickname.

Later, when Bernard returned to KelTour, he told his uncle, "He was very nice to me. Says I'd be a good artist." He told Salvador about each of the Abdell pieces—"like geometric snakes"—about the paintings he had seen and the beautiful space that housed them all. He talked, without giving it a name, about the sense of power he had seen at the gallery: the power of the towering artworks, the power of the man who owned them, the power of the clients who must flood the place during gallery hours. His first glimpse of the art world, and the embracing way he was received there, confirmed his confidence in his own future.

As they spoke, Salvador's phone rang, and it was Andrew Crispo, calling in admiration for the young messenger. Salvador said nothing about the call at the time, although later he announced he was troubled by it. Like other gay men who made the rounds from the East Side to Fire Island to Southampton and back, Salvador had heard rumors about Andrew Crispo, the gallery owner with a taste for young men, fair and dark-skinned alike.

But in 1977, Salvador had not revealed his homosexuality to his family in any way, and bringing up such a topic about Crispo would be like lighting a road flare. There was an uneasy truce surrounding the question among the Zapantas, despite the rush of Methodist evangelism that ran deep in their veins. Salvador's "friend," Jack Kelly, would find love among the Zapantas, as long as the nature of that friendship went unstated. In the Filipino culture, homosexuality was not an unusual thing; *talking* about homosexuality, though, was not done politely.

In New York, fewer than ten years after the Stonewall Riots, homosexuality had advanced well past the polite discussion stage. It had become a virtual staple of polite culture, transforming even the haute monde into what one matron called "the new Café Society." Best epitomizing the new social order of the late seventies was the eclectic, energetic mix inside Studio 54, on West Fifty-fourth Street, which emerged on the horizon "in a great puff of cocaine dust," observed attorney Roy Cohn's biographer, Nicholas von Hoffman.

Fifty-four stood alone as the institution that most popularized cocaine as the preferred recreational vehicle for this crowd. Dished out by the shovelful inside, coke was the disco's hallmark. A large illuminated man-in-the-moon ornament hung down from the high ceilings over the dance floor, and from time to time a cocaine spoon was lowered down toward its nose, which, when contact was made, shot a red cocaine toot up to its glowing eyes.

This was particularly true downstairs, in the catacomblike VIP rooms where Halston, Calvin Klein, Alan Carr, Roy Cohn, and Andy Warhol mixed it up with underage partygoers, nodded-out musicians, and sundry rambunctious, supercharged, well-dressed others (for those individuals who careened a little too fast through these rooms, the owners generously dolled out Quaaludes from a candy dish stationed in the cash safe).

Roy Cohn, not a drug-using man, found the place intoxicating, and, as the disco's attorney and most vocal barker, threw himself a birthday party there every year. Through him, the Studio 54 universe was widened to include top officials from the Democratic, Republican, and Conservative parties, elected officials on a local and national level, judges, columnists, millionaires of all sorts—each of them, somehow, ignoring that giant, indolent, coke-happy moon.

By 1979, Andrew Crispo had landed on Roy Cohn's most-intimate list, there for every birthday party, or Fourth of July bash, or New Year's Eve soiree. His inaugural invitation came on the infamous lawyer's fifty-second birthday. "The cake was a two-foot version of his face," began the *Village Voice*'s account of the affair. "The confectionery eyes were clear of the bloodshot coarseness that normally colors them, but the small, balding head still had the shape of a bullet."

Guests were invited by telegram: two hundred on the A list, who were asked to come early for dinner, and several hundred more on the B list, not welcome before 11:00 P.M. Crispo's telegram invited him at 8:30.

Comedian Joey Adams, columnist William Safire, budding billionaire Donald Trump, established billionaire Si Newhouse, and writer Sidney Zion were all A-listed. Top political officials were, too, including a handful of congressmen. The chief judge of the U.S. District Court was on hand, along with Kennedys, Rockefellers, Klein, and Warhol. Andrew Crispo and Ronnie Caran were easily among the most impressed.

Crispo would eventually find the coke moon unignorable, and unforgiving, though at first he kept his head. "He never, ever smoked a joint," said Philip Torini, a smooth-faced young artist who was Crispo's lover before the turn of the decade. "White wine, cassis, that kind of stuff," said another acquaintance about Crispo's mild tastes in mood-enhancers. It was universally said that Andrew Crispo retained an ardent sobriety no matter what—or who—was falling apart around him.

His sexual taste, meanwhile, showed a more experimental character. Besides Torini, Crispo kept limber with a string of one-night stands, picked up from Uncle Charlie's, the gay West Village cocktail lounge, or from the streets nearby. He also developed a long-distance variety of flirtation that occasionally snared him a handsome momentary tryst. "In his living room at the Seventy-ninth Street apartment," a frequent visitor to Crispo and Arthur Smith's home recalled, "he kept a telescope trained on the corner pay phone. When he saw somebody he liked, he'd dial the number and invite them up." Once, while pulling the stunt in Southampton, he got a local cop on the phone. (Officials contemplated a sting but decided against it.) But, as Ronnie Caran used to tell his friends, "he could pick people up all over the place—that's really the one aspect of his social persona that was fully developed. You'd be walking down Madison Avenue after lunch, talking about this painting or that client, and all of a sudden, he'd be gone! Just run across the street, pick up some trick, and wave good-bye!"

The trick, without embarrassment, might then be escorted right past the gallery's front desk, up the stairs, and into a very crowded storage room. "He would just trot them around afterward, like he was showing them off, like he was saying, 'Look at this one!' or 'Got another one!'"

one gallery worker said. "It was cheap and humiliating to us and to the tricks, who, you could tell, were really hot for him. I don't think they just wanted to get fucked over a couch in the storage room—and you'd have to really maneuver to fuck on that couch."

Patricia Hamilton often cringed at the scene, and was particularly repulsed by Crispo's detailed retelling of his exploits. On one occasion, after showing a momentary visitor to the door, he turned to her and sighed. "Boy, did I fuck him! Nice bones on that one, I'm telling you."

"Andrew!" Hamilton barked, and then made a referee's whistle. "Close the curtain right there! I *don't* need to know any more about it." Her hands became curtains, and she drew them in front of her face.

Tommy Martin, Crispo's friend from Philadelphia, last saw his old chum at The Big Top, a Times Square flesh emporium, in 1976. "It was a Saturday," he recalled in detail, "and my friend Peter and I had just spent the night at the baths or something, so on the way out of town we thought we'd just drop by one of the theaters near the bus station. One more nibble before heading back. And there was Andy, behind the movie screen, doing stand-up-and-bend-over sex. Andy was standing up—just the way I remember him! And he hadn't changed a bit; still hung like an ice sculpture, still had *the* best body. Still looked like he needed a meal in that really hot, orphanlike way." Tommy tried to join the action, but Andrew pushed him, gently, aside. Together with a handful of un-zippered men, Tommy Martin enjoyed the gala event from the sidelines, a cheerleader in the darkened arena.

Meanwhile, however, Crispo carried on serial relationships that some-times—often, to hear some say—overlapped by several months, continu-ing the tradition begun with Arthur Smith, his ever-present, extremely patient lover-turned-roommate. In the mid-seventies, Crispo had a love affair with Dennis Erdman, the young actor who was starring in *Equus* on Broadway at the time. Later, Erdman became marginally well known in a made-for-TV movie (*Friendly Fire*) starring Carol Burnett and Ned Beatty) that netted several Emmy Awards—he died in the first scene. They were a tight duo for several years, until the young man—blond, with a Ron Howard jutting jaw—moved to Los Angeles, a land Andrew Crispo was quite untaken with. "He was genuinely frightened *The Big Earthquake* was going to happen while he was there," said Peter Brown, who also relocated to that coast. "He came very rarely." Perhaps the earthquake trepidation was just a cover; Crispo was busy seeing Philip Torini, in what appeared to many associates to be his most romantic relationship since those early days with Arthur Smith.

But he was also seeing an actor who starred in *Fellini Satyricon*, and a photographer for *New Leader* magazine. And all the while, he kept that telescope finely focused on the dial of the neighborhood pay phone. Some of these young men became boyfriends who would accompany him to art openings, to Studio 54 events, to Southampton cocktail parties; some couldn't be left home unattended, so untamed were they. Each, however, seemed to hold a certain charm in Crispo's eyes.

It was precisely this mixture of the Andy Crispo of South Philadelphia coffee shops and the Andrew Crispo of Madison Avenue bistros that his friends admired. Peter Brown, the former Beatles manager, was one of them. As president and CEO of the Robert Stigwood Group, a massive British entertainment company (producers of *Tommy* and *Saturday Night Fever*; managers of Eric Clapton, Andrew Lloyd Webber, the Bee Gees), Brown was part of a social world peopled by some formidable personalities when the two men met. It was before Andrew Crispo had become a success himself. "I was connected with a lot of entertainment figures, and I gave parties at my apartment with a lot of high-profile people," Brown said later. "Andrew, who was one of the younger people around at the time, was never starstruck. I don't think that he was interested in celebrities—not in the conventional sense. And he never felt uncomfortable around them, either. He always seemed to fit in quietly; he was always himself: this bright kid from somewhere or another."

As his fortunes mounted, Brown said, his personality remained unaffected. "Certainly he would travel much more, and he would go to London and to Brazil and to Switzerland and all that kind of thing. And one knew that he enjoyed the fruits of the success by staying in grand hotels. But I don't think that he was ever flashy about it. Not a conspicuousness, certainly not. A lot of people show wealth because it gives them a persona; that would have been foreign to Andrew because he was so into creating a persona of his own. To be consciously flashy would have distorted whatever he was up to.

"Like the question about where the gallery's seed money came from— if he told the real story, a simple story, that would have been bragging; by not telling, he created a mysterious, enigmatic persona that was all his own. Don't you see?"

In business, those words Andrew Crispo pronounced before his very first gallery show still held true, more or less.

"We're not doing this for the money, but for the quality."

Now there was an added dimension, an incremental goal: fun. Potential employees clamored at the door, and a galaxy of kids was always available to hang a show, to be part of the history—not just of Andrew's history but the world's history. "I saw paintings come through the gallery that were better than the National Gallery had," said one assistant, "better than most museums had." Ronnie Caran frequently said, "I could stay here till I'm ninety-nine. It's home, it's comfortable, and it's the best time I've ever had." Andrew used to joke to Victor Ruggiero, the gallery's registrar in the late seventies and early eighties, "Vic, we need someone to do gallery work—scour the bars," and Victor would say, "By Monday you'll have somebody." Of course, this was unnecessary; this was play.

Dean Aarons worked in the stockroom, though he was only fourteen. He was part of a tag team of androgynous teenagers who had worked their way up from ashtray emptiers and vacuum operators, eventually carving out slightly more meaningful jobs upstairs. Upstairs housed the shipping and accounting department and spawned the truly playful rabble-rousing that took place at the gallery. When Aarons had to return to school or leave for a family trip, a friend would take his place at the top of the staircase, eager to ogle the celebrities shopping downstairs.

It was on the second floor, for example, that word first circulated that Patricia Hamilton, the deposed gallery curator, was opening her own space—the Patricia Hamilton Gallery. Just down the street! The news drifted downstairs gleefully. "Ronnie," Crispo said in a playful voice, "how can we make trouble for her?" The answer developed by committee.

Crispo printed up his own invitations to her first-night gala. They announced an anything-goes "leather and S&M party" at her address, for the very night. The kids distributed them around the meat-packing district, and, when the time came, Crispo sat across the street from the new gallery in a rented stretch limo, pushing champagne and caviar into his mouth, and pushing guffaws of vengeance out. Scores of motorcycles, cabs, and pickups deposited some of the raunchiest people imaginable at her black-tie fete.

That, to his way of seeing things, was the funny part. He had a serious plan, as well. Hamilton received a call, in those first few days after her unexpectedly funky reception, from a woman representing Corporate Art Directions, which at one time had been affiliated with the Crispo Gallery. "I wonder," said the voice, "if I could see slides of the sculptures you are working with?"

Hamilton, figuring this was one of Andrew's games, replied perhaps too quickly, perhaps too angrily. "I won't have anything to do with Crispo," she snapped. "I wouldn't give Andrew Crispo the time of day. I will not only not send slides, I will have nothing *what-so-ever* to do with Andrew Crispo."

A mutual friend, the lawyer working for both Crispo and Hamilton, called the twenty-six-year-old gallery owner within hours. "I don't know what you said, but he's going to sue," Carl Lobell told her. "Slander, he says. You'd better write him a letter, or something. You don't need this now."

"Fuck him! I don't have to do business with that sleazebag, and I don't have to apologize."

"He's crazy," Patricia remembered her friend saying. "You know him, you know he's crazy."

Patricia Hamilton wrote a terse note. It said: "I don't have any work available by any of my sculptors." It seemed to do the trick, judging by the fact that no suit was filed. But having to cry uncle made her so angry, she stepped up her bad-mouthing campaign.

Dean Aarons, the youngest and the most intense of the young men working for Crispo, was unaware of the second-level assault. He probably would not have believed it. Before joining the gallery, he was a student at the High School of Art and Design, on Fifty-seventh and Second, and worked as a delivery boy for a local dry cleaner, which brought him regularly to the building on East Seventy-ninth where Andrew and Arthur Smith lived. When Ronnie Caran decided to settle down in New York, and into his job at the gallery, he took a place in the same building, several flights below. It was he who suggested a job at the gallery, which Aarons's father, a divorced gay man, immediately found suspicious. He had heard of Andrew Crispo, and brought an insightful wariness to bear on the circumstances of the offer.

So the two of them—young, cute, tantalizing Dean and his handsome middle-aged dad—showed up for the interview. The elder Aarons stated his concern directly, with phrases such as "There's a whole gay society inside the art world, and my son's just in ninth grade." And, as it turned out, quite heterosexual, to boot. Convinced of the atmosphere's wholesomeness, Aarons's father eventually gave his okay, and the staff of the Andrew Crispo Gallery became part of the Aarons' extended family. They spent Christmases and Thanksgivings together, father and son and employer.

"It was one of the more incredible times I can remember in my life," Dean Aarons said later. "The most fascinating people in the world you'd ever want to meet. Billy Baldwin, Egon and Diane, Warhol, you know. Lowell Nesbitt and Charles Seliger and Hubert Long and Douglas Abdell. Mick Jagger and Jerry Hall. Everybody. Names I didn't recognize. I'm typing letters to people—So-and-so, from So-and-so—and I find out it's a wombo producer in Hollywood. When I started there, I had no idea how *wow* it really was, while other people were telling me it was like the middle of Madison Avenue society." He stayed for seven years, on and off until 1982.

To these young men, Crispo was more of a brotherly presence than a fatherly one. He talked like them, he thought like them, he dressed like them on Sundays and Mondays, when the gallery doors were shut. Other times, he appeared somewhat out of place in the couture suits that Arthur Smith handed down to him (always crisp, always floating around slightly on his athletic frame). He wore the suits on special occasions, but he still preferred the confirmation outfit for his everyday business attire: those gray slacks, that blue blazer, that simple Catholic-school tie.

He was wearing jeans the Monday that a babushkaed grandmotherly type walked through the towering gallery doors and asked for him by name. With the kids, and the other gallery staff, he was unpacking crates of Fred Eversley sculptures, cool-casted glistening phalluses. Andrew looked at Ronnie, and shook his head *no*. Ronnie said, "I'm sorry Mr. Crispo's not here. Can I help you?"

She pulled a trail of shopping bags around her swollen feet and announced, in a slight Germanic accent, "I'd like to see him myself."

Andrew made a face. The kids made faces. Somebody sniggered, choked, bellowed. Fred Eversley, large, dark-skinned, shy-faced, stooped over a statue in embarrassment.

"Well, he's not here," said Ronnie, still politely.

"I'd like to make an appointment." She was not unnerved. Andrew was laughing now, shaking his head in merry incredulity.

"I'm not sure when he will be here; I'll take your number and he can call you to make it himself." He took a pen from the reception desk. "Your name?"

She said, "Yes, please tell him that Mrs. Hans Hofmann stopped in to see him."

Crispo "did a giant bunny-hop across the room and almost kissed her hand," Fred Eversley said later. He apologized profusely. He invited her into the back room. He snapped to one of the kids, "Coffee!" She clasped her paper bags to her breast and slowly followed him into the gallery.

Her late husband had been art-world royalty, reclusive and legendary. "Steeped in the firsthand experience of Cubism, Fauvism, and Expressionism, and their various extensions," according to literature. Hofmann had left a warring Germany and established in New York the foundations for most twentieth-century American movements. He had pushed Cubism toward its postpainterly forms; he had embraced color, rejected automatism. His "abstract" became the next generation's Abstract Expressionism. Arshile Gorky and Matisse and Picasso and Miró had been contemporaries; Robert Motherwell, Stuart Davis, and Fernand Léger had been protégés. He had taught Jackson Pollack; it was Hans Hofmann who, in 1940, had first puddled and dripped paint on a plywood surface. It was Hans Hofmann who had created the art and the artists that were Andrew Crispo's specialty.

In his office, sitting on a red sofa, the widow Hofmann explained she needed to raise some cash. She reached in a bag and pulled out one of her husband's works. Then another. Then works by his contemporaries, by his friends, a mother lode of modern masterpieces painted in the forties and fifties that had never been out of this woman's home. Andrew Crispo wrote a half-dozen checks. The paintings had come out of the woodwork, as he had once predicted. She could have gone to the Guggenheim, or the Met, or the Modern. She went to Crispo instead.

Fred Eversley bumped into Mrs. Hofmann in the lobby downstairs. "I was kind of embarrassed about what I saw upstairs. I hope you're not doing business with that schmuck."

"Young man," the widow said, "in the art world, you get treated like that all the time. There's no avoiding it."

Sexually, Crispo kept to his unspoken promise to Dean Aarons's father and remained politely distant from his young staffers. Instead, he preferred to sate his urges by foraging the city's darker terrain for the overripe, feral youths he craved. There was something dangerously exciting about bringing untamed toughs into the splendor of his Upper East Side apartment.

Arthur Smith had decorated it, and his own adjacent apartment, and had each one laid out in *Architectural Digest* as examples of his work— without mentioning that there were no borders between them, or that there was any relationship between the one called Andrew Crispo's apartment and the one called his. (Of course, Crispo was listed as the owner of the prized art works in both layouts, and Smith was called the decorator; such mentions are worth gold to decorators and dealers.) Both apartments were as luxurious and forfending as velvet-roped showrooms. As severe as Andrew's tricks could appear on the street, or in the sex clubs or subways, once they entered his home, the intimidation of his possessions alone would hammer them into docility and awe, magnificence taming the beast.

But not all the time. Crispo left his apartment one Saturday morning after a frolicking evening with a leather-clad street kid he'd picked up downtown. The kid stayed behind. Smith was in Europe on business. With no discernible motive, the visitor went on a violent rampage, and ransacked *both* apartments.

Ronnie Caran, at home in his apartment just a few floors below the Crispo-Smith duplex, began to notice familiar pieces of debris floating past. "Andrew! My God," he screamed into the phone at his friend, whom he reached at the gallery. "I just saw the pillows from your sofa go flying out the window! And *Jesus*! There goes your *Franz Kline!*"

An incalculable amount of damage was done to several masterpieces, some of which Andrew owned personally and some of which were the property of the gallery (this was always a fine line). Antique statues were overturned and original Art Deco vases were shattered. Andrew's prized piece, a 1958 Morris Louis "veil" painting called *Beth Feh* that hung over his downstairs sofa, was scratched and misshappen; the Kline work was crumpled and soiled. Stuart Davis's *Rue Lippe*, a lighthearted work valued at three hundred thousand dollars, was knocked off the dining room wall, battered about on the hefty sideboard, and left in a corner, wadded up like a stiff towel.

But the damage was worse in Arthur's bedroom, which the designer considered a masterpiece of his work. The theme was deep red. A diamond-shaped red painting by Roy Lichtenstein (from his famed "Red Series") hung over a red-draped Russian antique bed, which grew majestically out of a plush red carpet. Even the walls were red—a glazed Oriental lacquer red, giving the room an erotic, gorgeous richness. But this was no ordinary brush-and-roller job; it was achieved with no less than twenty-two coats of hand-rubbed lacquer on a canvas-and-gesso base. The total cost for the finish alone: $22,000.

By the time Andrew arrived home, Smith's collection of avant-garde Russian knickknacks had been hurled around the room with such force that the red paint had been dented and marred beyond simple repair. The Lichtenstein was destroyed, having been slashed repeatedly with a knife.

Police officers arrested the young man, whom they found sitting dispassionately on the window ledge, dangling his feet out of Crispo's apartment, and Crispo set about making everything right before Arthur's return. The bedroom was relacquered from scratch. The vases were replaced with similar ones; the paintings were patched by a restoration company in Queens. (The diamond-shaped Lichtenstein, after patching, was sold to an unsuspecting Steve Martin.) What couldn't be immediately salvaged was taken off to a storage garage Crispo rented. Several gallery employees were enlisted in the hush-hush endeavor, all of which was charted in two file folders buried deep in Crispo's personal file cabinet back at the gallery. One, labeled BERSERK, PERSONAL, chronicled the expenses Crispo fronted from his own purses; the other, BERSERK, COR-PORATE, measured the hit to his business. The total added up to nearly a million dollars (one employee ventured)—and none of it was ever mentioned to Arthur Smith.

Victor Ruggiero, the gallery's registrar, was handed a pile of broken china, dismantled clocks, splintered frames. Caran told him, "Glue this, fix this, patch this."

"What *is* this stuff?"

"You're better off not knowing," Caran said. "In fact, don't tell anybody about any of this."

When Ruggiero eventually learned the truth (he found the "Berserk" files), he said to Caran: "He's lucky he didn't get himself fucking killed, bringing home guys like that. And leaving him alone in his house! What was he thinking?"

But the spectacle happened in the late seventies, by which time there was an answer to that question, one that most anybody who worked for the gallery understood deeply, and personally. Crispo was thinking that danger, in sexual matters, was exciting. He was thinking that intimacy was designed to be shared by strangers. He was thinking, as he often said, that the unfortunate, costly incident "could have happened to anyone."

PART

III

Criminal Passions

"Victor and I went down to have drinks at Windows on the World (cab $5). Drank and talked and looked out the window ($180). It was beautiful. Then we walked around the Village. In the old days you could go over there on a Sunday and nobody would be around, but now it's gay gay gay as far as the eye can see—dykes and leather bars with the names right out there in broad daylight—Ramrod-type places. These leather guys, they get dressed up in leather and go to those bars and it's all show business—they tie them up and that takes an hour. They say a few dirty words and that takes another hour. They take out a whip and that takes another hour—it's a performance. And then every once in a while, you get a nut who takes it seriously and does it for real, and it throws it all off. But it's just show business with most of them. Dropped Victor off ($5), stayed home and watched TV."

—ANDY WARHOL to PAT HACKETT,
on Sunday, June 19, 1977,
The Andy Warhol Diaries

CHAPTER
6

Nineteen eighty-two brought evidence of a new era. Down on Wall Street, and down in Washington, and across Ronald Reagan's America, wealth was beatified virtually overnight, climbing sainthood's tinder ladder like a flame. Money was nothing, and everything, making the difference between mere existence and full-fledged citizenship.

There was a cure for every ill ("Catsup is vegetables," the president said, eliminating hunger with the flap of a tongue), an explanation for everything evil (Mayor Ed Koch said, "The homeless *prefer* to live outdoors"). Everywhere, the bad birthed the good. Princess Grace perished when her car tumbled off a mountain road, but young, handsome, strong Princess Stephanie—model of a new generation—lived! The celebration, the music, and the sex was hard and coarse and plentiful.

That year, according to C. J. Scheiner, an observer of such matters, "sadomasochism hit its zenith, hit its stride. It was, for a time, no longer sub rosa, but part of everyday life." Halston and Andy Warhol at the Anvil, John Waters and Jerzy Kosinski sipping beer at the Hellfire Club. Only Renaissance France, whose King Henri III openly relished reports that he paddled his lovers for pleasure, had ever experienced such a phenomenon.

Arthur Bell's tart and naked *Village Voice* column replaced Bob Colacello's in *Interview* as the repository of important social facts attending these developments. The scene moved downtown, whipping right past Warhol's Union Square offices without even a wave. The hip were young, and the young lined up in front of Limelight, Area, the Mudd Club, the newest incarnation of the Peppermint Lounge, and The Saint, that all-gay dance emporium inside the old Filmore East on Second Avenue. Graffiti was king, and the East Village was exploding with galleries for the hot new artists—M-13 and Gracie Mansion and names that changed so often, no one kept an accurate list. Nineteen eighty-two, the year Keith Haring quit his job as the Mudd Club's doorman and parties were thrown in his honor at Limelight. The out were in, and the in were tumbling.

"Andrew Crispo wanted in," said Alan Rish, one of the architects of the changing scene. "I threw him a party. In nineteen eighty-two."

Nineteen-year-old Bernard LeGeros wanted in, too, and he went to Andrew Crispo, a man he'd met only once five years earlier when he delivered an airline ticket to the gallery. "I'm looking for a job," he had said over the phone, "maybe in photography, maybe in the art world." Andrew had invited him to the gallery, after hours.

"A glass of wine?" Andrew gestured toward a dusty case sitting on the floor, his stockpile for the baron's visits. "Or a toot?" His hand swung toward a four-foot-tall African fetish that stood on a pedestal just behind the red sofa in the Red Room, where they sat and where a slight disarray—a hill of open books, an overflowing ashtray—made the place more living room than office. The fetish was dark and blotchy, and caused Bernard to smile. The devil horns on the top were ominous, but the Jimmy Durante nose softened these; the stance of the fetish was aggressive, but a potbelly and stubby unformed arms were cartoonlike and silly.

Bernard gave a shy "why not" shrug, and Andrew tilted the statue back to retrieve from the hollow base a full bag of white powder. "This is made out of blood and mud," Andrew said casually over his shoulder, "*human* blood, from sacrifices. It's very valuable." He spilled some cocaine onto the coffee table.

Bernard gave a broad smile, which Andrew studied and compared to the face of the soft teenager he remembered so well. Round and dimpled back then, his face had become angled and highly defined. The teenage flesh that gave Bernard's eyes an Asiatic ellipse had since been stretched over high bronzed cheeks. He looked Hispanic, not Filipino, and he dressed very New York: black shirt and black jeans and black leather cowboy boots.

When he put a finger to one nostril and bent over the coffee table,

Andrew noticed tattered cuticles and a stubby nail. That first time they'd met, Bernard had chewed carnivorously at the ends of each digit. Always the same order, index finger to pinky, then thumb, as if he was playing out some unheard madrigal.

Andrew pinched some cocaine off his septum and wiped it on his tongue. "So, you bring a resume?"

"Well, no," said Bernard. An expansive sensation flowed through his brow, his stomach, his thighs, a spider crawling on his nerves. "I was gonna make one, but things just kind of came up." He laughed jolts of noise from behind his sinuses: *Heh-heh.*

"Things?" Andrew dashed more powder on the small table, moved it around with a bright razor blade.

Bernard bent down, rose up. "Oh, this and that. Heh-heh." He leaned into a soft chair and looked at his fingers, and looked at Andrew, who seemed kind and intense, who did not say a word, who seemed to be pulling the story out of Bernard, whose pupils were the size of dimes. Bernard, who felt very comfortable with Andrew, shifted involuntarily in his chair. He jerked forward, balancing on the seat's most extreme edge.

Andrew hoed out two more lines of cocaine. "Things?"

"Well," said Bernard, "I tried to kill myself. Heh-heh. Not the first time, either."

The young man told about his desperate love for Anya, who had been his girlfriend for three years; about how, when she left him two years before—went on a family vacation—he felt despair, felt an unbearable loneliness, felt terror. *"The act of suicide did not seem like that forbidden act that elders preached against. Death was the final action to end all action,"* Bernard had written in his journal. A security guard found him dangling off the edge of Waterside Plaza, thirty-seven stories above the East River. A city cop slapped him in handcuffs. *"I remembered crying for a dead dog, but my father soon stopped me, saying, 'It is the law of nature, my son.'"*

"I'm still seeing Anya," Bernard told Andrew, quickly moving to the recent saga. "And a couple of weeks ago, we were having dinner. See, she was like not there, distant, you know." He felt she was drifting away, maybe seeing another man, maybe dissatisfied with his sex. "I took two pills out. Potassium cyanide reagent. That I got from my mother's lab. That I put into capsules, purple and white capsules from an antibiotic I was taking." He had ordered wine. He'd said, "This is what you're making me do," and swallowed them.

Anya took him to Bellevue Hospital. He was not breathing; he slipped into a coma; he slipped back; he stayed there for several days. "No signs of organicity," a doctor wrote on his chart, "the patient's sensorium seemed intact although there were some deficits." Tests were done, showing him to possess a "high-normal" IQ (110), but low educational achievement. He was released at John LeGeros's insistence, and with the promise that the boy would seek therapy, though he never did.

Bernard was not laughing now. "My dad's a good man," he said, "but he just doesn't understand anything. Sometimes, I blame him." He leaned back into an upholstered chair and looked at his fingers and looked at Andrew, with whom he felt an instant and overwhelming intimacy. Andrew was stretched out on a red sofa, a knee crooked and locked in place with his elbow, absolutely motionless. With his other foot, he pushed around a stray shoe on the rug.

"Therapists," Andrew said finally, "don't know shit." It's a conclusion he had held fast since those early years, when social workers and others had pried into his life with thick voices, penciling their findings onto long pads. Perhaps he blamed those pads for keeping him in the orphanage all those years. He was, after all, a white baby, a handsome child. He had all his fingers and toes, a class-A candidate for adoption. Yet he languished through a cherubic childhood and into pubescence. Once, they sent him out on loan, more or less, to a local family who took him on for a few years as a foster child. They didn't adopt him, although for a period of time, he said, he adopted their name.

Andrew told only two stories about the years at St. John's, and he repeated them to Bernard.

The first one was about how he got there. His father was a man of French descent; his mother had been just sixteen, and unmarried, when he was conceived. He had declined an offer from Judge Bonnelley to be introduced to her.

The second story was more personal, and more telling. One sleety day, the young orphans were taken to a Philadelphia department store to meet Santa Claus and choose gifts, which the store gave to the kids. Andrew selected a small monkey that played drums. The next day, nuns lined up the boys to inspect their presents, and Andrew's appeared to be the smallest. "Will Andrew Crispo step out?" He did, and a nun gave a lecture about greed, holding up Andrew—eight years old—as a selfless counterpart to the others. Afterward, Andrew said, the other kids punished him mercilessly. This story was told so often over the years that, independently, a handful of acquaintances had given Andrew little furry wind-up monkeys. A cotillion of them sat on a shelf over the red sofa, above the African fetish.

After concluding his twin parables, Andrew walked across the room and retrieved a pen and paper, which he put down in front of Bernard.

"Tell you what," he said, "I want you to make two lists for me. On one, I want you to list all the things that make you happy, all the things you really like. And on the other one, write down what scares you, what pisses you off. All the things that really, really bother you. That way, you can look at everything all at once. You can face your fears, and you can face your shame. Face your fears and face your shame."

Bernard gave it a try. On one side, he wrote something he liked: Energy. On the other, something he wanted less of: Boredom, fatigue. Then his fingers went back to his mouth.

Andrew said, "What about money? Don't you want more money?"

"Well, I never thought about that."

"Why not? What do you mean?"

Bernard laughed uneasily. "I don't know. 'Cause I just don't ever think about money."

"Never? When you go to buy something, you don't think about money? We can walk right down the street right now and you can point out something and say, 'I can afford that,' and buy it right then and there?"

"Not exactly," Bernard said, a bit miffed by the challenge, and not at all sure where the conversation was going. "But I always have ways of working for it or gaining it."

"Okay, then," said Andrew. He was speaking very quickly, on coke time. "How about something that really, that you're really not proud of. Something very personal, something that maybe you're too embarrassed to talk about."

Bernard thought about this item, and couldn't imagine what Andrew had in mind.

"Something that only you know about yourself, that nobody else in the world understands. That you wouldn't want anybody else in the world to know about. Something"—that intense smile, that encouraging, prying voice—"that even you are still not completely comfortable with."

Again, Bernard drew a blank and the two men sat in a chaotic silence.

"Why," wondered Andrew, reclining again on the sofa, "did you call me, after all these years?"

"It's like I said on the phone. I thought you could point me in the right direction."

As quickly as he had begun it, Crispo abandoned the psychological probing of his young friend. There would be time for that later. Instead, he offered some specific suggestions for Bernard's resume and invited him back once he had typed something up.

"C'mon, Victor! Get out of here! The lot comes up at eleven. *Jesus.*" Crispo was fidgety. Sotheby's, the great British auctioneers, was putting up a set of hammered silver vases by the proto-Deco designer Josef Hoffmann. Crispo collected Hoffmann pieces. He snapped up every Hoffmann piece that ever appeared in an auction catalogue. They were stacked in his vault, in cabinets at home and in the office, on shelves over his Louis XVI desk. He was doing the same with Chinese enamel, George Ohr's turn-of-the-century pottery, anything Art Deco. As though he was proving the point to himself, Andrew Crispo purchased things he only marginally wanted. Because he could. No temptation was suppressible.

A set of furniture by the Swiss sculptors Alberto and Diego Giacometti was available; it went into one of Andrew's storage rooms. An acquaintance was bored with his collection of country jugs, and Andrew paid him thousands. He collected Georgia O'Keeffe paintings with such dedication that his holdings were among the largest repositories of her work anywhere. To accommodate the collection, he had his West Twelfth Street apartment made over immaculately, and then had it photographed and the photographs published.

"Victor!"

Victor Ruggiero jumped in a cab and raced over to the auction house, a block-long modernist structure on York Avenue. The set was already on the block when he claimed his paddle, and he began bidding from the back of the room. After outpacing the rest of the clamorers, sitting on folding chairs in the iron gray theater, Victor found himself in a war with an anonymous person furiously upping the ante over the telephone. "Eighty-five hundred," the auctioneer would say, and a woman connected to the phone would nod. "Nine." Victor's paddle waved. "Ten. Eleven five. Twelve." Winded but victorious, Victor headed for the cashier.

On his way out the door, the woman working the phones pulled his arm. "It was so funny," she began. "All of a sudden the man on the phone said, 'Is there a handsome young guy about five nine bidding against me?' And I said, yeah, and I read him your paddle number. And he said, 'Oh, my God. That's my guy!' " Crispo, bidding from back in the Red Room, had raised the price several thousand dollars.

Victor expected he'd be bawled out—for following orders!—once he returned to the gallery. But Crispo chuckled, instead. "At least we got it, right, Victor?"

Sometimes, it was even more complicated. At Christie's, the other leading fine-art auction house, Crispo had problems keeping up with his bills. Not that he didn't have the money. The gallery was doing millions a year in business, and the coffers couldn't have been more flush. Crispo just hated to pay. He held on to dollars the way he clung to canvases:

compulsively, desperately, needlessly. Christie's had eventually confiscated his bidding paddle and frozen his account.

Rent payments, which now totaled $17,000 a month, were habitually four to six months behind, and only relinquished after the second or third threatening call. Most of the time, he alleged the checks were in the mail, a line so frequently uttered that an elaborate scam developed around it in an effort to make it appear truthful. Postage was back-dated on the office stamp machine. Envelopes were wadded up, walked on, torn, and sent FedEx to a friend in Chicago, who would write "Please Forward" on them and drop them in a mailbox there.

New innovations on the antic, when they came from the staff, were rewarded with Crispo's highest praise. Victor Ruggiero dreamed up the Chicago angle. For his efforts, he was added to the gallery's sales staff, the first addition since Ronnie Caran. It meant that a part of the gigantic commissions flowing through the gallery would become his, at least in theory. Crispo fell behind on that, too.

There was only one area in his life where fiscal propriety would invariably prevail. Dearest to Crispo's heart, after the O'Keeffe collection, was his home in Southampton. In 1979, he paid $175,000 for a small stucco cottage near the beach in this exclusive Long Island enclave, and immediately set about doubling its size with bedrooms and living rooms and kitchens. He installed a pool outside (although he couldn't swim), and increased its value over tenfold. He spent most of his summer weekends poolside. The Italian terra-cotta tiles were the same as the ones used on the floors of the Uffizi Museum in Florence; the pool's deep blue walls were painted to match, in hue and cool richness, David Hockney's famous *Une Autre Piscine à Minuit*, which hung in the dining room.

The place was Andrew's East Egg mansion, tucked into the most exclusive street in that exclusive enclave: Gin Lane, Southampton. His immediate neighbors were Gloria Vanderbilt, whose enormous home shared a private driveway with Andrew's; local news anchor Chuck Scarborough and his wife, Anne Ford Uzielli; and Lee Radziwill, Jackie O's sister. From poolside, one could see their widow's walks, their chimneys, puffs of smoke from their barbecue pits drifting out over the ocean a block away. The owners of those houses, however, could rarely be seen except upon arrival or departure in long, chauffeured cars. Despite his proximity, despite his interest in the man's work, despite having owned and sold his most valuable paintings, Andrew Crispo had never met Roy Lichtenstein, the artist who lived two lots over. He told friends he had no interest in the man, just in the man's work.

Perhaps he wasn't being truthful. The great rewards for which Crispo had struggled, the material comfort, the untold possessions, were also very solitary ones. They had come with relative simplicity, alacrity, and ease—or so it seemed now. And this was the payoff: an unsettling tranquillity. A tall-hedged universe where anything he wanted, anything *commercially* available, could be his in a heartbeat, on his terms, no dollar amount insurmountable. It doesn't take a powerful man to write a check. Where was the sport? It was infinitely more rewarding to withhold the money.

Crispo had taken to telling people that "Down in the Depths on the Ninetieth Floor" was his favorite song. It was written by Cole Porter, himself the owner of many fine homes (and a client of Arthur Smith's). One of them was called "No Trespassing," and Crispo borrowed the name for his Gin Lane mansion. A small white sign carried those words at the foot of the driveway. That way, it would seem that Crispo retired alone behind the tall hemlocks by choice.

But the man whom nuns had once held up as an exemplar of selflessness could, by 1982, grow furious when denied his cravings. During a spring supper with Roy Cohn and a few of his friends at the lawyer's midtown town house, Crispo and Ronnie Caran were so distressed about one such denial, they could barely be contained.

For one thing, Cohn's home did not possess a very comfortable dining room. The building on East Sixty-eighth Street was also corporate headquarters for Saxe, Bacon & Bolan, whose offices were on the first floor. The dining room, in a sort of swing position on the second floor, served as the conference room during the day. It was not warm, certainly not as cozy as the formal living room, also on that floor, which the small handful of Cohn associates were allowed into only on special occasions. There was a feeling that business, not repose, took place in this room.

A course or two served, Cohn finally asked his younger guests— Crispo was then thirty-eight—what was on their minds. They spoke simultaneously.

Caran had struck a deal with Ileana Bulova Lindt, the Bulova watch widow who remarried into the Lindt chocolate fortune. At issue was a prized statue in her possession, for which she wanted eight hundred thousand dollars. It was a piece she'd been trying to unload for five years. "Fifteen years earlier," Crispo explained, "when Arde Bulova died, his will read that he gave all of his paintings and artwork to the Guggenheim, and she was livid. She maintained that all the stuff was supposed to go to the museum except this sculpture, which is a Brancusi called the *The Muse*. So she sued."

Caran added that legal skirmishing had stretched over the ensuing decade until she won the title. "Because Brancusi was Rumanian, and she's Rumanian, she said that Arde bought it for her, for sentimental reasons. Ileana, she's one of those very strong, very powerful Middle European women who can do the goose step. At age sixteen, she was apparently one of the great beauties in Europe, and the mistress to the dictator of Rumania during World War II, and she was in bed with him when he was assassinated, and within a few weeks, she was publicly the mistress of the new dictator of Rumania." There was no apparent historical foundation for Caran's brief biography—between the wars, Kings Carol and Michael (father and son) repeatedly exchanged trips into exile, dropping the scepter only briefly while fascists and communists battled for control; Michael left town one last time in 1947—alive—after the communists won elections. Caran's embellished story was a hit with Cohn nonetheless.

Crispo said, "We worked out this deal—it's all in writing—where I would give her one hundred thousand dollars up-front and the rest a few weeks down the road. She didn't want it all at once, for some reason."

"Capital gains," Caran said, adding that Crispo had found he needed an extra day for the remainder—a wire-transfer foul-up—and had negotiated a side deal. He'd give an additional one hundred thousand dollars on the final due date, and the rest the following day, with the understanding that if he missed the last deadline, she could keep the two hundred thousand *and* the statue. "This statue, also, is a major, monumental, *quintessential* work of Brancusi's," Caran stressed for effect.

This part was incontrovertible. One of his "primevalist" works, *The Muse* was a small, lumpy, marble carving in, more or less, the shape of an egg. It represented the artist's efforts to ignore nineteenth-century developments in sculpture, and start from the very beginning. Along with *The Sleeping Muse*, a bodyless goddess also shaped like an egg (which the Crispo Gallery had loaned to Adnan Khashoggi, then sold to a Midwest collector who promptly drilled a hole through its head and mounted the defiled object on his private jet), this piece was the artist's greatest triumph.

"We were supposed to meet her yesterday at three-thirty at her bank to make the final payment and take the item," Caran said. "The bank closed at three, the safe-deposit boxes closed at four downstairs, and that's where she has the Brancusi, in the safe-deposit box."

"Bank hates her," Crispo pointed out.

"Quarter past four, she arrives," said Caran, "and she titters, 'Oh ho ho ho ho. I'm terribly sorry I did this; I've been tied up all day long.'" Caran said these words in a Middle European, goose-stepping meter. "'I'll take the check today and you can pick up the sculpture in the morning,' she says. And the bank vice president turns to her and says, 'Mrs. Lindt, we knew how important this was to you, and we have Mr. Crispo's check right here, so we kept the bank vault open.' "

Crispo said, "Bank really hates her, wants this over and done with."

"Her face went wild, just insane. 'How dare you! I don't want this check; it's a terrible kind of check.' It was a bank check, one that you go in and buy with the cash. So she said, 'This is no good, I want a certified check.' The bitch didn't know what in the world she was talking about."

"So we went back today with the certified check."

"She says, 'I don't know about this check. I don't know if it's good.' The vice president was standing there; he says, 'Mrs. Lindt, this is a Federal Reserve–backed check. The only thing that could stop this check from clearing is if the government fell today.' Finally, she said it: 'I'm not taking the check.' "

"So I called our lawyers over at Weil, Gotshal and they called her lawyers," Crispo said, "and they said it was too late, because our agreement had expired yesterday. And then my lawyers say it will take three days to get any kind of court order for the thing!"

"We're pretty sure she's going to take it out of Morgan Bank tomorrow," Caran said, "and do God knows what."

Cohn, who had begun fidgeting, barked, "That's ridiculous," and pushed away from the table. "Let's see who's sitting tomorrow." He left the room.

When he returned, he announced, "I found a sitting judge, called him at home and told him I'd be sending papers down to him tomorrow. I said, 'This is the story; my guys are going to lose this thing and she's already got some of the money, so could I please get a restraining order on her bank vault by nine tomorrow?' He said sure."

Nine o'clock the next morning, Crispo and Caran sipped coffee from paper cups at the corner of Fifty-seventh and Madison, outside the Fuller Building. From there, they had a clear view of the entrance of the bank, two blocks up on Madison Avenue. They expected to see Ileana Bulova Lindt make the corner at Fifty-eighth Street, coming from her home on Park Avenue, and they were not disappointed.

"There!" Crispo was bouncing in childlike glee, the Andy from Philadelphia blistering at the surface. "I knew it! There she goes."

She wore a fur coat, her hair freshly coiffed, as she entered the bank. A younger man was with her. Fifteen minutes later, she exited empty-handed. She was gesticulating angrily to her companion and scuttling up the avenue. "Her *hair*"—Caran hooted—"is an absolute *mess!*"

The statue, eventually, belonged to Crispo.

* * *

Secretly, Crispo may have liked to compare his life to Cohn's. Both had gotten rich and well known as young men, Cohn as the twenty-five-year-old execrable general counsel to Senator Joe McCarthy. Both had a driving affliction for young blond men with broad shoulders (although Crispo, apparently unlike Cohn in this regard, could equally enjoy the short, dark, and handsome type). Both traveled in limousines they didn't own (Crispo's were rented by the hour, Cohn's by the month). Both had country homes. Both disliked paying their bills. Both had the fascinating misfortune of being tagged as murderers, in whispers and open gossip.

Cohn's "killing" had happened several years earlier, when the decrepit and highly insured yacht he bought from Malcolm Forbes sunk in the Atlantic, taking with it a young skipper. Said *Newsweek* at the time: "FBI agents who are investigating the sinking of the 97-foot *Defiance* off the Florida coast last June say they suspect 'crime on the high seas and possibly murder.' The facts beyond doubt are that the yacht—under lease to the law firm of Roy M. Cohn . . . burned up and sank off Port Canaveral seven months ago, and that the *Defiance*'s first mate, Charles Martensen, 21, was lost in the blaze."

Shortly before the fire, a tipster called the Palm Beach County sheriff's office, reporting that the yacht "would be taken out and scuttled for insurance." Roy Cohn, who pocketed that insurance money, escaped charges in the case. The alleged "killing" that hounded Crispo—the death of Franco Rappetti—proved equally profitable.

There were some marked dissimilarities between the two men. First, Cohn denied his homosexuality publicly, and actively campaigned in the political arena against gays. At Mortimer's restaurant, among a Who's Who of luncheoners, he used his high-profile friendship with Barbara Walters as his beard. Crispo, by contrast, was very open, a fact that sometimes cost him invitations to Madison Avenue parties because, as one acquaintance said, "He always had these boys around him."

Drugs were another departure. While both reveled in the heyday of drugs and disco at Studio 54, only Crispo fell into the cocaine trap that snared so many others, including politicians, judges, and celebrities of all stripes. Many gallery employees suspected he had begun to snort the stuff in the late seventies, with little proof. One, Vinny Marcus, said Crispo admitted trying coke in 1981, during a cleaning spree one Monday afternoon at the gallery. His crew of young staffers had agreed to work on their day off, he said, if he supplied the beer and coke. One of those young men denied the tale. "After hanging around with Andy Warhol? After Studio Fifty-four and everything else? You think we're the people he learned it from? Get real." Leave it to Andrew to pick his own time, Vinny Morcas reasoned; Andrew followed nobody's lead.

Except that he seemed to hang on Roy Cohn's words very closely. After the "world's most hated lawyer" (as he'd been called) made a very public salvo at the IRS, declaring that he could avoid paying taxes, Crispo devised a complex double-billing method that allowed him to reduce his taxes without the aid of Cohn's loopholes. One published account detailed Roy's penchant for buying, ignoring the bills, and, when the lawsuits came, offering fifty cents on the dollar; Andrew became even less responsible to his creditors and more reliant on his attorney.

It was in 1982 that, for a reason never elaborated, Andrew Crispo stopped all payments to Marty Ackerman, the financier who at the time held seventeen of Andrew's most prized paintings—including a handful of O'Keeffes, oils by Arthur Dove, Pablo Picasso, David Hockney—as collateral against $423,000 in loans. The paintings were worth nearly $3 million. Crispo defaulted on a debt to the Riggs Bank in Washington, D.C. He stopped interest payments on a $700,000 corporate loan from the Bank of New York and a $14,000 personal line of credit, also collateralized with paintings. Legal papers were flying into the gallery like ticker tape. Old friends like Ackerman were aghast; the Bank of New York's vice president who handled his accounts—now overdrawn by $136,000—was canned. Crispo was having much more fun doing things Roy Cohn's way.

Richard Pousette-Dart and his wife had been discussing a change of dealers for several months. "There's just not the attention being paid that there once was," Evelyn had reasoned. "These things happen from time to time. Change is good." They had noticed that sales were off, that gallery shows were more sporadic, and that between shows it was becoming increasingly more difficult to coax their dealer to the telephone.

Word was that the collagist Arman had moved on, and Richard Anuszkiewicz, the Op Art innovator, too. Fred Eversley had left two years earlier, angrily, and was still badmouthing Crispo. "He became like a big shot, or thought he did," he complained. "And I was supposed to be incredibly ingratiated by the fact that I was in his gallery. I wasn't going to put up with this shit. Every time I thought about the place, I wanted to fight. Where's my money? Where's the accounting? Where's the records of who bought this or that? And if I went over—this happened literally about eighty-five times—he'd make me cool my heels in the outer room. Real discourteous stuff."

The litany was not unusual, and many artists told similar tales about many dealers. But there was another part of Eversley's story that genuinely scared the artists who remained behind. When he decided, in the summer of 1980, to leave the gallery, Fred Eversley made arrangements to retrieve the statues that remained unsold. "He just refused to give them to me," Eversley told his friends. "They were just sitting in the storage room in boxes, for goodness sake. Not like he was actually trying to sell them, or show them to anybody. They had been in those boxes for years, but he wouldn't let me have them. Finally, after four months of this, I had to hire my own attorney to write a letter." The statues followed shortly.

Richard Pousette-Dart resigned from the gallery in early 1982, followed shortly by David Ligare, who had been the first artist to trail Andrew Crispo from the ACA Galleries. "I didn't fully know why I left," Ligare explained later, "but I could sense that other people, artists and museums or even employees who had trusted the place before, were kind of staying away. Things were no longer congealing."

Victor Ruggiero, in his fourth year as the Crispo's registrar, didn't feel any wariness. Or at least, he attributed any strain that existed between him and his boss to the fact that they simply were not friends. Still, of all the young, energetic, talented people who had joined the payroll, Ruggiero alone enjoyed the privilege of being in sales. Others could discuss works with clients, or suggest certain fine pieces, or write up bills. But since the gallery first opened, only Ronnie and Andrew had set prices and closed deals. It was a position of honor, and Victor knew it. He always figured that Crispo selected him because the two were so much alike. Both quick-witted, both Italian, both boyishly attractive. Both successful at winning over a client, or a young man.

There was something else these two men shared. They both liked to make up harmless stories about themselves for potential paramours, either to increase their chances of a score or just to live out some altered reality, if only for a single, passionate evening. Andrew liked being "Andy," a married man in distress, or in transition, or in mourning— desperate for any sort of affection.

Victor liked borrowing the interests of the man he was after. For example, he once shared a drink with a soft-spoken gentleman in his twenties who turned out to be an art dealer. "Really? I work for Andrew Crispo," he said. "What type of work do you deal in?"

"Vintage photographs, mostly," said the man.

"Really? I just got a vintage photograph, a Berenice Abbott," Victor said, stalking the prey. It was Andrew, not Victor, who had recently acquired the picture, but it gave the two strangers something to discuss.

"She's one of my favorites," was the man's reply, and he offered to represent the picture in the event that Victor wanted to place it on the market. They talked it over romantically that night in bed, and one other time about a week later, also in bed. The "negotiations" never became serious. It was their foreplay, the verbal buoy that marked the encounter long after the face, the name, the particulars had sunk into a careless and cluttered memory.

Until January 1982.

"Of course, I remember you," Victor Ruggiero said, unconvincingly, after an exhaustive effort and a conspicuously long pause. "The photo dealer, right? From a couple years ago?"

"Yeah," the man said on the other end of the phone. "The photo dealer, the kid from Ninth Circle." The word *kid* was obvious self-flattery, especially in the context of the Ninth Circle, a gay bar on West Tenth Street known for genuine kids: teens and younger, most of them there on "business." (In a gentler era, it had a more noteworthy reputation: In the basement bathroom, scrawled on a mirror in lipstick, Edward Albee found the words that he borrowed for the title of his play *Who's Afraid of Virginia Woolf*?) When he and Victor met there, although they were in their twenties, they represented the far side of the bar's age curve.

"Listen," the man said, "there's something I want to talk to you about." He was quite serious, and it was late at night. "You still have that photograph you told me about? The Abbott?"

The memory surfaced a little more clearly, and the purpose of the call was starting to make some kind of sense. But why call in the middle of the night? And where had he gotten this phone number, anyway? Victor had recently moved to an oceanside house in Belle Harbor, practically as far out in Queens as a person can get without entering the Long Island suburbs. "Well, actually, no. I don't. Why?"

"Because I think you stole it from Andrew Crispo," the voice said, "and I advise you to return it to him—get it back and return it to him—or I'm going to have to tell him that you've got it."

Victor thought the man sounded concerned, not angry. He might just explain the whole truth, that it was a come-on, a silly little game he had played. But that seemed too complicated. He chose to sidetrack the issue instead. "I didn't steal anything, really," he said.

Sensing that he hadn't made his point, Victor continued. "If you think I stole it, speak to Andrew and let him talk to me. I can straighten the whole thing out."

He never raised his voice—not his style—nor did he give any clue that the photograph was probably still in the gallery, in one of those many stuffed closets, or the vault, or behind hollow walls. When he hung up the phone, he felt he had narrowly escaped having to make an awkward confession about his cruising technique. Then certain questions occurred to him. Why did the phone conversation seem so—so *prompted*? As if somebody else was listening in, or whispering instructions? And why was this man involved, anyway? There might be a logical reason for the latter, which Victor tried to explain to a friend later. "Probably they met in the Hamptons. A lot of people look up to Andrew in the gay community— he's a colorful guy, he's wealthy, he's always with young boys. Maybe he thinks there'd be some kind of reward for returning the thing, if I actually had it."

The next day at work, a new tension existed between Ruggiero and Crispo, who seemed to be traversing the gallery on cat feet. Nothing changed as the week wore on, and the following Tuesday, exactly seven days after the first call, another came from the "kid from Ninth Circle." Again, it was late at night, and this time he demanded, "Did you give back the photograph yet?"

Ruggiero said, "Listen, I told you last time, I don't have anything that I'm not supposed to have."

"I spoke to Andrew," said the voice—pausing between phrases, speaking at what seemed like an unusual distance from the receiver—"and he said he can't find the picture anywhere. That means you've got it, and I'm going to have to let him know about this."

Again, Victor encouraged him to do so, and again he was haunted by the phone call. By now, he had come to the conclusion that Andrew was behind these intrusions. In the intervening week, Ruggiero had searched the gallery for the Berenice Abbott, and found it stuffed in a cabinet behind the stairs on the second floor. Crispo, he figured, must have known where it was located, too. Of course, he told himself, Andrew could misplace his head. Maybe he should confront Crispo with the print and bring this to a stop. No, couldn't do that; implicit would be Victor's unsubstantiated belief that Andrew was "lurking in these conversations," as he put it. He would just have to wait for the issue to explode, and then he'd set everybody straight.

That time never came. Instead, the morning following the second call, Ruggiero was called into Crispo's office and accused of swiping two books—bound volumes chronicling Baron Thyssen's collection of old master paintings—right out of the cardboard carrying case that now sat empty on Crispo's desk. "That's ridiculous, Andrew," he protested. "First of all, I'm not interested in old master paintings. And second, quite honestly, if I was going to steal something, I wouldn't have left the box." Crispo was red-faced, and told the other gallery workers he was sure Ruggiero was a thief.

"It seems crazy," Victor told a friend, "but this guy's got some huge bug up his ass about me, and there's no telling what's in his mind. He's fucking weird. Frankly, he's beginning to scare me." He explained that there were some people who believed Andrew had killed a man—Franco Rappetti—to advance his career. "Stories about him 'falling' out of a window, like it was the funniest thing," Victor said, "and it says *murdered* with a red crayon over his name in the Rolodex."

"You may be overreacting," said his friend.

"Kissinger says even paranoids have enemies."

"Then you should get out of there. There're plenty of places you could go."

Victor Ruggiero thought about it. He'd been idly planning to strike out on his own, but he didn't feel fully prepared. Besides, he felt that simply leaving would not bring anything to a conclusion. "You know, I think he's vicious. *Dangerous.* When the lawsuits starting pouring in, he used to come to work and say, 'Who can we fuck today, Victor?' You should have seen his face when he said that about the books—which even *he* must have found completely unbelievable. Something was really wrong there. It's like, I'm not worried that he's going to fire me. I'm worried he's going to *do* something."

He wasn't the only gallery employee who harbored such premonitions about the boss. One, who had worked there for years and considered Crispo a good friend, put it this way: "If you punch him in the stomach, he breaks your legs. A very resourceful man."

Perhaps Ruggiero saw in Crispo some deeply repressed part of himself that might enjoy some revenge over the uncanny physical resemblance, the little white lies. Besides these unintentional likenesses, Victor had modeled his business practices after Andrew's. *How would Andrew do it?* he often asked himself, about contacting clients, or throwing parties, or promoting an artwork. And in this case, he drew a dark, vague conclusion.

"I could get a little insurance," Ruggiero finally said, surprising his friend with the perfidy of the suggestion. "I could make copies of his books." *That's* how Andrew would do it.

Years before joining his staff, Victor had admired Andrew. Later, he hoped to rival him. "I'm a deal-maker," he once said, "I can sell anything." When he arrived in the office in 1978, it was to apprentice himself to the master. He didn't view himself as an infiltrator of the Crispo Gallery; he was an unabashed disciple of Andrew's deromanticized view of the field. If a fine point of the business confused him, he asked questions; when the answers didn't seem to be forthcoming, he dug further on his own.

For example, when the Andrew Wyeth ink study of a dead crow came into the gallery, he took particular interest, wanting to know about the larger work (*Winter Fields*), where that piece was exhibited (at the Whitney), how much the small drawing had cost Crispo (ten thousand dollars), who had sold it (Hirschl & Adler), and who had purchased it (the baron). The baron? Immediately, Ruggiero was struck with doubt. He knew that Thyssen had visited the gallery on a weekend, and the drawing arrived the following Monday. How could the baron have purchased this?

He did some research into the records and found the truth resting in a single file drawer mysteriously marked ST.

There was the bill of sale to Andrew from Hirschl & Adler, dated June 18. Stapled to that was another bill of sale dated June 12, showing that Andrew had paid $45,000 for a painting by Frederick Frieseke entitled *Hollyhocks*. There was a telex to the baron's bookkeeper requesting a wire transfer for the Frieseke. The stated selling price was $65,000. That meant Crispo made twenty thousand dollars on *Hollyhocks*.

But stapled to *that* was another telex, also to the bookkeeper, also requesting $65,000. Only on this invoice, the Frieseke's selling price was listed at fifty thousand dollars, and two other items—including the Wyeth study—were thrown in, making the bottom line jibe with the genuine invoice. Taxable profits were reduced from twenty thousand dollars on the single sale to less than ten thousand on all three. And the two items said to belong to the baron were now in Andrew's private hands, free and clear.

"So *that's* how it's done," Ruggiero had muttered to himself at the time, and continued leafing through the files. He found dozens of cases a month where Crispo had falsely listed items as sold to the baron. He even found why Crispo had gotten so steamed a year before when a Texas dealer purchased another Frieseke painting called *Lady on a Beach*. According to the phony records, it wasn't the gallery's to sell! A previous invoice had it going to the baron, "ST." Although it actually belonged to Crispo, he was forced to generate new paperwork to explain how he had sold the printing without cutting in the baron. And there it was, stapled to the back of those double and triple documents: a letter to the Lugano bookkeeper, apparently written only for the ST file. It purported to outline a trade the baron made with Crispo: Frieseke's *Lady on a Beach* for Preston Dickinson's *Still Life #1*. Undeniably complicated, and unbelievably undeniable.

With no clear idea of what he'd do with the "insurance," Victor Ruggiero spent the months of January and February 1982 photocopying the ST records (he took the letters to stand for "Shelter, Tax"—paralleling the "Berserk, Personal" formulation). Eventually, he had a stack of Xe-roxes three feet tall, which he kept in a crawl space behind the stairway in his Belle Harbor home.

On March 8, 1982 he was called into Crispo's office and was handed his own resignation letter, already typed. The charge: attempting, inde-pendently, to peddle a painting to a gallery client. He freely admitted the transgression. For some time, he had been floating trial balloons in anticipation of going independent. He was caught; he signed the letter and quite cheerfully said, "I guess it's time to split."

Crispo said, "I have a file on you," and held up a thin manila folder. His voice—challenging, boastful, clipped—revealed nothing about what the folder contained.

Now might have been the time to mention the alleged photograph heist, but Victor didn't say anything. Now might also have been an appropriate moment to discuss the tax files Victor had rifled, but again he chose not to. Instead, he offered an edgy smile and left the deep red office in silence. He was not angry.

And he was not vengeful. "This sounds silly," he told an acquaintance later about why the stack of Xeroxes remained in his crawl space, "but I'm just no hero. If the IRS wants that money, they're going to have to go for it without me."

He walked from the Red Room up the glass stairway to his desk one last time, and there he found his personal belongings already packed neatly into a box. Again, Ruggiero marveled: *So that's how it's done.*

For the first few months after leaving, as summer came to the city, Victor Ruggiero's paranoia seemed increasingly unfounded. Nothing hap-pened to him. There were no threats, or strange phone calls, or unex-pected happenings. Perhaps, he thought, he had misjudged his old boss. He felt badly about having drawn such a dark assessment.

Andrew Crispo, meanwhile, was acting just as hideously as Ruggiero had initially predicted. He chose as his victim a total stranger.

A man who signed his name as "Steve" wrote a letter to a reporter that began with the words, "I *vividly* remember my 'encounter' with Andrew Crispo." In the summer of 1982, Steve was working as a "model/escort" and advertising his services in *Screw* magazine.

> One muggy evening a man named "Andy" phoned to make an appointment. About twenty minutes later he arrived at my apartment in Chelsea. I offered him a drink and we chatted a while before getting down to business. He said that he lived in the Village and was an art dealer. I liked him—he was attractive,

conversant, warm, and charming. Eventually we undressed and went to bed.

By his own admission he was straight (a lie I hear frequently) and initially seemed somewhat passive. I performed oral sex on him and asked him if he would like to fuck me anally. He concurred and I spread out flat on my belly.

He was quite practiced and it was clear to me that he was an old hand at it.

As things progressed, his sexual movements became more aggressive and frenetic. I closed my eyes, enjoying myself.

Suddenly I became aware that one of the many oversized pillows on my bed was covering my head. At first I thought it had just fallen there by accident and I reached with my hand to brush it away. It was then that I felt his hand holding the pillow firmly on my head. I tried to push his hand and the pillow off, but he pushed down even harder, making it difficult to breathe.

Plainly, he was literally trying to suffocate me! I struggled and tried to slide off the bed. At that moment, he reached orgasm and collapsed on top of me. He eventually withdrew from me and I stood up. Verging on hysteria and rage, I told him to get dressed and get out. Looking rather sheepish he complied and left without saying another word.

CHAPTER

7

Perhaps things were tight throughout the art world by 1983. Perhaps money just wasn't flowing as it had been, or people were losing interest in the modernist movement that Andrew Crispo loved and Victor Ruggiero was trying to join. Ruggiero took a job selling real estate on the side to supplement the slim salary he was making peddling pictures in the months since leaving—or being asked to leave—Crispo's gallery. Co-ops and condominiums and canvases, the three Cs. Not a bad time to enter the home market, though. In Manhattan, it took no genius to sell an apartment; deeds were changing hands as quickly as a beanbag toss. Donald Trump turned his millions to billions in this market, Victor reasoned happily, then sold and sold and sold. Two-bedroom apartments, studios, de Koonings. Seven crazy days a week. He never knew what to expect, which hat to don, which commodity to push each time the phone rang.

Once, on an early winter morning, a voice on the other end asked, "Victor, do you know where I can get some cocaine?" It was a routine question, and it came from an acquaintance, Glen Cerrato, whom he'd met at Agawam Realty, the office that now employed him. He considered taking on the challenge before concluding, "Nope, you've got the wrong guy." He wasn't against coke. He'd tried it—repeatedly—and never learned to like it much. But that's not something you advertise when everybody who appears daily in gossip columns is shoveling it down by the ton, when the powder, more than a name or a string of accomplishments, could open the tall doors of success. No, Victor Ruggiero was not against coke. If that's what other people were into, he wasn't going to stand in the way, the law be damned.

Even Susan Slack, the tame receptionist at the Andrew Crispo Gallery, was involved with the stuff, and from time to time found her hands so full, she needed to unload it. Mostly, it was Crispo who bailed her out, casually, a few grams at a pop. People had noticed that he liked to spread around his business, never filling the base of that African fetish with single purchases, or with the wares of a single dealer. Seven grams was his usual purchase, an amount that, by most estimates, would barely last through the day.

Besides, Crispo enjoyed the negotiation, the pursuit, as much as the score; he liked his drug dealers to be dusty and *street*, he liked them young, handsome, and, whenever possible, gay. There was another important consideration: The more dealers there were, the more he could scatter around his IOUs, ensuring that his supply would never be challenged.

Two weeks after the out-of-the-blue call from Glen Cerrato, Victor answered the phone and it was Susan Slack. He and Susan had stayed in touch—twice in the previous year, they'd had dinner together; often, they'd gossiped on the telephone. Her standard greeting was, "You got out of here just in time."

Now, though, something else was on her mind. "Vic, I'm kind of stuck. I hope you can help."

"Sure," he said.

"See, this friend of mine's got four ounces of stuff she's trying to unload. You see . . ." She told an intricate tale that involved a friend's boyfriend, an overly optimistic coke order placed with some tough, a party that drew fewer guests than had been anticipated, and an outstanding drug bill that needed to get paid. "I said I'd try to help him, but I just don't know anybody who could buy in this quantity." Four ounces was a dealer-sized amount, not party coke. It filled a large Baggie.

"Why don't you ask Andrew? He can share it with his boys," Victor suggested with pronounced animosity.

"Oh, I tried, but he wasn't interested, he said. You know how he can be. Fact, I asked everybody at the gallery, and they looked at me like I was crazy."

"Listen," said Victor, reluctantly pulling out his deal-maker's voice, "I got a call a couple weeks back from a man I hardly know—he suddenly disappeared from this real estate office I work for, and then he calls asking for drugs. Told a story about how he's dealing in Suffolk County, but lost his supplier and his customers keep calling him up. His name's Glen Cerrato, and I've got, I think, I've got a number for him here. Somewhere—"

"Oh"—an exaggerated sigh of relief—"could you be a darling and call him for me? Please—just this once—and let him know what I've got? You know how I am on the telephone, Vic."

On the telephone, she was a shy woman. And easily excitable. It was an odd handicap for a receptionist. Victor acquiesced.

With Cerrato, he pushed the product. "I've got a friend," he said, "who may be willing to sell a couple of ounces, if you're still interested."

Cerrato said, "Okay, but I'd like a taste first. See if she'll give me a little taste, so I can find out just how pure it is."

Victor called Susan back. "It occurred to me that there's not even any money in this for me," he said. He was beginning to get that rush of emotion that selling provided. Even without the money. "He wants a taste."

"Fine! Great," said Susan. "When and where?"

"Susan, call him and find out!"

"Oh, oh, oh, oh, okay. Thanks, you've been a prince."

Minutes later, Susan was on the phone again. "It's set up. It's all set. But he says he's not coming into Manhattan, and I wondered . . ."

"You want my car."

"I wondered," she said, "if you'd mind too terribly driving it out to him. You live so close to Long Island, you know, and you have a car, and you *know* I'd make it up to you." Although not an attractive woman, Susan Slack had a way with gay men. Most of her friends were gay, except for that older boyfriend of hers whom Crispo ridiculed ceaselessly.

"I'll meet him halfway," Victor said, not altogether refusing, and on the evening of March 30, 1983, he pulled into a parking lot off the Long Island Expressway, just over the Suffolk County border, and climbed into the back of Glen Cerrato's Mercedes. He handed a small cellophane envelope over the seat. On the passenger's side, a man Cerrato introduced as one of his key buyers grabbed it, tasted it, and nodded to Glen. "We'll give you a call," he said to Victor, "and thanks."

The call from Cerrato's principal client came on Thursday, the morning following their meeting. He liked the goods, and wanted to conclude the deal. The conversation moved to price, and Victor gave him Susan Slack's phone number, though the gentleman seemed not to want to bother with an additional phone call.

"It's my understanding," Victor said, "that she's got four ounces, and she wants ninety-two hundred. But I've never seen it."

"Kind of steep."

"This is not my deal," Victor explained. "You've got to talk to her."

"Then," said the man, "there's nothing in this for you?"

"Frankly, I'd like a couple hundred for my time," he said. "Car time, you know."

"Go ahead," the voice said, "set it up."

Susan once again begged for a ride, and on a cool Saturday morning, after conceding the slim commission, she jumped in Victor's car and the two headed back out the Long Island Expressway through Queens, through Nassau County, and over the Suffolk border. They turned off on exit 52, making the first right and pulling into the Howard Johnson's parking lot in Commack.

Victor got out and took a stool at the restaurant counter. He ordered coffee. He could see Susan through a window. He watched as Glen Cerrato and his client pulled up. The two men got out of the Mercedes and climbed into his car. He watched as a team of police officers surrounded them. He watched as Susan Slack was taken from the car and handcuffed.

Behind him, two uniformed officers appeared, each with a gun drawn. He could see their reflections in the window.

"Don't try anything stupid," one said, "just *ease* your hands into the air."

A waitress holding a cup of steaming coffee backed away slowly.

One of the cops patted down his sides while he sat on the orange Naugahyde stool, staring out the window. He watched the so-called client give high-fives to the cops. He watched Glen Cerrato crank up the Mercedes and, with a wave, drive out of the Howard Johnson's parking lot and up the expressway ramp.

According to the arrest report, Glen Cerrato, who owned a window-washing service in the Southampton area, was known as Confidential Informant #1810–83 to Suffolk County narcotics cops. Weeks earlier, he had made the mistake of purchasing a small amount of cocaine from an acquaintance at his health club—a Ford Agency model who was himself a confidential informant. Cerrato was arrested on February 25, 1983. He resigned from the real estate office, where he was supplementing his income, the next day. The setup with Ruggiero and Slack was his first sting, a sign of good faith, which—he was told—might earn him five years' probation instead of certain jail time. He arranged several other deals over the following months, and in November he was rewarded. He pleaded guilty to criminal sale of a controlled substance, fifth degree, and was given a "narcotics conditions" probation.

Victor and Susan, independently (for they were instructed not to discuss anything relating to their arrests), agreed to a similar arrangement. Suffolk County, it seemed, was in a strange racket. With a small narcotics staff, the district attorneys regularly flipped petty dealers, creating an untrained army of very desperate narco-cops, sniffing out the white powder as far away as the city, Connecticut, Massachusetts—it didn't matter where they lived, so long as the final transaction was conducted within the county limits. The real cops, the ones with badges and guns, sat back in a small office in Yaphank, waiting for the calls to pour in.

At his first meeting with agents and the DA's people, Victor Ruggiero explained he had few contacts in the drug world but would be willing to develop them. He was a deal-maker by nature; he was confident he could perform for them. In May and June, he said, he twice arranged buys, and twice he was stood up by police—leaving him to make up some excuse for the sellers, trying to keep them on a hook. Through his attorney, he complained about a lack of undercover support, but things didn't seem to get much better. On July 11, he was indicted for criminal sale of a controlled substance, second degree, an A-1 felony, and at his arraignment, bail was set at $50,000—up from the paltry sum of $250 he had deposited on the day he was first nabbed.

Susan Slack was arraigned on the same day, and her bail—just ten thousand dollars—was posted by a bondsman that afternoon, collateralized with one of Andrew Crispo's paintings.

Also that afternoon, Victor's attorney informed him that his "cooperation was no longer wanted" by the DA. The only bargain available to him now, a pretrial plea of guilty, would win him a minimum of three years and a maximum of life. Or he could take it to trial. If he lost there, the minimum would be fifteen years. And a loss would be guaranteed—there were tape recordings of him negotiating prices on the phone with Glen Cerrato and the undercover cop, negotiations in which he had asked for the small kickback. When he asked why the original deal had fallen through, his attorney said, "The DA's going on vacation. Says he wants to clear his desk."

Victor Ruggiero pleaded guilty on August 11, 1983, with the explicit understanding that he'd get the minimum. The court, showing some lenience, gave him until September 26 to get his things in order before sentencing and induction.

In the interim, he received a call from Andrew Crispo. They had rarely spoken since Victor's unceremonious departure the year before. "You still in real estate?" Crispo asked hurriedly. "I got a deal for you; you're never gonna believe it."

Roy Cohn, he said, was putting his famed East Sixty-eighth Street town house up for sale. The one he lived in and the headquarters for Saxe, Bacon & Bolan, law firm to the mob. "There's a huge commission in this," he said, "absolutely gigantic. Be good for you, good for Agawam, good for Roy, good for me. 'Cause what's good for Roy is good for me. See? I told him about you, what a hustler you are, and he said to bring you over. Could be a big listing fee in this, Vic."

The consummate deal-maker couldn't say no. Not even to the former boss he'd once called "vicious" and "crazy." Especially not when he'd just paid ten thousand dollars to his lawyer, and forced his mother to put up her house against his fifty-thousand-dollar bail. He agreed to a sit-down meeting with Cohn and Crispo. Before entering the state penitentiary, he had time for one last deal.

They met in front of the building. Crispo was puffier than he had been a year earlier, and disheveled. His pants, unfastened and wrinkled, rolled over his belt. His nose was florid with veins and his eyes darted nervously over Victor's shoulders as he offered disjointed small talk about a mutual acquaintance. Cohn, apparently, hadn't yet risen from his bed.

"I told you I got Larry as a birthday present, right? Just gave him to me, like that," Crispo said wildly. He was plucking cigarettes and antacids out of his suit coat with great speed. "Anyway, once, we were in the elevator at the Fuller Building, and there was . . . Anyway, one construction guy who worked there, very straight-looking, and you should have seen him fuck Larry! He had a thing with this one construction guy. Wow. Not just simple intercourse, I'm telling you." One description of the act after another stretched on into the next hour.

Ruggiero studied his old boss with compassion and pity. Seeing Crispo like this cast a new light on Victor's arrest, he figured. It's terrifying to watch a human being, even one who was once hated and feared, sink so far into a drug-driven depravity. It made him feel guilty in some indirect way. It made him feel criminal.

Finally, the two were summoned upstairs to the living room. Cohn was wearing a white terry-cloth bathrobe; a very muscular blond man stood in a doorway, which seemed to lead to the bedroom, clad only in a very white pair of underpants. Crispo complimented him to Cohn, who smiled a smile that seemed to say, Oh, *this* old thing? Ruggiero looked but said very little. He was more confused than embarrassed. He was unaccustomed to doing business in such a casual atmosphere, with such casually attired clients.

Furthermore, this was his first visit to Roy Cohn's legendary sex corral and he was surprised about how old-lady the decor was—lots of rickety Victorian-type furniture, ruffles everywhere. A very large piano dominated the room, and "about seventeen hundred pictures" of Cohn with Francis Cardinal Spellman dominated the piano. Roy and the cardinal at a political function, Roy and the cardinal in Rome, Roy and the cardinal on a Circle Line tour.

What small amount Ruggiero knew about the lawyer came from Crispo. Roy had his entire house bugged, Crispo used to say. Or: Roy rubs out his enemies; Roy controls the mob; Roy can get any boy—straight or gay, rich or poor—he fancies. For a man of such clout, Victor thought, his town house was in quite a state of disrepair: marred walls, stains on the rugs. If there was going to be money in this sale, it would come only from someone willing to drop down cash for the right to say they owned Roy Cohn's bachelor pad.

Ruggiero was instructed to sit on a long, lumpy sofa, and Cohn and Crispo sat on chairs facing him.

Crispo started, clearing his throat aggressively. "This is not about . . . Well, this is about a different kind of real estate. This is what we want from you." His words raced out now, no longer light and staccato, as they had been during their hour downstairs.

Cohn spoke next, in gruff gangster intonations: "We know your circumstance in Suffolk. You're about to be sentenced to three years to life. This we know. A friend of mine sits on that bench."

"A friend of Roy's," Crispo stressed, wagging his head.

"It seems that you had some kind of deal worked out, and it mysteriously fell through, right?"

Victor was astonished, mute.

"Apparently," Cohn said, "that attorney of yours is not very well connected in certain circles."

Then Crispo, emboldened, screamed, "Listen, you! I want those papers you've got. *That you stole from me.*"

Cohn put a spotty hand on Crispo's arm, calming him. "Andrew tells me you've got something of his, and we'd like to ask for it back. We—Andrew, myself, and my friends—would all be very grateful. We're not interested in cocaine or anything like that," he said, "we're simply interested in knowing what you know about Andrew's business affairs."

Victor stood up tentatively, glancing around the room for the rumored microphones. In the plant? Under the cushion? He moved toward the door, backing up slowly with a hand stretched behind him. He thought, so that's it! It was these guys! His mouth was opened and he heard himself say, "Go fuck yourselves," as he bumped into a wall.

Crispo, too, was on his feet, and he was crimson. "Don't walk away from me, Victor," he was shouting. "Victor!" Cohn, still seated, had both hands on Crispo now. "Victor, don't fuck with me, Victor! You know what I'm capable of!"

"Hey, Andrew! It's Bernard LeGeros," he shouted into the pay phone. "I'm just in the neighborhood with my friend Lisa, and maybe we could stop up." It was a Sunday afternoon in July 1983.

Keeping in touch with Crispo became an exciting part of Bernard's routine, performed with a regularity that fell somewhere between changing the oil in the Command Vehicle and brushing his teeth. About every other month, they would have dinner together—Crispo paying—and on either end of the meal, without fail, there was limitless cocaine, passed around like mints. Later, they would go to Limelight, where Crispo and his guest were whisked into the VIP room, or back to Crispo's apartment. There, more cocaine and soft storytelling would consume the night.

Sometimes, another guest would attend, usually older, usually holding out the vague possibility that there might be a job for Bernard. Because Bernard was only vaguely petitioning for one, a vague possibility suited him fine. This search for employment had become little more than a pretext for Crispo and Bernard to get together. And each time it was brought up, Bernard seemed to be entertaining a different career. He'd been awarded his associate's degree in political science from NYU in early 1983, and was heading back for a B.A. in the fall. Maybe he'd study cinema. Or modeling or fine arts.

Sometimes, Bernard brought along his own friends to introduce them to the powerful benefactor. Lisa, a plain-looking woman in her mid-twenties, had heard a great deal about "my friend Andrew Crispo." She was eager to meet him. She had also heard a great deal about Elana Martos, Bernard's full-time girlfriend, whom she was convinced she'd never meet. As the "other woman," she had been introduced to few of Bernard's friends.

Hanging up the phone, Bernard said it would be okay for the two to pay a visit. "But he says two things. First, we have to go to his dealer's apartment and pick up some cocaine. Second, he says there's somebody there he wants us to arrest."

"Arrest?"

"That's what I said. But he said it would be a game."

"Well," she said, pushing her glasses up her nose. "I don't know."

"C'mon. It'll be a kick," he said, and together they walked a small circle: up to West Fifteenth for the drugs and back toward Crispo's West Twelfth Street penthouse. Along the way, they ducked into a sex-supply shop and purchased a pair of handcuffs.

Besides Crispo, there were two other men sitting in the open living room area, laughing over a tray of powder. Bernard leaned his head over the coffee table several times before asking their names. Hal Burroughs and Hank were introduced as old friends from the art world, themselves chums from high school days. Crispo introduced Bernard as "one of my oldest, most trustworthy friends." The adulation, coming from someone whose friendship Bernard so hoped for, caused bubbles to percolate on his gums. Smiling, he put an index finger to his left nostril and cleared his sinus.

"This guy's coming up," Crispo said shortly. "I want you to bust him. Pretend you're a cop and bust him for drugs."

"Well, you know, okay. But tell me why." Bernard was nervous, and Lisa bristled on the sofa. She felt a strange distance from the other people in this room, felt that being *female* here was wrong, felt that she could never explain this sensation. She laughed loudly.

"It's my friend Gordon," Andrew said. "He likes this kind of stuff. He just went down to the video-rental store. It's like a big surprise."

Crispo ushered Bernard and his date over the terrace that connected his large studio to the duplex penthouse owned by Arthur Smith. Hal and Hank stayed behind.

"Here," he said, pointing to a police uniform on Smith's sofa, "wear this," and then to Lisa, he said, "You can play a lady cop. Gordon will never suspect that." She laughed again. "I'll be right up these stairs, watching," he said, ascending with a finger beside a nostril, snorting puffily, Santa Claus–like.

On the sofa was a full-dress police uniform, complete in detail right down to the patches on the sleeves and, on the front pocket, a police badge. It said: "City of New York Police Detective Endowment Association." Without hesitation, Bernard stripped to his underwear and pulled on the outfit. He snapped the handcuffs on the belt. "What do you think?"

Lisa smiled approvingly. Bernard had often spoken to her about his many sexual fetishes—leather, uniforms, games. These fantasies they shared. Of all Bernard's girlfriends, Lisa was the furthest advanced sexually; the irony was that she was also the one of whom his parents most approved. "Pretty sexy, frankly," she said.

The knock came just then, and Lisa moved to the far side of the room, striking a strong silhouette against the picture window. She tucked her fists into her armpits. Bernard opened the door and demanded, "Who are you?" He flashed the badge.

Gordon stammered, "I'm a friend of Andrew's," and held up the video as proof. He was slight and young, and had insecure eyes. Bernard threw him against the wall and, twisting the man's arms behind his back, slapped on the cuffs. "You're coming with me," he barked, and dragged him into Arthur's bedroom, threw him on the bed, and pillaged his pockets. "Hey," he said, menacing. "Look at this! Look what I found! Could this be coke?" He tossed a small envelope of coke on the floor and pushed Gordon's head into a pillow. Lisa, standing at the door, giggled.

Then Crispo entered the room and replaced Bernard's hand with his own on the back of the visitor's neck, while motioning to Bernard to keep up the dialogue. Gordon was shivering, whimpering, but said nothing. "You're gonna do a long time in the slammer for this shit," Bernard continued, backing away. "And that ain't gonna be a pretty sight. And don't even *think* about looking up or I'll blow your fucking brains out, faggot." Bernard looked over at Lisa, who was virtually doubled over in laughter now.

"The interrogation begins," he barked. "What's your name, faggot!"

The man answered immediately.

"Are you now, or have you ever been, a homo? Faggot!" More snickering.

"Um," the man said into the pillow. "Yes."

"What! You admit this transgression?" Bernard said this while looking back at Lisa again. But her expression had changed; she pointed, in astonishment, toward the bed. Bernard looked around and saw Andrew yanking down Gordon's pants; his own already hung loosely around his white knees. "Oh, shit," Bernard said. "I'm getting out of here!"

Bernard had never watched homosexuals "in the act," as he put it; he'd certainly never witnessed his new friend so compromised before. Once, several months earlier, he and Elana had fucked on the outdoor terrace under Andrew's picture window, and Andrew had stood over them silently. That was one thing. Being watched "in the act" was not in itself sexual, did not constitute a threesome, did not mean that he had shared an intimacy with Crispo. Bernard was, unquestionably, engaged intimately with Elana, just as Andrew had been—as the voyeur—engaged with Bernard. It was a single-pathed, linear event, and Bernard took no responsibility for any pleasure Andrew may have stolen from the scene.

Standing at a distance from Andrew and Gordon, that would be different. That would place Bernard at the end of the chain, signifying a direct sexual liaison. He would not play witness. He was not gay. Lisa and Bernard scurried across the outdoor terrace to Andrew's apartment to finish off a few lines of coke. Lisa, dumbfounded at what she'd seen, kept rolling her head. "I just can't believe he did that," she said. Over and over. Into the night.

Mostly because Elana thought it would be a good idea, Bernard had had pictures taken for a modeling portfolio and had passed a few off to Andrew. In the pose both men liked the best, Bernard was reclined against a white background, wearing black leather pants and a V-necked sweater. Although he was quite handsome, in an exotic way, he didn't possess a model's countenance or physique. His nose was just the tiniest bit too small and, together with the rest of his facial features, took up only a small quadrant of his face, which had grown heart-shaped over the years. Despite his work on the free weights, which had bulked up his body substantially, he still looked wispy when fully clothed, in part due to his five-foot-eight stature. Perhaps in compensation, he'd developed an exaggerated Brooklyn accent that lent a steeliness to his appearance, but the camera did not capture that.

Instead, he seemed like a soulful, skinny, beautiful young man, his shiny black hair swept back with gel. In one shot, posed in a white polo shirt, white sneakers, and white tennis shorts that gripped his thighs, he seemed uncomfortable and unflattered. In another, squatting in a European pose on a sidewalk, his shoulders rose up toward his ears as though he was ducking bullets. A lighted cigarette dangled nervously from his hand, which was between his legs.

Crispo praised the pictures nonetheless; he even requested several prints for himself. And, in the late summer, he introduced Bernard to Sam Collins, a formerly handsome ex-boyfriend of his, with the hope he'd be able to find Bernard a modeling gig at Coast Productions, the video company where he worked. Bernard carried his modeling portfolio over to Sam's house, at Andrew's suggestion.

During the course of this job interview, in Bernard's recollection, he'd grown light-headed and had fallen asleep. He had lost time, had lost consciousness, had lost a handle on what had transpired there. He remembered having nursed a frozen drink. He remembered being offered no job. He remembered rising on rubber legs, apologizing, and exiting. He remembered Maria Callas singing in the background.

Sam Collins, at least according to what Bernard was led to believe, remembered more. Bernard told a friend this way:

"Month later, right? Andrew comes to me and tells me that Sam slipped me a Mickey Finn in that drink—and that he fucked me, this and that! And that there were pictures. Whipped me and stuff. I mean, I wanted to go after the faggot! I wanted to get him, you know? Of course.

"But Andrew says, nah. He'll take care of the guy, he'll do him in. 'I'll take care of Sam,' he says, 'I'll get you the pictures.'

"I said, 'I'll meet you at his apartment,' and he goes, 'No, no. I'll take care of it.' Long run, Andrew comes back to me and says, 'I took care of it. He's in a mental home in the Midwest.' "

Bernard never again saw the "offending party," as he was then known. But from time to time—over at Crispo's, or during a quiet dinner out— Crispo introduced him to men who he later said were friends of Sam Collins. "How I'd like to get my hands around his neck," Bernard would say, "and let him know what I think about Collins."

Crispo, angry and earnest, would say, "I can arrange that for you."

When Bernard called Crispo from the street a few weeks later, he was invited up to the apartment to "interrogate a victim." Initially, he objected, saying he was too busy, or not interested. His first glimpse into Crispo's sex life, that evening with Lisa, was not altogether pleasant. He had explained to Crispo afterward that it was not appropriate for him to be in a room where Crispo was fucking.

Then Crispo announced that the "victim" was a friend of Sam's. "And you remember Sam Collins, don't you?"

"That fucking faggot scum."

"Oh, come on, Bernard. You could teach him a lesson. Come on!"

"Okay," he said, and took great joy in kicking a man whom he found in the large shower, naked except for a leather hood encasing his entire head. He pressed his knee into the man's side, made dents with his boots on his thighs. He rolled his wet body over and said, "Tell *that* to Sam Collins," and he left the apartment with an unspent rage.

"None of my other friends would have done that for me," Bernard said later. "That's the way Andrew was, the way he looked after me."

Sam Collins was never committed to a mental hospital; he disappeared, instead, to a coke rehab clinic in New Jersey, of his own accord. There, he was known as a recidivist patient. In each of his two previous visits, he stayed for nearly a month before returning to life in the city's fast lanes. And Collins's life included Andrew Crispo, as a center focus.

He had first met Crispo in the Hamptons, in the seventies, while still an extremely handsome man in his twenties. For a time, they were lovers, but that arrangement didn't work out well. "He's got what they call *performance* problems," Collins told a friend candidly. They remained friends, and their sex lives were sporadically entangled over the ensuing six years. Frequently, through 1983 and 1984, they "did the loop" together, beginning at the home of their mutual cocaine dealer, then heading to the Boy Bar, or some other popular hangout for handsome gay youth, like Uncle Charlie's or Rounds. "We'd start picking up boys," he said, "some who we knew and some we just met. Coke whores, mostly, like twenty-five or twenty-six or twenty-seven. And when we had enough, we'd take them back to Andrew's apartment. As long as Arthur wasn't around—Arthur didn't approve of our little exploits. He knew, always, though—after the fact. I think he was doing his best keeping Andrew under control—he was working hard at this. But he would come back afterward, and whether it was a sixth sense or what, I don't know, but he'd figure out what had happened."

It couldn't have been too difficult, as these orgies frequently took place inside Arthur Smith's half of the penthouse. "He had an amazing bathroom in that apartment with a shower that would accommodate twelve people easily, and most of the times the party would wind up there," Collins said later.

Occasionally, Collins and Crispo found fun in shared business endeavors as well, such as the benefit they cosponsored in late 1983 for a small AIDS foundation headed by Dr. Mathilde Krim. Crispo had convinced Lowell Nesbitt to play host in his downtown studio, and to donate one of his four-foot-by-four-foot flower paintings to the cause. Collins took care of selling tickets, and used his high profile to get one thousand dollars each. The event, even before the night of the raffle, was a success. The drawing took place at a bright little party, with few art-world notables in attendance.

Collins was there with an extremely handsome young date. Blond and very Nordic looking, the man (whose name nobody could remember) was said to be a fashion student at FIT. He was an impeccable dresser, and possessed a seductive, fresh smile—paper-white teeth, spaced slightly distant from one another, all seemed to be about the same size. His smile alone caused many of the guests to remember him, despite the fact that he spoke to almost nobody. It was assumed he didn't have a very strong command of the English language.

Crispo showed up late, and announced, quite frenetically, that he had been trying to get Nancy Reagan on the phone for an endorsement. He was speaking very quickly, on an obvious coke jag, and was universally ignored. Collins, meanwhile, had been selected as the person who would reach into a barrel of small green cards—stubs from the raffle purchases—to choose the winner of the painting, which was worth an estimated twenty thousand dollars. He dipped in and produced the name of a man from Los Angeles, reportedly a friend of Tony Richmond, who was the husband of former Charlie's Angel Jaclyn Smith.

Crispo immediately and insistently announced that the gentleman was unavailable to claim his prize, and volunteered to take it for him. Officials from the AIDS group rejected the offer with suspicion.

Quickly, the operation began to unravel. Efforts to reach the winner by telephone were fruitless. Each time, a woman claiming to be his secretary said he wasn't interested in the Nesbitt painting, and would like to donate it back to the foundation. This, however, would have been impossible without talking to the winner. There was the matter of the taxes that had to be considered, the officials said.

Then, according to people familiar with the gathering, another strange twist was discovered. The winner's ticket had been purchased the night of the party, with a check drawn on the account of the Andrew Crispo Gallery.

Meanwhile, Andrew Crispo made frequent calls to the foundation in an effort to claim the painting. Long after the AIDS group changed its name to the American Foundation for AIDS Research, and took on Liz Taylor as its honorary chair, the controversy remained unresolved. And the painting—of large red and pink hibiscus petals with white dots—remained behind a desk in AmFAR's small New York offices. "Frankly," confessed Sam Collins long after the fact, "I just don't recall what happened there."

And just as Sam Collins wasn't in a mental hospital, he was not exiled from New York, either. He stayed in the New Jersey clinic for twenty-eight days, leaving early in the back of a limousine sent to him by his Manhattan coke dealer. "There was a package for me," he said, "and when I opened it up, it was a gram of coke! How sweet!" Thus relapsed, he returned to the city for a wild party—which included Andrew Crispo—that went on for several days. Although he never saw Bernard again, he remained in frequent contact with Crispo.

In fact, Sam Collins was one of a shrinking handful of people with the patience (and the coke capacity) to be counted as one of the art dealer's close friends. The others, besides the cadre of teenagers who supplied him with drugs and bravado, were Hal Burroughs, Crispo's regular Hellfire companion, and Bernard LeGeros. What each of these four men had in common was an ability, a need, to stay awake for two, three, sometimes four days on end snorting up thousands of dollars of crystal powder until, eventually, they crashed.

Victor Ruggiero went directly from Roy Cohn's town house back to his Belle Harbor home. He was shaken, confused, and, mostly, disbelieving.

He couldn't imagine how Crispo had figured out he had stockpiled copies of the ST files. The way Cohn talked to him was completely beyond belief. That he could pretend to suggest a connection between Victor's bad fortunes with the Suffolk County justice system and Crispo's own interventions was so farfetched as to appear comical.

When he arrived home, his mother was waiting for him. She said she had received two calls at her nearby house. "One was from Roy Cohn," she said. "Is this *the* Roy Cohn?" An Irish immigrant, she spoke with a soft, melodic brogue. "And the other was from that Andrew Crispo. He's crazy," she said. "He said you have something that belongs to him."

As they spoke, Ruggiero got a phone call from his Southampton lawyer. "I got a message that Roy Cohn's office called, reference to your case," the lawyer said. "Who's Roy Cohn?"

Suddenly, Victor Ruggiero knew that what Roy Cohn had said to him was dead-on. His lawyer was no good.

The following days were spent in a scrambled attempt to find someone who could pull him out of this mess, and on Friday, September 23, 1983, Victor met with a former U.S. Attorney, hot out of Rudolph Giuliani's office, who advised him there might be some interest in trading the tax papers for a light jail term. His fee would be fifty thousand dollars, cash, up-front, nonnegotiable. And unattainable. On Saturday, Victor placed sample pages of his Xeroxes in a Federal Express envelope, addressed to the IRS.

On Monday, September 26, he was sentenced as scheduled—three years to life—and was immediately remanded to the windowless Suffolk County jail.

A month later, Susan Slack was sentenced for her role in the crime that foiled Victor Ruggiero. She got probation, "narcotics conditions," and was released on her own recognizance. She returned to her job as the gallery receptionist with the instruction to keep in touch with the narcotics division. Her probation would last the rest of her life—as long as she played the game. She turned to her boss.

James Bradford ("Brad") Learmonth, a slight, soft-spoken, undistinguished actor/waiter with a history of nervous breakdowns, moved to New York City from Boston and experienced a sizable culture shock, owing mostly to what he called "that whole real slick New York scene." A year later—three days after his thirtieth birthday in September 1983—Brad met Susan Slack. In an interview, Brad said:

> I think Andrew Crispo's regular dealer went away or something, and he knew these two guys who used to get him coke. He told

them that if Susan Slack needed anything, they should help her out. She called them, and they called me. I didn't know them very long. I was only in town for a year—a very rough year and I got into coke for a couple of months and I got on the edge. A little strung out. And at the time, I wasn't thinking very clearly. I had quit my waiter job to get into acting, but that was going nowhere. *I* was going nowhere. Not that I was dealing, I certainly wasn't dealing. Never dealt. But I always knew where to get the stuff. When I needed it. And I was really, really, really short on cash at this particular point in time.

So this friend calls and wants to know if I've got anything, which I don't, and wants to know if I can *get* anything. Naïvely, I said I had some access. I had been buying through a friend who was from Colombia, who had some family, or something, some connection that sent stuff to her. This was supposed to be for a friend of Andrew Crispo's, he said, whom I had only met once, at Uncle Charlie's down in the Village. And a friend of mine who saw me talking to him there took me aside and said, "Stay away from him. He's trouble." But I knew at least one other person who was like a major dealer for Andrew and hung out with him. And when the call came saying he had said this about this Susan—and this coming from some regular suppliers—it seemed aboveboard.

Then Susan calls, and she wants a large quantity, she says, more than a few ounces. I came up with a pound from my Colombian friend, who spoke terrible English, and the price was given at forty thousand dollars for a pound. Then I get a call from Paul, who's supposedly Susan's friend and going in on it with her, and who turns out to be the detective. He's supposed to be a businessman. And he says that was terribly high. I said—I ad-libbed—I said that it's real good stuff. He said he'd check. So I went back to my Colombian friend, and it finally came out that she thought a pound and a kilo were the same thing. What I thought was a pound was actually a kilo, so I wound up with a kilo because of broken English. This Paul then says that was a very small price. He played it up, played it pretty well.

Then he set up a rendezvous. Susan engineered the whole thing on the phone with me, over and over. She's coming to pick me up in a cab, and for some reason we're going "just outside the city limits" to meet this guy, this businessman. I remember it was a Friday. It was pouring, pouring rain. It took

us two and a half hours to get out there. I had no idea where I
was. I'd never been to Long Island, and because of the traffic,
I had no idea how much distance we traveled because it was
just bumper-to-bumper.

We just ended up at this hotel all of a sudden. The Smithtown
Sheraton. It was happy hour, I remember, and I was terrified.
I'm carrying more cocaine than I'd ever seen before in my life,
size of a football, which I've got in a bicycle bag, from between
the handlebars on my bike. And, of course, I've never met this
Susan face-to-face before, that's how stupid I was. I asked her
something like, "Who's paying for this cab?"

Anyway, we pull into the happy hour, and this businessman
has a Tiparillo hanging out of his mouth. I handed him my
bicycle bag, and he took it into the rest room, and he came back
to the table. When he slid the money across the table, and
when he got the acknowledgment from me it was all there, he
lit his Tiparillo and, in his best Clint Eastwood bravado, he
says, "One thing I hate is a cocaine dealer." Fifty cops came
running, and I remember him saying, "Watch it, he's got a
weapon." I had a Swiss army knife in my bag.

Susan was just sitting there, terrified. She was extremely
nervous when she came to pick me up, but I figured that's the
way she was. Somebody said to her, "Nice job, Susan," and
then, so I could hear it, "I don't think she's got anything on
her, just hold her here." But they had guns on me and handcuffs
and everything, and she was just sitting there.

I guess she had told him that I was gay, because somebody
handcuffed me in the lounge and dragged me out the door,
where there were these two six-foot-five, ugly, dry-look guys
with gold chains. One of 'em said, "Here she comes!" I thought
I was dead. I was sure of it. My senses shut off. I was convinced
I was going to be killed very shortly.

Anyway, I got out on a small bail, finally, and I was sitting in
a bar with a couple friends of mine. And I got paged by this
friend who was also a friend of Andrew's. I don't know how he
found me. And he says Andrew wants to talk to me. It was
urgent that he speak to me. Definitely urgent. And I kept
saying, "No, no, no, no." And he kind of insisted. My friend,
he—I'm not sure why—thought it would be beneficial for me
to get some more information.

So I went to his apartment in the Village. He was sitting

there trying to convince me that Susan had nothing to do with my arrest, and that *he* had *nothing* to do with it.

And I was just, like, kind of dumbfounded. I was like, "Andrew, I don't know what you had to do with it, if anything, and I really don't care. I mean, she's your *friend*. If you tried to help her, that's fine with me. There's nothing I can say about that, except I think it's disgusting. But don't tell me she had nothing to do with it. She was sitting right there." So we went through this for about an hour, and he was really pushing it.

I think he was probably afraid that I was going to start talking about him. I imagined he was probably a little nervous about getting connected with cocaine, or any kind of weirdness. He managed to cover his ass on that pretty well. But that's the only thing I could figure out.

Right after that, I remember, I got a phone call from my lawyer, who claimed that someone had called the DA and told him that I had threatened Susan's life, which is absolutely ridiculous. I never saw her again, so I put these two things together.

I stayed out on bail for five months, into 1984, stringing them along about the busts I was going to make. They wouldn't accept . . . I couldn't turn in somebody with a half a gram of coke and expect to get off. It had to be something big. It had to be an A-1 felony, which is anything over four ounces, I believe, which is what I was convicted of. Finally they just got tired of me and threw me in the county jail while I was waiting for my sentencing.

First thing, I meet this guy Victor Ruggiero, which I thought was another very strange coincidence. "Fucking Susan," "that cunt Susan"—he was saying stuff like that. And he indicated to me that Andrew was wanted by the feds, and mixed up in all kinds of tax things, so I thought this guy may have been a . . . like a *plant* to try to get some information from me. It was just too coincidental that we ended up on the same floor, next to each other. I thought that if Andrew could somehow do this to me outside, I wondered what he could do inside this place. My God, I thought, there's no telling what I could have gotten myself into.

Brad Learmonth served out a five-year sentence in Fishkill, New York, where he worked in the legal library and earned a college degree. "It was a productive time for me," he said later, "it turned me around."

Whatever his reasons, Brad Learmonth *had* agreed—perhaps only once—to involve himself in a narcotics transaction. In that sense, he considered himself a guilty party who deserved punishment.

Nonetheless, he remained convinced he had been drawn into a trap set by Andrew Crispo, that Crispo had fed him to Susan Slack to be passed up the food chain.

Whether Crispo provided others to help Susan's handshake with the law was not known, but there was *one* indication. A month or more after making her deal with the authorities, a noticeable demographic change occurred among the individuals brought before the county's lead trial judge. He put it this way: "I am sending away the elite of our society; I am not sending away the people who have no connections, people who can hardly read and write, and people who are substandard in intelligence. I am sending away smart people, educated people, people with the whole world ahead of them."

Victor Ruggiero was equally convinced of the conspiracy, though far less forgiving, especially after his freak run-in with Brad Learmonth at the county jail in early 1984. Instead of settling in for his own sentence, he hired an appeals attorney, who in turn hired a private investigator to ferret out Andrew Crispo's role in Victor's arrest. With a two-thousand-dollar retainer, and on the eve of filing his report, the detective, Herman Race, died "a legitimate death," according to Louis Rosenthal, the attorney. "It was a brain tumor." So the appeal, which sought to roll back his sentence, was forced to rely instead on Ruggiero's own interpretation of events. And his story seemed absurdly paranoid.

In an affidavit, he complained of a lack of cooperation in his efforts to gain probation, and cited his Cohn meeting as a probable cause. He pointed to the fact that Susan Slack served no jail time, while he—"as neither owner/seller nor purchaser"—was locked away for three years to life. He wrote about meeting Brad Learmonth in the county jail, saying he "related to me how Slack with the aid of Crispo arranged to have him arrested. . . . The potential for a conspiracy is compounded by the fact that Crispo has a house in Southampton, Glen Cerrato lives in East Hampton, and Crispo and Cohn have a real interest to place me out of communication and out of reach."

The court, of course, found Ruggiero's assertions farfetched, and peppered its appeals rejection with uncharitably tart phrases such as "striking," and "incredible," and "not worthy of belief."

CHAPTER
8

On New Year's Eve, 1984, though he was invited to a handful of parties, Andrew Crispo stayed at home with a few close friends, and then headed out to the S&M clubs. It showed his new priorities: He would rather stay up through the night with half-dressed, whip-burned strangers than commune with the art-world acquaintances who had crowded into his life.

Art itself seemed of little importance to him now, and he was paying scant attention to operating the gallery he had labored so hard to build. The lawsuits which had entertained him in the past were now left to languish, with only an occasional challenge, in civil courts around the city. Only the escalating IRS battle remained of any measurable concern—perhaps because of the stakes, perhaps just because the scuffle animated him.

The drugs and the S&M clubs gave him a stronger charge, and so did a string of little diversification schemes that kept him busy, and kept his mind as alert as possible. He invested more than a hundred thousand dollars—and lost it—with Sandi Franklin, the mother of a graffiti-writing tough with whom he was hanging out. She had developed a board game she was sure would rival Trivial Pursuit. With several friends, he'd gotten involved in a scam that produced plaster castings of famous sculptures, which purchasers were donating to museums as originals—taking huge tax deductions worth fifteen and twenty times their initial investment. Also, some spare cash went into a horse farm in Southampton, bought in partnership with old friend Carl Lobell and several other attorneys, including Arthur Jacobs and the notorious Peter Schmidt, whom a federal judge once dubbed New York's "fraudsman extraordinaire" and the *Times* called "intrinsically venal." Several years later, Schmidt simply vanished—perhaps to a new life in Haiti or a quick death in Brazil, according to rumors—leaving behind dozens of clients who claimed he'd robbed them blind. Constantin Dumba, an Austrian count, was out a cool million; the heirs of Michael Burke, chairman of Madison Square Garden, lost twice that.

Crispo even assumed a five-figure debt that a famous rock star owed to their mutual coke dealer. He charged her substantial interest, Bernard LeGeros said later, and sought unsuccessfully to take over her home as collateral.

But the project that had completely consumed Crispo was an under-the-table movie deal he was trying to strike with René Arlington, a slight and handsome blond man who had become a close confidant, drug buddy, and sexual interest of note. A year before, Warner Books had published a book for which René and his adoptive father, Paul Murphy, shared the byline. Called *La Popessa*, it was a true story of the pro-Nazi nun who was said to have controlled the papacy of Pope Pius XII. The nun, Sister Pascalina, was cast as the Pope's life partner, his Haldeman in Third Reich malfeasance.

While there had been a great deal of buildup for the book, there was also trouble brewing at home. Julie Murphy, who was Paul's ex-wife and ongoing friend and research assistant, felt she had done more work than René, and resented her stepson's byline. Recognition of her contribution was limited to a one-sentence nod on the acknowledgments page. There were squabbles over the advance, and marked differences over how the royalties, and potential movie rights, would be split.

In the long run, the book was something of a flop. " 'Sixty Minutes' wanted to do a segment; the *Times* was calling all the time. There was great interest in movie rights," said one of the editors who worked on the manuscript, adding that Crispo was not among the formal bidders. "There was a feeling that this thing was going to hit hard, that there was going to be a lot of explaining to do at the very highest levels of the Church." Anticipation mounted until the final days before publication, and then dried up. Murphy, a high-strung former Catholic, blamed influence from the Holy See. His agents at William Morris, somewhat more skeptical, drew no conclusion whatsoever; Warner was merely disappointed, and was taking a pass on Murphy's next book, a full-fledged conspiracy theory connecting the death of John Paul I to the collapse of the Franklin Bank in New York. "Paul was very concerned," said Owen Laster, his literary agent. "He was afraid of something."

Warner editor Ross Claiborne said, "He feared dying, and told everybody about it. And then, suddenly, he did indeed die." Of a heart attack, perhaps brought on by the lurking shadows he had begun envisioning everywhere; perhaps a result of the family bickering.

Or perhaps, as Crispo suggested to one person (using the passive voice), Paul Murphy "was slipped an overdose" of the medication he'd been prescribed for his nerves. Another remembered him saying, "It was done to look like a hematoma." According to another, "Andrew said he got a nurse to inject air or something into him, to speed up his fricking heart rate, and that it was untraceable."

Whatever the truth, Murphy was certainly dead, and his passing touched off a race to grab up any of his belongings before the ex-wife claimed rights—to his future stake in *La Popessa*, and to the new manuscript he'd developed. Many gallery employees were unwitting and unknowing accomplices.

Crispo used Ronnie Caran's financial imbalance (which he'd created) to rope him in. "René's stepmother's apartment's for sale," Crispo told him one afternoon. "A really good buy—and I know you're having trouble with your landlord. You really should own something. I could help you out. This is a place you should consider."

"Go look at it. René's there now."

Caran, who had considered René "a sweet kid," had heard the scuttlebutt about how his father, in the months before his death, had turned against him. But he paid it little attention. Uptown, he and René poked through his stepmother's apartment, and Caran loved it. A large studio on a high floor on Central Park South, it was bright, quiet, and beautifully decorated. Julie Murphy's things were still there, some of them packed in boxes near the door.

"She's in Europe now," René Arlington explained, "and she's moving to Boston when she comes back. I had been staying here with her recently, and I'm going to have to find another place, too."

The phone rang, and it was Crispo looking for Caran. "Could you do me a really big favor? René's moving out of there, and, uh, he's got no place to put his things yet, and uh, I was thinking of letting him store some stuff here. He doesn't have any money or anything. The favor is, could you help him bring some things back to the gallery?"

"Sure," said Caran, happy to be doing Crispo that favor. It might mean a real payoff when he returned.

So he hoisted a large open box—papers, files, notebooks—and cabbed back. Bernard LeGeros, who had begun hanging around the gallery lately, met him at the gallery elevator. "Oh, great. Listen, René needs help, you know. He doesn't have any money."

"I know, that's why I carried this!" Bernard took the box from him.

"Could you go back one more time for another armload? Just one more trip?"

"Why isn't he doing any of this? He was just standing there when I left. I don't see him taking cabs back and forth."

"Just this one more time, please? Even better, just take the stuff back to your house, and he'll pick it up there from you over the weekend."

Ronnie made one last trip, this time burying himself under two boxes and a canvas bag. On the ride to his apartment, the bag made marimba noises from what might have been half-full pill containers, many of them, scudding around in the bottom of the satchel.

Bernard, not René, showed up for the bundles, sharply commanding that Caran turn them over immediately. "You didn't look in 'em, did you?" Confused and angry, Caran pointed the young man to the door.

Within days, a frantic Julie Murphy began calling everybody she knew with reports that René Arlington had looted her apartment. To a Warner executive, she appeared "extremely upset, not only over Paul's death, but that René was really causing a lot of serious trouble. He'd broken in, she said, and stolen some papers. She was worried that any subsequent earnings from movie rights would be—in essence—stolen by him."

Owen Laster, the agent, got a similar call. "She told me she thought he might have stolen the papers," he said, "but I explained there was no ongoing interest in any movie deal. To my knowledge." René Arlington called Laster next, and explained he was in desperate need of cash. He requested that he be notified the minute a royalty check arrived, and that he'd be over that afternoon. He didn't mention his father's death at all.

While Crispo chased new challenges, old friends were chasing him, chief among them Marty Ackerman. Since their first factoring deal together, Ackerman had loaned Crispo a total of $423,000. In exchange, he and his wife "owned" seventeen of Crispo's paintings, works by David Hockney, Pablo Picasso, Stuart Davis, Arthur Dove, Charles Demuth, and all those paintings by Georgia O'Keeffe—worth an estimated $3 million. For a reason nobody could explain, Crispo had simply concluded that he was done paying Ackerman anything.

For two years Ackerman tried diligently to get Crispo to resume the payments, and refrained from placing the paintings on the market. "Because they were friends," Ronnie Caran explained to a friend later, "and he couldn't believe this was happening."

Then, months before Caran resigned from the gallery, Marty Ackerman showed up personally to try to find out what was happening with the money he was owed. Crispo, who had refused his phone calls for nearly a year, kept him waiting for more than half an hour before swinging open the door to the Red Room. Looking pale and slightly puffy, he ushered in his old friend.

Ackerman began with these words: "You'd better come up with some money, Andrew, or I'm selling your pictures. There're buyers waiting on line." He was pissed off, and a good deal injured, by this treatment. "C'mon, Andrew. I know you bought an O'Keeffe drawing yesterday for forty-five thousand dollars. You think the art world is so big? All you've got to do is pay *me* the forty-five and you could have had one of the deals back, or you could have cut all of your option repayments and started fresh." Then he exploded. "What are you doing to me?"

Crispo denied the new purchase outright.

"Look," said Ackerman, finally sitting down, "I've talked to Rosenthal"—Marvin Rosenthal, another factor Crispo had stopped paying, was also going after an old debt—"and we can get together and take you out of a lot of your jams. Give you a real substantial amount."

Crispo thanked him, but added, "I don't need your kind of help," and stood up, signaling the end of their meeting.

As the elevator doors closed behind Ackerman, Crispo shouted, "You and Rosenthal aren't going to take over the Andrew Crispo Gallery! That's still my name on the door, bastard!"

Within a few days, a formal final notice came to the gallery, delivered by certified mail, announcing a deadline for repayment or rescheduling. If the date was ignored, according to the letter, the entire bundle in Ackerman's possession would be sold that day.

When that deadline passed, most of Crispo's prized paintings went to Steve Koman, a millionaire collector who had been a regular gallery client but who had slipped away recently. Koman had even loaned Crispo money himself once.

Privately, other gallery employees felt it was fair turnabout. For months, Ellery Kurtz and Susan Slack and Ann Marie Scully, who had been hired on as the gallery's social secretary (and spent much of her time scheduling what appeared to be disgruntled coke dealers), were sworn to secrecy on Andrew's purchases: "Don't tell Ronnie, whatever you do," he'd say, "Ronnie and I are having some trouble; I'm getting a lot of flak from Ronnie." Within hours, someone would whisper in Ronnie's ear, "You know that Burchfield that was in here this morning? Well, Andrew just wrote a check out for eighty thousand dollars for it."

Nevertheless, at the time Caran was not one of the people gloating. "Andrew fucked him royally," he said, "but the punishment's *much* greater than the crime. Marty could have sold just one of those paintings and recovered his losses."

He took it upon himself to call Marty Ackerman and complain, and the two of them—through several weeks of negotiation—devised a way out of it for all of them. Crispo would pay $1 million to Koman to get back the fourteen canvases now in his possession (Koman bought them for a fraction of this in a deal nobody at the gallery was able to figure out), and Ackerman would turn over the three remaining ones in exchange for a $150,000 check, which represented outstanding debt. The net cost to Crispo would be something less than a million dollars above what it would have been had he not defaulted, but (Caran kept assuring him) he'd be getting $3 million in artwork in return. And he'd be in control of his precious Georgia O'Keeffe collection once more.

The day came for the deal. Koman had flown into town, and was waiting at Ackerman's office; Caran was going to sign all the necessary papers, with Crispo's approval. "It's the best deal we could have gotten," Caran said. "You swallow your pride, and you get three million in pictures for a small price." Crispo replied, "I should have listened to you all along. I always get in trouble when I don't listen to you. Go."

Caran took a cab to Ackerman's office—twenty blocks, maximum—and found Marty smoking a cigar and laughing a wicked laugh.

"Hey, kid," he said, "I don't know what's going on but I know one thing. Your boss is crazy." Marty's carriage was always "a little more garment district than Harvard," as one acquaintance put it.

"I just got off the phone with the son of a bitch. He says, and I quote, 'Tell Ronnie to come back when he gets there, because I'm not going to do any *fucking* deals with you.' Says, 'You're a thief, and I'm taking you to court, and I'm filing papers against you, and I'm filing papers against your wife, and I'm going to put your daughter in reform school!' Man's a crazy bastard. Tell him for me"—he puffed his cigar—"to go ahead and sue. I've got all the time in the world, being my own lawyer. And I've got his paintings to pay for it."

The papers were drawn up rapidly, and Crispo had them served on the Ackermans in their Connecticut home, instead of the Manhattan office. The move was his idea: It sent a signal that it would be an ugly, unforgiving war. He wasn't going to allow them to rest; there would be no weekends off, no relaxing vacations, no family member—or former family member—unencumbered.

After some research, Crispo learned that Frances Ackerman, Marty's first wife and mother of his kids, was pursuing Marty for a million dollars in back alimony, and that Ackerman had declared personal bankruptcy to escape it. Crispo paid for copies of the legal papers—dating back a dozen years—and attempted to negotiate a buyout of her interests in the case, according to a gallery employee.

Eventually, this route was abandoned. Instead, he routinely updated his charges against the Ackermans, alleging "miscalculated and despicable acts" such as usury under federal law and "disproportionate" penalty. In February 1984, he added this charge: that Martin J. Ackerman had taken his knowledge of the Crispo Gallery's accounting practices and, "in violation of the Code of Professional Responsibility," turned Andrew Crispo over to the Internal Revenue Service. "He was absolutely convinced this was a possibility," said a former employee. "He kept noticing a coincidence between the dates the IRS wanted to audit his books and the dates he was supposed to have paperwork done for the Ackerman case. He called it evidence."

The outpouring of Crispo's coked-up fury was unparalleled. He threw more into this battle than ever went into his gallery, or the jobs before that, or the mischief in Philadelphia's Rittenhouse Square. The O'Keeffes were gone! If that wasn't a casus belli, nothing was.

Meanwhile, he took seriously Roy Cohn's motto in such matters (although not necessarily his instructions) and ignored all court dates. He refused to appear for depositions, denied, as a matter of course, ever having received service of anything. The tactic, however, was never explained to the young associate from Cohn's office, who was frantic. On more than one occasion, he'd had to explain to the judge that he expected his client to show up at any minute, while Crispo (he told gallery workers later) was roaming around the bowels of the courthouse "signing things. See, as long as I can prove I was in the building, they can't touch me!" It was unclear where such a thought had originated.

Irate, the judge finally ordered an in-court deposition, one of the harshest sanctions short of contempt. Again, Crispo didn't show, and the attorney was handed an affidavit that said, "Mr. Crispo has to be in Houston tomorrow on business, and cannot make the deposition."

The judge exploded, and gave a deadline of a number of minutes, with contempt charges—perhaps even jail—as his sword.

Ronnie Caran answered the attorney's phone call to the gallery, and grew quite concerned. "He's here," Caran said, "and he says he's ready to testify, but listen. I know this is not my place or anything, but you've got to stop this. This man can't go anywhere."

The attorney said, "We can't do that; he'll lose the case. You should see this judge—he's livid."

"I don't care what happens, but Andrew's in no condition to do anything. If he goes in today, you're definitely going to lose the case. He's as high as you can imagine—on coke. So unbelievably high that he'd make a fool out of you, make a fool out of Roy, and you'd lose the case. He'd probably get himself arrested at that."

Interviewed by a reporter, the attorney gave a lengthy account of what happened next: "He came down to court. We started the deposition. Within fifteen minutes, Crispo had created so many contradictions in his story, he was sweating profusely. I was sitting next to him. I could literally look through his nose. I could see all the veins in his nose, red and blue. Within about an hour, he destroyed the whole lawsuit."

On his way out of the courtroom, Crispo began screaming that Roy Cohn, his good friend, would have the judge decommissioned for the way he had treated him.

Back at the gallery, Caran went over Crispo's remarks in amazement. "How can you tell so many lies? You think you're going to get away with this?"

Crispo was brittle, combative. "Who are you calling a liar?"

"Well, not me, that's for sure. You told them that you never got the final notice from Marty saying he was going to sell your works on such and such a date. But Andrew, I was with you! I signed the receipt!"

"I'll just say you don't show me everything that comes in here."

"You're not going to drag me into this. Didn't someone ever tell you that the only time you should lie is when you know you're not going to get caught? All they have to do is subpoena your papers and say, 'This is a lie, this you made up, I don't even know what this is based on!' "

Crispo decided to refuse any future requests for his appearance. Only months later, following Caran's departure, did he offer a written explanation, which blamed his escalating IRS battle for his lack of cooperation. What began as a simple audit had turned into a full-scale tax-evasion investigation, headed by the U.S. Attorney's office.

In a statement to the judge in the Ackerman case, his lawyers wrote: "Plaintiffs had been served with Federal Grand Jury subpoenas and upon advice of counsel . . . Mr. Crispo will not testify. . . . Since the Grand Jury subpoena specifically requires documents and testimony relevant to transactions to or from Mr. Crispo and/or the Gallery, these issues would be relevant to this proceeding and, therefore, we are going to clearly instruct him not to answer those questions and to invoke his Fifth Amendment privilege."

His suit against Marty Ackerman and Steve Koman was thrown out of court, a judge concluding that if Crispo couldn't, or wouldn't, produce any paperwork or testimony to back up his charges, then there was no reason to continue with any of it.

Simultaneously, a similar drama was playing itself out in another courtroom, with another attorney representing the gallery and another creditor—the Bank of New York—laying claim to Crispo's art collection. For months, Crispo didn't even file answering papers to the bank's twenty-nine-page opening salvo. When a court order to do so was issued, Crispo had his attorney—he wasn't using Cohn on this—tender a two-sentence rebuttal: "Defendants . . . deny that they have any knowledge or information sufficient to form a belief as to paragraphs 7, 8, 11, 13, 14, 16, 20, 22, 25, 27, 28, 31, 34, and 35. WHEREFORE, defendants demand judgment dismissing the complaint, together with costs and disbursements of this action."

Within a month, he had dumped his previous lawyer, taken another Cohn associate, and sought to amend his account of the bank's dispute. This time, he told a story that was entirely unbelievable.

Three Bank of New York representatives, two men and a woman, came to his gallery, he said in the papers. "They addressed members of my staff in a loud and obnoxious manner, demanding them to locate me at once. When I came from my office, they descended upon me in such a manner that I feared that they intended to physically accost me.

"They announced that they were from the bank and that they had a truck outside and were 'here to collect' various pictures because I 'owed [them] more than one million dollars.' They made these statements to me in a loud, threatening, and abusive manner, in the presence of my staff and numerous clients. This assault caused me to become extremely stressful, frightened, and embarrassed as I explained to them that I didn't know what they were referring to, and pleaded with them not to remove any pictures. They demanded that I sign numerous forms that they had brought with them, which they claimed would allow them to renew certain letters of credit that had long since expired. They threatened that if I didn't sign them at once, they would have the 'crew come up and begin removing pictures.'

"Because I believed that they would actually carry out their threat and based on their assurances that by signing the forms I would not expose myself or the gallery to any harm, I acceded to their demands. They presented me with four standardized forms and directed me as to where and how to sign them. They did not allow me to read the forms, and explained that they would 'fill in the blanks later.' "

Evidently, these were not your typical bank loans whatsoever.

Even if a court had swallowed Crispo's newest explanation, it would have been too late. He neglected to inform his current Cohn attorney that a temporary restraining order, and an order of seizure, had already sailed through the system. The state supreme court ordered him to turn over nine paintings he had promised the Bank of New York as security; he had tried to convince the court he no longer owned those works.

Indeed, two of them, *Cleveland*, by Louis Lozowick, and *Silver, Ochre, Carmine, Green (River Bottom)*, by Arthur Dove, had been collateralized twice: Rosenthal & Rosenthal, the factor, was holding on to them against *its* loans.

Another painting on the court's list was Preston Dickinson's *Still Life #1*, the painting that had been transferred into one of the ST files Victor Ruggiero had discovered, in order to cover for the Frederick Frieseke, which was supposed to belong to the baron but had been sold inadvertently to a Texas buyer. So Baron Thysson was the owner of record. "I was just storing it for a client," Crispo was now arguing—armed with bogus receipts to bolster this assertion. The paperwork had become so complicated, even Crispo couldn't keep up.

Ronnie Caran, meanwhile, spent his remaining time at the gallery trying to put out the fires. He arranged a buyer for the marble Brancusi head—*The Muse*—willing to pay $3.5 million. When the papers were drawn up, Crispo decided he wanted $4 million, and called the whole thing off. Then, a bank in St. Louis grabbed Edward Hopper's famous *Hotel Lobby* to make good on a four-hundred-thousand-dollar loan. Caran had a standing offer for eight hundred thousand dollars for the piece, but Crispo wouldn't let it go. The Riggs Bank—the bank and its chairman were both gallery clients—was holding an important Degas pastel (*The Two Dancers*) as collateral against a loan, and Crispo was months behind in payments. About to lose the work, along with the goodwill of its chairman Joe Allbritton, Caran found a buyer with a certified check totaling $625,000. But Crispo said, "I'll sell my paintings when I'm good and ready to sell my paintings."

Then he bellowed, "I came from an orphanage with nothing, and if I lost all of this, so what? *You* can't tell *me* what to do; that's my name above the door. *My name! Mine!*"

This line, on a moist fall evening, Caran repeated to his friends at Beulahland. "*My name! Mine!*" His face grew pink and he jabbed a thick finger into the air, illustrating the significance of the line, which was lost on the listeners.

He explained: "In the old days, it used to be 'That's my name over the door,' like he was absolutely thrilled by the fact that he had made it. Then it became 'my *name*,' you know, like with pride. Now—now, it's like a threat, a club!"

In the months since Roy Cohn hosted the town-house meeting, after meddling in Ruggiero's criminal case and actively pursuing the legal matters that his longtime client Andrew Crispo now preferred to ignore, the rapport between the two men began to sour. Cohn had hung on longer than Crispo's other friends and associates, putting up with the ill-advised courtroom tantrums and private irregularities. He had even been willing to go to bat with the IRS on Crispo's behalf, despite his knowledge of the intricate paperwork that had first landed him in such trouble. And despite Crispo's strange reactions to it.

First, Crispo had announced that he had scattered the gallery records around New York—in friends' houses, or friends' parents' houses, or in secret storage bins he had rented around town. "If these are ever subpoenaed," he had explained, "the gallery would be ruined! It took us a decade to put these records together—where paintings are, who bought what for how much. Without them, there's no Andrew Crispo Gallery."

Then he had taken to telephoning Cohn for legal advice, most often in the middle of the night while Crispo was strung out. (Cohn kept a short list of favored clients over his secretary's telephone. Anyone on this list was entitled to know how to reach the attorney day or night. Crispo had been there for years.)

But perhaps a more serious matter to Cohn was the rumor, muttered around town, that Baron Thyssen-Bornemisza had severed ties with the gallery. Although Crispo would never confirm it, a gallery associate said it was true. "Andrew owed the baron several million dollars," he said, "both for works that he sold on behalf of the baron and that the baron had paid for but Andrew wasn't able to deliver. So Andrew gave him a number of paintings as collateral, but Thyssen's lawyers were worried that the paintings were not his to give, that the IRS would grab them and he'd be out."

By June of 1984, Thyssen had indeed disappeared, instructed by his board of directors to wait out the legal wrangling if he intended to continue doing business with Crispo. Through intermediaries, he had cautiously broached the subject of the outstanding debts, and had secretly tried to track down the whereabouts of his paintings. "Andrew was crushed," the associate said. "He viewed it as infidelity."

It was the same charge of treachery bestowed upon so many former friends and gallery employees. Now Crispo seemed to blame Ronnie

Caran for the baron's departure, despite the long years they had served together in the gallery's trenches. "I'm surrounded by liars and thieves," he'd bellow at imagined transgressors. "Nobody can be trusted!"

The ties with Roy Cohn were not destined to last. "Without Roy knowing it," said a mutual friend, "every time a lawyer came into the gallery to discuss collecting money for their client—whether it was an artist or somebody Andrew sold a painting to and never delivered or paid, et cetera—Andrew had a unique ability of getting the lawyers to forget what they came for and help him out. He got the Bank of New York lawyers to advise him on this case, or somebody else's to advise him on that one, and they would spend hours with Andrew for no fees whatsoever. Andrew had a phenomenal ability to enlist these people. But all of a sudden, Andrew was giving Roy advice." Apparently, he was encouraging the other attorneys, those who were dunning him for money, to offer off-the-cuff comments on the work that Saxe, Bacon was performing for him. "He became convinced Roy was not the person to handle the tax case," the mutual friend said.

Worse than that, he apparently hired Stanley Arkin, a noted tax attorney, to double-check Cohn's work. "When you were a client of Roy's, you played by his rules," said a former Cohn associate. "And the cardinal rule is that Roy is never the number-two lawyer."

"Andrew double-crossed Roy," the mutual friend said, "and that spelled the beginning of the end."

The end of the end came shortly, after one last midnight call. "Andrew had been on a coke party for probably several days and had been reading something about Nostradamus," said the mutual friend. "Some part of one of his predictions said something like the bear was going to lie down with the eagle, and the world would be ruled by a man in a turban with a star on it."

A couple of years earlier, the gallery had been trying to sell a huge diamond for Baron Thyssen called the Star of Peace, considered the world's largest uncut diamond. It was 171.3 carats, and rather yellowish. The gallery had it for about a year, but had no takers. "Andrew gets it into his head that the man in the turban is Qaddafi, and that the Star of Peace is *the* star," said the friend. "He got Roy on the phone and explained this to him, and said, 'You've got to get me in touch with this man. You've got to put this deal together.'"

Perhaps he thought that if he could sell the diamond, Thyssen would resume his lucrative relationship with the gallery. "He was coked up out of his mind, literally screaming into the phone!"

Cohn, enraged by the call and astonished by Crispo's bizarre idea, furiously removed Crispo's name from those coveted lists: Crispo was no longer over the phone on the secretary's desk, no longer on the invitations for the Fourth of July, or New Year's, or February 20, Roy's birthday bash. In the summer of 1984, Crispo was shoved out of the loop.

Within a week, Cohn messengered Crispo's case files over to the gallery, without so much as a cover letter.

August 1984. The heat and humidity in New York mounted a conspiracy against the city's tenuous civility. Fumes from restaurant waste, piled on the street corners of Chinatown, snaked low through the hot, dripping air as far north as Fourteenth Street. The blood and fat splattered by day over the streets of the meat-packing district in the far West Village resisted all efforts to be hosed down the sewer at night. A thick, sticky film leached into the cobblestone there, and there it remained, pinned under the weight of a blue-orange haze. The dark alleys and narrow side streets were permanently wet; the smells were sickening. Everywhere there was the particulate remains of urban decay suspended at shirt level, nose level, pore level, pouncing at will.

High above West Twelfth Street, Bernard sat in Andrew's air-conditioned apartment, complaining. His targets were many: His mother was on his case about Elana; Elana was on his case about a career; his father, disappointed that Bernard wasn't developing a focus to his life, or at least a good job, had announced he was "ready to put a line through your name" in the family will. Employed as a models builder for a computer company, Bernard had given up asking for more creative work, waiting, he said, for a possible assistant's job at Andrew's gallery. To his mother, he had explained that Crispo was planning to open a satellite gallery in Washington, D.C., and to appoint Bernard its director, at forty thousand a year. She brushed the comment off as wholly unbelievable, which pissed him off.

But what was truly consuming him now was his relationship with Elana. "She and me hardly ever have sex anymore," he told Andrew. "And you know, I've got Lisa, so whenever Elana doesn't give it up, I go off to Lisa's house."

"What's Lisa like sexually?" Andrew asked.

"You know, she's pretty hot. And I do things, tell her things, lots of things. Just to keep her away from me, I think. Like head games. Like I'd tell her, 'Get ready, we're going out.' Then I would say, 'Listen, I'm going to be a little late, I'm going to be a little late,' and I don't show up at all, see?"

Crispo seemed to understand.

"Because she'd get mad at me, but continue to fuck me," Bernard explained, his conversation full of speed. "I mean, I'm going through stress right now. Elana's fucking with my head *major*, but I can't retaliate against Elana because I love her too much. Lisa is just something I picked up along the way, when I was in school. I like Lisa. The one time I started blowing her off is when I found myself falling in love with her. I'm like, Shit, what's going on here? Now I've got one, two . . . And I say, No, I can't get involved, because the second I start getting involved with somebody who needs somebody, forget it. I'm lost in that person. I don't want to leave Elana. Elana has the kid. I couldn't do that to her. Or to him. Every Sunday we take little Julius for a walk in the park."

Andrew offered more coke, wine, attention.

"See, I call Elana my Ice Princess. Because she's that cold. But it's gotten to the point where having sex with her is like jerking off. I'm the kind of person sexually where her pleasure is my pleasure. If she doesn't get anything, I don't get anything. That's why Lisa's such hot sex. But Elana, one time I guess I insulted her. It was after I had sex with her. I took a wad of bills outta my wallet, and I said, 'There ya go; this was about as good as using a whore.' That's what I told her; I told her, 'If I wanted to have sex, I'd go see a whore. A whore would give me better sex.' I kinda felt bad about it."

It was an unqualified act of betrayal for Bernard to be telling Crispo about Elana. From the start, Elana had nursed a negative impression of the older man. Their first meeting took place a year earlier in a small coffeehouse called Miracles on Greenwich Avenue in the Village; it was the young couple's special place. Bernard, who had begun to talk about Andrew Crispo frequently, asked whether she'd like to meet him, and left their table, left the restaurant, and went next door to Uncle Charlie's to fetch his friend. Elana was confused about how Bernard knew Crispo would be in the gay bar, though she didn't ask.

When the two returned to the table, Crispo seemed disdainful. "So you're the famous girlfriend of my kid brother," he said. She had no idea to what Crispo was referring, but politely acceded. Bernard then explained: They had decided that John LeGeros had fathered Andrew, then abandoned him in Philadelphia.

"Oh," said Elana politely, confused, taking Andrew's hand. "Nice to meet you." Afterward, she joked about the farcical claim, which needled Bernard. And in recent months, she had frequently and belligerently accused Bernard of spending more time with Crispo than with her. "Why aren't you with your homosexual wife," she'd say, "why don't you two get married?"

But Bernard himself felt betrayed by Elana, and did not feel badly about crafting a conspiratorial alliance with her nemesis. His girlfriend, he explained to Andrew, had decided—unilaterally!—to return to Rumania for a cousin's wedding. "First, of course, she says it's up to me and wants to know what my opinions are," he said, "and while I'm thinking about it, she goes ahead and makes her plans. Like it didn't matter what I was going to say at all! She quit her job. She got the airplane tickets for her and Julius. She's just abandoning me, just like Anya did before, and just like my mother. . . ." As he spoke, his dark eyes welled up uncontrollably; he stared down at his torn and quivering cuticles.

Crispo produced several sheets of paper. "You remember how we did this before? Remember how you . . . if you make a list you can see with your own eyes, you know what the pros are and what the cons are of any situation?" Bernard nodded. "On this sheet of paper," he continued, "put down all the good aspects and all the bad aspects of your relationship with Elana. All the things that bother you about the relationship and all the things that you like about the relationship." Bernard sipped from a wineglass and cleared his throat. "You do the same with Lisa on this piece of paper, and on this one you do a list of the good things and bad things about your parents."

"I'll need a couple of pieces of paper for them," Bernard joked.

Smiling, Andrew explained his belief in lists, his disbelief in shrinks, his theories of independence, of loneliness in a crowded world. "With lists," he said, "you're in absolute control. And nobody has the information except you. Unless you want to show it to them. But with psychiatrists, they just want the money. They're not your friends; it's just their business. And you go to them weak, and they take, take, take. Kindness," he said, "is weakness. Same thing. And in you, because you're so kind, people will see that and try to hurt you for it. Like Sam Collins."

Bernard looked squarely at Andrew and felt safe. "You wouldn't do that? Hurt me?"

"Don't worry about it," he said, and left Bernard alone to think and to enumerate.

What Bernard thought about was how Elana was never there to help him but always demanded that he help her. About how he had helped Lisa get a job, and had—despite the coercive tricks he had played on her recently—gone out of his way to provide for her. He reviewed that long high school relationship with Anya, who just sort of disappeared after visiting him in the hospital, where he was being treated for cyanide poisoning that *she had caused.*

And then he listed the things about Elana that he adored. Her cherubic face and her hazy blue eyes and the sweet, melodic accents of her voice when she loved him. She was his type of woman. Curly brown hair, perfectly round eyes. Full shiny lips and skin as white as a Hummel statue. Quiet. Soft. Almost perfect helplessness. Their weekend photography project was dubbed "Abstract Visions of New York." Elana, dressed in her most delicate attire, would pose before demolition sites, broken walls, wrecked cars. "I would probably think of taking a picture of flowers, and pretty things," she would trill to Bernard, "but not you! You prefer a garbage dump!"

When they spoke, their conversations touched on politics, God, their future, and young Julius, who "had no name," Bernard would say, because the father had skipped long before the boy's name had been inked onto a birth certificate. For the woman he loved, and for her son, he signed the affidavits his parents drew up, waiving the LeGeros-family inheritances as long as he stayed with them. For them, he had sacrificed his parents' love. And she responded to this with treachery, deceit, and frigidity. She refused him sex! She was leaving him, alone and terrified!

By the time Andrew reentered the room, Bernard had worked himself into a frenzy. "I just want to kill myself," he announced flatly, "just to show her what she's doing to me."

Crispo attempted to cheer him up. Finally, he said, "I can understand why you'd want to die. But I want you to know this: All you have to do is come to me and tell me that you've decided it's time. And I will pull the trigger for you."

"Really? You'd do that for me?" The unequivocal dedication of the offer resonated in Bernard's melodramatic mind. "Nobody's ever said that to me before."

Andrew explained that he only wanted to help his young friend, and that he would go to all extremes to prove that. "We're friends," he said, "we're half brothers."

Before he left Andrew's apartment that night, Bernard folded up the pages and passed them across a cocaine-dusted coffee table. He wanted this man to know him intimately; he trusted this man as he trusted nobody else in his life. He felt as though the items listed on the sheets were the keys to his soul—what made him happy or sad, full or empty, enraged or sated, safe or endangered. And he felt as though Andrew Crispo was the one individual he knew who, wanting nothing from him in return, would safeguard their contents.

A month later, when he called from the limo and requested his job with Crispo, Bernard was fully aware that a commitment to his new boss would involve much more than traditional employment dictated. He was aware that a mutinous wave had gripped the gallery, and that Andrew's enemies, detractors, and besmirchers were everywhere. It was tacitly understood that the twenty-two-year-old was promising unframed personal devotion, loyalty without bounds.

Bernard LeGeros would accept the title of "executioner" just as seriously as that of "bodyguard." And his targets, from the very beginning, would include Andrew's business rivals and sexual partners equally, though the latter group was by far the largest.

In a typical scenario, Crispo would ring up the number of a pay phone—either a public booth on Abingdon Square in the Village or one of the several phones outside leather and S&M clubs nearby—and invite whoever answered to a "party" at his West Twelfth Street apartment, or in the Fifty-seventh Street gallery, or in the smaller Galleria apartment next door. When the visitor arrived, Crispo would socialize for a while before finding a reason to leave the room. Then LeGeros would enter, dressed in an SS uniform, or like a security guard or a cop, and begin the assault.

A steady stream of street-trained teenagers—members of Crispo's "club," such as John Parker and Kenny Morales, there for the drugs more than the action—would take turns chaining the victims, beating them, and screaming antigay epithets before turning them back over to Crispo, who would sometimes force them to renounce their homosexuality. Often, he would have them perform fellatio on him before letting them go.

"Andrew told everybody he was gay, but he was a good gay, somehow," one of the kids said. "He promoted this antigay theme in about every conversation we had. He promoted the idea that homosexuality, in everybody but him, was weakness and gross. He liked us to be straight, and with a kind of in-your-face attitude."

Andrew Crispo would also play his own victim from time to time, insisting that LeGeros or one of the others torture and humiliate him. Billy Mayer, Bernard's high school friend, participated in several of these scenes. Once, he was a "Nazi" who beat Crispo's back and legs. Another time, he and LeGeros played "New Order" thugs interrogating Crispo, who was bound and blindfolded and wearing an elaborate leather harness.

Billy Mayer, who described himself as "only semi-normal" and whose shabby attire and violent locutions bore this out, detailed their first meeting. "Because I had heard all these stories from Bernard, I said to Andrew—this I remember distinctly—'So I hear you like to beat people.' And he said, 'Yeah, but actually I'm more the other way.' " Mayer sat comfortably in a chair as Bernard and Andrew "kinda disappeared for a couple of minutes, and worked things out."

When the two men returned to the room, Mayer said, they invited him to engage in a "scenario" with Crispo. The older man would play the role of "a scum Jew art dealer fag" whom Mayer, a "Nazi" guard, would interrogate. He accepted, and Bernard handed him a toy gun and vanished.

"And essentially what it was, I went outside and I came in the door with a gun, and he hid someplace. He wasn't funny-looking, but he had a funny, overweight way of moving. He'd be standing real still, and then he'd be like in a leaning position, like *stooping*, and move around like that. He was really funny that way. So I came in and he was behind the screen, and I could just see his head. And I had the gun at that point, and I started speaking in, you know, German or whatever. And he . . . he . . . he had this, was it a belt? I whipped him on the ass with this belt.

"I was interrogating him, I was a gestapo officer—it was very, I don't know. He was playing that he had to take his medicine, which was the coke. Had a little bottle with a spoon that screwed out. It's like a game. I'm like, 'Tell me where it is,' without ever really saying what 'it' is. He's, 'I won't tell you where it is! I won't tell you.' Like that, gamelike. There's no clues. Then he would say, 'My heart! I'll have a heart attack if I can't take my medication!' 'Okay, you sonabitch mothafuckah; I need you alive, so take it.' Crack!"

Like Bernard, Billy Mayer enjoyed obfuscating all experience: It was Billy who first dubbed the LeGeros family's Oldsmobile Vista Cruiser the "Command Vehicle," and who instituted phrases such as "a communication" or "a transmission" to mean a telephone call. Sex was "a mission accomplished." The game he was invited to play with this older man, which he did not view as sex, exercised the same quadrant of his brain.

"Andrew was wearing these tiny black shorts," he recalled, "but he took them off after a while. He wanted to take them off. I didn't . . . I couldn't—I didn't hit him hard. I just couldn't see hitting him hard. I had been an antique dealer for a while, and most of the people in the antique business are gay, or so it's been represented to me. So I was used to gays. Even women, I know a lot of women who like to get slapped really hard on their ass during sex. And so I didn't see that as any real— not too bizarre.

"But he had this eighteen-inch dildo, he wanted me to—I didn't even want to touch it! I wouldn't touch it. He wanted me to fuck him with it. Then he said something about having a twin brother who could take the whole thing. 'If my twin brother was here, he would just walk over to that dildo and stick it up his ass. Just like that.'

"After all of this, we went over to Arthur's—right over that balcony thing—and had Chinese food. Arthur, apparently he was very much more proper, started picking on Crispo. Something trivial, like he left the spaghetti out. And Andrew was like, 'Arthur, I didn't mean anything, I didn't do anything.' Like it was his father."

Over the next few weeks, Crispo called Billy Mayer often, suggesting they "do that again," but Mayer declined. "That was once," he told Andrew, "and I'm not interested anymore."

Nevertheless, it did happen again in the fall. This time, Bernard controlled the scene, and it appeared to get a little out of hand.

Bernard and Billy began the evening with an outing (an "operation") to see *The Inheritors*, a movie about a neo-Nazi youth growing up in Germany. Crispo showed up—he wasn't expected but had apparently overheard the evening's plans. The three sat in the back of the theater "acting out all those parts," Billy said later. Bernard had brought his AR-7 collapsible rifle along in a nylon gym bag, and assembled it in the darkness. Each time a gun was fired in the film, he pulled the trigger wildly, causing Crispo to cackle like a child. "And somewhere along the line," Billy recalled, "it was decided we'd keep doing this back at the gallery.

"What happened then was, Crispo reached into this thing he called his bag of toys and pulled out the same clothes. He changed into the black shorts, and was wearing this black cap on his head." Around his soft chest, he fastened a leather harness off of which hung a half-dozen steel rings.

"Me and Bernard were 'New Order' cops, right? So he ran around for a little bit. Bernard was there, so I didn't have to hit him at all. Didn't have to do any physical touching, because Bernard didn't mind hitting, like getting down and punching him a little bit, like on his ass, or his back, or the fatty part of his arm." For twenty-five minutes, Mayer humiliated Crispo, threatening untold torture, promising death. Then LeGeros reached into Crispo's nylon bag and produced a long black bullwhip and began lashing out in full-arm swings. The noises were loud; Crispo struggled to his feet but Bernard kept whipping—thirteen, fourteen, fifteen times.

"Crispo apparently must have felt different," Mayer said later. "There's three people this time. And one of 'em's Bernard. When I did it with Crispo, we could break out of the role instantly. I think he felt that Bernard had a harder time stopping. I think he was scared.

"So he went into the office—*ran* into his office—and locked the door. Maybe it was him playing a manipulative game, saying, 'Stop.' But I doubt it. He called from the phone upstairs to make sure it was over, and he took fifteen minutes before resurfacing, just to be sure. 'I'm coming out, I'm going to come out.' He called the whole thing off."

On social occasions, Billy said, Crispo would needle Bernard, taunting him in an apparent test of his limits. While watching television, for example, Crispo would announce to one of Bernard's friends, "You know who gives the best blowjobs? Bernard does, just incredible." Initially,

Bernard's response would be something like, "Andrew, just shut up, you know I'm no fag."

"He could be very persistent in a line of conversation such as this," Mayer said, "and after a while, even if you're joking with people, it gets a little aggravating.

"But with Bernard—Bernard would grow *very* upset. Andrew knew just how to make this happen."

On September 20, 1984, Andrew Crispo called Kenny Morales, extending a familiar invitation to make some money. He was one of the "dozens and dozens" of like-minded kids, according to young Kirk Green's count, introduced to the powerful art dealer by John Parker. Kenny was known as "Ken 007" among fellow graffiti artists in the Bronx. Andrew called him "Sergeant."

Morales accepted the invitation with pride—he'd never been called directly before—and ordered a cab from the O.J. Cab Company. He swung by the house of two other kids, "Zeal" and "Dax," and headed to Manhattan for a "party" at the gallery. September 20 was Kenny Morales's twentieth birthday. He was dressed in tight-fitting pants and a crewneck sweater, and wore his hair, which was dark and wavy, in a short Tony Orlando style. Zeal and Dax were also twenty, the latter being blond. All three were extremely well groomed and attractive, and physically imposing for their age. "Ernie, the guard in the lobby, paid the cabbie," Morales said later. Bernard LeGeros walked them through the foyer.

"We arrived at the gallery at about 7:00 P.M. that night and saw a white guy on the couch. He was handcuffed behind his back. The white guy was about twenty, skinny, with a short beard, wearing jeans and a white pullover shirt." Another Bronx kid called "The Leak," described as nineteen and blond, was also present.

"The guy's shirt was taken off and he was put up against the wall. The guy was whipped. I saw a mask somewhere in the room. Bernard had a starter's pistol out. I was told to whip the guy—I did, a couple of times. The Leak and Dax also whipped the guy."

Later, he said, "The guy's head was held in the toilet and pissed on and the guy was told to sing 'Happy Birthday' to me, calling me Sergeant Slaughter because of my time in the army, and told to kiss the Sergeant's boots. . . . The guy thanked us for not killing him after the whipping. He was scared, did not want to get whipped, and was scared of Bernard's gun.

"I left about midnight with my friends, and the guy was still there in the gallery. We took a taxi home and I paid with my own money. I was usually paid cash, a hundred and fifty dollars," he said, indicating there had been similar transactions. "The other guys got coke, no money."

A day following this incident, Crispo gloated about it to Kirk Green. "Andrew said, 'You should have seen the victim we had last night. It was great!' And Bernard sat there laughing. Then Andrew said, 'I got him to the gallery and stripped him naked and Bernard came out in a security guard's uniform and beat the shit out of that queer. Then I fucked him! You should have seen it.' " Kirk Green figured it was the coke talking: "You couldn't believe a word they were saying."

Paul Jeffries had trouble believing it, too. He was the skinny man who, from inside the toilet, was made to sing to Kenny Morales.

At somewhere near 7:00 A.M. the morning before, Paul Jeffries went to the coat check at the Anvil, a meat-packing district gay bar frequented by "leather queens" and drag queens alike, and retrieved his leather bomber-jacket. He had been dancing and snorting coke all night; his T-shirt was soaked with perspiration, and he felt nauseous. He walked outside and turned east on Fourteenth Street, toward the subway, but a block later he turned south again, in search of a stoop or a loading dock where he could sit and get his head together. He was a soft-spoken, college-educated Canadian native who worked in a Manhattan gay restaurant; he did not seem out of place on the glistening streets.

At the corner of Washington and West Thirteenth Street, before dawn, he stood unsteadily against a wall, resting. "A pay phone outside a working man's bar, called Howlie's Bar and Grill, was ringing," he said later. "It rang, I don't know, maybe a dozen times. And at some point I decided to pick it up."

He said hello; a deep voice on the other end asked how he was feeling. "Not too well," he said. "I was dancing all night at the Anvil, and I guess I did too much coke."

"What do you look like?" the man asked. "What are you wearing?"

Jeffries answered without hesitation. "Well, I'm twenty-five, you know, dark hair, a beard. Generally, I'm considered handsome, or hot." Although he had never answered a ringing pay phone before, he knew about the practice; friends of his had met people over the telephone at the corner of Christopher and Seventh Avenue South, the one that seemed always to be ringing. "Blue jeans, a T-shirt, and a black leather jacket," he said.

"How'd you like to come up to my place?" the man asked, but Jeffries hesitated. "I'm right around the corner, Washington and Twelfth. We could just talk. And I've got some coke."

Jeffries arrived at Crispo's apartment building and pushed the buzzer on the intercom; a voice boomed out, "Back up a little and stand in front of the camera." He complied, and heard the lock click open on the door.

Upstairs, when the elevator opened, a puffy, pale man greeted him: "Hi," he said, "I'm Andrew," and he ushered Jeffries into his penthouse apartment. Several lines of cocaine were already drawn on the coffee table in the living room area, on top of a catalogue that was inscribed "The Andrew Crispo Gallery."

Over the next several hours, they snorted lines of coke in five-minute intervals; they talked about their pasts, about Jeffries's work as a waiter and his desire to complete a master's degree in cinema, about the Crispo Gallery and the tax mess. The lines of drugs were the size of fountain pens. Several times, the telephone rang and Andrew Crispo spoke to a man he called "The X," whom Jeffries took to be a very close friend.

At noon, Crispo handed the telephone to Jeffries and asked him for a favor. "It's The X," he said. "Tell him, 'Fuck you,' or 'Go fuck yourself.' " Jeffries balked at first, then agreed. It didn't seem like a big deal.

"Hi," he said into the phone.

"Hi," came the reply.

"Go fuck yourself," Jeffries said, and handed the phone back to Andrew, who smiled at first. Then he seemed different, changed. Paul Jeffries had trouble keeping up.

"You know what a snuff film is?" Crispo asked. "You ever watch one?" Jeffries hadn't. "Would you like to see one?" Jeffries nodded yes.

"Me and The X," Crispo said, "we have this need to kill somebody every once in a while. It builds up every so often."

Jeffries cleared his sinuses, but Crispo did not pause. "You don't know of anyone you'd like to see dead, do you?"

The visitor shook his head. "No, of course not," he said.

"Surely there's *some*one you know of, someone who's hurt you badly."

It sparked a coke-driven memory in Jeffries, a recent memory about an ex-roommate who had thrown him out of the apartment when Jeffries refused to have sex with him. It made his stomach churn. "*He* hurt me," Jeffries offered. "I was very hurt by that."

Crispo asked his name, and where he lived. Crispo asked if Jeffries would like to see the person hurt, and he said yes. Crispo asked if he and The X could hurt this person, if Jeffries would take them to this person, if Jeffries would mind filming it, if he had the technical expertise to film it, if this person could be brought to them today, because "the need has built up to the point where we have to kill *today*."

"I said," Jeffries admitted later, "I guess I said yes. I was very, very stoned."

Then Jeffries told Crispo, "It would be difficult to commit that kind of messy, bloody murder in this apartment, because of having to cover everything up."

Crispo said, "That's no problem. My friend and I have access to this place up in the country where we could do this. That's no problem." Then Crispo called up his friend and announced, "I think we've got a victim." As they spoke, Jeffries roamed to the back of the apartment and, in the bedroom, removed his shoes and his pants, intending to climb into bed.

He felt Crispo's hand on his buttocks, and turned around. "Lean over the chest," Crispo commanded, and he did. "Pull down your underpants." Crispo then slapped him with a black leather belt three or four times, and Jeffries—no stranger to S&M—allowed it.

Then he stood up and turned around, and the two men fondled each other. Neither got an erection. Laughing uncomfortably, Jeffries apologized and asked if he could take a nap.

It was nearly three when he awoke with a buzzing headache and an embarrassing flashback to the murder discussion. Dressed, he searched the apartment to find Andrew Crispo and apologize again. Crispo was in the kitchen. "Listen, Andrew. I'm sorry," he said. "I know we talked about killing someone, and I realize, you know, that I could never go through . . . I'd always thought that if I did not work in art, that medicine would be my second choice, you know?"

Crispo chuckled. "It's no big deal," he said, "just something we talked about. It's not important." They consumed another round of cocaine in the living room, and Crispo invited his new friend to a birthday party "for a small group of friends of mine uptown. I'll have some more coke. And these are nice guys. Hot, young guys. You'll like them." He gave Jeffries a piece of paper with the address and phone number of the gallery. "Please come."

Jeffries accepted. He arrived after six, and was not released until after midnight.

When he returned to his apartment early the following morning, bloody and in obvious pain, Paul Jeffries told his roommate, Karl, an incredible story about six hours spent with Andrew Crispo.

"When I got to the gallery, he asked me to wait, said he was attending to some business. So he took me to this small brown room. 'Make yourself comfortable,' you know, so I sat in one of the chairs and waited.

"The objects around the room, first thing I noticed was a portrait of Roy Cohn—that famous one taken by Robert Mapplethorpe—sitting on a bookshelf. It was signed by Roy Cohn on the bottom. And there was an old crucifix, looked like an old icon from a church, that was hanging on the wall at about head level. Anyway, I waited for about thirty minutes here, it could have been a little longer. The door was closed. I decided to leave, finally, because I was impatient. I gathered up my things, and a young man burst in the door, in a brusque kind of way, and he had a gun in his hand! He pointed the gun at my head. He was dressed in some kind of dark shirt—blue or brown—and he looked like he had a uniform on, so I didn't think he was a burglar. He asked me, in this very angry tone of voice, what I was doing there. Accused me of breaking in. I assured him that I was not. And he said there was nobody else there but me. He pushed me around, he kept the gun on my head.

"When I kept insisting, you know, that I was there by invitation, he had me stand up and he frisked me, then he reached down to the bag where the wine was—I brought this wine—and my wallet was, and he pulled out a very small brown bottle that had some coke in it, I guess. I mean, it wasn't mine. 'What's this! Is this yours?' I said no. 'How'd it get there, then?' I said I didn't know. He said he'd have to take me down to the station, and then he said, 'Are you saying that this is Andrew Crispo's?'

"I said, 'No, I just don't know how it got there.' And then he slapped some handcuffs on me, really roughly, put my hands behind my back. I kept insisting . . . But then he started pushing me around, accusing me of being a liar.

"After a short time of this—like five or ten minutes—he left and then came back in the room with Andrew Crispo. And I said, 'Andrew, what's going on here?' I said, 'I did *not* ask to have this happen to me, I did *not* ask to have these handcuffs on, and I did *not* ask to be slapped around!' You know?

"And he said, 'This is my friend, Bernard LeGeros.' He said, 'We told you this afternoon that we needed a victim. You promised to give us one, today!' He said, 'You lied to me, you betrayed me.' He said, 'If you don't give us a victim, then *you're* it.'

"That's when I started praying, hard. He left the room. And that left me with Bernard—he told me that while they decided how they were going to kill me, that Bernard would be my master, that I would have to call him Master.

"So he left, and Bernard hit me. He kicked me, pushed me off the chair, called me a liar, a faggot scum. Said, 'A chair's too good for the likes of you,' that kinda stuff. And he kept going in and out of the room— at times he was very enraged and shouted at me that I had betrayed him and Andrew, didn't I know they needed a victim, and that I deserved to die because of it. He said over and over again that they were going to kill me.

"At one point, while he was beating and kicking me, he flew into a rage, saying, 'You're the person who told me to go fuck myself, aren't you?' And I said yes, that I'm sorry, but that Andrew Crispo made me do it. He kicked me while I was on the ground. This goes on for forty-five minutes, and then he left the room and closed the door, and Andrew came in again about ten minutes later with three young men this time. He introduced me to them, told me their names, told me these were the men who were to have been at the birthday party. He told me he was going to leave me with them—they were going to do with me as they wished—while he and Bernard were going to decide how they were going to kill me. He told me that one of them, the birthday boy, would be in charge.

"They called me all kinds of insults—they pushed me around and kicked me. They called me faggot, scum, slime, other things like asshole. They screamed at me as well that I had betrayed Andrew Crispo and that I deserved to die. One of them, all of the sudden, had what looked to be a circus whip—another one took off my shirt and told me to go and kneel under the crucifix on the wall. I was still handcuffed, with my hands behind me.

"They told me that they were going to whip me for Andrew. And they took the whip, and each took turns and whipped my back for a count of ten each—there was a count. I was in a lot of pain. The one who looked youngest was whipping me really hard and I was screaming, and the older one told him to cool it a little bit, to be not as ferocious. So at first, this was like thirty times or so in total, on my back. Then the whipping continued. Andrew came into the room with Bernard and I was told I'd have to be whipped some more, but I was in a lot of pain, so one of the young men came up to me and helped me stand up and pulled my pants down so they could whip my ass instead of my back.

"When they pushed my pants down, they also unlocked my handcuffs and brought my hands around in front. I was directed to spell out a phrase, a word or two, with a number of letters in it, like Fuck You, or Asshole or something, while someone whipped my buttocks this time. Like, 'A,' and they'd swing at me; 'S,' and they'd swing again. I was crying so hard I could barely speak, but I did it. I just kept doing it.

"After that, Bernard and Andrew left the room, and I sat down on the chair and the kids started this conversation with me. Like, one wanted to know if I was just, in their words, faggot scum, or if I was bisexual and was interested in fucking pussy with them. I said no. They wanted to know, asked me if I had ever fucked a woman. Asked me if I ever got off on women. I said something like, 'Sometimes they're very beautiful, but I prefer men.' One of them invited me to gang rape some woman with them. Like fifteen minutes passed doing this, and they finally went looking for Crispo.

"I could hear them talking outside the door. Then Andrew came in again, and he was really angry this time. He had this gun in his hand, the one Bernard earlier had held against my head. He shouted at me, 'Don't you believe we're going to kill you?'

"And I said something like, 'What would you do with the body?'

"He said he would put it in—that *they*, not he, would put it in a box and weigh it down and put it in the East River. Said bodies disappear all the time in the East River. Then he left, and Bernard LeGeros came into the room next and closed the door. I begged him for my life. I said I would give, I would *do* anything they wanted. I would give them the victim they wanted. I would do anything. I wouldn't say anything to anyone about what would happen—just please, please, *please* don't kill me.

"Bernard sat there for a while, several minutes, as I begged over and over again. I kept pleading for my life: 'Don't kill me. Please don't kill me.' And he looked up at me. He looked very, very sad, his face was down-fallen, downcast. He got up then and left the room, and again I was left for some time, maybe fifteen minutes. And then Crispo came in. He was alone. I said the same things to him, begging for my life. Over and over again. I would do anything, I would never say anything about what would happen to anyone. After he listened he left and returned again. He said to me, 'It's all right. Bernard has decided that we shouldn't kill you,' or 'Bernard has decided to let you live.' Something like that.

"He told me that there were a couple of things I had to do in return, though, before they would let me leave. First was that I would have to agree to go out cruising for women with the young men. That I would go to Limelight with the one who was having the birthday.

"And second was that I would have to go into the bathroom and put my head in the toilet and sing 'Happy Birthday' to the guy while all three young men were there, and I agreed. I got up. Someone unhandcuffed me—I don't know who—and I was led into the washroom in back by Andrew and the three men followed. I went into the washroom area, Andrew stayed outside, and the three men followed me in. I put my head in the toilet, you know, and I started to sing over and over and over and over: 'Happy birthday to you, happy birthday to you, happy birthday to you,' while the men urinated on me on my head, and then when they finished urinating, they pushed my head in the toilet and flushed while they called me names and when I pulled my head out they were all laughing very loudly. They left the room after that.

"And I went to the wash basin and soaked my head and upper body with water. I kept trying to clean myself off. And after, I left the washroom area and I was in a much longer inner-office sitting area, with a sofa in it. Andrew Crispo was the only person in that room. He was sitting on the sofa and he was clothed except for his genital area. He was masturbating, and he said, 'Come here.' So I went to where he was, and he gestured with the hand he wasn't masturbating with toward his penis, and he said, 'Go on, do it.'

"I went down on him. I felt that I had to do anything I was told or I would be killed. Almost instantly he came, and I got up and spat it out in the bathroom.

"I spat and spat and rinsed my mouth, and I left the room to look for my stuff, and Andrew came in, pointed at the picture of Roy Cohn that I had noticed earlier. He asked me if I knew who he was. I said yes, that I'd studied Joe McCarthy, you know, and the Hollywood Ten, and that he was well known for defending important people in the Mafia.

"He said, 'That's right.' He said, 'He's a very good friend of mine.' He said, 'We've got a lot of friends in common.' He said that if I ever told anyone about what happened there that his friends would find me. 'The family exists anywhere.' He said it wouldn't matter where I moved. 'The family would reach out and exterminate you if you ever say anything.' "

Karl, the roommate, listened intently, sympathetically, while he put warm compresses on the welts, which cut hatches in Paul's flesh from his shoulders down past his knees. His was an exceedingly thin, athletic body, a runner's physique with pronounced muscular development only on the lower end. His back, unpadded and vulnerable, had sustained the worst damage.

Friends of Karl's had spoken about Crispo before. "A fiend," said one acquaintance who had met him; another called him "a notorious leather queen, and not the good kind, either."

"You just picked up a pay phone, and all this happened?" Karl asked in a high voice. "There was no indication? He sounded normal?"

"Not like this." Jeffries's cerulean eyes were damp, inflamed. "I mean, I expected it was going to be a little rough, you know—a little S&M, a little B&D. But not like this."

CHAPTER

9

Months after leaving the gallery, Ronnie Caran was more concerned about his safety than ever. Through January and February 1985, he continued to spot Bernard LeGeros outside his window occasionally, and he understood there had been inquiries about him at Beulahland, his neighborhood hangout. More than once, he found Bernard sitting in a nearby subway car, having apparently followed him into the station. "I took the train to Thirty-third Street and got off," he told his friend Susan one night. "I stood behind a pole on the platform, behind a pillar, and let two more trains go by. I think I may have ditched him. But instead of using the Astor Place stop, which is closest to my house, I'm starting to go to Fourteenth Street now. Even then, I look down the block in all directions before going down the stairs."

He could not explain why these occurrences continued, now that he had left the gallery.

"Bernard was, you know—he could be affectionate with me, put his head on my shoulder or whatever. But I, on the other hand, believe this completely: He is absolutely, totally capable of pushing me in front of a subway car *if Andrew tells him to do it*! Not on his own, but you've got to see it to believe it, that he's a total product of what Andrew wants.

The point is, I can't figure out why he would want that. I haven't done anything!"

Caran saw Bernard again, a day or two later, and vowed never to leave his apartment without one of two friends, who—having concluded that his fears were well founded—accompanied him virtually everywhere: the video store, the bank, the pay phone (his home telephone was cut off in November, such were his finances).

Caran suspected that his name was now on Crispo's shortlist of possible IRS collaborators. While he didn't clearly understand its exact nature, he knew that the others on that list—Marty Ackerman and Victor Ruggiero—had paid dearly for their alleged treason. He had a real sense of the rank, and the reach, of Crispo's temper.

He knew a little about Crispo's taxes, having learned about it in the weeks before he resigned. And it was Andrew who had explained it. Crispo had taken him to a file cabinet marked ST on the gallery's second floor. "It means, in shorthand, Sold to Thyssen," Andrew had said. He explained how false bills of sale were generated to make it look as if Thyssen owned a large part of the gallery's—and Crispo's—inventory. "But only I knew it was sold to the baron—me and the IRS. Of course, the pictures were really mine." Caran didn't understand how the files worked, or how that affected the IRS. As interested as he was in the matter, he had asked no questions. The more he knew, he figured, the worse shape he'd be in.

At Crispo's bidding, he'd already filled out several affidavits attesting to the gallery's bookkeeping, about which he was utterly unsophisticated. In one of them, involving the suit Crispo had brought against Marty Ackerman, he even went so far as to allege that Ackerman's wife had blown the whistle on them. At the time, he thought there was a possibility that this was the case. But he was also adamant in his belief (for he never, apparently, researched this) that there was no tax fraud going on at the Andrew Crispo Gallery.

So, as a kind of parting challenge, Crispo had given him the key to the scam, and apparently was now convinced Caran was sharing his firsthand knowledge.

Caran, of course, had no way of confirming this. Nor would he have particularly cared, if it weren't for the matter of the money he felt he was due. He had no phone, and his new landlord, like the one before that, was growing tired of missed payments.

He called the gallery from the corner phone booth regularly, demanding the pay, and was told, variously, that it was in the mail, or that it wasn't his to claim, or that it would be available in a few weeks. These messages came from Bernard, who refused his requests to speak directly to Andrew.

By mid-December, Caran had seemed to be making progress. He was instructed to come to the gallery for a partial payment. Bernard made him wait for nearly two hours in the reception area, made him explain why he needed the money, made him (Bernard acknowledged later) "squirm mercilessly." Finally, Bernard walked back to Crispo's Red Room and returned with a four-thousand-dollar corporate check and a dense one-page statement detailing the reason for the payment. Ronnie signed without reading it, and as he was leaving, Bernard said, "Where are you going with that?"

"To the bank!"

"You don't have a signature at that bank anymore."

"How do you even know what bank I'm going to?"

"Doesn't matter. I've got to go and cash it."

"That's ridiculous."

Bernard, who was slightly taller than Caran, moved between him and the door. "I'll take the check and deposit it for you, in your account."

"Bernard, this check is mine. I'll do with it whatever I want to do with it."

"Andrew says this is the way it has to be done," LeGeros said. "The orders are, I cash the check and bring you the money. The orders are that you sign it over to me."

"Fine," said Caran, resigned, "let's go."

"No, you can't leave the gallery."

"*Now* what are you talking about?"

"If I go to the bank with this, nobody will be at the gallery. So if you want this now, you've got to stay here and watch the phones."

As the gallery director, Caran had never had to watch phones. It seemed unbelievable to him that now there was nobody on hand to perform the task, and even more unbelievable that he—a persona non grata—would be left in charge. Where was everybody else?

"You wait here," Bernard said, "and give me twenty minutes." It was 2:30.

At 3:15, the phone rang. Bernard said, "I have to go meet Andrew. He just told me."

"Fine, I'll meet you wherever you are."

"No, no, no, no, no. You wait there. I'll be in touch."

At 5:00, Bernard finally returned. "Andrew's got your money," he announced, "he's going to have it sent to your house tonight."

Of course, the money never was delivered.

The absurd part was that Caran went through the same cagey paces again in January, signing away a large check and acknowledging receipt on one of Crispo's forms. That night, when the call came from Bernard to Caran at the reception desk, he was instructed to exit the gallery, leaving the doors unlocked. "Arthur Smith had to borrow the money," Bernard explained. "Somebody will get back to you."

This had become a strange nightmare that, for some reason, Caran was incapable of escaping. He kept calling right through February, from a phone booth that now was plastered with large pictures of Eigil Dag Vesti, one on each side, proclaiming that the handsome FIT student was MISSING, FOUL PLAY SUSPECTED.

Bernard again invited him up to the gallery, and again left—after a pitched battle—with an endorsed check, this one for fifteen hundred dollars. While Caran waited at the gallery, Crispo called. "I'm taking that money," he announced, "but there's fifteen hundred in my beige jacket, and I think I left it on the red sofa in the Red Room. You look, and I'll hold."

Caran hadn't been inside the Red Room since September, when all the nonpublic spaces were suddenly locked, off limits to him. But the door was wide open, and Caran found no jacket.

"That really bothers me," Crispo said. "I wonder . . . I thought I left it there. Check around, would you? The Green Room or the Brown Room. Maybe it's there. I'll hold."

The entire gallery space was strangely unlocked, and he was apparently alone. He peered into rooms downstairs, but he found no beige jacket.

"I've got to retrace my steps," Crispo said. He was mumbling and breathless. "I can't imagine who might have stolen it. You wait there; I'll make some calls." Fifteen minutes later, he was on the line again. "Everybody says the jacket was there—there in the Red Room. So I have no option but to conclude that you found it, and you took the fifteen hundred. It's in your hands now, so don't come back to me for it again."

Manhattan, of course, is no place to suffer poverty, and Ronnie Caran would have been unfamiliar with such a state virtually anywhere. But what was happening to him was greater than that. His spirit had been crushed by the absolute betrayal he had suffered after a decade of marriagelike reliance on his friend and boss. Then it was dismantled piece by piece and scattered to the wind by the residual threats, taunts, trials, and treachery. This was not mere unemployment; it was a disentanglement, a divorce.

And like other divorces, Caran's experience since leaving the gallery entailed a step-by-step reassessment of his entire relationship with Crispo, and with the gallery. It entailed perhaps too many outings to

Beulahland, past the dulling gray MISSING posters that shivered unnoticed now in the unusually warm winter breeze, perhaps too many vodkas, too many stories told too many times. Through the winter, he did not look for a new job.

On the morning of March 22, 1985, like other mornings, Caran woke late and swung his legs off the edge of his mattress, with no particular agenda for the day. He would make some strong coffee—Bustelo, strained through a paper towel—and shuffle around the small apartment until his pack of Kools was depleted. Then perhaps he'd buy the *New York Daily News* and clip coupons, one of the few hallmarks of poverty he had actually learned to enjoy. "There's no thrill like finding pasta three boxes for a dollar," he told a friend in earnest.

The cellophane wrapper lay flat by noon, and he ran out the door without a jacket. At his first stop, the local East Village bodega, he paid three dollars for two packs. At his second, he dropped thirty cents for the paper and had almost left the newsstand before glancing at the cover. He had expected another front-pager on Bernard Goetz, the "subway vigilante" whose story had fascinated every New Yorker but Caran. Instead, he found a more provocative headline—UN WORKER'S SON HELD IN SEX DEATH—and the promise of details on page five.

He folded the tabloid under his arm and dashed home, past the phone booth, past the pictures of that handsome missing person that had, over the month since they arrived on the horizon, refused to recede into the city's woodwork. Other handbills, those promoting parties and discos and political upheaval, seemed to disappear long before they yellowed, seemed to be buried beneath more visual posters for more pressing concerns before anybody could get used to them. On the side of the door at Caran's local bodega, the accumulation of paper grew so dense that it frequently slid off in chunks, like paper and wheat-paste bark. Perhaps nobody could bring themselves to plaster over the blond boy from Norway; his mysterious fate and perfectly beautiful face, his bare chest and gentle, wide hands had four weeks to sear themselves into the city's conscience.

Back home and warm, Caran recognized Eigil Dag Vesti's picture immediately beneath the inside headline: HELD IN MALE MODEL'S S&M KILLING. It was the same picture used on the poster. His eyes swung to a larger photograph, on the lower-left-hand side of the page. An attorney, dressed in a dark suit, was holding at arm's length an eerie leather hood. There were cutouts for eyes, a blocky patch of leather for a nose, and a wide silver zipper covering the mouth. The attorney cupped it gingerly. A caption read: "Rockland County District Attorney Kenneth Gribetz shows hood worn by victim." Caran studied the picture for a long time before scanning across the page to the final photograph.

It took him a moment to recognize the young man whose hair stood tall in disarray on his head, and who was wearing a crewneck maroon wool sweater with no shirt collar showing. His face was drawn and showed exhaustion. His lips were pressed viselike together, thin and dry. "Oh my God," Caran said slowly, unable to focus on the text. "Oh shit."

"The son of a United Nations employee was arrested yesterday on charges of murdering a Norwegian modeling student in a 'sado-masochistic sex rite,' " the story began. "A second suspect was being sought in the slaying of Eigil Vesti, 26, a student at the Fashion Institute of Technology. Vesti's body was found by hikers in Rockland County last Sunday—naked except for a leather 'bondage hood.'

"Bernard John LeGeros, 22, of 10 Waterside Plaza, Manhattan, was arrested after contacting police several times 'to give clues and hints as to who he suspected was the individual who committed the crime,' said Rockland County DA Kenneth Gribetz. 'We soon determined he was not the informant, but the murderer.' Gribetz said that about a month ago, Vesti, LeGeros and an unidentified male went to a two-and-a-half acre estate owned by LeGeros's parents 'for the purpose of engaging in sado-masochistic sexual activity.' "

Caran grabbed his coat and headed for the pay phone on the corner, where he called his attorney and demanded an emergency appointment. "I'm leaving the country," he said. "You're the only one that knows."

The following day, March 23, 1985, a plane carried Ronnie Caran toward England, where, according to friends, he was given sanctuary by Baron Heini Thyssen-Bornemisza in a guarded London town house.

Andrew Crispo at an art opening in 1977, a year before his Andrew Crispo
Gallery lured the world's biggest collector, Baron von Thyssen-Bornemisza.
(CHRISTOPHER MAKOS)

By 1985, Crispo preferred using pay phones, assuming his personal lines were tapped. (*New York Daily News*)

Crispo during a court appearance, September 24, 1985. (*New York Post*)

Eigil Vesti and friend at a party at the Limelight, May 13, 1984, nine months before his death. (PATRICK MCMULLAN)

Vesti kept a modeling portfolio, though he aspired to be a fashion designer; the picture on the right was used on the missing person poster.

Bernard LeGeros briefly considered a modeling career before becoming Crispo's gallery assistant, "bodyguard," and "executioner."

The Stony Point police arrested LeGeros in the Vesti murder on March 24, 1985. (AP/WIDE WORLD PHOTOS)

At his trial, September, 1985. (AP/WIDE WORLD PHOTOS)

The entrance of Crispo's Greenwich Village apartment building.

The LeGeros family home, nicknamed Buckberg, which overlooks the Hudson River from Tomkins Cove, Rockland County.

The entrance to the Hellfire Club, just a few blocks from Crispo's penthouse.

Inside the Hellfire Club.
(ROCKLAND COUNTY BUREAU OF CRIMINAL IDENTIFICATION)

The Revolutionary War-era smokehouse behind the LeGeros family home, as it was on the day Eigil Vesti's body was found; his remains are barely visible. (ROCKLAND COUNTY BUREAU OF CRIMINAL IDENTIFICATION)

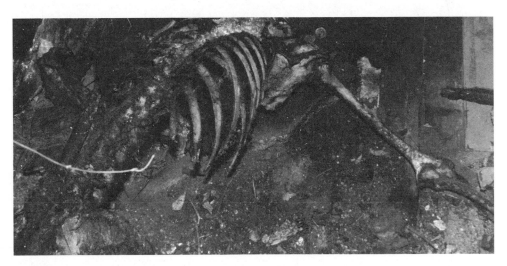

Vesti's body had been burned twice and devoured by wild animals inside the smokehouse. (ROCKLAND COUNTY BUREAU OF CRIMINAL IDENTIFICATION)

Kenneth Gribetz, the Rockland County District Attorney, holds the hood found on the body. (*New York Post*)

PART
IV

Murderous Passions

Should the young man yield? To whom? In what conditions and with what guarantees? And can the individual who loves him justifiably hope to see him yield easily?

—MICHEL FOUCAULT,
The History of Sexuality, Volume II

CHAPTER
10

On March 17, 1985, Det. Sgt. Billy Franks bounced onto the front seat of his blue Chrysler, which was parked on the shoulder of Buckberg Mountain Road. Though young and fit, he was not a limber or slender man, and he moved his towering body around in unjointed sweeps, bending his legs under himself only after he had landed on his rump. He radioed for backup. First, there was the chatter that small-town cops don't edit out of their broadcasts, then the update: The medical examiner was on his way. "I hope he's got a strong stomach," Sergeant Franks said. More chatter, and he shared his excitement: "This is certainly going to be interesting."

Withdrawing himself from the unmarked car, the police officer took a moment, his first that day, to appreciate his surroundings before returning to the body. He was standing next to a New York State historical landmark on the roadside, proclaiming this nub of the Ramapo Mountains, this apogee of the Hudson Valley, to have been the staging ground for George Washington's successful Battle of Stony Point—the general, bunking at the old Eyrie Hotel, had rallied troops for the first key victory of the revolution. "Standing here," said the peeling cast-iron letters, "Generals Washington and Wayne surveyed the British Fort at Stony Point and planned the victory of July 15–16, 1779."

From the signpost on Buckberg Mountain Road, a well-tended lawn rose up slightly before beginning a westerly plunge toward the Hudson River. A small white guest house stood between Franks and the overgrown remains of the Eyrie Hotel: three pillars, a crumbling stone wall, and a small, brimming cave—a stone smokehouse where the Eyrie cooks had prepared their meals. One hundred forty-eight feet to the north stood the old Potter house, built (along with the guest house) by Mr. Potter himself in the 1920s. Two stories, white clapboard, country Colonial with a green slate roof, the main home sat on the crest of the highest knoll in this part of the county. Low walls made of mossy stones marked the driveway.

One hundred Buckberg Mountain Road was an imposing old house. A rocky path from the driveway twisted past the red front door (which was really on the side of the house) and around to the back, where a bay window looked down onto a clay tennis court cut into the side of the slope and surveyed the woods, the Hudson, and the rest. Soon, the dogwood trees would flower and a steady breeze would send down dime-sized locust blossoms to blanket the tailored gardens outside the front door like sea foam. But for now, there was an earthy New England smell: wet leaves, mold, stones, worms. The Potter lawn lay flat, each whip of grass matted to the next. Where the clearing met the trees, brown patches of snow remained unvanquished by the sun.

Sgt. Billy Franks balanced a pair of aviator shades on his nose. It was the kind of day, and the kind of place, that had convinced him he'd never again leave Rockland County—his home since birth, thirty-three years ago. He strayed once, a dozen years before, to take an apartment in Queens and a job in a loud nightclub on the Upper East Side of Manhattan, where he was the bouncer. As a brief experience, he had treasured it: the late nights, the post-sixties wantonness. Drugs were passed around like currency; sex was invited with a glance. It was not a way of life that could be sustained, though. And Franks never touched the drugs. He took the job with the Stony Point police force, and married Margaret when he returned.

Pausing on the hilltop, he lit up a Vantage and, if his thoughts meandered for a moment, he must have thought about fishing—he was always thinking about fishing. Winter was mild, could the spring run be near? Could he slip his boat into the river soon? He may have scanned the water for recreational craft, a reflex, but only freighters were moving that day—toward the Saint Lawrence Seaway, toward Erie, Detroit, Chicago, or the other way to the Atlantic. Just an hour earlier, the sergeant had been at a friend's house, where his own boat was parked for the winter. The two were working on the hull when Margaret, a schoolteacher, called with the message: The station had summoned him; there had been another bone sighting.

"Shit," he had said impatiently. "More kids and more bones. Just how I wanted to spend my friggin' Sunday."

Rockland was full of skittish newcomers who couldn't tell the difference between a deer carcass and a chicken—all of which they took, out of fear or hapless adventurism, for gangland slaying victims. In recent years, such calls had been coming more often, in inverse proportion (the sergeant said once) to the diminishing population in New York City. Reluctantly, Billy Franks laid down his tools, swung past the station to grab an official vehicle, and arrived on Buckberg Mountain Road with an insular grudge. It was, after all, St. Patrick's Day, a marginal holiday. But more to the point, it was his day off, and such times were reserved for the boat, religiously. He was already counting days to his retirement (just under three thousand remained), at which point he planned to fish full-time, instructing and entering small competitions for the prize money. "A person could make a fine living, fishing," he had told his wife, especially with a twenty-year police pension underpinning his income. A delicately featured woman with simple brown eyes and a twenty-inch waist, Margaret Franks may have accepted this plan, though she appeared a little less thrilled than her husband, especially as she entertained no similar desires to leave her post at North Rockland High School. She taught computer science there—it put her in contact with children, and Billy had repeatedly said he didn't want to have any of his own. They'd get in the way of his fishing.

So perhaps there was resentment scattered among Frank's thoughts as the winter sun grew dim, but there was ample anticipation, too. Plenty of crime reports had crossed his steel desk as head of the township's small detective squad, but few had been very challenging. And even a cop who dreams of a charmed riverboat life feels a professional surge from time to time.

"This is going to be *real* interesting," he said, this time to himself, tossing his Vantage and sucking his long mustache into his mouth before lumbering across the lawn, which now belonged to the LeGeros family. He passed the guest house and descended the embankment, around the corner of the clay tennis court that now was not vital enough to keep weeds from pushing up (a small roller sat in center court, completely encased in rust). Where the court met the woods, a twenty-foot chainlink fence held the line immutable. Franks bowed his head and lowered himself down the footpath that led, in just ten strides of a tall man, to the two-hundred-year-old stone smokehouse and the uniformed officer stationed there.

"You didn't look, did you?" Franks asked Officer Patrick Brophy. "Didn't touch anything, right?" Billy Franks stuffed his shades back in a pocket, revealing green eyes surrounded by radiating lines—not wrinkles, but tan lines showing where wrinkles would eventually dig in. They gave his face a look of constant tenderness. A tuck of flesh at the far corners of his eyes stretched smooth when he smiled. Mustache whiskers curled over thick lips, masking an expressive mouth that, except when sucking on facial hair or cigarette filters, was always open.

"Nope, Sarge," said Brophy, playfully intoning the title. Franks led his squad with a jocund demeanor that won their respect and friendship. He didn't even get on people's nerves when, as it frequently did, his voice took on a tutorial edge. Franks, not the oldest member of the force, was the tallest (six two) and the most decorated. In 1983, he had been selected to study at the FBI's behavioral sciences laboratory in Quantico, Virginia. During three months there, he practiced investigative techniques, studied the criminal mind, and learned a lot more about sexual perversion than his wife would let him mention socially. His subordinates, unarguably more appreciative, hung on every word.

"Lesson one in detective work: Never let your curiosity get out of hand," Franks would say. "Gotta show some restraint, chief." (Everybody was "chief," or "boss," or "buddy.")

As Brophy watched, Franks leaned toward the smokehouse opening and sniffed—he had smelled worse. Mostly, it smelled of charred wood, charred leaves, charred flesh. A fire had left little of the corpse untouched: Some tendons at the shoulder and little shocks of red meat sporadically gripping bone could be seen from under the green screen door. Earlier, when Franks first got down on his knees to peer under the door, he had spotted the masked head and some evidence of remaining flesh there. But he had left it at that. "The facts will come by themselves, in time," he said again.

Shortly, the hillside below the tennis court was congested with inspectors, detectives, officers, and medical examiners from the township, the county, and the state. Tomkins Cove, like most tiny hamlets near Stony Point, had no police force of its own, so Franks's team often found itself spread thin. On homicide cases—and this seemed like one of those right from the start—the Stony Point department regularly called upon the sheriff's men and the state troopers. Nine cops raced the darkness. Some combed the area for weapons (they found none), climbing down into the old foundation and sifting through the well with flashlights. Others put soil samples in small tan envelopes; one detective lifted a single brown sock, discovered just a few feet down the path, and folded it into a Baggie.

Another spotted a scorched leather cowboy boot ("apparently brown suede"), lifted it gingerly, and noticed with repulsion that it still contained a foot. The other boot, frayed and reduced to a collection of flapping talons, persevered firmly on the end of the corpse's remaining leg.

Edward Starkey, from Rockland County's Bureau of Criminal Identification, took pictures of the green door and the bones that buckled underneath it. He chose three different angles, including a close-up of the victim's femur. Billy Franks gave the okay, and the door was removed. Light reflected off something—a filling?—in the region of the skeleton's mouth. More pictures. Another okay, this one from Chief Medical Examiner Frederick Zugibe, and Franks and his men pulled on rubber gloves and dragged the stiff tangle of bones out of the cave. They placed it faceup on a sheet of white plastic, rigid as a tree trunk. It was disgusting.

The black hood was bondage-style. It had shifted back on the victim's head so that instead of starting its encasement well below the chin, it grabbed under the nose and sheathed everything above that, clear around to the back of the neck. It had been laced up so tightly that the leather straps and the metal grommets through which they were yanked made deep cuts beneath the hair. Above the exposed teeth (white and meticulously formed), a grotesque zipper created a solid ridge of aluminum teeth that curled upward in a smirk on the right side, where the oversized tab had been yanked open, and parked.

A triangular nose patch floated above that, held firm (and made more menacing) by a thick frame of double-stitched seams. Because of the jockeyed positioning, the eye cutouts revealed only forehead and a protruding wisp of blond hair. The victim's eyes were covered, preserved enough for the ME's office to conclude later that they had been blue, Mediterranean blue, although they had turned a milky haze in the flames.

So compelling was the image that it took a long while for Zugibe, the medical examiner with fifteen thousand autopsies under his belt, to glance downward and study the surviving bones, particularly toward the ends of the crumpled arms. The right hand was simply gone—by all appearances, burned off by the flames that had engulfed these remains. The other one, frozen in a loose fist, carried the only other bodily adornment: a very thin gold wedding band.

Zugibe took notes. "A mild surface carbonization was present over much of the skeleton with much of the distal tibia and fibula burned off. The left hand was badly burned and shriveled. The right hand and distal aspects of the ulnus and radius were missing, having been burned up to this point." He noted that "light-color hair" pushed out through the back of the mask, besides the strands that were apparent through the eye holes. "This is a skeletonized body, almost completely devoid of flesh from the maxillary area to the feet." Or at least the foot. The only exception, he wrote, was a long strip of "dehydrated, leatherized" skin on the left forearm—and both areas showed evidence that small animals had nibbled away at the fringe.

The cause of death was not yet apparent.

"Hi!" A shout came down from the guest house to the swarm of officials poking through the woods. "What're you doing there?" Franks dispatched an officer to talk to the glassy-eyed young man, who was waving both arms at the crime site. This was David LeGeros, twenty-one, who had the yapping nervous energy, and the bulk, of a St. Bernard. Round-chested and round-faced, there was nothing particularly striking about David except for his intense gaze and breathy, direct voice. The fact that he was half Filipino would have been more readily evident had he not cropped his shiny black hair right down to his skull, giving his entire head a singular and sallow complexion.

After an afternoon visit with his uncle and cousin in nearby Tappan, David had returned to "Buckberg" intending to hammer dents out of the Vista Cruiser's fenders. He spent the morning scouting a wooded section of Westchester in preparation for an "Orienteering Convention" the ROTC was sponsoring, and David (a lieutenant) was in charge of hanging numbered tags on trees for the recruits to ferret out. He still wore his camouflage uniform.

A uniformed officer made it up the muddy hill, puffing. "Who are you?"

"David LeGeros," the young man answered. "What's up?"

"Get out of here, Mr. LeGeros," came the response, directly, and the cop made a grand swooping motion with his arm.

"Well, this is my house. We live here." His voice showed fright, not indignation.

Minutes later, he was on the telephone with his uncle, whispering, "That's when he told me to come into the house, and to stay here, I don't know why. And then he said, 'We found a body, a body down here.'" Uncle Andy was asking for details, but David interrupted, panicked. "And just a minute ago, they carried a body bag up the hill and took it away!"

Racquel LeGeros needed to retrieve a suitcase and some summer clothes for a trip she had scheduled for the following Wednesday. John, her husband, had planned to drive her from the city to Buckberg to help pack. So when David called and told John—again in a whisper—that the police would like to have a word regarding a body found on their property, they were not inconvenienced. They would meet up later that night, at the country house. Any other day, it might have proved impossible. John spent most of his time under buzzing fluorescent lights in his office at the United Nations headquarters. Racquel, now a noted biophysicist at NYU, spent time in France, Japan, or London giving papers at scientific meetings at least several times a year.

That was why she needed the suitcase. At an upcoming meeting of dental researchers in Las Vegas, she was to deliver six papers and lead a panel on "Hydrolysis of Octacalcium Phosphate to Apatite." She hoped to load her things in the car and hurry back to their two-bedroom apartment on the ninth floor of 10 Waterside Plaza, where she planned to reread the papers she was expected to deliver. Presentations always made her nervous, less about standing up before her colleagues and addressing some of the top minds in her field—artificial bone production and its application in dentistry—than about having them read her written work. Dr. Racquel LeGeros worried obsessively about her English grammar, and found herself showing her papers to half a dozen laypeople (her sons David and Bernard included) before having them photocopied for her peers to review. John called her Kelly. It seemed to fit her softer side.

During their hour drive over the George Washington Bridge, along the Palisades Parkway that passed briefly through a corner of New Jersey and into Rockland County, up the steep inclines of Buckberg Mountain Road, and past a little chapel where they had once been parishioners, Racquel and John did not speak about the body that had been found on their property. Racquel, in fact, was still in the dark about it. When David told his father, he had suggested not telling her. John, perhaps miscalculating, agreed.

As they approached the narrow driveway to their weekend home, their headlights found two officers, sitting in a squad car on the edge of the property. Racquel got excited. "What on earth?"

John, pulling in the driveway, explained briefly. "Now, Kelly. There was a body found, this is what Davie says, in the smokehouse. Probably a hunting accident. Don't worry about it."

She found it an odd request—not to worry about a dead man on her property—but rushed into the house for her things, nonetheless. Inside, David explained more.

John walked up to the squad car, and was promptly whisked off to the station house 3.1 miles away, where Det. Sgt. Billy Franks took down some information. John had most recently walked around his property the previous Sunday, March 10, and when he passed the smokehouse, he saw a "green door inside same, and recalls that the far end of the door was raised up but he did not see any body." Police Officer Brophy then escorted John back to Buckberg, and checked the house for any signs of a break-in, "with negative results."

As Brophy was leaving the house, John called after him. "You know," he began, "it doesn't make any sense for you to have to sit in the car outside. Here, take this set of keys. You can use the house as Command Central for your investigation!" It was a coy suggestion—John LeGeros, indeed, was excited about being so close to a police investigation, in the thick of things, and this would ensure a direct flow of information. Besides, he felt it his patriotic duty to help out where he could. He held out the keys, occasionally jerking them forward and swaying back on his heels so rapidly that it seemed as if he needed to use a bathroom, until Brophy relented, and pocketed them. Pleased, John then pressed his palms against his upper thighs, and put on the face of a satisfied youngster, which did not suit the rest of his appearance: white hair worn in a crew cut, powdery sacks of flesh beneath bushy eyebrows, pants hiked up and cinched above a slightly round stomach.

Within a week, he would wish this investigation had never touched him. His wife felt it immediately. In the car on the way back to the city, she found herself unable to concentrate on her work, and by the time she and her husband and David were home, she was obsessing. David, too, grew excited again. "Look, Mom. This must be the guy!" He held out a story from that day's *New York Daily News* about a blond-haired man of twenty-six from Norway who had disappeared weeks earlier in the city. The story mentioned the concern of his friends, who had conducted a citywide poster campaign. "I bet that's it!"

Racquel pulled up a pair of tinted square-lensed reading glasses that swung on a lace around her neck. She studied the picture. "He is from so far away," she said, chirpy traces of Tagalog syntax showing through. "He died so far away, and he was young, and . . ." She placed the newspaper in her lap and offered up a brief, teary prayer.

Partway across town, Dallas Boesendahl was in his large two-room apartment on East Fifty-eighth Street, working at a desk. Well, sitting at a desk. He hadn't truly accomplished anything since February 22, three weeks earlier, three weeks in which the idea of hyping one of his parties—Dallas was a private-party thrower for the city's leading clubs of the moment—seemed completely inappropriate. Most of those days passed very slowly, with his slightly textured face wrapped in his gentle hands.

Nights, he walked the streets till two or three, pasting posters of Eigil Dag Vesti on phone booths and lampposts all over Manhattan. MISSING! they declared in two-inch letters above a black and white portrait of a striking young man, his hair windswept, his chest shirtless beneath a denim jacket. Under that, in serif italics: "Foul Play Suspected. Norwegian F.I.T. Student Last Seen Friday, February 22, Midnight, in Chelsea/West Village Area." To the right of the picture, a caption listed statistical details—Eyes: Blue. Hair: Blond. Height: 5'11". Weight: 135. Age: 26.

Through the efforts of Dallas Boesendahl and a small cadre of friends—and aided in no small way by the dramatic juxtaposition of those frightening words and Eigil Vesti's purely handsome face—small gatherings throughout the city felt caught up in the fate of this young man. At certain cocktail parties, health clubs, and offices, the unusual name had become nearly as familiar as Bernie Goetz, the subway vigilante. Even the newspapers had begun to take notice of this chilling street theater, and Dallas had encouraged the *New York Daily News* to write the small story (and run that picture) in its St. Patrick's Day edition. The article, neatly clipped, sat on his desk as the phone rang.

It was Sgt. Marcia Stanton, the Missing Persons official whom Dallas had been calling daily, and prodding ceaselessly, since the Saturday morning he reported his friend's mysterious disappearance. She had been pretty upset about the posters. In those first few days, while he was convinced that something had gone very, very wrong, she took a wait-and-see attitude. He had last been seen on Friday, she reasoned, and might reappear in a few days. By Monday, the posters were back from the printer and already dotting the city. She had been second-guessed, and overtly pressured.

That wasn't their only source of tension. From the start, there seemed to be an endless loop of misunderstanding on the officer's part. Dallas described Eigil Vesti as his "intimate," an effete term that she apparently took to mean lover—but they were close friends who dined together several times a week, that was all. Dallas explained that Eigil liked to smoke an occasional joint, causing Sergeant Stanton to suspect a drug problem ("It could be just a long, lost weekend," she suggested to Dallas. "Give him time to resurface"). But perhaps the most bristling misinterpretation came over Dallas's recounting of Friday, February 22, 1985, the last time he had seen his friend.

There had been a small dinner party at Rick's Lounge, a popular Tex-Mex restaurant in Chelsea. Eigil joined the gathering at the last minute, after spending an afternoon at the Metropolitan Museum, and introduced himself for the first time to Dallas's friends. He only nibbled: sesame chicken fingers, guacamole, nachos. The meal was not all polite, Dallas had explained. Two of the guests, who were cousins, exchanged words and a drink was thrown. Things calmed down quickly, but the scene seemed to deflate Eigil's mood, which was already flagging.

As Dallas and Eigil parted, just after midnight, Eigil had suggested they have another nightcap. "He asked me two or three times," Dallas said. "Normally, I would have said sure, but I was so tired. We took a cab past his apartment, and I dropped him there. And nobody's seen him since."

Sgt. Marcia Stanton took it down in her notebook, and asked who else had attended the dinner. But Dallas didn't want to give the names. "They didn't even know him," he insisted. "They shouldn't be bothered." But he relented, and named Maria Burton (daughter to Elizabeth Taylor and Richard Burton), her husband Steve Carson (the talent agent), clothing designer Roger Forsythe, Ty Smith (a young model), and Jonathan Moor, from *Sportswear International.* They went into Stanton's book as people to question—just what Dallas had hoped to spare them. These were the kinds of people for whom police questioning was a grave and unnerving experience.

Yet somehow the entire dinner party had wound up on a police list alongside suspects; Dallas Boesendahl later opened a phone bill and found a note explaining that his conversations had been tapped, by court order, for several months.

If these false starts spoiled his relationship with the Missing Persons squad, the fact that they had turned up no real leads in three weeks made matters worse. Dallas and Eigil Vesti's two sisters had hired their own detective, Mort Sussman, to beat the bushes. But that, too, was unrewarding. Sussman seemed to want to follow only gay angles, as if homosexuality alone was a motive in his disappearance. Every time he learned of another gay bar Eigil had visited, it went into his notebook; each bar was described in minute detail. What Sussman had compiled after several weeks' work was something Dallas Boesendahl could have written from memory.

Sergeant Stanton's call was greeted icily. "What!" snapped Dallas.

"I need to know if your friend wore a wedding band," she said.

Dallas replied softly. "Yes, a small gold one. I think it was his grandfather's."

"Was anything engraved inside?"

"Some letters. But they were on the outside, in a repeating pattern around the circumference."

"Fine. I'll call you back in a few minutes," she said, and at about nine that evening, she informed him that Eigil Dag Vesti's body apparently had been found, in Rockland County.

CHAPTER
11

March 18, 1985. For a Monday morning, it was unusually hectic at the police station in Stony Point, a boxy sixty-by-sixty-foot redbrick edifice with one floor and few windows. Already by 8:30, a second team of officers had returned to the LeGeros home to conduct another sweep of the wooded hillside; the Rockland County Bureau of Criminal Identification (called RCBCI) had flown a photographer over the crime site in a helicopter, recording all possible access routes to the smokehouse; seven uniform police were out canvassing the area for eyewitnesses, suspects, and leads. Their flurry of telephone calls and radio transmissions back to the station's communications center lent exigency to the bluster.

In the station's lunch room, which doubled as the "interview" room (a polite reference to the place reserved for interrogations), Sgt. Billy Franks sat over a crumpled pack of Vantages, facing Stony Point's other detectives. Lt. Frank Tinelli, Franks's immediate superior, and Stephen Scurti, the chief of police, were there, too. Their purpose was to "brainstorm" the developing case.

There was good news, and bad, Franks began. First, the corpse would "probably" be identified in the coming hours as Eigil Dag Vesti, based on the ring that was found on the skeleton's bony finger. "There's a sister, and she's coming up here to make a positive ID," he said. This was an unusually quick turnaround, given the fact that the medical examiner had already put the time of death at some three weeks before, in late February. But they had been extremely lucky. When the leather hood was removed, the ME was astonished to find the entire upper portion of the victim's head fully intact, preserved from the elements and shielded from the fire.

Where the hood ended, below the nose, the flesh ended, too. A ridge of meat dropped down to the cheekbones and exposed teeth. It created a hideous special-effects spectacle: What remained of Eigil Vesti's face seemed like a latex hood itself, affixed to a dirty biology-class skeleton. Even the two small bullet holes—one in the back of the head, the other in the neck—had failed to cause disfiguring exit wounds on the other side.

"We lucked out," Franks said.

There was more good news. The Vesti family's private detective had been able to piece together some facts about his last day. "There was a dinner party with Maria Burton," said the usually unimpressible Franks, "daughter of Richard Burton. This was on February twenty-second. Then the deceased went to her apartment for a cognac, and shared a cab home with a friend"—he shuffled through papers for the name of Dallas Boesendahl; the names so far involved in this case were all entirely too uncommon, he thought—"who dropped him at his apartment, a loft building in Chelsea he shared with"—another strange name—"one Steve AuCoin. At that time, apparently, Eigil Vesti had asked Boesendahl to accompany him for one more drink, but the friend refused."

That led to the bad news. "If this turns out to be our guy, this investigation is widening to include the city. Means *a lot* of hours."

The detectives threw around various game-plan proposals. To Lieutenant Tinelli, it seemed clear the killer had some familiarity with the area behind Buckberg Mountain Road, so remotely located was the smokehouse. He suggested seeking out suspects with homes in the city and in Rockland. Scurti, the chief, wondered whether they were searching for cult-type connections in the case, and Franks said that wasn't ruled out. "We're still trying to get the skinny on the mask, Chief. It seems something strange was behind this."

As they spoke, Anne-Margrethe Vesti stood in a conference room at the Rockland County morgue, several miles away, facing a television monitor. Police officers, sheriffs, coroners, and prosecutors had been addressing her—about the cleaned bones, about the black hood, about the camera in the other room trained on the part of her little brother's face that had been preserved, about being braced for the worst. They were not certain how well she understood the language, which she did very well. She just wanted this over, wanted the smooth forehead she was about to see to belong to anyone but Eigil. She was grateful they had arranged it so that she didn't have to stand in the same room as the corpse.

The screen brightened with a frozen image: cheek, eye, hair. A white sheet had been pulled up to his upper lip, leaving exposed only part of his waxen face. A plum-colored lividity blemish mottled his left temple; the hair was mussed and strawlike. One eyelid lifted into a groggy dusty blue peep.

Anne-Margrethe said nothing for a long, long time, then reached in her bag for the dental records she had brought with her from Oslo two weeks earlier. "This will confirm it," she said in methodical, accented English. Anne-Margrethe's hair and eyes were somewhat darker than her brother's, and her body was a bit more full. But when she set her jaw determinedly, as she did that moment, she was unmistakable kin: unapologetic, unpretentious, untouchably pretty. Climbing into the car Dallas Boesendahl had rented for the trip, she wept stealthily.

It grew dark on the brief drive toward the Stony Point police station house, and as each ray of lowering sun brushed her face, Anne-Margrethe seemed to change. Her skin was taking on a new, angry pallor just as colorless and just as permanent as her brother's.

The news reached the station before her, in a call from Frederick Zugibe, the medical examiner. Det. Sgt. Billy Franks had only a few moments to prepare for the interview.

Her statement was brief and, it seemed, steely. While her brother had accepted his homosexuality many years ago, she said, she was convinced the hood had nothing to do with his proclivities. She saw it as a kidnapper's device more than a sexual one. "That's interesting," Franks said, chain-smoking with one hand and stroking his ragged mustache with the other.

Franks, who considered himself "not easily impressed, and hardly ever shocked," had not known any homosexuals personally, although the concept didn't raise in him any of the macho rage that other Rockland County–bred men let fly from time to time. This was 1985, and particularly in the greater New York metropolitan area, it was difficult to avoid the growing enlightenment around the issue—movies such as *Making Love* and news footage on Manhattan's annual Gay Pride March had seen to that.

Still, homosexuality was considered "funny"—as in "odd," and as in "humorous"—and Billy Franks would laugh along with his colleagues when they ribbed fellow cop Dougie Coles-Hatchard for smoking "faggot cigarettes," Salem Ultra Lights. And why not? For all the positive gay images in the media, there were even more hostile ones. Plus, there was this "funny" gay disease going around, first called Gay-Related Immune Deficiency, GRID, the gay plague, now known as AIDS. It killed Haitians, too, and junkies, but according to well-known scientific evidence, it preferred homosexuals with 1,100 sexual partners, the magic number.

A homosexual victim. It raised more questions than it answered. Because the body was found unclothed, except for the hood and charred boots, it seemed to Franks that sex, at some point, had entered into the killing scenario. He repeated this thought later that evening to the detectives and RCBCI officials, gathered once more to brainstorm. "I think we're looking for someone with these three characteristics," he offered. "He's familiar with New York City. He may live in Rockland. And he may be gay."

One officer asked whether they were going to have to inquire as to whether or not their subjects were "fags."

Franks smiled. "Just try to figure it out yourself—you know, look for clues." All laughed. Then, checking himself, Franks added, "Hell! We ask heterosexuals whether or not they've had relations with people, don't we? Like, 'You haven't been stepping out on your wife, have you?' Stuff like that's okay; why not for gays?"

Still, the idea seemed hysterical to the others. Sure, more than one of them must have thought, and they'll punch us right in the nose.

It got more complicated still. In a final conversation with Sergeant Stanton of the Missing Persons division in the city, Franks learned something about Eigil Vesti that his sisters hadn't known. In his leads book, he wrote the following: "Sgt. Stanton advised EIGIL DAG VESTI, W/M, DOB: 12/21/58 . . . is a homosexual who frequented homosexual and S&M clubs on the Lower West Side of Manhattan."

Eigil Vesti, the only son of a Norwegian ship's captain, developed two finite goals during his childhood in a big house on a quiet street in Oslo. One: Find a career in the fashion industry. Two: Live in New York City. Both fit in nicely with the other truth about the teenage Eigil Vesti—his early recognition and warm embrace of his sexual yearnings, which were toward other men. Anne-Margrethe, his eldest sister, was alone in the family in her unconditional support. A liberal herself, she was a reporter for one of Norway's leading liberal publications and had said to her brother those words many sisters have spoken: "As long as you're happy." That's not to say that Tone Vesti Wilse, Eigil's married sister and the middle child in this tightly knit family, was anguished by her brother's declaration, but neither was she thrilled; the parents, both in their late seventies, were kept in the dark. Eigil had broken the news selectively in 1975, almost immediately upon returning from a year as an exchange student in a Kalamazoo, Michigan, high school. He was seventeen, and the assumption (though it was probably never discussed) was that he had experienced certain liaisons there that had opened his eyes to amorous tendencies.

The Fashion Institute of Technology, a small and prestigious state-financed college tucked into the quiet side streets of Chelsea, on Manhattan's West Side, became the logical fulcrum for Eigil Vesti's dreams. On top of the fact that the school was widely respected in the fashion field, it had a reputation of being quite gay—just 20 percent of the student body was male and, by most estimates, an even smaller percentage of that group was heterosexual. "Fashion schools have that reputation," one admissions officer said candidly, "and that reputation, in our case, is not unfounded." So openly acknowledged was this fact that, when a group of senior girls planned a "Men of FIT" pinup calendar to raise funds for a student group—which was to include thoughts from the men on their ideal woman—a faculty adviser quipped, "Golly, I don't think we have twelve straight men on campus! Maybe you'd do better with a bake sale."

In 1981, after Eigil's first application was rejected—a poor showing on the English exam at root—his father helped arrange a job aboard Oslo's *Sagafjord*, a "five star–plus" luxury liner. He was appointed sales clerk in the ship's boutiques, where he practiced his English and cultivated a mesmerizing Continental charm.

And he put both to work for him during a particular transatlantic cruise. A middle-aged passenger, well known in Californian menswear-industry circles, took a shine to the exceptionally beautiful shiphand, and when they docked on the Florida coast, he gave a call to his friend Jack Hyde at FIT. "He's a very smart, very nice-looking Norwegian. I think you should talk to him," the passenger said. "It would be nice if you did." Hyde obliged—this was nothing unusual—and, impressed, endorsed the young man's bid for admission. What Eigil's native intelligence hadn't been able to pull off, his physical prowess had. He matriculated in February 1982, in mid-semester, and for three years he scored exceptionally average marks.

Jack Hyde, the fussy, fiftyish head of FIT's Menswear Design and Marketing division, described the young man this way: "I would call him a thirty-eight regular, which would mean about five ten and a half. But he was thin; he was very thin. And he had very fine features, and that means, well, he was a very nice-looking fellow who was Scandinavian." It was those Scandinavian features that made Eigil Vesti unforgettably handsome. A very slight surplus of pale flesh wrinkled under his eyes, which could appear nearly a royal blue, depending on the outfit. His lashes were long and feminine. His mouth was slender, and full of expression; he smiled almost perpetually, except when posing for a snapshot, when he preferred a somber, reflective, affected pose. All this under a crop of white-blond hair, bowing graciously over his forehead. When he read or watched television, his right hand grabbed the locks and stroked them toward the sky, slowly, absentmindedly, his elbow raised over his head.

Eigil Vesti stripped down to his undershorts was not quite the same as Eigil Vesti fully clothed. In the former state, he looked no more exotic than anybody else who might go unnoticed in a campus crowd. Skinny, not lithe, his shoulders rolled forward, exaggerating the unremarkable qualities of his chest and the pronounced dimple in its center. His arms and legs were hairless and untapered, and his hands, though broad and veiny, were prone to turning pink around the knuckles and cuticles in all sorts of weather. A percussive symphony could be tapped out on the many places where Eigil's bones strained against the surface: sternum and ribs and clavicle and scapula and coccyx and all thirty-three verte-brae, easily enumerated. Clothing did more than compensate; it trans-formed this gaunt physique altogether. Whether in loose-fitting jeans slung casually low on his hips or tight leather trousers, Eigil's stringy lower body billowed out with a sensual gust of strength. Shirts righted his shoulders and a spring jacket lent his torso an elliptical fullness. Always, he wore cowboy boots, jutting out his buttocks, squaring his back, rounding out a presentation that had many of his inexperienced classmates at FIT believing, falsely, that he was a forty long.

Dressing, which Eigil did studiously, had another, equally important effect: It gave him that "cultivated attitude," as one professor said, that's considered a requisite building block to fashion-industry potential. "Right or wrong," the professor said, "our kids learn that the individual is as much a fashion statement as the accessories." (Among themselves, gay FIT students joke that the school's acronym might better be spelled out as "Faggots in Training," for that very reason.) This is a particular truism in marketing and retailing, which was Eigil's major.

"He was the talk of the school," Elise Browning, his best friend there, told a reporter. "He was just so striking-looking, everybody was talking about him." And studying him. "He was always miles ahead of every trend," said another friend. "Fashionwise, he was absolutely princely." Dallas Boesendahl put it this way: "When he walked into a room, the sterling clattered, the drapes shook."

There is somewhat less agreement on the young man's character, and definitive description was hindered by his problems with the language.

He was loving but unquestioning; thoughtful but slow in conversation; worldly and polished and naïve, too; "pleasant," yet on the far side of vapid.

Jack Hyde summed it up: "He frequently dropped by my office, as all students do, to ask for an explanation of something, what have you. And after a question or two, he never had very much to say. 'Hi, Eigil, how are you?' And he'd say, 'Fine.' 'How's everything going?' 'Fine.' That was his word; he said 'Fine' *all* the time. And then he'd just sit there, smiling! It got to the point where I told my student aide that if Eigil came in, to give us about five minutes and then call me and tell me the dean wanted to see me or something. Because it was embarrassing! He would sit there with a nice smile, very congenial, but there was no way to have a conversation with him!"

By late afternoon on the eighteenth, Monday's edition of *The Journal-News* was scattered across lawns throughout Rockland with a B-1 story headlined SKELETON FOUND BY HIKERS AT BUCKBERG. The small article began:

> The skeleton of a white man, whose death was labeled suspicious, was discovered Sunday afternoon by a group of hikers in the woods near the top of Buckberg Mountain in Tomkins Cove.
>
> Stony Point police said the remains were discovered at about 3:30 P.M., but would provide no other details about whether it was clothed or whether any weapons or other physical evidence had been found nearby.
>
> Nor would they elaborate on why they considered it suspicious.
>
> Detective Sgt. William Franks said the skeleton had been turned over to the Rockland County medical examiner for review today. "The death is suspicious at this time," Franks said.

Billy Franks enjoyed the notoriety briefly—there was just enough time to call Margaret, his wife (who had begun a scrapbook of her husband's appearances in print), before calls began to flood the station with tips. Among the Tomkins Cove neighbors reporting "unusual occurences" was one man who said he saw "some black youths" wearing "construction-type clothes" walking up Buckberg Mountain Road in late February, an unusual occurrence indeed. Another saw a suspicious Ford Granada, and one woman called to say that an Hispanic acquaintance, whom she named, was most certainly the gunman. Several neighbors reported hearing gunshots, each at different times. A Queens resident wrote an unsolicited letter with several suggestions, including the location of a Satanic coven in the city. On the bottom of her note, she added: "P.S. I have no personal knowledge of this man, the case, or Satanists."

Each lead was typed onto three-by-five index cards, their dispositions pending. Two police officers were assigned to locate the Hispanic (who turned out to be an inmate, currently and for some months past, of a state correctional facility); the black kids were not found, though much effort went into the search. The letter writer was classified as a quack. Still, more tips poured in. The stack of index cards eventually grew four and a half inches tall.

Franks walked out of his tiny office into the Detectives' Squad Room, and motioned for the men to circle their chairs. "It's going to be like this," he said. "People are going to be calling in names and descriptions of people they just want to get in trouble." Then he hiked his light blue cotton slacks into his crotch, lifted a very large foot onto Det. Joey Denise's desk, leaned forward. "That aside, let's have some ideas, fellas."

Denise, a sallow-skinned man with half-mast eyes and curly black hair, began it. "It's *got* to be somebody from up here, because of where the body was. I mean, how's somebody going to find that place, unless they been there before?"

"I agree," Franks said. "There're tons of places you can dump a body around here and nobody'd ever know. Like Cedar Flats or Mott Farm Road. At night you could see car lights fifteen minutes away on Mott Farm Road." He unfurled a large aerial photograph of the LeGeros estate, and pointed to the two paths leading up to the smokehouse, one logical (right over the front lawn and a few paces into the woods) and one circuitous (the overgrown route taken by the five young hikers). "I think they went right past the house, and around the tennis court. It's enough for me to want to check out the LeGeroses again. Meantime, you canvas every house that comes anywhere near either of these two routes." And Franks went back to his telephone.

He reached John LeGeros at his UN office, and asked him once again about the last time he had been to the Buckberg home, prior to the discovery of the body the day before.

"Golly," he said. "My wife and I were out of the country; we were in France for a scientific conference where she was delivering a paper. That would have been fourteenth until twenty-second February. After that, I was up to the house on the first two weekends in March."

Franks asked, "When did you last walk past the enclosure, the smokehouse?"

"I think . . . well, I know I walked around the property on tenth March, to see what kind of work will be needed in the spring in order to clear out the overgrowth. I guess I walked past the smokehouse then, but I didn't see anything. Which interests me. Could you see the body clearly? I imagine it must have been tucked in there or I would have seen it. But either way, you'd think I would have smelled it, some odor of decomposition."

Franks explained there was no heavy smell when he was there, and pressed on. "How about the rest of your family? Any idea when they last walked around that area?"

"Well, I think I told you, or Davie did, that Davie and Katherine, my oldest daughter, and myself were down there in December 1984. That's when we saw the fish tank; there was a fish tank somebody had put in there for some reason."

"When was the last time your sons were at the house?"

"Well," John LeGeros said, "you'll have to ask them yourself. They're quite independent." And he gave Sergeant Franks the phone number of the apartment that his two sons shared, and a daytime number for Bernard. "But good luck reaching him," he said.

The sergeant had such luck, and found a talkative Bernard at 4:00 P.M. Monday. Because it was the first time they had spoken, Billy Franks began with the foundation questions, such as date of birth (April 6, 1962), and place of employment (Andrew Crispo Gallery, 41 East Fifty-seventh Street), and duration of employment ("since September 1984"). Then to the meat of the issue: "When were you last at the Buckberg home?"

Bernard LeGeros gave a reply in his usual long-winded fashion. "Probably two or three weeks ago on a Monday, like the twenty-fifth of February or March fourth, with Josephine, one of my girlfriends. We went to spend the night there. This was not my regular girlfriend, though, so I didn't tell anybody about it. So we were having sex in my room, the bedroom on the first floor, right off the living room, when I heard a car pull into the driveway. It must have been two in the morning, and I got up to look out the window, and there was a vehicle—full-sized, possibly Chevrolet, possibly a 1971, dark-color vehicle. It didn't stay long, though. Just backed back out onto Buckberg Road, and turned around in a neighbor's driveway, and headed down the road toward Route Nine W. I didn't see the occupants, nor could I tell how many people were in the car."

He did not pause. "The time before that would have been during the second week of February, and at that time I noticed footprints in the snow going across the tennis court toward the grotto."

Franks interrrupted. "Grotto?"

"Grotto, yeah. The smokehouse."

Bernard said the last time he had climbed down to the smokehouse was in the fall of 1984, at which time he had first noticed the fish tank

and the old green door, which he said was once on the front of the
abandoned guest house.

"There was something about his voice—I can't put my finger on it—
that seemed suspicious," Franks said later. "Like he had rehearsed it,
like he tried to sound convincing. That stuff about his girlfriend! And at
the end of the conversation, there was this pause, an inquisitive pause,
like he was trying to figure out whether or not I bought the story." It's
not that Franks suspected Bernard LeGeros—not at this point, anyway.
But there was ample indication that, as he noted on his private pad,
"LeGeros might know more."

Bernard had been trying to get Andrew Crispo's attention since the
morning, when he showed up at work and whispered, in a frightened,
elastic voice, that "they found the dog."

Crispo said, "The dog?"

"You know, the D.B." Then he mouthed the words *dead body*. "Yesterday," he added aloud.

"I want you to meet somebody," Crispo said immediately, and turned
toward the Red Room. "Somebody I'm thinking of doing some business
with." He showed absolutely no concern, not even the slightest amount
of interest in the news Bernard had brought.

Bernard followed behind, passively, and paid no attention as the two
men discussed a joint venture. He chewed his cuticles methodically,
beginning with the index finger and ending with the thumb. Recently,
he and Crispo had begun almost indiscernibly to drift apart. Now they
could go several days without seeing one another, and Crispo could go
weeks avoiding the gallery. The first week of March, he called in daily
from his bed, complaining of a bloody nose from cheaply cut cocaine.
Although he had a major show scheduled to open on Friday, March 22,
he had done virtually nothing to prepare for it. Invitations had not been
sent; paintings had not been hung. A shipment of silver plates, designed
by Pablo Picasso, had not even been opened yet. The show's centerpiece,
an exhibit of white faces and face masks done by the artist Robert Courtright, leaned unorganized and scattered along the brown walls in the
main viewing area. It was for that exhibit that the show had been named
"Masks."

Bernard, too, had gone his own way recently. Instead of showing up
at Crispo's Galleria apartment or his West Village penthouse each night
after leaving work, Bernard was spending time again with Elana, although
they had broken up almost immediately after her return from Rumania.
They were no longer having sex, but a new romance had blossomed
between them—a tenderness and apparent honesty that was new to both

of them. Often, he would roll his head onto her shoulder and cry. "I never should have let you go," he said once. "I never should have left you for Andrew."

He had been with Elana the night before, when his parents and his brother were scouring Buckberg for any evidence of a break-in. David had told him about the grizzly discovery the following morning, when he returned to Waterside Plaza to shower and change clothes before heading off to the gallery.

Not until late afternoon did Crispo return to the morning's topic, and he did so with a surprising lack of gravity, Bernard thought. When Bernard explained he'd just spoken to the police, Crispo handed his young employee a red file folder and several sheets of lined paper. "I want you to write down everything that was said between you and the police. Question and answer, question and answer, question and answer."

As he struggled to recall exact words and phrases, Bernard said later, he glanced over at Crispo, who was sitting on the red sofa in the Red Room, and watched the man draw lines of cocaine on a sheet of paper, gesturing for Bernard to partake. He put down his pen. He rose and walked toward Crispo, toward the coffee table and the cocaine and the sheet of paper.

With a thin straw positioned in one nostril, he leaned his head over and vacuumed the dust off the black and white face of Eigil Dag Vesti. Andrew then cleared the lines that covered the words FOUL PLAY SUS-PECTED, leaned back on the sofa, and folded his hands behind his head.

CHAPTER
12

March 19, 1985. Formalities over and assignments made, Det. Sgt. Billy Franks headed down the Palisades Interstate Parkway on Tuesday—two days after the sparse remains had been hauled out of the smokehouse—for a protocol meeting with New York City higher-ups at the Thirteenth Precinct, in Chelsea, where Stony Point would be given an office to use as their city base. He also planned to compare notes with the Missing Persons squad, and to find Mort Sussman, the private eye who had been looking for Eigil Vesti. By day's end, Franks headed home with a great deal of information about Vesti's last day alive, but very little about his last few months.

On the morning of February 22, 1985, Eigil Vesti rose late and shuffled around the loft he shared, just since the first of the month, with photographer Stephen AuCoin, author of the previous season's fastest-selling coffee-table book, *Man Alive!* AuCoin was out working a photo shoot, so the place—located on a low floor overlooking West Twenty-sixth Street—was all his. The goal for the day was to write out a resume. He was between jobs, having been let go by Richard Gaines, a young designer, and again in mid-January by Nicole Miller, a designer and retailer with a Seventh Avenue showroom (she called him "not a hard worker. More like a spoiled kid"). To make ends meet, Vesti had been filling in as his roommate's assistant: setting up shoots, primping models, fetching rolls of film. He enjoyed the work, and was good at it (his contributions to *Man Alive!*—pretty clothes and pretty men—also included posing for two spreads). But it was a detour from his professional ambition, and friends were pushing him to look for another fashion-related job.

The Sussman notes informed Sergeant Franks of other pressures on Eigil. According to friends, the twenty-six-year-old's parents were imploring him to return to Oslo, apparently worried that he had fallen into the wrong circles in New York. Simultaneously, his student visa was expiring because he had changed his status, in the last FIT semester of his senior year, from full-time student to continuing education at nights—a resident alien's no-no. His parents, unaware of the change in his schedule, continued sending eight hundred dollars a month; they believed it was going toward full tuition. None of his friends could explain these discrepancies, but they all agreed Eigil was not ready to leave the city. "He believed that saying, 'If you can make it in New York, you can make it anywhere,'" Dallas Boesendahl had explained, "and he felt that he wasn't finished making it here yet."

Eigil and Elise Browning, a friend from FIT, had spoken about getting married so that Eigil could get a green card. But abruptly, a week or so before he disappeared, he told her to forget about it. "I've figured a way around it," he said, without elaborating.

Dallas Boesendahl told the authorities that the visa solution Eigil had found was a vague promise of financial backing from "some rich investor" for a line of accessories Eigil had designed. "I don't know exactly who it was," he said, "but there was talk. Eigil knew enough people of means that this did not seem at all unusual." But until the money was in hand, Dallas told Eigil over and again, he should continue pounding the pavement for work.

Boesendahl also told authorities that when the two of them met at Rick's Lounge for supper that night, Eigil admitted he hadn't spent any time on the resume. Instead, after rising late, he walked a block or so from his loft to the McBurney YMCA, renewed his membership with a sixty-dollar check, and enjoyed a half-hour workout. There, he reportedly told acquaintances he was excited about a trip to Florida, slotted for a week down the road, with Stephen AuCoin. He was to help on the photographer's next book.

After showering, he spent the rest of the afternoon at the Metropolitan Museum of Art, and made it back downtown a little after the scheduled eight o'clock rendezvous at Rick's Lounge. It was his first meeting with Maria Burton-Carson and her husband, who were friends of Boesendahl's; they got along very well. "He was sweet, and very quiet," said

Steve Carson. "We did all the talking." Eigil ordered a martini before dinner, sipped two glasses of wine during his meal. After the altercation, when one of the dinner guests threw a drink at another, the party wound down quickly. The Burton-Carsons invited Boesendahl and Vesti up to their place for a nightcap, and they accepted.

Shortly after midnight, Boesendahl and Vesti shared a cab back downtown, and that's when Vesti was made to account for his irresponsibility. "I guess I was very angry," Boesendahl said. "I guess I sort of yelled at him. He was supposed to have finished the resume, and he just didn't!" So, when the cab pulled up in front of Eigil Vesti's West Twenty-sixth Street home, and he suggested they might go out for one more cocktail, Boesendahl rebuffed him. "I'm just too tired," he said. "Maybe some other time." But Eigil was insistent, and pressed the issue. "I think he was depressed about something," Dallas Boesendahl told the cops, "but I didn't have the energy to get into it right then."

Up at his apartment, Eigil phoned Elise Browning. "I told him, 'No, I'm too tired. You go and have a good time,' " she recalled for the police. She did not think he was despondent, she said. AuCoin, who was awake when Eigil came in, said Vesti changed his clothes quickly and left. He wore brown suede cowboy boots, a skintight pair of dark jeans, and a green leather jacket with superpadded shoulders and a zipper that cut across the front diagonally.

Nobody knew what happened after that. Though the city police and Mort Sussman had spearheaded two active and independent investigations, they hadn't unearthed a clue. Except that there appeared to be two separate Eigil Vestis. The tame Eigil, the "A-List" Eigil, the one that Elise and Dallas and Stephen AuCoin knew so well, who enjoyed evenings in the VIP room at Limelight, or at Private Eyes, or Area, a downtown happening spot known for its bank of video screens and ever-changing and very expensive decorative installations. He occasionally dropped by Uncle Charlie's or Boy Bar to socialize with friends. "I went with Eigil on a half-dozen changes of scenery at some of the clubs," Dallas explained to the police, and to the reporters who followed them. "Mostly, he liked to see the fashions, that kind of thing. He wasn't a big party person. Walking down to the pier and smoking a joint was a big evening for Eigil. He was that reserved."

Seth Fletcher, his roommate for two and a half years before throwing him out over the Christmas holidays, told investigators about the other Eigil Vesti, a victim of the dark seductions of New York high life and the traps set for handsome young men. It was this rendition that most fascinated Sgt. Billy Franks, the club bouncer turned detective, because he had seen such things happen before.

A year younger than Eigil, but more than a year ahead of him at FIT, Seth Fletcher became roommates with the handsome Norwegian the first day he arrived in New York. Since graduating, in the spring of 1984, Fletcher had become an assistant promoter at Limelight. Quickly, though, he had begun to develop a dim impression of the denizens of that place, and the other clubs of the moment that had sprung up in the days following Studio 54's great success of the seventies. Not Eigil—he had begun using Seth's position at Limelight for frequent, and free, passage through the door.

"When this came out," Seth Fletcher explained, "I wasn't shocked. He had led this other life. I was his closest friend, but I probably only knew twenty percent of the guy. Nightclubs. That's all he lived for. Works out, showers, puts on an outfit, shops at Barney's, then he'd come back to the club and party till four. Go home, pass out, wake up, and go back to the gym. He was totally caught up in it to the point of not being able to see that it wasn't real, that it was a fantasy world. All he wanted to do was be a society boy, running around drinking wine and champagne and not working for it, hanging out with the stars and the celebrities."

Seth, dark and just as handsome as Eigil, breathed in shallow puffs. "It's a very sick place, the nightclub world. There's no virtue, no morals. A new code of social behavior operates in that world, and it's not healthy. There're drugs everywhere, and there's nobody going to save you. There's no one to take Eigil's hand, to lead him out.

"He started falling into this in the fall, last fall. Just started disappearing for two or three days at a time. Once I came home and he was passed out on the floor, and he had tried to cut himself out of his tuxedo. With scissors. Because the cuff links, silk ball cuff links, were too tight!

"And we were fighting. He didn't have money for bills, wasn't showing up for things. I would say, 'Where've you been?' And he would tell me about these people in midtown, Arabs or Saudi Arabians, who had a lot of money, lots of cocaine, and they would party all night. This guy liked music and would play music all night on two turntables. I never met them; they never called the house. I never even learned their names. Physically, Eigil was looking horrendous. He started to fall, to crumble. Never stopped dressing well, though. He loved beautiful clothes.

"He did have one pair of sexy faded jeans and brown suede cowboy boots. When he put those on, I knew he was going out somewhere nasty—like the Anvil, he liked the Anvil." The club, which was all gay and all male, was described as being more of an S&M fashion show than a true rough-and-tumble sex establishment. Upstairs, there was dancing and drinks and lots of posing; in the basement, dirty movies were shown and, periodically, a few revelers would openly engage in some rather uncommon sex. Beyond one dark corner, and behind a cinder-block wall, there was a large room penetrated by absolutely no light. A steady stream of individuals roamed back there.

Seth Fletcher continued. "All this was getting worse and worse, and he left just before Christmas to visit his family in Norway. And I wrote him a six-page letter about how he had to grow up, how he was living in this fantasy world. How he had failed at the school thing, because he had dropped out, you know? And I told him he was running in a bad track, heading for danger. And if he couldn't turn it around, that we couldn't be roommates anymore. Of course, he didn't answer it, so I just got rid of the apartment.

"I saw him one time after that, because he owed me money. We met on the corner of Twentieth Street and Sixth Avenue, and he gave me it in cash—maybe a hundred or so for the phone bill. And it was remarkable how different he looked! Drawn. Haggard, Eigil was. I think it was on some level a suicide. He was so distraught, and his fantasy about life and what was going to happen in New York was so shattered that his physical beauty was gone. I think he just threw his arms up in the air and said, 'Shoot me, take me away!' "

To Sergeant Franks, Seth Fletcher's gray assessments of the clubs and their various inhabitants rang true to his own two-year experience as the "cooler" at that Upper East Side dance club. His stint, however, came in the early seventies when the New York club scene was far less stratified into in crowds and out crowds, before Studio 54 introduced VIP rooms and celebrity nights and social climbers and the "coke whores" who accessorized this mix, before orgasm became a form of entertainment one might expect inside one of these places. By 1982, the year Limelight opened, nightclubs had become Café Society's showplaces, particularly for the worlds of fashion, rock, art, and literature, the four corners of the new haut monde. In 1985, popular clubs were scrambling to put the names of artists on their invitations. Keith Haring and Jean-Michel Basquiat could draw a desirable crowd. An ambitious club required a large staff of social engineers to anticipate the trends.

Seth Fletcher, clearly, did not have a stellar future in the field. He accepted that. What he had not anticipated, however, was that by elucidating his dark critique of Eigil Vesti's slide downward, he would be putting himself at odds with Dallas Boesendahl, himself a party promoter who shared none of that distaste for a world he helped build.

Dallas showed up at Limelight looking for Seth the day following Eigil's disappearance, and it was Seth who called the Missing Persons unit. But in the days and weeks that followed, he found himself iced out of the investigation. "Don't you think that if this was true," argued Dallas, "his friends would have noticed? I saw him three or four times every week, in the end. And I had no such indication. It's absurd."

That may be why Seth Fletcher never told police that he knew that Eigil Vesti and Andrew Crispo were close. Vesti's sisters had pointedly told police that Fletcher was unreliable and unliked "by the Norwegian community."

Sgt. Billy Franks arrived back at the Stony Point station house with just enough time to prepare for the first formal interview of the LeGeros men, who were scheduled to arrive from New York City around six. He would have visited them at their Manhattan apartment, but for one of the maxims he had learned in police school—and later at the FBI academy: "Whenever possible, bring the subjects in for questioning." Sitting in the stark interview room (another maxim: "Never *interrogate*, always *interview*"), uneasy subjects were apt to become increasingly tense. Tension produces interesting answers.

And he was expecting something interesting, particularly from Bernard. Call it cop's intuition. First, there was the strange quality to Bernard's voice that Franks had noticed when they spoke on the phone the day before, and after that came two subsequent telephone conversations with the boy's father, one at 8:05 P.M. and the other at 8:50 P.M. In the first one, John LeGeros said he "just wanted to let" Franks know that the front door to the main house may have been left unlocked during the week of February twenty-fourth to March third, or from March third to the tenth. "Bernard must have left it unlocked," he said in the first call, "from when he went up there with his friend Billy Mayer."

"When was he up there with this Billy Mayer?" Franks inquired.

"He tells me it was either the twenty-fourth or the third, that they had gone up to spend the night. This, of course, would have been right after my wife and I returned from France, from the conference."

Franks double-checked his notes from his own chat with Bernard, finding the first contradiction in his story. Bernard had said he was last at the house on a Monday, either the twenty-fifth or the fourth, not a Sunday. In fact, he seemed emphatic about the day, having explained that galleries are traditionally closed on Mondays.

At 8:50 P.M., John LeGeros had called again with some additional information. "Detective Sergeant Franks, I just spoke to my wife, and she tells me that Bernard told her that he had a feeling that someone was in the house, or had been in the house, when he was there over the weekend of March third. I thought you might be interested in that."

Franks asked, "Are you sure about that date?"

"Which, the third? Yes, absolutely. Why?"

Franks said he was just trying to keep things in order.

"As I told you, I was there myself on the third, and Bernard was planning to come up, but we left there before he got there. I think we missed each other by a half an hour or so."

"You're right, Mr. LeGeros. I *am* very interested in this. You don't suppose you and your sons could make a trip up to Stony Point—say, tomorrow—so we can check out the house for any signs of a burglary or such?"

"I'd be happy to help in any way. David and I will go up right after work. But," he said haltingly, "if you want Bernard to come, you'd better call him yourself."

"Not getting along with your son, Mr. LeGeros?"

"It's just, you have to understand Bernard. We can never get him to come to Buckberg with the family, not even for holidays anymore. But if I were you, I'd tell him you needed his help in this investigation, his insights; maybe that will kindle his interest." Franks, reaching Bernard at work, did just that, and Bernard agreed to catch a ride to Rockland County with his father and brother the following evening.

Investigators T. J. McGowan and Dave Shae from the RCBCI, along with State Police Senior Investigator Sandy LiDestri, were selected to sit with the LeGeroses. "Dates, dates, dates," Franks instructed them. "Go over everything they've already told us, and get as many specific dates as you possibly can."

McGowan sat in a small dark office behind a black metal desk, and interviewed John LeGeros, who seemed nervous but eager to assist. And his brief retelling of events seemed to be evolving slightly, over time. Again, he said he was last at the house on March 10, at which time he had walked past the enclosure and noticed nothing unusual. When he was there a week earlier, he said now, *he* found the front door unlocked, and questioned his son Bernard about it. "He said that he was up there for the last time—well, last time before all of this—on Thursday, February twenty-first, but he was emphatic about saying that he never used the front door, used the garage door instead. And he told me that he found urine in two of the toilets in the house, and fecal matter in another. This, see, is consistent with a break-in, because I turn the water off at the source each time before I leave—to avoid pipes freezing and cracking in the winter—and nobody who hadn't watched me do it would be able to find the spigot.

"You might ask Bernard who he knows that might have been up to the house—he's got so many friends that he's brought up here; maybe one of them came back. That's possible. I told him to make a list for you, but I don't think he did it."

While John LeGeros was being questioned, David sat in the formal interview room, across a heavy scuffed-up wooden table from LiDestri and Shae. And Bernard, who would follow his younger brother, chattered uncomfortably with Franks in the main detective's room.

"What do you thing about Bernie Goetz, huh? Looks like they'll hang him," Bernard said, pacing from one desk to the next and lighting his third Benson & Hedges. Goetz had become the fascination of New York City tabloids. That day's *New York Post* cover page screamed the interrogative on everyone's lips: WILL BERNIE FRY? Bernard's concerns about the issue seemed gruff, street-tough.

Franks replied studiously, using an unusually high voice. "You can't take justice into your own hands. But," he added, "there's always ways you can help justice along. Take this case, for example. We could really use your help on it. Who knows? Maybe I'll make you an assistant detective."

Bernard's steely exterior dropped as fast as old shorts. "Really? That'd be great! Can you really do that?"

Franks was shrugging, fishing for a reply, surprised at how childishly exuberant the subject had become. Then David LeGeros appeared at the door to the Detectives' Squad Room, smiling and bouncy. "Your turn, Bernard," he announced, and as his brother walked past him, he leaned in to whisper, "I told them that you did it, so why don't you just go ahead and confess and go to jail—they've got a cell waiting for you."

"You're not fucking *serious*, are you?" Bernard grabbed him by the collar. "Fuckin'-A, David, what did you do that for?"

Bernard's reaction angered his younger brother—he'd only been joking, hadn't said any such thing. But he pushed Bernard slightly away from him and said, "Because this is a waste of my time, and I've got an exam tomorrow." Then he laughed a loud, rattling laugh and slapped Bernard playfully on the shoulder.

Relieved, Bernard laughed, too. Then he held up his right hand, with his fingers crimped, and said, "Big Bear Paws."

David returned the secret salutation, the memorial to Major, the reminder of their youth.

The false alarm from David did little to ease Bernard's mind as he sunk into a brown leather chair across from Sandy LiDestri and Dave Shae in the small cinder-block interview room. LiDestri, a tall, soft-spoken veteran with short-cropped hair, rose to shake his hand. "I'm Detective Sandy LiDestri, and this is Detective Dave Shae," he said, introducing his unimposing older partner. Shae, thin, blue-eyed, with a pinkish, ministerial complexion, was by far the gentler of the two, though neither seemed to Bernard to be coming on too strongly. The game plan, as laid out in the brief conference before Bernard LeGeros arrived, would be to avoid a good-cop/bad-cop grilling.

After some small talk about Bernard's employment, Shae, operating on some body-language signals, stepped in as the questioner. The session lasted nearly three hours. LiDestri handed his notes over to Billy Franks, who later read them into a bulky Sony tape recorder and had a secretary type them into his official logbook under the simple headline DETAILS.

> BERNARD said that he was at the Tomkins Cove house some-time between February 11th and the 15th, 1985, with a girl named JOSEPHINE, who he had met at the LIMELIGHT, located at 20th Street and 6th Avenue, New York City. BER-NARD stated that he was having sex with JOSEPHINE when an unknown car entered his driveway. BERNARD said he stopped the sex act to watch the car in his driveway, and he observed the vehicle back out of the driveway and travel back down Buckberg Road. BERNARD further advised that he lost his house keys when he was at the house with JOSEPHINE. BERNARD advised that JOSEPHINE works for a sex phone service, and her work number is 212-976-8484. BERNARD advised that he was last at the Tomkins Cove house on February 21st, 1985, to pick up some clothes. BERNARD also provided INV. LiDESTRI and INV. SHAE with the following list of people he had taken to the Tomkins Cove house:
>
> 1. EDO, last name unknown, approximately 33 years of age, a white male. EDO does photography and is a partner in a boutique in the area of Bleecker and Lafayette streets, New York City. EDO was at the Tomkins Cove house for a couple of hours on one of the following days: February 9th, 10th, or 11th, 1985, and BERNARD had brought him up from New York City to see the house.
> 2. WILLIAM "BILLY" MAYER, age 22, address unknown. BERNARD stated that he was classmates with MAYER at the LASALLE ACADEMY and that MAYER was at the Tomkins Cove house on one of the following dates: February 5th, 6th, or 7th. BERNARD stated that the reason that he went to the house with MAYER was to pick up two bronze dogs (statues) and return them to New York City.
> 3. JOSEPHINE, unknown last name, white female, approxi-

mately 24 to 25 years of age, 5'5", black hair. BERNARD stated that he brought this girl to the Tomkins Cove house sometime between February 11th to the 15th, 1985, and that he had met her at the Limelight, located at 20th Street and 6th Avenue, New York City.

4. ELANA MARTOS, age 22, resides at West 47th Street, New York City. BERNARD stated that she is his girlfriend and she is employed as a waitress at a club on East 60th Street, New York City. BERNARD stated that he had been going out with ELANA for the past two years, that she is a native of Rumania, and she has a child, but BERNARD is not the father. BERNARD stated that ELANA was last at the Tomkins Cove house in 1982 or 1983 and that there is a problem between BERNARD'S parents and ELANA. BERNARD says he picks up ELANA from her job between 8:00 and 8:30 P.M. every working evening.

5. EMIL MARTOS, who is ELANA's brother, and according to BERNARD, EMIL is in Rumania at this time and left in early February.

6. ELLIA, unknown last name, late twenties, heavy build, 5'8". BERNARD advised that he is a friend of EMIL MARTOS, and ELLIA works as a dishwasher. Last known address was S.R.O. Hotel in the West 50s, New York City. BERNARD advised that ELLIA was last at the Tomkins Cove house with him in 1982 or 1983. BERNARD mentioned that they had fired his .22-caliber rifle from his back porch during his visit. BERNARD stated ELLIA is into cults, the subject reads cards, spins Bibles and other weird things. BERNARD said that EL- LIA had slashed the tires of a car owned by EMIL MARTOS following an argument. BERNARD will attempt to learn the last name of ELLIA. ELLIA is known by a man named FLOR- IKA, who is a dishwasher at the TRINON DINING ROOM on 50th Street and Madison Avenue.

7. PETER SANDE, age 30, resides on East 7th Street be- tween avenues B and C. BERNARD stated PETER was last at the house with him in May or June of 1984 and that PETER is a homosexual.

Sergeant Franks asked the LeGeros gentlemen to be patient and wait in the interview room while he and the RCBCI people compared notes. "And then we'll go over to the house, if you don't mind, and see if anything there has been disturbed."

"That's fine," John said, adding: "But I think I gave you keys to the house, which, you know, you can use whenever you need to."

"Yeah, thanks," replied Franks. "And our guys appreciate it; they've been using the bathroom and stuff."

David said, "When? Just when they're driving past it?"

"Oh," said Franks, "we've got a car stationed out front, and an officer has the smokehouse area secured at all times. Just a precaution, so that nobody disturbs any evidence we haven't found yet."

"Help yourself to anything," said LeGeros senior, his face lighting up. "Use the refrigerator, whatever. Like I said before, it's your command headquarters."

Smiling slightly, Franks excused himself and joined McGowan, LiDestri, and Shae in his small office. "What have we got here?" he said, studying the handwritten reports he and his men had accumulated since discovering the body. "Different dates, still, huh?" Bernard first told Franks he went to Tomkins Cove last on a Monday, either February 25 or March 4, with a woman friend. Then his father said he was there last on a Sunday, February 24 or March 3, with Billy Mayer. But just moments ago, Bernard said the Billy Mayer trip was earlier in February, and that he was last at the house on February 21, 1985, to pick up some clothes. That would have been a Thursday—and, coincidentally, the day *before* Eigil Dag Vesti disappeared. It seemed like a convenient date, Franks noticed, and a wise date to choose—except for the fact that he had already given so many other dates to so many other people.

The others agreed it was "interesting," and Shae brought up another point. "David LeGeros gave me a list of guns that are kept in the Buckberg house, including a thirty-two pistol, a shotgun, and—get this—a twenty-two-caliber assault rifle."

McGowan jumped in. "The father called it a 'piece-of-garbage' gun, said he had no respect for it. Said it couldn't hit the side of a barn from ten feet."

"Either way," said Franks, "we got a deceased who was hit with a small-caliber weapon at contact range. I'd like to see that gun," he said almost melodramatically.

Then he asked what could be made of the names Bernard had supplied. They studied the list, pondering over any similarities, or oddities, or red flags. Mostly, they concluded, it seemed to represent a rehearsed recitation, a red herring. But the fact that Bernard pointed out the homosexuality of Peter Sande seemed noteworthy. So far, it hadn't been revealed that the victim was gay, or that the hood found on his head was believed to play a part in sex rituals. Even the way Bernard pronounced it—with a "can you believe it" sneer—suggested discomfort, and knowledge.

Sometime after 11:00 P.M., a uniformed officer accompanied John LeGeros and his two sons back to their Buckberg Mountain Road house, but the gun—a collapsible AR-7 assault rifle, made by Charter Arms and sold as a campers' accessory—had apparently disappeared. But nothing else seemed disturbed. John and the officer searched through the den, located just to the left of the front door. They rummaged through the stone-walled rec room in the basement and the cluttered garage, which was used mostly as a work space, to no avail. The boys said they were checking the closets in Bernard's room, and when the two teams met up again, Bernard said that the AR-7 might be at his Waterside apartment. He promised to check there. "We're going back tonight."

The officer, Sgt. Robert Manasier, returned to the brick station house with only the .32 handgun, and, at 11:45, placed it in the Detectives' Evidence Locker.

Franks, smoking and dictating his case updates into the recorder on his desk, waited until nearly two in the morning—more than enough time for the LeGeros entourage to return to Manhattan—before calling Bernard on the phone.

"Hey, buddy. It's Sergeant Franks."

"Oh, hi," Bernard said, apparently not asleep.

"How about that gun, buddy. Any luck finding it there?"

"Well, you know, I looked in the briefcase, under my bed, where I thought it might be—because that's where I put it, when it's here in the city—and it wasn't there. Sorry."

"Any ideas where it might have gone, Bernard?"

"I suggest," he said, "that you recheck Buckberg, because I think I remember that it might be in one of the closets there, from that time that Edo and I shot it up at the house. Maybe it's in a dark green, olive drab–type bag."

"Okay, Bernard, let me send somebody over there. Just hold on a second," Franks said. He commandeered Sergeant Manasier, threw him the keys, and ordered him back to the LeGeros house. When Franks returned to the phone, he said, "Let's say it's not there, then what do you think might have happened, Bernard?"

"If it's not there, I'd suggest you look around again in the woods. Maybe somebody broke into the house and stole it, and that may have been the killer. Maybe he stole the AR-Seven, and then threw it in the woods."

"That's interesting," Franks said. "Tell me more."

Bernard's mind wandered off into unchecked hypotheses. The killer found the keys that Bernard had once lost. Or the door was merely left unlocked by a family member, and when the killer arrived he just walked right in. Or the killer had discerned the one way to gain entrance to the house without a key (a wood panel on the garage door, off the driveway, was easily removed, giving access to the knob on the inside). "We've done it lots of times, and maybe somebody was watching, and took note of it."

As their conversation was winding down, the word came from Manasier: The military duffel bag contained tent poles, no gun. "Well," said Bernard, "I'll keep looking around here. I'll let you know tomorrow, you know, one way or the other."

"Alrighty," said Franks. "And thanks for all your help, chief."

John LeGeros began to fume as he listened to Bernard's end of the conversation. He had escorted his boys back to their apartment, and poured glasses of orange juice for them. He knew that Bernard had not yet searched the apartment, and immediately lashed into him for misleading the investigator. But a buzzing intercom cut his lecture short. It was three uniformed officers from New York City's police department, asking for permission to look for the gun themselves. Evidently, Sergeant Franks drew the same conclusion as had Bernard's father.

The three LeGeros men and the three officers walked down a narrow hall to the bedroom. Bernard pulled a briefcase from under his bed, and opened it. "Not here," he said. "I guess it must be up at Buckberg."

After the city officers reported their findings to Stony Point, sometime near 2:30 A.M., Franks wadded up an empty pack of Vantages and tossed it in the trash. It was the third spent pack that day. Billy Franks piled his tired body in a red Corvette and drove to his cedar-shake ranch house in town. There, he "climbed in the crib," in his jaunty phrase, for a three-hour nap. It would be his last rest for another three days.

CHAPTER

13

Det. Joey Denise was nowhere near bed, as Tuesday became Wednesday, and wasn't very close to home, either.

With a picture of the living Eigil Dag Vesti in hand, he had been sent down into the city in the midafternoon to the clubs the deceased was said to have frequented. He had the names, their addresses, and only a vague idea of what he would confront there. The Anvil, the Hellfire, Cockring, Alex in Wonderland, the Mineshaft—names that an elderly attorney associated with the case would eventually condense into the generic "Death-knell." If only by virtue of the dark downtown neighborhood they inhabited, Denise expected they would be a little seedier than Boy Bar, Uncle Charlie's, and Rounds; when he showed up at the latter, a mirror-lined piano bar, the owner had greeted him wearing a silk ascot and leather shoes as soft as velvet.

A dark-souled cop given to careless utterances such as, "I'd bang anything warm," Denise was, in fact, a traditionally married suburban man in his early forties whose sex life was probably no more reckless or experimental than that of his Rockland County neighbors. Nonetheless, it was from his desk, in the two-desk detectives office in the square police station, that foulmouthed whoops arose each time certain young women were escorted through the building. His heavy, dark eyelids would lower dramatically and from his thick Greek lips, connected to his nose by an inch-long fleshy canal, a filthy sucking noise erupted more than once.

Despite such failings, Denise was not a menacing man. Just under five ten and just over 180 pounds, he appeared to be growing even more bantamly as his years advanced, a result mainly of the thinning of his black hair, which once stood high on his head, Afro-style. His nubby hands looked more natural when clutching a cigarette than a pistol, and his attire of choice suggested he spent more time on a golf course than in a saloon or a dark alley. Indeed, Denise seemed loved and admired by the area residents he bumped into daily. Under a cloudy sheet of Plexiglas covering the counter at Dee's Country Deli, a stroll away from the station house, Polaroids of him, and of Dave Shae and the other cops, showed there was appreciation for all types of characters in Stony Point.

He was the perfect candidate for this nocturnal mission in the city. Before enjoying a late repast at a Greenwich Village steak house, he had poked his head into a dozen bars, mostly gay and many of them specializing in leather-loving patrons. He directed his canvassing along West Street, the thin patch of concrete separating lower Manhattan from the Hudson River, and then up Christopher Street, the main drag for gay New York, stretching seven blocks from the river toward Sixth Avenue. He marveled at how so many in the eddying crowd would appear heterosexual in any other environment. Hairy male fingers were zippered together, or touched behind an ear, or crossed languidly behind a friend's back, filling the wallet pocket of his dungarees, open-palmed, sinking and bobbing with each stride.

The bars, and along this strip there were many, had been surprisingly full and festive, given the day (Tuesday) and the weather (cloudy and damp). Ty's and Boots & Saddles, both western-theme haunts on the south side of Christopher, looked a lot alike, except that the crowd at the latter was a bit more shrill—accounting for the bar's nickname, Bras & Girdles, coined by the uniform officers who patrolled outside. There was a warm camaraderie, too, at the more upscale pubs on the north side, such as Trilogy and Christopher's and the Village Stix, the white-tiled bar on the corner of Greenwich Street where floor-to-ceiling plate-glass windows looked in on a handful of neatly dressed young men sipping from beer mugs around a crackling fireplace. It all seemed so orderly and congenial, and private. Denise, perennially in command, had felt as if *he* was the deviant on a dusk orange street in a city he had apparently not yet fully experienced.

And he wondered where the women were.

There were a few establishments here that appeared to have roots outside this parallel world, owned by Arab and Korean sellers of fruits and cigarettes and deodorant sticks, the standard merchants of such goods throughout the city, and even in some parts of the suburbs. Still, other shops along Christopher Street had no semblance to any Rockland County reality; for example, the adult bookstore on the corner of Hudson Street. Its shiny glass cases brimmed with sex devices ("They looked like nightsticks," Denise said later) in an array of flesh tones, each offering unique services. In the back, beyond the magazines and video racks—there were no books in this bookstore—was a dark doorway and a very active turnstile, which Denise did not venture past. A block and a half to the east, at a green sign reading 78–80 CHRISTOPHER, a flight of stairs descended to the basement entrance of an "entertainment center" with no discernible name. Inside was another turnstile and a bulletproof window, both filling a tiny black anteroom just large enough for two broad-shouldered men, unless they both were to reach for the six-dollar entrance fee simultaneously. Handwritten signs promoted the various items that one might find helpful on a sally through the turnstile: LUBE, and LOCKER ROOM, and COCKRINGS, $1.

This was all before dinner, and Denise hadn't learned much that would serve his immediate purpose—which was to locate anyone with a three-week-old knowledge of the last moments of a handsome blond Norwegian man. Indeed, he found no one who recognized the photos he carried, beyond an occasional "He looks familiar, somehow." Those secrets, he supposed, might be lurking, if at all, within the after-hours establishments in the meat-packing district.

The first such place on his list was the Mineshaft, considered by New York City authorities to be a "hard-core S&M club for gay men." It was located on the corner of Little West Twelfth Street and Washington Street inside a weltering slaughterhouse in the meat-packing district—a six-block-square neck of the Village, just south of Fourteenth Street, where huge frozen animal carcasses, shipped in from the Midwest, were reduced to familiar shapes and marketable sizes. During working hours, hundreds of great refrigerator trucks inched up to crowded loading docks; at nightfall, after the trucks pulled away and the cobblestone streets had been hosed down, men wandered wordlessly over the skids and beneath the awnings and under the clamor of peeling tin signs: WELL-CUT BEEF and STEAKS, STEAKS, STEAKS and SHELL STRIPS, TOP BUTTS, FILLETS, CHOP MEAT.

For this leg of the investigation, which began after midnight, Denise was not going in alone. Det. Pat Barry, a New York City cop with some experience in "morals work" (as patrols of the city's sex pockets were called), led the way to an unmarked door off an unlit, unpeopled stone-paved alley that squeaked under car tires and stuck to the bottom of the cops' shoes. Lt. Frank Tinelli, second in charge in Stony Point, was there, too. All three wore street clothes, including no small amount of polyester.

Behind a heavy black door, distinguished only by a white painted arrow pointing to it, a narrow wooden stairway led up to a doorway framing a bright, unsheathed light bulb. A burly, fortyish man sat there on a stool. Hand-painted unevenly on the door behind him was the name MINESHAFT and a listing of the club's dress code. The roster began at about eye level and stretched, item after item, toward the grimy floorboards:

NO cologne or perfume or designer sweaters.
NO suits, ties, dress pants or jackets.
NO rugby-styled shirts or disco-drag.
NO coats in the playground.
NO horizontal stripes.
NO dress pants, including Chinos or pleats or designer
   jeans.
NO formal shoes.
NO sneakers or tennis shoes.

Offending items, the sign concluded, could be checked free of charge.

Reaching the top of the steps, winded, the officers produced badges and asked for the manager. "That'd be Wally," said the weathered bouncer, and momentarily Wally Wallace appeared, in jeans and a leather vest. He wore no shirt, and yards of gray chest hair and facial hair spilled all around him. A round-bellied man in his fifties, Wally Wallace was the gay male S&M community's elder statesman—sponsor and perennial emcee of the annual Mr. Leather contests, longtime contributor to gay causes, father confessor to a community of people he called, collectively and in a kindly, gravelly voice, "the kids." This was a fortuitous place to start.

Wally Wallace said he had never seen the person in the picture, "except in those posters all over the place. Sweet kid. I've been wondering what happened to him."

"So, he's never been here?"

"Oh, I can't tell you that. But here, come talk to some of the kids. Maybe they remember."

The three cops rounded the corner into the roaring main room of the Mineshaft. Along one wall was a long, wide plywood bar with hitching-post devises hanging above it and attached to the side. A drum of Crisco sat next to the cash register with a notice advertising the price of a fistfull.

There was a row of bar stools but nobody sat on them. Nobody, it seemed, spent much time in this first dark room, which was the brightest, except to pass to other darker passageways, or to refill a drink or dip into the lube bin. Most of the men in the other rooms, and there were many, were shirtless. Some stood naked, or else in jockstraps or leather cowboy chaps with nothing underneath, so that just the sides of their legs were covered, strangely shielding only the least vulnerable quadrants of their anatomy. Hands, firm on beer cans or whip handles or doorways, made the only rapid motions as they swooped down on dangling penises and pink buttocks and narrow waists pulled out of the crowd.

No one spoke, but the chambers were packed with relentless disco cadences. A wild smell spoke of armies of visitors to this body biologic: gallons of piss and beer and sweat and come, miles of leather, flesh, and mold. Amyl nitrate was uncapped everywhere, casting a vague orange halo over the happenings; it was strong enough to give a first-timer like Denise a spontaneous headache.

The officers followed their guide through a small doorway to the left of the bar, which opened onto a room with a prison theme where men stood in small cages or were handcuffed to bars or strapped to chairs. "My God," Denise said later. "This is somebody's idea of sex? Talk about your dens of iniquity." But inside the Mineshaft, he masked his astonishment, and when a half-dressed man brushed a little too close, he muttered only, "If that's what turns your clock, go to it."

The establishment had three bars on two floors, and Denise, Barry, and Tinelli passed through a dazzling number of nearly empty rooms and crowded, nearly impassable catacombs before arriving, finally, at Wally Wallace's office. Only one bartender along the route said he recognized Eigil, but he called him an "infrequent" customer who hadn't been around in some time.

In the office, which was really the large concrete room with a floor drain where beer cans were emptied, stacked, and readied for return to the manufacturers, Wally Wallace talked about sadomasochism. "These boys come here for some fun," he began, not convinced he could adequately explain. One of the cops snorted, and Wally Wallace began again. "What they're doing here is safe, sane, and consensual," he said. "They're doing exactly what they want to do, in exactly the way they want to do it. Don't you see? It's a game. And it's got rules—the bottom sets the rules, like how much pain is too much pain, and when the scenario will stop. Then the top takes it from there."

Gently, he explained the concept of S&M "contracts," the negotiations that should proceed an encounter, and the "safe words" that are adopted. If one person says, "Stop, you're hurting me," that might be part of the scenario. It might not be heartfelt. So people agree on a word—*mercy* is a common one—that *really* means *stop*.

The cops had been listening intently, struggling to understand, and Denise finally interrupted. There's a dead body, he said, and it seems he was killed during some kind of sadomasochistic ritual. Wally Wallace said, "Murder is to S&M what rape is to sex. Don't get this confused. You may want to play with danger, but you want it to be a game in the end. These kids," he said, motioning a big arm toward the Mineshaft's clientele, "want to be able to come back and do it again next week."

Back on the slick streets of the meat-packing district, Denise, Tinelli, and Barry walked silently to their cars, passing doorways where men were taking blowjobs from other men, or women, or men dressed as women, doorways filled with couples, threesomes, crowds; passing the Polarized windows of long black limousines; passing light posts and telephone booths and heavy warehouse doors where Eigil Dag Vesti's face could still be seen peering out from behind more current posters: parties at the Ritz, the River Club, Danceteria, and Limelight.

Det. Sgt. Billy Franks was back at work by 9:15 on Wednesday, March 20, not having rested very well in his few hours off. He hadn't been able to shake his belief that a LeGeros, probably Bernard LeGeros, knew something, probably everything, about what had happened to Eigil Vesti on February 23. He obsessed on the possibility, which was unusual for him. "Never get tunnel vision," he would remind himself, mantralike, "never let one hunch overshadow other hunches."

He increased the number of police, from his station, from RCBCI, and from the sheriff's department, and had them continue questioning neighbors, looking for a witness, a clue, a person who looked guilty. For the second day in a row, he ordered "rescue dogs" back to 100 Buckberg Mountain Road to sniff around the woods for more bodies, or more of Eigil Vesti's body.

The mounting suspicion was that the fire and hungry animals alone could not have accounted for the condition of the victim's body. His left leg had been found inside the charred boot, severed midway between knee and ankle. His right hand had still not been discovered. If animals had aggressively torn these appendages off the corpse, wouldn't the corpse have been dragged out of the smokehouse in the process? Wouldn't scavengers have carried the leather boot away, or torn it open to get to the flesh hidden there? How had they been able to clean the corpse of internal organs without disturbing the bones?

Det. Joey Denise was rustled from bed and sent back to the city, and investigators Sandy LiDestri and Jimmy Stewart, from the district attorney's office, were sent there, too, in a separate car, to help piece together the deceased's last hours.

But Franks stayed behind—an elbow pressed into the blue desk blotter, an eyebrow skewered on his middle finger—working the phones, sucking on a Vantage, sucking on his mustache. Briefly, he talked to Bernard LeGeros, whom he reached at 9:30 and who told him the AR-7 assault rifle had not yet turned up. An hour later, Franks called John LeGeros, who suggested Bernard may have hidden it in David's Buckberg bedroom, under a broken floorboard in a closet. "He's a little silly about the durned thing," John had explained, "he treats it like his teddy bear, carries it around with him all the time. He took it to Virginia with us once, for a family reunion! So you see, it's a favorite thing of his. Maybe he just doesn't want to lose it, so he's refusing to turn it over to you. If you think it would help, I can have a friend, who is an intelligence officer in the air force, talk to him about it." There was a drumming impatience in the elder LeGeros's voice.

John had first had it out with Bernard in the car the night before, as the three LeGeros men headed back to New York City after their lengthy interviews with Rockland officials—and before the surprise police search that Billy Franks had apparently ordered. They had been cruising down the Palisades Interstate Parkway in the Vista Cruiser station wagon for some time in silence when Bernard began to fantasize. "I bet it was a truck driver, some old fat guy," he said, "who picked up this young kid, like a hitchhiker. Picked up a hitchhiker and they had sex, and then the truck driver probably killed him after and dumped him in our woods."

John became instantly furious. "All this conjecture! Why do you always persist in so much conjecture about such foreign subjects? Truck drivers and young men. What makes you do things like this?"

"What do you mean?" Bernard was impudent. "You've heard of old guys who have a thing for young guys, right?"

David, in the backseat, had a phrase for it: "Ass bandits."

Sure, John said. In the service, he had watched fellow soldiers "roll homosexuals" for fun. That wasn't the strange part. "For what reason would you tell *this* story?" he demanded. "You're so full of stories, really, Bernard. And this is the most weird story I've ever heard. And if you go repeating a story like this to the police—some cockamamy theory!— they're going to think you know something and we're going to have a heck of a time getting you out of jail." John pulled the car left, where the Palisades Parkway swoops onto the George Washington Bridge, and the city skyline twinkled in his windshield. "Jiminy! We'll have a hard time getting you out of jail, and it will distract the police to boot."

These tensions peaked when, sitting up at the apartment at 40 Waterside, John stood by as Bernard brushed off the police who were looking for the rifle. Before going to bed, he issued his son a stern dictum: "Find that dang gun, and get it to the Stony Point police." His flat gray face grew slightly animated and his voice shook. "If you're worried they won't get it back to you, that's just dumb."

It never once crossed John LeGeros's mind that Bernard's gun had played any role in the Rockland incident, despite Detective Franks's insistent pressures to get a hold of it. "I just thought that the sooner we found it and turned it over," he said later, "the sooner the police would see the gun wasn't used for anything."

The 9:30 call from Franks had come moments after Bernard had arrived at the gallery, and before anybody else had reported for work. Besides himself and Crispo, there were just two other employees working there now: Ellery Kurtz, the registrar, and George Perret, the elderly gentleman who was the first person hired on, thirteen years earlier. "George's a lech," Bernard told a friend once, "but he's harmless. Ellery, he proved his loyalty to Andrew, so we didn't worry about him." The others, one by one, had been fired (or forced to resign) in the six months since Bernard's first day on staff.

Ellery Kurtz arrived at ten, and Andrew Crispo rushed through the heavy front doors nervously a few minutes later. It had been a very long time since Crispo had made it into work before late afternoon. His pupils were huge and restless. He appeared to have been up all night, or perhaps for several nights. He wore a crumpled brown suit jacket and a graying white shirt. He snapped a finger to Bernard, commanding him to order up breakfast. "Eggs and sausage," he said, and strode into the Red Room. The food arrived at 10:25. Bernard carried it to the dark, curtained office.

"What did they ask you last night?" Crispo said wildly. "What'd they want to know?" He bolted up from a chair involuntarily, it seemed, wobbling uneasily over his food. Then: "Don't tell me. Write it down; write down every word. Question and answer, question and answer, question and answer." The red folder containing Bernard's earlier script lay open on the coffee table.

As Bernard scribbled down the conversations from the night before, in screenplay-style, his boss stood over him, reading each word as soon as Bernard's small, chapped hand moved past it. When he was done, Bernard was dismissed and instructed to prepare the gallery for an upcoming show. "We're opening on Friday," Crispo announced. "There's a lot to do."

At 11:30, David LeGeros called and said the pressure was intensifying over the AR-7. "Either find the thing or buy another one," he said.

"Okay," said Bernard, with no intentions of following through.

At 12:30, Crispo emerged from the Red Room and found Bernard in the Brown Room, where he was unpacking the Picasso silver plates. "Here's what you've gotta do," he said. "Call the Stony Point police and tell them where you bought the gun. You remember, right?"

Bernard agreed, and dialed Sergeant Franks. A secretary said he was out, and took a message.

At two, Crispo again pulled Bernard aside. "Franks called," he said, "call him back."

"Okay."

"Are you scared?"

"Yeah."

"How'd you like to be known as the late Bernard LeGeros?"

"Heh heh."

"I'm serious."

"I am prepared to die, if necessary," Bernard said, "but take care of Elana and the kid for me."

Andrew said, "Don't do that. Who am I going to get to replace you?"

Franks seemed overjoyed to touch base with Bernard this time. "I need your help on this case, buddy," he said in a voice that was both friendly and commanding. "How'd you like to come up to the station and talk about a few things with me?"

"Sure," said Bernard, "but I've got a dinner reservation with my girlfriend, with Elana, this and that. But I can come up after. That's too late?"

"Oh, no," said Franks, "that would be fine. Just call me here when you're ready, and I'll have somebody pick you up."

At 8:15, Bernard called Franks from a pay phone. "Yeah, it's Bernard," he said. "I got a message you called?"

"I don't think so," Franks said. "Where are you?" He was on the corner of East Sixty-sixth Street and Madison, still waiting for his girlfriend to leave work. "I've got a team right near you," Franks said, "I can have a car meet you in a couple of minutes."

"That'd be okay," said Bernard, "but I'm going to have dinner with Elana, when she gets off work. We do it every workday, and then I walk her home."

Franks seemed to understand. "Well, at least you'll have a warm car to sit in while you're waiting for her."

Investigator Sandy LiDestri entered Franks's office shortly before ten that night and closed the door. "We've got the LeGeros kid," he said, explaining how they had waited a half hour for his girlfriend, then convinced him to give up on her and leave the city. They whisked him up the West Side Highway toward the bridge and the hour-long drive north. "And you should hear this guy's *theories*. He just started to ramble!"

"What kind of stuff?" Franks asked.

"Really incredible stuff, like about 'chicken hawks,' and how the killer was probably a homosexual, *prepared to kill*. That's his words: *prepared to kill*. And then he said this thing about how the killer probably returned to the scene the day the body was discovered." He showed his boss two pages of nearly illegible notes he'd taken in the dark while Bernard gabbed on in the backseat. More than a dozen "theories" were listed there.

"Let's go talk to this boy," Franks said with jubilation.

The interview started at 10:10 P.M., on Wednesday, March 20, 1985, in the cinder-block interview room under a buzzing fluorescent bulb. Bernard elaborated: The killer must not be an upstate person, or he wouldn't have burned the body. "Attracts attention," he said. He supposed that the weapon was a small-caliber gun, and that the "perpetrator probably didn't like homosexuals, although he might be a fag himself. Maybe even a chicken hawk."

Franks had been jotting notes. "Chicken hawk?"

"Yeah," said Bernard, who showed a kinetic eagerness to be speaking with these two men. "That's a fag who likes younger guys, or guys who look like they're young. It's an older homo who goes after boys."

"That's interesting," Franks said, offering to light Bernard's Benson & Hedges. "What else?"

"Well, this guy, the killer, is probably psychotic, right? And he probably hangs around in the gay bars in the city—places like the Mineshaft, or the St. Mark's Baths in the East Village. Like in that movie *Cruising*, where the psychotic picks up guys and kills them while fucking them. Probably he was prepared to kill. Either that or it was an S&M thing that went too far. Mineshaft, that's an S&M place, and so's the Anvil, and Badlands. You're probably going to have to do what Al Pacino did, and dress up like one of them and start hanging around in their places. Because fags blend into the city. Unless you've got a gay cop who could do it."

"Tell me about the bondage hood, Bernard." Billy Franks lit a Vantage as Bernard rolled the end of his cigarette in an ashtray, first knocking off the ember and then reattaching it nimbly.

"The hoods are worn during the scenes, and they can be worn either by the master or the slave. Either one. But mostly it's for the slave, because it dehumanizes the victim, the slave. You don't see the face, and they become less than human, or you don't have to think about them being humans, anyway."

"Bernard"—Franks approached the subject carefully, kindly—"how do you know this stuff, about chicken hawks and bondage masks?"

And Bernard had a quick answer. "Movies," he said. "You never saw that one, *Choirboys*? Well, they had this one scene in there, it was a comedy, about a guy at a police academy, I guess. They had a scene where this guy sees a hooker, and she was into S&M, and she's whipping him and he's crying and screaming. It was a laugh—me and my brother saw it—and he had on one of those masks. He was, 'Ow, ow, ow, ow.' " Bernard laughed aloud. "It was a slapstick thing."

"Do you know anybody who might be involved in that kind of thing? In S&M?"

"No," said Bernard, nearly spitting.

More than an hour had passed before Franks and LiDestri began pressing for specifics, something to nail Bernard with, a trap to snare him. What they got instead was a windy list of people Bernard didn't like, for one reason or another, many of whom had been his guests up at the Tomkins Cove house nonetheless. A former teacher at LaSalle Academy "once put his hands on my back and started to massage my shoulders. I thought he was getting queer, you know, so I slapped him and told him not to ever do that again." A man named Robert who had been a LaSalle student "may have gone up," or Luke, a black student from the same class. "He's straight, but he hangs with gays and he's into heavy leather and likes young white girls, like fourteenish."

Franks gave up on this line, and asked the point-blank question: Where was Bernard the night that Eigil Vesti disappeared?

There was a very detailed answer, accounting for every minute of every day between February 22 and February 24, in which Andrew Crispo seemed to be Bernard's constant companion.

"You've got a terrific memory, Bernard," Franks said. "Can you also tell me what you were doing the Friday after that?"

"Friday? I think I went out with Dean Aarons, the guy who was staying with me that weekend. Or no. That was before."

"How about Saturday night?"

"I, we went to my Aunt Virginia's to work on some furniture. Or maybe that was Friday night and I went out with Dean on Saturday." Bernard began chewing on the nail of his index finger, feeling confused, reaching for his depleted cellophane pack. He wished he had some coke to clear his mind. Right after work, down at Crispo's house, his boss had razored him out a few lines. That was a long five hours back.

Franks grew obviously upset, convinced that Bernard was holding out but not yet sure of what he knew. "Do you realize the seriousness of this? That this is a criminal investigation?" Bernard nodded, and Franks pulled out a small card from his wallet and began reading. "You have a right to remain silent. Everything you say can and will be used against you. Do you understand this right?" Another nod. "You have a right to an attorney. If you can't afford one, an attorney will be provided to you at no cost. Do you understand this right?" Bernard nodded again. "Now, Bernard, did you have anything to do with this homicide?"

"No."

"Do you have any personal knowledge of the homicide, either directly or indirectly?"

"No," Bernard repeated in a firmer voice.

"You're so full of shit, Bernard!" Franks exploded, theatrically slapping his hand flat on the table. "You haven't been honest with us since the minute you got here." Turning to LiDestri, Franks said, "C'mon. This is a waste of our time. Let's get the fuck out of here," and the two stormed out. In the other room, Franks immediately paged Detective Denise and Lieutenant Tinelli, who were asking questions in a bar in the village, at the time, and when they called back, he had them head over to Andrew Crispo's house, on West Twelfth Street, to check the alibi.

As he was hanging up the phone, he heard Bernard calling from the interview room. "Sergeant Franks! Sit down a minute, I have something to say." Bernard took a deep breath and tears filled his eyes. "I have not been totally honest with you," he said. "I know what happened. Billy did it. Billy Mayer killed him."

The tale Bernard LeGeros then told, and elaborated on throughout the night, was a bizarre account of a complicated, not altogether fathomable evening in Manhattan, traversing the watering holes of the haut monde and the after-hours establishments beneath them. It came to be known as the Billy Mayer version.

He and Mayer, his LaSalle chum, met at 6:00 P.M. on February 22, 1985, and went to Hellfire for "a look around." But, finding it a bit tame, they moved on to Limelight, which Bernard described as a "church desecrated by the presence of this disco."

At the door, they bumped into Andrew Crispo, who escorted them past the doorman without paying and gave them entrée to the VIP room, which was located three flights above the expansive dance floor in the main worship area of the converted church. There, they were introduced to Claire, a manager, and to Freddy Rothbell-Mista, who was in charge of seeing that the assembled notables ("movie stars, political figures, people that accomplish things," in his words) had full glasses. It was inside the VIP room, Bernard said, that Crispo and Mayer decided it would be a good idea to kill Freddy Rothbell-Mista.

One at a time, they each attempted to convince Freddy (who "liked" Billy) to "come with us to a party over the bridge." Each time, he declined.

So the plan was abandoned, and Bernard descended to the dance floor and flirted with a young woman. He said he didn't look for Billy Mayer again until after 4:00 A.M. But then, unable to find him, Bernard left the club and headed for the Vista Cruiser—which he discovered was also missing. He said he walked around the side streets looking for it, and finally spotted the car at about 5:30. Billy was asleep on the front seat.

"Hey, asshole! Where did you go?"

Billy woke up. "Get in and shut up."

"Billy, I was looking all over the place for you. Where the hell did you go?"

"I went out. For a cruise."

"Didn't you think I would look for the car? What possessed you?"

Billy turned to face him, and whispered, "You're gonna shit."

"Why?"

"I blew away a scum-sucking fag!"

"Yeah, sure. Where?"

"Up around your house."

"Waterside?"

"No, asshole, up in the country."

"Billy, stop fucking around and tell me the truth."

"Really! Upstate. I opened the gates of hell and shoved the Jew-loving slime in. Oh! I wish you could have seen it!"

Sergeant Franks noticed that Bernard seemed to register no horror in this telling, suggested no hint of apology for having stored away these details for so long. What did show clearly on his face was an urgent desire for Franks to believe the story. But he did not. The sergeant gave Bernard a yellow legal pad and instructed him to write out all the details he could recall. Bernard put it down in dialogue form, including stage directions.

ME: (Thinking about a past visit to the house, in which he called the smokehouse a gas oven, my first thought was: did he really do it? And if so, did the flames catch to the trees? I didn't see any blood on Billy's clothing except for what appeared to be red dots on his white trousers). Billy, what's that on your trousers? (Hoping against the possible: *blood.*)

BILLY: Nothing.

ME: Billy, why would you do that?

BILLY: 'Cause he was a sick little faggot! And Freddy's next, the scum—

Then Franks told Bernard to sign each page, attesting that they were "a true and accurate" representation of the facts as he knew them. Bernard did, finishing the task after 3:00 A.M. on Thursday. That's when the real "interview" began, with Billy Franks picking apart every line, every word, every insinuation and allegation and inference. For twenty-five hours, with each man taking only short naps, they went at it, Franks calling Bernard a liar, Bernard amending his story, the sun rising once more and then setting over the cold environs of Rockland County.

When it was over, Bernard LeGeros—twenty-two, handsome, confident, cocky, well spoken—had confessed to pumping two bullets into the brain of Eigil Dag Vesti, "once for the body and once for the soul."

Early on Friday morning, March 22, Kenneth Gribetz instructed his media liaisons to schedule a press conference. As Franks, Denise, Shae, and Tinelli filed into his office in the county's district attorney building, he seemed ebullient. He asked who had brought the mask. He played with the zipper on the mouth, and joked about how eerie it appeared. Then he told each of the officers where they would be standing once the cameras arrived. They would form a semicircle behind his desk, where he would sit, holding the death mask, as it had been dubbed by New York City papers.

Gribetz, the forty-one-year-old DA, loved the media as much as, or more than, any other elected official. He played them pretty well, eliciting favors and dropping hints, all in an effort to maintain control of the eventual story. This story, though, seemed to be flying just fine without him.

Reporters had gotten calls from his office, or had learned about the press conference from the Day Book, an electronic bulletin-board service provided by the Associated Press. He was announcing that Rockland County had nabbed the killer of Eigil Dag Vesti and charged him with second-degree murder.

Reporters began arriving after two, and he introduced himself casually. Before his statement, he made himself available for photos. For television crews, he cupped the ugly mask in his hands, holding it steady. For newspaper photographers, he stretched it long and raised it to the height of his nipples. That way, his face would also fit in the frame.

"Eigil Vesti was shot twice in the head," Gribetz said in his statement. "He was shot after he had engaged in sadomasochistic activity with individuals at this particular location. He was stark naked when he was shot, except for a matter that was placed over his head." (If you don't describe the thing, the reasoning goes, they're sure to have to show pictures of it cradled in your hands.) He announced that Bernard LeGeros had confessed to the slaying, had said he helped burn the body—had even confessed to returning a week later and torching it again. "We are looking for a second suspect," Gribetz added.

Nobody asked the identity of the second suspect, but one reporter wondered about the significance of the mask. "Detective Sergeant Franks is our expert on sadomasochism," Gribetz said, with a gesture over his shoulder. "He can answer that."

"Wow, no," Billy Franks blurted out, waving his large hands in front of his green eyes. "Uh-uh. You can call me a ballistics expert, or a homicide expert, or an expert on narcotics or anything else you want. But nobody's labeling me an expert on sadomasochism. No way."

The other cops standing behind Gribetz leaned forward and spilled their laughter freely. But not Kenneth Gribetz. This was his press conference, and his stakes were considerably higher. The look on his face was unmistakable, humorless, and ferocious.

That evening, Racquel LeGeros returned to her hotel room in Las Vegas exhausted. The scientific conference had been tiring, and might have worn her out under any circumstances. But her mind kept going back to that photograph she'd held in her lap, the one in the paper that David showed her of the young, handsome blond man whose remains they believed were found at Buckberg. On several evenings, she had actually tried to compose a letter to the boy's parents. *I'm so sorry. He was so far from home.* There were times when oceans had separated her and her children, times she'd worried about catastrophe hitting her own family. But it was a meandering fear that kept permeating the letter she was writing to Oslo. Selfish things tried to push their way out of her pen. *I pray it never happens to my family. I'm so sorry it happened to yours.* How else could she respond? How do you console the grieving without showing your overwhelming relief that it had not happened to you?

In Las Vegas, she had mentioned the episode only once, to a close friend and colleague who had accompanied her to a dinner. "Racquel," the friend said, "they could make a TV show out of your life." It was the only time she'd laughed.

But this night she was not laughing, and was attempting once more to compose the proper letter when her brother Salvador—Tito Sonny—called. He said he wanted to find out how her work was going, wanted to take her mind off that grisly discovery up at Buckberg—wanted to fly with her to New York. Often, he and Racquel had talked about meeting at one conference or another, in this country or another, and flying home together. As an employee of an airline, he was able to travel free from his home in Dallas, where he now lived. "It's been so long," he said, "I want to see my nieces and nephews."

He arrived a day later, on Saturday, and during their flight, which wasn't going to arrive at La Guardia until nearly midnight, they exchanged soft-toned updates. Though he had been in the country for a greater portion of his life than Racquel, Salvador's accent was much more pronounced, and his diction more stammering. He was a slender man and was considered cute, even as he was approaching forty years old. He was a crisp dresser and an intense, very direct, conversational partner. Finally, he asked her about the body.

"I told you everything I know," his sister said. "Except . . . usually when I'm away on a conference, I call home every night at the same time. But I called Wednesday night, and no answer. I called Thursday and Friday, same thing. I guess they've got a lot going on back there."

"Then you don't know anything else?"

"No," she said. "What should I know?" Questions always seemed didactic to her, implying an already formulated answer.

He placed his hand over hers on the armrest and said, "Whatever happens, be strong."

"What do you mean? Sonny!"

"You know, that incident about your house."

"That was so terrible. I don't know . . ."

He said, "Whatever happens, be strong."

John greeted them at the airport in New York. Sasha, Kara, and David were there, too. "I'm surprised," she said. "I was only gone to Las Vegas, and only for four days."

"We're here for Tito Sonny," John said as the girls jumped all over their uncle.

Then Racquel spotted her sister from Virginia, and Uncle Andy, her brother from Tappan. "At the first excuse, we have a party," she said in her most melodic voice. "What are we celebrating now?"

"Just having you home," someone said, "is reason enough." But something was clearly wrong.

Later, she said, "They all looked at me so strangely, there was something not very wholesome about this."

John sent David to fetch the luggage. "Where's Bernard?" Racquel demanded. "Everybody's here, but no Bernard."

John moved her toward a coffee counter, saying, "He's being questioned by the police."

"That just serves him right," she said. "For having such stupid friends. You don't think Billy Mayer, or someone like that, had something to do with this? Bernard's always so protective of him. Remember when he called us in the middle of the night? Saying that Billy was in some kind of trouble? I certainly hope that Billy Mayer didn't have anything to do with *this*."

John and Racquel rode together into Manhattan, and headed for the Upper West Side, where their lawyer, Murray Sprung lived. John said he needed to retrieve some legal paperwork. The rest of the clan, packed into a single conveyance, headed straight back to Waterside Plaza. Racquel spoke proudly about the conference, and merrily about her flight home with Salvador.

Mary Sprung, Murray's wife, opened the door. She was unusually bedraggled, and unusually affectionate: She gave Racquel a long, powerful embrace. Murray was sitting in the dining room, also looking physically traumatized. He had had a stroke several years earlier, and now needed an aluminum walker to get around. Arthritis kept his fingers from bending at the smaller knuckles.

His eyes, though, were more shrunken and darker than normal, rings of tired flesh draping down his cheeks. Seeing him frightened Racquel for the first time. "You haven't slept! What on *earth* . . ."

Murray addressed John: "Did you tell her anything?"

John shook his head. "No."

With slow, trembling hands, the lawyer reached for a file folder and, opening the cover, slid it across the long mahogany table to Racquel. Inside was the front page of that day's *New York Post*. UN EXEC'S SON ON MURDER RAP, it said in huge type. Below that was a four-inch-high picture of Bernard, looking absolutely horrible. His eyes were nearly swollen shut; his hair stood straight up on his head.

Next to his picture was the face of that young man whose parents Racquel had wanted to console. In a very dark frame was another picture, this one depicting a gruesome, zippered, formless black hood.

Beneath this clipping was another newspaper story. The cover of the *New York Daily News*, in equally large type, read: UN WORKER'S SON HELD IN SEX DEATH.

Racquel LeGeros screamed. "No! No! Oh, my God. God, no no no no." She reached for the table, a chair, her glasses, a wall; she clutched the air. John moved toward her, but as he did, she released a wail that startled him. She then said, "What are we going to do? What are we going to do!"

Very slowly, expending a great deal of concentrated effort, Murray

Sprung lifted a pair of glasses off his nose and placed them on the table. "I think," he said, "that we'll talk about this some more after you've all calmed down." He, too, was weeping openly.

Later, Racquel opened an envelope holding the few things that had been removed from Bernard's pockets after he was fingerprinted and locked into a small cell: a wallet, some keys, a handful of change. Inside his wallet, next to a pink dry-cleaning ticket, she found two pieces of folded yellowed paper. She opened them carefully. "My God," she said, "they're the birth certificates of Major and Gypsy! He kept them! Why?"

She looked desperately into her husband's face and back at the pedigree papers for the dogs she had disposed of so many years ago. They rattled in her shaking hands like a ransom note. Her eyes pleaded for an answer.

And then one seemed to come to her. "What have I done?" she asked in a deep, accusing, genuine voice. "What have I done to B.J.?"

CHAPTER

14

Keeping tabs on Bernard had not been a part of John's ordinary parenting practices, at least not since returning from Yemen. There were no bed checks at the other Waterside Plaza apartment, no monitoring of hours or of nutrition or of lifestyle. The only accounting he required of his son, starting on his eighteenth birthday, had been a weekly budget session in which the younger LeGeros had reconciled his expenditures with his earnings.

But even those meetings had slacked off once Bernard landed his lucrative gallery job. John had been impressed by the three-hundred-dollar-a-week salary, the new suits, the apparent responsibility. He even seemed to respect Bernard's new boss, although with some reservation. Two or three times, John had called Andrew Crispo and invited him to dinner at the United Nations delegates' dining room, a very exclusive, though not very fancy, eatery in the UN's main complex on the East River. He wanted to thank Crispo for offering encouragement to his son, but Crispo declined each time, citing a full schedule. Once, Crispo claimed he was having a dinner meeting with Fidel Ramos, the Filipino general; other times, he said he was busy negotiating a sale to Imelda Marcos. "A common name-dropper," John had complained. "I think I was supposed to be impressed."

Nonetheless, certain things about this man kept panning out: When Bernard spoke of the royalty that frequented the gallery, the assertions went ignored; Andrew Crispo in those brief conversations had confirmed their presence. Bernard bragged about limousines and great expense accounts and luxurious apartments and, well, John himself had seen the long black cars picking his son up some mornings. The boy's wild imagination seemed to have found a wild reality, John felt. This was good.

He once thought about going up to the gallery, just to meet this man, but decided against such a paternal intervention. Perhaps—although he'd never say this—he was baffled by the fact that anybody would want to employ his son, a kid who had disappointed him intellectually and otherwise.

Racquel had a similar undercurrent of distrust for the relationship Bernard claimed to have with his boss. Often, he was out through the night, or through the weekend, with this man, and she had wondered aloud to coworkers about the normalcy of this pairing.

One of those coworkers, the mother of a marginally renowned artist, had heard of Andrew Crispo. "He's a notorious homosexual," the woman said, brows arched high.

"Homosexual! Homosexuals," Racquel said, revealing a 1940s sensibility, "when they get involved in ugly things, they're *very* ugly things."

At least that's the way she remembered the conversation after the body was found.

John, in recent months, knew very little about how his son had spent his time, and only intervened when it seemed clear to him Bernard was concealing the AR-7 collapsible rifle. After their first visit to the Stony Point police on Tuesday, and the surprise arrival of cops at Bernard and David's apartment later that night, John had made Bernard promise to turn over the gun.

Again, John was entertaining no suspicions. He had convinced himself that the people who had rented Buckberg from them a decade ago, while the LeGeros family was in Yemen, had something to do with this. After moving back into the big country house, he found signs that witchcraft had been practiced there: candles and pentagrams and books on sorcery and "thousands and thousands of those little brochures they give out at Sunday school." He had mentioned this during his interview with Officer McGowan, who remembered the tenants.

John then added that he had also found industrial-strength spotlights in the basement. And in the smokehouse, he found "melted wax, drawings, hocus-pocus things." To John, the satanic angle was key. To McGowan, it was a fascinating aside. He was more curious about what role those spotlights—and those tenants—had played in the reports of UFO sightings over the Indian Point nuclear reactors across the river.

John hadn't seen Bernard on Wednesday, even though he had agreed to have breakfast in the family's apartment to bid his mother a safe trip. David joined John for the drive to the airport. On their way back, John showed his first signs of concern about his older son: "Why doesn't Bernard give up that dang gun?"

David said, "Suppose Bernard knows something about this?"

"What could he possibly know about this?"

David had just shrugged his shoulders.

John worked late into that Wednesday night, arriving home well after one in the morning. Three hours later, at 4:00 A.M., the phone rang. Andrew Crispo was on the line, apparently drunk. John wasn't awake enough to pay close attention, but Crispo's concerns about Bernard's alibi came across clearly. "I can account for every minute, every hour," Andrew told him, "except from one to five. One to five is a problem. I don't know anything about Bernard during those hours."

"My son doesn't need an alibi, Mr. Crispo. But I appreciate the call."

Insistently, Crispo pressed the point. "You should come over here, so I can explain the times, the whole schedule of times, to you," he said. "You really should."

"Thank you again, but do you know what time it is?"

John shuffled off to bed, making no effort to sort out the significance of the call.

Shortly, the phone rang again. It was Dean Aarons, who had been Bernard's guest in the adjoining building several weeks before. After a week there, Racquel had asked him to leave by fabricating a story about the imminent return of Bernard's grandparents—they would be needing their room back, she told him. She suspected the young man was a heavy drinker and saw no reason for him to stay. Bernard had objected to the eviction, unsuccessfully, saying he was "a friend of Andrew's, I'm helping him out for Andrew."

Aarons's call seemed long distance, and he was apparently quite frightened. "Mr. LeGeros? Look, I heard about the, about them, them finding a body on your property. I just wanted to let you know how sorry I am about it."

"Mr. Aarons," John said. "It's four-thirty in the morning. If you'd like to talk about this, call me when the sun comes up."

Still, John developed no theory to explain these coincidences.

But come Thursday, he was certainly very interested in finding his son. He spent most of the day on the phone, first with the gallery (they said Bernard hadn't shown up for work), and then, repeatedly, with the

Stony Point police station. Each time he called there, he was told they hadn't heard from Bernard. But at four that afternoon, the story had changed; Investigator Jimmy Stewart, from the district attorney's office, had called him. "Bernard is here, Mr. LeGeros," he said. "He's talking to us. I think you'd better come up here."

"You don't think he's involved, do you?"

"No," he said unequivocally. "But I think he knows something."

After making an unsuccessful effort to reach the family attorney, John raced up to the suburban police station, where, unexpectedly, he bumped into David, cooling his heels in an empty office. "What in blazes are you doing here?"

David said, "Just like you, looking for Bernard. I just got here, and he's on the other side, in a conference room."

John knocked on the door and was invited in by Officer Pat Barry, the New York City cop. "He's telling us a story," Barry said, "that you should listen to."

Looking deflated and solemn, as if he hadn't slept, Bernard took it from the top of the Billy Mayer version, starting with the section about how he, Bernard, had roamed around the city, cutting ever expanding circles away from Limelight in his search for the Vista Cruiser.

Later, outside of Bernard's earshot, an officer said to John, "Of course, this story doesn't ring true. I think he's shielding somebody, but who could it be?"

"You've got to understand," John said. "It's possible he would say anything. . . ."

"Why can't he find that gun?"

"I'm telling you, it is a favorite thing of his."

John LeGeros didn't volunteer to tell about his two unexpected phone calls. Their significance still baffled him. He hadn't even discussed them with his youngest son, who would have been able to offer a fascinating explanation. David had gotten a call from Crispo immediately after his father had. And David accepted the invitation to "come over here so I can explain the times."

Fifteen minutes before John received his middle-of-the-night call from Andrew Crispo, and twenty minutes before David received his, Crispo was awake and fully clothed, talking to Det. Joey Denise and Lt. Frank Tinelli over the intercom at 380 West Twelfth Street. "Dressed," Denise mused later, "as though he'd been expecting us." It was 3:45, very early Thursday morning, on March 21. The officers' instructions, just received from Det. Sgt. Franks, were to double-check the alibi Bernard had just given for the weekend that Eigil Vesti died. He had just written out details of the Billy Mayer version, a story in which Crispo's role was small but significant. Franks and the others didn't quite buy it—they were still grilling the subject—and Denise and Tinelli were in the Village on a mission to discredit the account.

It was also a way for the two Rockland cops to leave behind the peculiar world of sex and S&M they'd been milling around in for the last several nights. Denise had thought he'd find the clubs fascinating, even titillating, but his response was much more melancholy. "Sad life these people have to live," he had muttered. "Having to drag themselves out for this. I can't imagine it."

Andrew buzzed them past the doorman and into the elevator. On a notepad, Tinelli had written the salient facts needing confirmation: After leaving Limelight in search of Billy Mayer, LeGeros didn't see his boss again until nine the following morning, at which time the two of them holed up at the Twelfth Street apartment "working on some papers"; he napped there, and showered; they had dinner that night with a man named Edo Bertoglio and his girlfriend, Lynn, at Van Dam Restaurant on Varick Street. He was not clear on how the rest of the evening was spent, except to say that in the predawn hours of the following Monday, Andrew and Bernard rode in a rented limo to Southampton ("driver's name was Alan"), where they spent the rest of the day at his Gin Lane home. He said he had watched the movie *Witness* in a Southampton movie theater before returning, again with his boss, this time via the jitney bus.

Inside his apartment, an anxious Andrew Crispo seemed nervous and strange. Before the officers could begin their questioning, he frantically blurted out an apparently prepared statement. In it, he was stressing a bizarre caveat.

"They say it was this Norwegian guy," he said, "but I think it was somebody else." He held up the sensational MISSING poster for Eigil Vesti next to an eight-by-ten head shot of a man with a striking resemblance to the deceased. His hair was blond and mussed, just like Vesti's, and he, too, was wearing a jacket with no shirt. In both poses, the lips were slightly parted. This new fellow, though, had a deep cleft in the chin, making him look a little bit more, well, American. Like Robbie Douglas from "My Three Sons." "This is René Arlington," Crispo said. "I think somebody's trying to kill him. Enemies of mine," he said excitedly, "might be trying to block a movie deal—he wrote a book, explosive book, about the Church, the Pope. I'm in negotiations, and there are people who don't want to see this thing happen. I think somebody's trying to kill René Arlington. This," he said about the poster, "is not a picture of some FIT student. This is René! Don't you see it? Look closely."

He argued that the posters were put up not because somebody was indeed missing but in order to send a message to him, to Andrew Crispo, that if he was serious about following through on any film, there would be a great price.

Detective Denise, perhaps just as disturbed by this apparently psychotic rendition as he had been at the Hellfire Club down the street, was growing even more resolute in his distaste for New York City as a whole. "You got to be a weirdo to live so close to all these other weirdos," he concluded later, snapping his head. He let Lieutenant Tinelli talk.

The lieutenant said, "We need to talk to you about the weekend of February twenty-second through the twenty-fourth."

For twenty minutes, Crispo showered the officers with a nearly indecipherable string of times and places, delivered in jolting sprints of recollection.

A block away, Denise and Tinelli regrouped on a dark, windy corner and called Franks from a pay phone to inform him that the story, more or less, jibed. From Crispo, it seemed unrehearsed.

"I also asked him if he'd ever been to the LeGeros house in Tomkins Cove," the lieutenant said, "and he said no. Emphatically said no."

Franks asked him, "What are you doing tomorrow?"

"I guess I'm working on this," said his boss. "Why?"

"How'd you like to go to Florida?"

"Are you kidding? I'd love to go to Florida."

"Well, good, because we found Billy Mayer there, and somebody should go get him."

Immediately after Tinelli and Denise left his apartment, Andrew Crispo called Bernard's father, and once again reviewed his list of times and dates. Apparently unfulfilled by that exchange, he called the other Waterside Plaza apartment, and woke David.

"Where's Bernard?" he demanded.

"Who is this?"

"Andrew. Andrew Crispo. The police have just been here."

"Well, he's not here." He checked the clock; it was well after four. "He doesn't always come here."

"I want you to listen to me. I think—I'm worried about your brother, I think he might try to hurt himself. I'm looking all over for him."

"Sometimes he stays with Elana. You can try him there."

Crispo said he already had. "Bernard's—your brother's—been acting weird lately. Since they found the, you know—found it upstate. Maybe— I, I think something serious has happened to Bernard."

"You mean," said David, "since your little adventure was made public." It was the first time David had allowed himself to acknowledge aloud the story Bernard had told him four weeks earlier.

For a long time, only breathing came over the phone line. Heavy, erratic breathing. "David, I want you to come talk with me. This is very urgent. Now! Up at the gallery."

David threw on a heavy green army jacket, and was there by 5:00 A.M. So was Crispo, wearing a rumpled suit that had been torn out under the armpit. It was only their second meeting.

The older man ushered him through the large doors of the gallery, and seemed a physical wreck. He was jumpy, and his eyes were dark and shallow. Crispo leaned close to David, inventorying the young man. "You wired?" he asked, and touched the full pockets of the green coat.

"What?"

"Wired, wired. Tape recorder or anything?"

David said no, and was led into the gallery. They walked past the reception desk, through the cluttered main space—Picasso silver plates, African-type masks, collages—and around the stairs, to a small room with red carpeting and deep red walls. At the door, Crispo asked him again, "Are you wired?"

"No, of course not."

"You're sure?"

"Don't you think this is something I would know?" With David, aggressiveness came off like apology. His eyes grew very large instead of narrowing.

"You want anything?"

"Like what?" Crispo explained he was about to order up breakfast from a local deli. "Oh, no, thanks. Nothing."

He called down for coffee or tea. "How about a toot?"

"What's a toot?"

Crispo laughed seditiously. "A toot of *cocaine*."

"Oh. No. I don't do drugs."

"Well, excuse me, then. Because I'm real nervous and I got to take a toot," he said, leaving the room with a small container. He returned shortly and sat down. He stood up and moved toward the phone, took it off the receiver, and returned to his seat.

Then, still silently, he stood up again and picked up the telephone, moved it outside the room, and closed the door.

Sitting back down, he said, "It might be wired. Or there might be a tap; the whole business might be tapped. I want to show you something," Crispo said, telescoping a thousand thoughts. He reached beneath the sofa and pulled out the photograph of René Arlington. It was in a wood frame. "This," he said pointedly, placing it on a cushion. He reached down again and produced the MISSING poster. "And this. Don't they look alike?" He glanced earnestly at David, who was motionless. "The poster and the picture. Don't they? Identical, they look." Crispo turned them toward himself, reexamined the two, convinced himself once more, turned them around. "Identical. You know why? This"—he pointed to the poster—"this isn't Vesti."

He told the long story about the book, about his enemies. "René's father was killed, I think, by the Vatican and his body was burnt somewhere outside the country. Now"—eyes growing wild—"they want him, want René! Eigil Vesti, his body was burned, and because Paul Murphy, who was René's father, well stepfather, because his body was burned, now they're putting René's picture on the poster to capitalize on this fact. The burning. It's all part of trying to scam me out of a million dollars. Look at the cheekbones, the eyes, everything. They are the same."

"I guess so."

Andrew reached under the couch one last time, surfacing with a copy of *La Popessa*. The paper cover was brown, with white lettering. A painting of a nun in a white habit stared out from the front, the back, and the spine. "I could stand to lose a million," he said. "More. A million or more."

He placed the evidence down purposefully on a coffee table. "There's a strong possibility of Vatican involvement here. Your brother was with me and I can have Claire at Limelight verify this. All night, he slept over here—or at my apartment, I mean—the whole weekend. We never left the city. This can all be verified."

"Mr. Crispo. I already know about the party, the adventure of yours up at Buckberg. Bernard told me about it."

With a sudden intensity, Crispo walked across the room and returned with a red folder. "This is where we were," he said, "this is everything."

David opened the folder and leafed through a stack of paper written in his brother's hand: question and answer, question and answer. David recognized the entries as Bernard's account of his conversations with the Stony Point police. Dates and times were underscored. On the top was written "For Andrew."

As David read the first entry, Andrew Crispo whispered, "Just a minute. I think your brother may be upstairs! I can't go look, I'm too scared." He seemed genuinely terrified.

David slapped the folder on the table and bolted through the door, up the stairs, calling his brother's name. He went from room to room, all dark, and gripped the doorjambs, calling out. Winded and angry, he returned to the entrance of the Red Room, where he saw Crispo recapping his coke vial.

"Did you look in the bathroom?" He pointed to a small door off the office, and David checked there, too. "Close the door, then. I have something to tell you. Something about the burned body you should know."

After an emphatic pause, he said, "You know how some parties can get—kind of wild, you know. Out of hand."

David nodded, although he didn't understand.

"Three of us, we're in the car, we're at Bernard's house—*your* house, and . . . and . . . A game. Role playing. I don't know how much you know. We were playing. And your brother went off. *Killed* this guy—bam, bam. Do you understand?"

David fidgeted. "Well, what were *you* doing?"

"Just stuff, normal little games, with Vesti. Do you understand this mess now?"

"No," he said with resolve. "Not at all."

"Are you wired?"

"I told you . . ."

"Okay, okay. Okay. From out of nowhere—*from out of nowhere*—came the life-form. *Ssshhhhhh.* Just like that! And then Bernard went, 'Oh, we have to eliminate this,' the body, 'have to eliminate this.' We . . . the gasoline scheme, threw wood and everything else, and set the item on fire."

David was quite terrified, and said nothing.

"Your brother snapped. What's his snap coefficient?"

"His what?"

"Snap coefficient. I ask, because I think he snapped. He was going to throw away the you-know. But I told him, you throw something like that away, you never know when someone's gonna find it. I told him to hide it in a safe place so that twenty years from now he still knows where it is. For twenty years, we can have some peace."

David felt caged in this strange, halting monologue. An unfamiliar rage was growing in him like algae. Though he had been the instigator, David did not want this confirmation of the murder story his brother had told him. He hated Crispo now for giving it. The fact that someone had died was infinitely less hateful than this. David stood up nervously as though to leave, and found some pleasure in having inadvertently startled Crispo in the process.

"The marijuana plant," Andrew Crispo said—lifting his hands as if to shoulder a rifle—"has been moved to a safe place"—jabbing both index fingers toward the ceiling, toward the gallery's second floor. "The marijuana plant. Safe place."

David was back at his apartment for a few hours when Crispo called him again, ordering him to return to the gallery immediately. He arrived by cab at 10:45 A.M, more helpless than angry. A man sat at the reception desk, attempting to make a call to Brazil. Another stood in one corner of the main gallery space.

Crispo took him aside and again asserted his belief that "Bernard cracked, flipped." Now, though, he was arguing that René Arlington looked nothing like Eigil Vesti, and tried to get David to concur.

"I guess so," he said.

"Somebody's got to clean the house," Crispo said abruptly. "Clean up the house."

"What are you talking about?"

"And the car. I'm telling you, if they find one little piece of evidence in the house or the car, your brother's fried. This is what I want you to do," he said. "I'm going to paint a little design on the back of your jacket with special glue. It'll look like artwork, like a design. Then you've gotta get in the car and roll around on the seats and the floor, being very careful to touch everything possible with the coat. Pick up every last piece of hair, or whatever."

David balked.

"Look," Crispo said. "Your brother is a very marginal and unstable person and he may have gotten himself in some trouble. Did he tell you where he might have gone?"

"No, he told me that you two went up to Buckberg."

"I don't mean then, I mean today."

"Oh, no."

"I think—there's a chance he may have gone to the West Side. He might be lying in an alley or something like that. Or by the water, by the piers, the docks."

"What makes you say that?"

"A hunch. If I were you, I'd go and look."

David left, but not for the West Side docks. He went to work, where he had been expected hours before. Like his parents, David could sublimate any troublesome, untidy matter in order to make room for paid labor. It's the way he had first dealt with Bernard's obvious drug habits, how he had handled his brother's suicide attempts and peculiar, insistent fabrications about sadomasochism, torture, murder.

* * *

At the same time David LeGeros headed off to work, his brother sat slouched in a green leather-covered library chair in the Stony Point interview room. It was mid-morning on March 21, the day following the onset of his interrogation, and Bernard continued talking. Through the night, he had tried to take catnaps by pulling another chair up to the one he was using and spreading his tired body over both. But he had not gotten rest.

At about 10:25 A.M., he asked for a pen and paper, and he updated the Billy Mayer version in long hand. Additional information had Bernard visiting the smokehouse a week following the incident "for possible signs of a killing." Indeed, he said, there was a charred body inside the structure. "I got a sledgehammer and tried to knock down the smokehouse, to conceal what my friend Billy Mayer claimed to have left behind. I was not able to do so, and I then decided to torch it, it meaning the remains."

He admitted to taking logs from the house and throwing them "in the chest area of the body to try to burn the remaining flesh from the bones." Using a white Bic lighter, he reignited the corpse and "stayed at the smokehouse for about an hour making sure the fire was still burning."

Two hours after this admission, Bernard called Sergeant Franks back to the interview room and asked to amend his comments again. He admitted, for the first time, that he had been present, that he was an eyewitness to the murder. Franks, feeling he was getting closer to the truth, dictated this version into his tape recorder:

> Bernard stated that while at the Limelight disco on Friday, February 22, 1985, into Saturday morning, February 23, 1985, Billy Mayer states to him that he wants to kill Freddy, the employee. Bernard stated that that conversation takes place in the crowded disco, and he tells Billy to be quiet and that someone would overhear him. Billy Mayer then said to Bernard that they could invite Freddy to a party upstate and that they could get the "fag" up there to Bernard's Tomkins Cove residence and kill him. Bernard stated that Billy attempted to get Freddy to leave the club with them, but that he was very busy and said that he was unable to leave.
>
> During the evening, Bernard states that he and Billy Mayer meet the deceased, Eigil Dag Vesti, and invite him to a party upstate, and that he agrees. Bernard stated that they entered his parents' Oldsmobile station wagon, traveled north through Manhattan to the George Washington Bridge and north on the Palisades Interstate Parkway. Bernard stated that as soon as

they left the city, Billy started belittling Vesti and exerting his master (sadist) behavior over his new "slave," and Bernard stated that he was calling him a "Jew fag," a "Jew-loving cocksucker," "scum-eating Jew," et cetera; and that Billy Mayer always plays the part of a German Nazi and refers to his S&M partners as "Jews."

Bernard stated that while traveling north on the Palisades Interstate Parkway, Vesti states, "This is nice up here. Where are we going?" And Billy Mayer says to him, "You're going to Norway—in a fucking box." Bernard states that he realizes that they are going to kill Vesti, and they continue to his father's house, known as 100 Buckberg Mountain Road, Stony Point, New York. Bernard further advised that he was in the area of exit 12 on the PIP when he is convinced that Vesti will be murdered.

Bernard states that they arrive at his parents' home and the three of them enter the residence, at which time he shows Vesti and Mayer an assortment of knives, swords, and rifles, including what he knew to be a loaded .22 caliber AR-7 rifle. Bernard states that he allows Billy Mayer and Eigil Vesti to go downstairs to the downstairs living room and engage in their sadomasochistic activities. Bernard stated that he could hear strapping and turned up the radio upstairs to override the noises coming from the basement. Bernard stated that a short time later, he observed Eigil Vesti come upstairs wearing only a jock and a full bondage hood, and then Billy Mayer came up behind him and struck Vesti several times with a belt. Bernard stated that he called Billy Mayer in the other room and asked him to take Vesti outside because he didn't want the homicide committed in his parents' house. Bernard stated that Billy Mayer and Eigil Vesti went outside and he observed Vesti giving a blowjob to Billy outside his residence on the porch near the downstairs living room. Bernard stated that he then observed Vesti being led on a belt-type leash by Billy toward the smokehouse, and that Billy is carrying the AR-7 rifle. Bernard states that he follows the twosome down the embankment across the tennis courts to the smokehouse, and he observes Vesti on his knees in front of the enclosure, noted that Vesti's hands were bound behind his back, and states that he watches Billy execute him by shooting him twice in the back of the head.

Bernard LeGeros states that he said to Billy, "Now we have to take care of this mess." Bernard LeGeros states that he

returns to his residence with Billy Mayer, that they obtained
gasoline from the garage and returned to the smokehouse and
set Vesti on fire using gasoline, logs, and twigs. Bernard stated
that they left the residence, traveled to an area north on Route
9W from Buckberg Mountain Road, making the first right turn
onto an unknown street, and that he threw the rifle into the
backwaters of the Hudson River on the west side of the railroad
tracks. Bernard stated that they then traveled to the Palisades
Parkway via the back roads, traveled south on the Palisades
Parkway to exit 1 or 2 on the Jersey side of the PIP, drove
around for a while, found a dumpster, and Bernard said that he
threw the victim's clothing into a dumpster at a construction
site.

Although he had spent a great deal of time dictating the entry into
his tape recorder, and although his secretary would spend even longer
transcribing it, Franks went through the motions only procedurally. He
didn't believe this story, either. Cop's intuition.

Early on the afternoon of the fourth day of his vacation in Florida, first
in Miami Beach and now at a friend's home in Tampa, Billy Mayer spent
the morning completing the most implausible account he'd ever entered
in his journal. After capping his pen, he carried the red spiral notebook
with him on an errand to the local convenience store, reading it over for
accuracy and spelling.

In it, he had described his first meeting with Eigil Vesti, at Crispo's
downtown apartment. When Mayer and Bernard had arrived, Vesti had
been sitting naked on a sofa, masturbating languidly, his thin white thighs
splayed on the cushion. Mayer wrote in detail about participating in what
he called "not more than a few minutes" of whippings and beatings and
verbal abuse of the skinny blond, before Bernard had driven Mayer
home. And he recalled how, a day later, Bernard had boasted to him that
he had returned to Andrew's apartment for some more activity. "We
snuffed the guy," Bernard had told him, but, Mayer wrote, "I didn't
believe it for a minute."

That changed one afternoon in the Village more than two weeks later
when Mayer had spotted his first Eigil Vesti poster pasted to the side of
a telephone booth. He had recognized the face immediately, and lowered
himself to the curb in absolute disbelief. "Could he have really done
this?" he had asked his companion on the stroll. "Could this be real?"

The day the body was found in the smokehouse, there was no more
room for doubt. Billy Mayer had decided to take a little vacation; he had

left from Newark Airport the following morning. He'd figured he knew too much. He'd felt his life was in danger. He'd feared Andrew Crispo.

Still three blocks away from the Tampa condominium where he was staying, Billy Mayer watched a group of men ascend the stoop at 11617 North Fifty-first Street. Lt. Frank Tinelli was knocking on the door. Behind him were a Rockland ADA, a New York State special investigator, and two Tampa police. "Undercover," Billy Mayer said later, "but they might as well have had *cop* tattooed on their foreheads."

Mayer had actually been expecting them. He said, "Looking for me?" And when they said yes, he handed over the notebook. "This says it all," he said, "the whole ugly story."

Tinelli read the first few pages right there.

> Thursday, March 21, 1985.
> —Miami Beach.
> Here I am in Miami and it is the 3rd day I've been here.
> "I threw the body in the grotto and lit it on fire. The flames blew up all around me but did not touch me. It was as if the gates of hell had opened up and I was the keeper."
> "When you kill, it has to be done totally without emotion— you can't be angry. You have to do it as if you were lighting a cigarette or driving a car."
> "After I was finished, we got in the car. I told C— to shut up. He didn't say a word as I drove at 100 mph to his house. We turned out the lights and lit some candles. I went to bed and slept like a baby."
> "I walked into the room like death itself."
> These are various quotes from you-know-who. I have to admit that he is a gifted poet, but it seems that he is probably psychotic since he committed a bizarre murder namely for the thrill or the experience or whatever and is displaying absolutely no remorse for it. Quite to the contrary, he plans to kill again.

After placing a brief call to Stony Point, Lieutenant Tinelli, clutching Billy Mayer and the spiral notebook, boarded a late-afternoon flight back to New York City. Billy Mayer would be kept as a "guest of the State of New York" for several days, and would submit to a series of acrimonious grillings.

Det. Sgt. Billy Franks returned to the small room where Bernard had spent nearly twenty-four hours. "We've just spoken to Bill Mayer," he said, offering the young man a cigarette, "and he says you did it." Ber-

nard's father was in the room at the time. John LeGeros did not call off
the interviews at this time. He did not try again to reach Murray Sprung,
the family attorney. Nowhere in his thoughts did he harbor the slightest
suspicions about his son's personal involvement. This was just another
product of a "fantastical mind," more of Bernard's "dreamy nature."

Personally, he resumed the interrogation of his son. He asked about
times, about whereabouts, about witnesses and names and alibis.

"There's something wrong with this time sequence," he said to one
cop; to another, he said, "I think he knows something, but I can't get to
the bottom of it."

When, close to midnight, Franks came into the room where John and
David LeGeros were waiting for Bernard, John's genuine assumption
was, without question, that the officer was there to announce Bernard's
release. Instead, Franks said, "He has confessed to being the gunman—
pretty much the same story, but he substituted his name for Billy's, and
Andrew Crispo's name for his own. I believe this is an accurate account.
I believe this is how it happened."

Furthermore, he said, this ultimate version dovetailed with the story
that he had given Billy Mayer, and Billy Mayer put in his book, independently.

David LeGeros began to fall apart. "He told me he did this," he blurted
out, crying. "He told me, but I don't believe it! He hates blood. This is
impossible."

His father prodded for details, still playing investigator; David continued: "I told him I didn't believe him. I said, 'Sure, I killed a guy, too. I
shot two people today.' But he kept telling me, like four different times.
Once, he even acted it out."

Only then did John LeGeros show a father's reaction. He was shaking
visibly. Later, he realized how completely and skillfully he had convinced
himself of Bernard's innocence. That is, until he forced himself to picture
Bernard acting out the slaying. Then it seemed clear, and entirely possible. Then he felt sure his son had lost his mind.

LeGeros encouraged his youngest son to follow the county stenographer into a quiet office and give a statement—a statement against his
beloved brother, Bernard.

In the presence of an assistant district attorney, several cops, and a
stenographer with a steno machine, David began by telling about a visit
he had made to the Crispo Gallery just that morning. There was another
meeting between them, several hours later. According to David, Crispo
had told him a story that—for the first time—gave some credence to
what Bernard had said a full month earlier.

On February 24, in the early morning, Bernard had bounded into their room while David was asleep. "I shot someone," he'd shouted, and "we shot someone," freely alternating the two pronouns. David had begged him to turn off the light and let him sleep, but his older brother had persisted. Frustrated, David had said, "C'mon, I shot two people today, too," and he had tried to fall asleep again. But Bernard had shaken him wildly, saying, "You've got to hear this."

"He said he was at the smokehouse with Crispo and the AR-seven," David told the officers. "I figured, Well, you woke me up. I might as well get up. I got up and washed up and went to the car, because he had to wait for a limousine to pick him up to take him somewhere." David explained that, though it was before dawn, he had errands to perform in New Jersey and had planned to get an early start. The two sat in the family car in the driveway of Waterside, chatting.

Thomas Zugibe, the assistant district attorney (and nephew to Frederick Zugibe, the chief medical examiner who had done the autopsy on Eigil Vesti), interrupted. "What car was that?"

"A Vista Cruiser, Olds."

"Seventy-four Olds?"

"Seventy-six."

"What else did he say to you regarding the shooting?"

"I said, 'What happened,' and he told me this guy was shot in the smokehouse. I said, I started to get serious, I said, 'You just don't go shooting people.' He said this guy was harassing him or something like that and I said, 'Well, what happened?' He goes, 'Well, there they was in the smokehouse and he shot him.' I said, 'With what?' He said, 'With his AR-seven.' "

Over the ensuing weeks, David said, Bernard had continually entreated him to go to Buckberg and check out the smokehouse, which he finally did. "There were bones in there, but it looked like a Great Dane or a deer or something," David said. "I figured they had shot this animal, so I told him to go and clean it up."

When the body was discovered, and the rifle was not, David had begun to assume there was some foundation of truth to what Bernard had told him—"like maybe Crispo did this, and told him about it."

He had confronted Bernard often about locating the gun. There was a particularly angry exchange upstairs in Buckberg, the night the LeGeros family had gone there with the police. "I said, 'Look, you're wasting everybody's time. Just give up that gun so they can prove that you had nothing to do with this.' And then later he said it again. They shot this guy and then, uh, then they cut him in his side and let blood drip out into a wineglass. This they drank."

Investigator Shae had previously been among the most skeptical about the belief, promulgated by the medical examiner's office, that the body had been mutilated. Not anymore. "He did what?" he asked in a loud voice.

"Again," David said, "it was four in the morning, I told him he was full of shit." Then he looked over at his father and added, "That's when he acted the whole thing out for me."

The statement taken, John and David were told they could leave; they spent the rest of the night in a twenty-four-hour coffee shop. At some point, John asked his son why he hadn't told him about Bernard's involvements earlier, to which David replied, "I tried to," and then, "I don't know," and then, "I didn't really believe it." Otherwise, they did not speak much.

At daybreak they were at Murray Sprung's Manhattan apartment. John gingerly tucked the old attorney in the car at the curb and flung his aluminum walker in the backseat; David went home, in case Racquel was to call from her conference. John hadn't spoken to her since her departure, and he was feeling a great need for her company, and a pounding terror about how she would react. He instructed David to tell her nothing.

The two older men headed for Rockland County immediately, up the Palisades Interstate Parkway toward exit 15. Murray Sprung did not seem to believe that David's statement to authorities was inappropriate. But then again, David was not the only person to whom Bernard had offered up a confession. Although Sprung didn't yet know it, Bernard had told the same story to Billy Mayer. He'd even bragged about it to Edo Bertoglio, a photographer friend of Crispo's from Switzerland, and Dean Aarons.

Before arriving at the police station on Central Highway, the two men went to a church together and exchanged private words with a minister. Sprung undoubtedly asked for the strength and wisdom to handle the case, aware that his physical weakness, coupled with his inexperience in criminal court, made him a poor choice for Bernard's defense.

CHAPTER
15

By combining Bernard's, David's, and Billy Mayer's stories, Stony Point police pieced together this, the most complete accounting of Friday night, February 22, 1985:

Andrew Crispo, Bernard LeGeros, and Billy Mayer did meet at Hellfire and took turns roaming through its dungeonlike basement rooms. On the stage, a black woman dressed in a leather bikini was paddling a naked, older, paler man; a crowd gathered around another couple, watching as they engaged in oral sex. The Crispo group was just browsing, Andrew in a business suit, Billy in work pants, Bernard wearing jeans and black Italian combat boots. None wore coats or jackets; a bizarre heat wave had engulfed the city, bringing the February temperatures up to sixty-two degrees, a record high.

By their standards, it was a tame evening at the club, so they did some coke and agreed to head over to Limelight. They jumped in the Vista Cruiser, joked about it being their Command Vehicle, and drove toward the Sixth Avenue disco. Their route brought them within a few blocks of Rick's Lounge, where Eigil Vesti was sipping a martini with friends.

On the way, according to Mayer, "Andrew Crispo offered the suggestion that that would be a good night to kill Freddy." Andrew and Bernard had promised to help their friend Edo Bertoglio exact some sort of revenge against Frederick Rothbell-Mista, one of Limelight's managers. Freddy and Edo and Edo's girlfriend had had a disagreement weeks earlier in Palmas del Mar, a Puerto Rican resort town. By some coincidence, they had found themselves simultaneous guests in the home of a "rock star" who was not present. Rothbell-Mista had felt the other two were mistreating the host's property, and had so informed the host. There was, apparently, a subsequent showdown outside a nearby club, in which the girlfriend ("quite drunk and screaming") approached Freddy, who was in a car. Words were exchanged and the girlfriend claimed she was butted with the vehicle, though not harmed.

Back in New York, when Bertoglio had gone to Limelight and attempted to settle the score, Rothbell-Mista had had him expelled. Edo Bertoglio vowed to get even.

Early in February, he had first brought the subject up. "They were trying to figure out ways of getting vengeance on Fred," Billy Mayer said later. "Edo felt that Bernard was kind of like an expert in the field." Crispo had first proposed sending anonymous and frightening letters, then suggested taking him to a wooded area, stripping him, and tying him to a tree and whipping him. "Who knows," somebody said, "he'd probably like that," and it was rejected.

In a predictable bluster, Bernard announced, "There is only one possibility: He has to be eliminated. Why don't we kill the fucking fag?"

Edo Bertoglio, of course, opposed that plan, saying he'd be content with punching the man in the nose. "Besides," he said, "this is my problem. I'll take care of this."

Such objections notwithstanding, a plan unfolded inside the Vista Cruiser on February 22, on the short drive to Limelight, which combined the worst of those suggestions. Freddy Rothbell-Mista would be taken to the country, tied up, and killed there.

The three men, looking more or less presentable, were ushered into the VIP room, which Rothbell-Mista ruled as host and manager. He knew Crispo from his previous visits to the club, and was introduced to Bernard and Billy Mayer for the first time. He personally served a wine to Crispo, a beer to Mayer, and a Coke to Bernard.

Crispo repeatedly invited the host to a hot party "just over the George Washington Bridge." Each time, Rothbell-Mista declined: "No, I'm too busy. I've got to work here."

Crispo was persistent, offering Freddy "all the blow I wanted" and "his boys for sex." He insisted that Billy was quite interested in Freddy, and described his testicles as large and cool. He added that Bernard "gives good head" and that the party would include others, mostly college-aged boys. "It's gonna be hot," he said. "Really hot."

At around 3:45 A.M., with the VIP room still crowded, Bernard—with Crispo at his side—made one last entreaty. "Billy really likes you; he wants you to come with us." Again, Freddy Rothbell-Mista politely declined.

Crispo seemed injured by the rejection. "Maybe you'd like to come some other time," he offered, and Rothbell-Mista nodded. "How about giving me your phone number, and we'll call the next time we're having a party."

The host agreed and jotted down his numbers, both home and work, on a napkin.

Then Crispo called his team aside and instructed them to leave the club. If he was willing to give a number, perhaps he could be convinced to come along, Crispo said. He vowed to try one more time, and said he would meet them back at Hellfire in forty minutes. Mayer and LeGeros piled into the Vista Cruiser and headed for Bernard's apartment at Waterside Plaza. There they picked up the dismantled AR-7 and placed it in a black nylon bag, stopped at a neighborhood coffee shop for a container of coffee, and headed south again to find their friend.

P.J., the doorman at Hellfire, told them that Crispo had already come and gone—with a thin blond man in tow. So Bernard and Mayer got back in the car and drove the few extra blocks to Andrew's nearby apartment. P.J. rode along on the hood, with no jacket. His shift was over, and he was on his way to the Mineshaft for an after-work drink; when they swung past there, he slid off. It was a balmy evening, a beautiful, playful night in the Village.

At first, when Bernard buzzed, Andrew was hesitant. "I've got somebody here," he said after a long pause. Bernard buzzed again, and the door was finally opened. They took the elevator to the top floor. Crispo, in dark running shorts, a black T-shirt, and a black NYPD baseball cap, let them in; a wiry blond man with a striking Nordic face sat naked on a sofa. His legs were tucked under him and his knees were spread wide. Slowly, seductively, he was milking a slender, fully erect penis. He looked inquisitively at the newcomers.

"Bernard," Andrew said, gesturing, "he doesn't believe I'm a fag."

Eigil Vesti, still masturbating, said, "What the fuck are these guys doing here?" His tone of voice was conversational, not commanding.

Bernard said, "Bill. Tell him who this is."

"This is only the biggest fucking queen," Mayer said, referring to Crispo.

With that, Vesti turned around and leaned over the back of the sofa, presenting himself.

"He thinks you guys are faggots," Crispo said, handing Mayer a five-foot bullwhip. "You going to let him get away with that?"

Billy Mayer gave a swipe. It landed on Eigil's shoulder blade, and he seemed to thrust his buttocks out farther, indicating what Billy took to be his preferred striking zone.

"What the fuck are you guys doing?" Vesti asked again.

Bernard said, "Billy, man. That's not the way," and took the whip from him. "Let me show you how to do that." Bernard unfolded a full-arm swing. The braided end of the whip grabbed Vesti's flesh into a bright red welt.

Crispo was standing to one side of the developing scene, half-smiling, apparently pleased. "Bernard," he said, "he's a friend of Sam Collins's."

Bernard swung again, and again, tearing a great noise from the end of the lanyard. Eigil tried to turn around, apparently concerned. Bernard knee-dropped him against the far side of the couch. Using a handful of his hair as leverage, Bernard cocked back Eigil's head and planted the hard butt of the whip's handle square on his shoulder. Once. Twice. Andrew stooped forward, as if to place his ear close enough to the victim's rib cage to hear the echoes of the blow.

Billy Mayer had disappeared into the bathroom, several yards away, and when he came back out, he loudly announced that he was leaving. Crispo hushed him, worried his booming voice would wake Arthur Smith and his other neighbors. "I'm leaving," he said again. "I'm getting outta here."

Bernard said, "Nah, Billy, don't. Wait!"

"Nah, I'm taking off."

"All right, wait! I'll drive you, I'll drive you."

"Listen, if you want to hang out, man."

"No, I'll drive you."

"Okay, listen. See you, Andrew."

"See ya', Andrew," Bernard said, glancing over to see the victim, still kneeling into the couch, let out a shallow breath of relief.

At this hour of the morning, the streets were virtually empty of cars, but the sidewalks were still surprisingly well peopled. Having withstood winter, New Yorkers in every neighborhood from the Village to the Upper East Side seemed incapable of letting go of the springlike day.

The drive took just ten minutes, and was marked by a tense argument. Billy Mayer felt Bernard got too excited about Crispo's "little games." He was mad at Andrew—perhaps still ticked off by the testicles comment—and he wanted Bernard to see it his way.

"Like Freddy," he said, "he's not gonna kill Freddy! He's just telling you that, and then sitting back and watching you. He's using you, man. He says this shit, and this shit never happens."

"He's gonna get Freddy, Bill. You don't know him."

"This guy, he makes you wait, he makes you do shit for him, he plays games with you, he's not really your friend. Like that time he called you and told you to get coke from Edo. Remember? And when you get back to his place, he says, 'Not right now. I've got somebody up here. Come back in a half hour.' And you just do it, man. Why do you do it?"

"Oh, he is! He is really my friend. He'd do the same shit for me."

Mayer snorted. "Bernard, man. You dropped out of NYU for him, you know? You put things on hold for him, like your friends and stuff. You think he'd do that?" He ridiculed Bernard for putting up with Andrew's frequent "blowjob" comments and the Sam Collins taunts, for becoming his apparent "lapdog." "This guy's forty and you're twenty-two. He's playing with your mind. Like that guy up there, he wasn't no friend of Collins."

"Andrew's a good guy; he's nice. He'd protect me," Bernard said combatively.

Then he repeated an assertion he'd made to Billy Mayer before, and which Mayer had repeatedly dismissed. "He's my half brother, Billy," Bernard said. "My dad was his dad, and my dad abandoned him! Now you're trying to tell *me* to abandon him!"

"Well, I know one thing for sure," Billy said, changing the subject back. "Crispo has no plans to kill anybody."

"Bullshit," Bernard said.

It was 5:00 A.M. when Billy Mayer got out of the car on East Eighty-first Street. He assumed Bernard was heading home.

There were only slight and (from a police standpoint) unimportant variations in Billy's and Bernard's account of events up to this point. Bernard said that he warned Eigil Vesti to escape, but Billy did not recall that. Billy said there came a time when Vesti seemed to be jerking against the pain; Bernard's account had him angling for more. Independently, however, both agreed on Crispo's conduct—including his exact words—throughout the time all four players were together in the apartment, which was estimated to be less than ten minutes.

The rest of the story, gleaned from Bernard's various confessions—to the police, to Billy Mayer and David LeGeros, and, later, to his lawyer—struck the investigating officers as credible, as far as it went.

They believed Bernard arrived back downtown at 5:15, and found Vesti kneeling in the foyer. He was wearing the leather hood around his

head and handcuffs on his wrists, which were in front of him. The zipper
was open, and Vesti's tongue slithered in and out of the grotesque opening, pink and damp.

Bernard commanded, "Stop fucking around," and kicked Vesti hard in
the side. "Enough is enough! I warned you, Andrew. I'm getting tired
of this *shit*!" Bernard tried to walk around Vesti, who had righted himself
again, to get to the bathroom, but Crispo pushed the hooded man into
Bernard's path. Bernard kicked him again, this time on the backs of his
thighs, before entering the bathroom and slamming the door behind him.

"What are you doing?" Crispo yelled through the door. "Crying? Hey,
the little girl is crying."

"Fuck off, Andrew. I'm not playing this game. I'm sick of your fuckin'
games!"

He turned on the water in the sink but could still hear a Norwegian
voice: "Crying, crying, the little girl is crying." It enraged him. He flung
the door open and swung his boot far behind him, a pendulum driving
into Vesti's stomach. Vesti doubled over and knocked his leather head
mutely against the hardwood floor.

Crispo let the crackling tension subside some before helping Vesti into
the bathroom and approaching Bernard on the sofa. He screwed open a
brown vial of cocaine; connected to the inside of the cap was a small
spoon, the way hoops are attached to bottles of soap bubbles. Crispo
filled the spoon with a small heap of powder and raised it to Bernard's
nose. "Let's really kill him," he suggested softly.

"Bullshit, Andrew, you're always so full of shit!"

Crispo spooned a pile into each of his own nostrils decisively, and
joined Vesti in the bathroom. Several minutes passed before the two
men reappeared. Once again, that red tongue was flicking between the
zipper's edges. "So we're going for a ride," the tongue said. "Where?"

"Who the fuck you think you are?" Bernard said, hurling the words
like lashes. "I didn't invite you anywhere."

"We're taking him for a *ride*," Andrew said. "For a ride. Can I talk
with you a moment?"

Bernard reached for the vial, and now he was joining Crispo in the
bathroom.

But Crispo was no longer using measured tones. "You're going to take
that shit from him?" He shook his head violently. "That fag stuff? That
stuff? A friend of Collins? Take that shit from him and do nothing?"

Bernard was lifting and lowering the little spoon. "What the fuck,
Andrew," he said.

"How do you want to do it?"

"You tell me."

"Let's drive him some place and dump him."

"Okay, okay."

"Get dressed," Crispo commanded Vesti when they returned to the living room area. "We're going upstate!"

"Where? How far away?" He seemed genuinely excited to make the journey.

"Here," Crispo said, thrusting a nylon bag at Bernard. "Take my bag of toys down to the car, will you?"

The Rockland authorities believed Bernard when he said he headed down to his car, and waited there for fifteen minutes. Vesti, dressed in a green leather jacket, dark jeans, and brown suede cowboy boots, slipped into the backseat. Andrew Crispo got in the front. "Okay, let's go!" He slammed the door.

They believed it when he said Crispo was afraid of passing the tollbooth on the Palisades Interstate Parkway, and when Bernard explained that, on the way out of the city, there was no toll collected.

Crispo was celebratory: He passed around a bottle of white wine and the brown cocaine vial. Near exit 12, Eigil Vesti's head was buzzing, electric, alive. "This is beautiful up here," he said. "Where are we going?"

"You're going to Norway," Crispo said, "in a fucking box." He laughed. Vesti and Bernard did, too.

Bernard pulled the car onto Route 210, through Stony Point, past the four white buildings of Tomkins Cove, and up the steep inclines of Buckberg Mountain Road.

He was the first out of the car, and the first to enter the house, which he did through the back door. Vesti and Crispo were ushered in through the side door, the one off the driveway, to the right of the garage. Inside, they were technically in the basement, although this room—walls of stone, linoleum floor—had been made over into a damp den. A narrow stone hallway and a steep stairway led to a door that opened onto a central foyer. Straight ahead was the large kitchen; to the right, the front door, the stairs to the bedrooms, and another den filled with a small sofa, an ottoman, a television, and an ornamental gun collection. In the other direction was a small dining room alcove and, down two steps, a very large living room with gnarled wood walls. A wide bay window looked over the tennis court, the woods, the Hudson. Crispo and Vesti made themselves comfortable on a long bank sofa and looked out. The sun was beginning to rise over the river.

On a glass coffee table, Crispo razored a half-dozen coke rows; each inhaled two. Vesti filled glasses with wine. Crispo shouldered an invisible gun. "Did you bring it? Do you have it?"

"It's in my knapsack."

Crispo held up his glass for more wine as Bernard noticed Vesti filling his own glass to overflowing. "Hey, faggot! Watch! It's too full and you're going to spill it, damn it!"

As if on purpose, he let the glass spill a pool of wine onto the carpet. "Fucking *ass*hole!" Bernard shouted, and attacked Vesti with his hands and feet, pummeling him around the head. But he likes that, Bernard thought. Can't punish him if he likes that. He stormed toward the front door.

"If you leave," Crispo shouted after him, "I'll throw this in the fireplace." He was dangling Bernard's rifle and nylon bag over the dirty pile of soot.

"Give it to me," Bernard said, approaching him slowly. "You stupid fuck."

Laughing aloud, Crispo returned to the sofa and splashed more cocaine on the tabletop. To Vesti, who was kneeling by his side, he said, "What are you going to offer the master of the house?" Then he whispered something in the Norwegian's ear. "He wants to suck your dick, Bernard. For being such a good host."

"Goddamn you," Bernard said. "Fucking faggots." He pressed his nose to the table surface. "You make me sick."

Crispo and Vesti laughed gently, cocking their heads toward the window. Vesti shifted in the sofa to study the view. "Is that for tennis?" He turned to Bernard.

"Yeah, can you play?"

"Yeah, but not on that piece of shit."

"Fuck you, then!" Turning to Crispo, he said, "Andrew, I'm not fucking playing. I'm not in the mood for this shit."

Crispo pulled Bernard's knapsack up onto the couch suggestively. Bernard opened it and began snapping together the AR-7 as Vesti watched. "Is that real?"

"Fuckin'-A," Bernard said with great impatience. "It's an assassin's rifle, asshole."

"Did you ever kill anything with it?"

"Yeah. Birds, deer, and assholes, asshole."

"It doesn't work," Crispo added quickly, "it's a fuckin' toy."

"Yeah, Andrew. I'll show you a fuckin' toy," Bernard said. He threw back a door on the veranda. "Watch this, motherfucker," he said, locking, loading, and firing a couple of rounds. The gun made a cheap clacking noise, with very little recoil. "Look," Bernard said, "deer! Hey, I shot one, I think. I think I hit one."

"You hit shit," Crispo said, and took Vesti by the arm. "We're going downstairs."

Bernard didn't follow. From the living room, he could hear the familiar sound of leather stinging flesh, of breathing peaked and suspended. He went into the television room and turned on the stereo to blot out the noise. He loaded a second clip into the AR-7, shouldered one of his father's antique rifles, imitated deep discharge noises by rushing air between his teeth and cheeks. He went to the kitchen for a towel to clean the wine-soaked rug.

Outside the window, between the house and the tennis court, Eigil Vesti was kneeling in the grass, wearing a jockstrap and handcuffs. Some sort of rope had been tied around his neck. As Crispo tugged on it, his penis was disappearing behind the silver teeth on Vesti's mask, which twisted with great animation from one side to another. In a minute, they were gone; Bernard could hear them again in the basement. He preferred them to be outdoors.

"Hey," he yelled down, "let's go look what I got. Find the deer I got." Then he opened the front door, ran across the terraced lawn, and headed down the hill toward the tennis court's south side. Over his shoulder, he could see his friends ambling slowly, Crispo too overweight to take the slippery hill without caution; Vesti, still in the hood but wearing pants and boots now, unable to see clearly through the small leather holes over his eyes. They opened a gate on the north side of the dirt court and walked across it toward Bernard.

"So where is it?" Crispo was panting now. "You didn't get shit."

Bernard ducked his head into the woods that abutted the tennis court. He moved quickly over a path crowded with crusty unmelted ice, fallen limbs, woodland debris. He heard Crispo tell Vesti to hand over his nylon bag, heard Crispo uncork the bottle of wine. Bernard wound past Turtle Turn, the curve in the path named by his father; he stopped in front of the smokehouse. "You're right, Andrew," he said, "I didn't hit shit. Either that or it ran away with lead in it."

"I like the way you said that," Crispo said; then, "What's this?"

"That's the smokehouse."

"A what?"

"Smokehouse, dummy. Where they smoke meat." Crispo raised his brow and moved a puffy hand to his crotch, smiling. "Not that kind of meat," Bernard said. "Jeeze!"

Turning to Vesti, Crispo said, "Tell Bernard what you did to his car."

"Come on," Bernard said.

"I pissed on it." Vesti's blue eyes twinkled from behind the mask.

"Come on. I said stop fucking around. I mean it, I'm getting tired of this shit."

"Now tell Bernard what you called him."

"I don't remember. . . . Oh, yeah. A fucking wimp."

"See what he called you? A fucking *wimp!*" Crispo roared. It was 7:30 A.M., and the sun had fully emerged over the horizon. Bernard threw closed fists into Vesti's bare chest, easily causing his thin neck to snap forward unnaturally. Bernard hiked farther down the hill with large strides, heading toward Revolutionary Road, named by his father, the place where old LeGeros family cars are parked for eternity.

He was gone for many minutes, and only returned because he wanted more blow. Crispo filled his spoon five times. Vesti, his pants unfastened and bunched up at his knees, knelt passively in the narrow muddy clearing in front of the smokehouse. His hands were cuffed tightly behind his back. His black leather head rocked slightly in the damp breezes, breezes that caused his skin to pimple and his small pale nipples to point.

The police believed this about Crispo: that he was there, that he had established the groundwork for a sadomasochistic scenario that he controlled. They believed (as Bernard had told them) that Andrew Crispo had forced Eigil Vesti into a kneeling position outside the stone smokehouse. They believed that, as part of the ritual, Andrew Crispo had ordered the execution of the handsome Norwegian fashion student with these words: "He's ready, now. He wants to die. Shoot him." They believed Bernard had followed those orders with two tugs on the trigger.

But in preparation for his own defense, Bernard soon obfuscated key aspects of the story. In one new version, he said Vesti was already dead when he pulled the trigger—the result of stab wounds inflicted by Crispo. In another, it was all a grave mistake; the gun went off without warning as it was being passed from Crispo to Bernard. The Stony Point police felt that the more indicting elements of Bernard's story were more apt to be true. He had nothing to gain from telling them, and everything to gain by having them forgotten.

Det. Sgt. Billy Franks and others were particularly fascinated (and equally repulsed) by what Andrew Crispo was said to have done to Vesti in his last moments. On the night of his arrest, as officers were fingerprinting Bernard, he called one of them over and offered this detail: "I just want to say I'm sorry I killed him. And no matter what I say, I want you to know Andrew was holding Vesti on his lap. They were both nude, and Andrew was holding Vesti on his lap. He was *in* him. Then Andrew turned and said, 'Okay, he's ready. Hit him.'"

But a week later, even this story changed. When Bernard returned to the smokehouse with his loaded gun, he now said, Eigil Vesti was kneeling again, his wrists cuffed behind his back. In his hands was the base of an enormous dildo, the rest of which was planted deep inside his cavity. When the shots rang out and Vesti fell forward, it was Andrew who retrieved the device.

The clothing was then cut off with a razor, and the boots were left on his feet ("We tried to remove them," Bernard said later, "but either he was already stiff or his feet swelled"). Bernard removed the handcuffs, using a key to free the blue arms. His delicate fingers, curled loosely behind his back, quivered inhumanly during the process. Andrew Crispo attempted to dislodge the hood, but decided instead to wipe it clean of prints.

Then, according to what Bernard told his brother and Billy Mayer (and later recanted), a hole was dug in Vesti's side with a black-handled hunting knife and his blood was let into one of the cups Crispo had packed in his nylon bag. "I tried to drink it," Bernard said, "but it was pulpy—I spit it out."

Bernard then fetched shovels, but the woodland floor was still frozen, despite the heat wave. Digging a grave was impossible. The body was moved inside the smokehouse—a very small enclosure—and, when a sledgehammer failed to collapse the structure, Crispo suggested the use of lye to destroy the remains. Gasoline was the only available alternative, and both men made several trips back and forth to the garage on the top of the hill carrying cans and logs, according to each statement. Bernard lit the match, which was plucked from an "I Love New York" matchbook, and the two returned to the house under the white haze of morning. Before leaving Buckberg Mountain Road, Crispo wiped fingerprints off everything that had been touched.

Along the route home, as Bernard drove, Andrew Crispo threw various items out of the car window. Off exit 1 of the Palisades Interstate Parkway, they pulled up to a blue Goodwill box and deposited the green leather jacket Eigil had been wearing, along with his razored blue jeans and jockstrap. A T-shirt was also placed there.

They drove a little farther into the country, in a section known as Devil's Elbow, and Bernard pulled off on a side street. There, Crispo found a storm drainage grate and attempted to stuff the dildo inside it. He got all but about four inches of the latex device through the metal slats before giving up on it, and left it there. The large flexible testicles dangled ungracefully under their own weight.

After returning to the highway, according to Bernard, Andrew lifted his hand—the one that still bore the rubber stamp from the Hellfire Club—and touched it to Bernard's hand on the steering wheel. "We're married now," he said softly as their ink blots united. "We're husband and wife."

* * *

They arrived in the city on Saturday morning after ten, having again avoided all tollbooths, and went directly to Andrew's West Twelfth Street apartment. There, they bathed and napped in separate beds through the afternoon. That night, they had dinner at the Van Dam Restaurant with Edo Bertoglio and his girlfriend, Lynn. On a stroll to the cigarette machine with Edo, Bernard told an abbreviated version of their story, which Edo dismissed out of hand. Unconcerned, Edo invited Bernard back to his apartment after dinner to watch television—just the two of them.

Bernard left there for a midnight meeting with Billy Mayer. He confided the long version of the story, which Billy, like Edo, did not take at face value. They spent several hours talking about it, nonetheless.

Then Bernard went back to Waterside Plaza, where Andrew had planned to meet him at 5:00 A.M. for a limousine drive to his Southampton home. That's when Bernard woke David and announced, "I killed a guy. We killed a guy." Like everyone else that long evening, David LeGeros did not believe his brother. Apparently bothered by the string of dismissals, Bernard acted out the entire scene, including the cutting in the chest and the sipping of the blood.

"I killed somebody, too," David said dismissively. "I killed two people. I do it all the time."

The limo arrived on time, and Bernard and Andrew didn't return to the city until Monday night. Three vials of cocaine were consumed during the days since the killing, and Andrew engaged in three liaisons with three separate young men (one appeared to be about thirteen) while Bernard went to the movies, read the papers, and went for walks. One man who saw Andrew and Bernard in Southampton said he noticed nothing unusual. "They seemed their regular artsy selves," he said.

The revelry was temporarily over, though, by Tuesday, when Crispo took to bed for three days. Bernard, who continued going to the gallery during business hours, spent most nights at home, entertaining an unexpected houseguest. Dean Aarons had once worked at the gallery, and had recently returned to New York with no accommodations. Because Andrew was not feeling like himself, he asked Bernard to put him up.

One evening that week, Bernard told Dean, "I killed somebody. You don't believe me?" He didn't.

Andrew, in the weeks before the body was found, brought it up once, too, although very obliquely, to Hal Burroughs, his regular Hellfire Club cohort. Hal stopped by his house one evening that week, and found a morose Andrew in bed. When asked what was bothering him, Andrew first mentioned a nosebleed, caused (he ventured) by some cheaply cut cocaine.

"And," he said quietly, "a friend of ours died." Burroughs didn't ask any other questions. By Friday, Crispo seemed better. Back to work, he was energetic, exuberant, and "mumbling a lot more than usual," one visitor noticed. His cocaine intake had staged a drastic rise. "He entered a 'bad week,'" Hal Burroughs said later, "that went on for several weeks." But that meant the coke was flowing, and Hal saw Andrew frequently through the first half of March. They went out to the clubs, visited at the gallery or at Crispo's apartment. They spent a weekend at his Southampton mansion with Hal's friend Hank. Except for one afternoon there, Hal never suspected that anything had changed.

On March 21, just before noon, a week after his weekend in Southampton, Hal Burroughs dropped by the gallery, having been promised the loan of several art texts. He found Crispo in bad shape, apparently having gone without sleep, apparently strung out on coke. A man at the reception desk was dialing Brazil over and over.

Andrew asked his friend a few questions about the items he hoped to show in an upcoming exhibit. And without any forewarning of the leap he was about to make in the conversation, he held up Eigil Vesti's MISSING poster and said, "Do you recognize this?"

"What, the poster?"

"This person, the person here. This person."

Hal Burroughs didn't. Andrew put the poster down, resumed discussing the upcoming event, and then picked the poster up again in a rapid swing back to his original, unclear thought. "I think I know who did this," he said.

"Did what?"

"This!" He waved the poster. "I think Bernard did this."

As he spoke those words, David LeGeros appeared in the main gallery space, his second visit of the day. He and Andrew walked to the far end of the gallery, and Hal, who could not hear their conversation, studied their theatrical arm movements. The two disappeared momentarily into the Red Room, and when the door opened again, David wore a grave face. He rushed out of the gallery.

When Andrew approached Hal again, he took him by the arm for a walking tour of where his paintings would hang—next to the Picasso plates, next to artists far more prominent, in plain view of the door. There, amid the light chatter, Crispo said abruptly, "I think Bernard is going to kill himself."

Having weathered these "bad weeks" before, having heard so many gory stories before, having not taken it upon himself to judge Andrew's erratic behavior, Hal rolled his eyes visibly. Nine months before, when

Bernard told him he had slaughtered beggars in Libya, or Lebanon, or Yemen, Burroughs rolled his eyes, too. And he had done it again when, as Crispo's guest recently in Southampton, the art dealer had pointed to a large lawn sculpture by Douglas Abdell and said, "I bury my enemies there." "A circle of liars," he told his friend Hank once—almost admiringly. "Can't believe a word they say."

While Burroughs never believed the stuff about buried enemies was true, he nonetheless experienced a nondescript, unfocused, confusing chill while napping in the Southampton guest room. *Maybe he's dangerous*, this chill seemed to suggest.

But he eventually dismissed the thought, just as he was dismissing his friend's morbid assertions now. In this instance, Hal assumed Andrew was trying to distract him for some reason—the Eigil Vesti information as McGuffin, a red herring, an intentionally unimportant yet highly stressed tidbit. He changed the subject back to the show, and Andrew followed along seamlessly. For a short time.

Then he grew very agitated, and dragged Hal through his Red Room into the adjoining bathroom. He turned on the faucets in the sink ("in case there's a bug," he said) and motioned for Hal to huddle with him next to the toilet. He began speaking half in mumbled, whispered words and half in giant arm motions. "You know how these things"—he made cocking motions with his wrist—"can be *games*?"

"Uh-huh."

Andrew hushed him. "For some people"—he pointed an index finger dramatically, probably aiming at where David LeGeros had just been standing, probably suggesting the boy's brother—"this wasn't a game." He gave a meaningful glance. "He snapped," he whispered.

"Uh-huh."

Andrew lifted his arms as if holding a rifle; then he took one hand, his palm flat and yellow, and made two karate-chop motions to the back of his own head. "Chew, chew," he said.

"Uh-huh," said Hal.

"I know where it is," Andrew said, shouldering the rifle again. He was flushing the toilet frequently. "I'm concerned it should be moved."

"I don't even want to think about it," Hal said, "I'm not gonna think about it." He was beginning, finally, to panic. It amazed him that it had taken so long to muster this reaction. "Why do you even want to think about keeping something like that, anyway, Andrew?"

Very quietly, Crispo said, "Might want to use it again, might want it another time," and in a louder, stilted mutter: "So, take those books, and you can return them to me tonight. Just drop by my house."

Oddly, incautiously, inexplicably, Hal showed up at Andrew's apartment at about 8:30. Later, he said he went for the coke—and because Andrew seemed to need him around. But at the time, he had managed to convince himself that he was just delivering the books.

Andrew appeared to be in his third or fourth day on coke time: nervous, superenergetic, unfocused, unrested. Sweat squeezed out of his pulsing temples, cut slug trails down his neck. He was racing through his studio apartment gathering up items and throwing them in the black nylon bag: a stack of porn magazines (*Drummer, Blueboy, Honcho, Mandate*); dozens of love letters with René Arlington's return address; a leather harness; a set of handcuffs; a white glove made of plaster. He produced a Pan Am flight bag and packed it with two five-foot bullwhips, two cockrings, a small toothpaste bag that contained two brown vials that had been full of cocaine. Hal sat on a sofa watching.

"This stuff wasn't used," Andrew puffed. "Just some S&M stuff. You know, homosexual stuff. With this Bernard thing, I'm worried the cops are going to search my apartment. I don't want the police to find this." His coke jitters were coming in torrents. "You must do this," he pleaded, "you've gotta help pack."

Hal finally agreed, and tucked away several other brown vials, and the black disklike coke dish that was Andrew's favorite. An official police badge, clipped to a standard-issue leather wallet, was tossed in the nylon duffel, along with a brown hip holster and a small starter's pistol.

When the gear was zippered shut, Andrew asked Hal to talk to a downstairs neighbor and ask him to store them. Hal carried the bags to the neighbor's door, but when nobody answered the bell, he continued on to the mirrored lobby, beseeching the doorman to hold them in the package room behind the front desk.

Back upstairs, Andrew begged Hal to take the bags away with him. "I guess," he replied, snorting a line of coke through a small straw. "Do you want me to destroy the stuff?"

"Oh, oh. No! Just—just *hold* them for a while. I want to keep them."

After another line, Hal retrieved the bags from the doorman and put them in the trunk of his car. When he returned to the apartment, he hoped to talk about the upcoming show—set to open in a number of days—and to ask some advice from Andrew on the paintings he had selected. Instead, he was instructed to walk across the terrace to Arthur Smith's apartment. "Wait there just a little while," Andrew commanded impatiently. "I've got some business to take care of over here."

Shortly, Andrew called him back and introduced him to a woman in her twenties, his newest cocaine dealer, and instructed Hal to "take a ride with her and pick up a package."

Again Hal agreed, and headed for the door just as two detectives began knocking. Hal eyed them through the peephole and informed Andrew, who was hysterical. "Shit," he said, "fuck," panting. "Don't open that door!" Slapping the air with his hands, he grunted, "Okay, okay. I'm gonna call my lawyer. Hal"—he gripped his friend's arm—"you've gotta tell them it's the wrong door. Just say, 'If you're looking for Andrew Crispo, you've got the wrong door.' You've got to do that."

He obliged, and as the detectives retreated, Andrew did not thank his friend. Instead, he had him complete the drug mission.

In about twenty minutes, Hal returned with a sandwich bag weighty with a dense white powder, just as Andrew was concluding a telephone conversation with Debbie Harry, the lead singer in the rock group Blondie. His entire demeanor seemed altered, relaxed, casual. He had invited her over for some coke. For no apparent reason, Andrew was throwing a party.

"Hank's a Blondie fan, isn't he?" Andrew asked Hal. Andrew seemed to have a crush on Hank. Once, he hired him to do some last-minute picture framing for an exhibit; another time, he paid him to stash some of the incriminating tax files in his Brooklyn apartment. Recently, Hank had accompanied Hal and him to Southampton. "Why don't we ask him over and surprise him?"

"You don't know Hank," said Hal. "He'd get a kick out of it, but if we just call him up and invite him, with no reason, he's not gonna come."

"I've got an idea, then. Tell him that Bernard killed somebody and that I want him to come over to talk about it."

"Fine, Andrew. You do it."

Andrew did, hiking up his frantic voice once more, this time for show. "Bernard was arrested for killing somebody! I really need you to come over right away." He told the story as a ruse; the killing of Eigil Vesti had become a fantasy pretext for a coke party with a mystery guest, a lighthearted facade, an irrelevant detail in a larger plan.

Andrew smiled broadly when Hank agreed to rush into Manhattan.

Indeed, a pleasant evening unfolded. Hank was visibly overwhelmed by Debbie Harry's presence. She autographed an album for him; he professed to be one of her biggest fans. They uncorked a succession of wine bottles and dusted coke onto a tabletop until 2:00 A.M., laughing idly as their sinuses grew into tunnels and their brains sizzled within tingling heads. Debbie spoke about her hard decision to drop out of sight to care for Chris Stein, a former boyfriend and band member who had taken ill; Andrew told an orphanage story or two. The plastic bag Hal Burroughs had fetched earlier in the evening was quickly depleted.

It wasn't until after the rock star departed that Crispo brought up the killing again with Hal and Hank, their minds shrunken to useless masses, their skin jumping right off their arms, their eyes dry and saucer-wide. Sitting on the sofa across from their host became a chore, and they alternated side trips to the terrace, to the elevator, the bathroom— anything to keep moving, to spend this high. They asked few questions. As a result, the stories they heard about the killing were fragmented and, on several key details, contradictory.

Hank remembered Andrew saying he had been up in Rockland County at the time of the slaying, but that he didn't know how he had gotten there. Hal heard him say the party had begun in the Village apartment and continued north in Bernard's car. "He didn't say anything about a mask or a whipping," Hank said later. "He said he didn't see any blood." Hal heard descriptions of the sex games and sex aids. Andrew told both of them he had been at "the grotto," and that Bernard "took a gun out from under his coat and shot this guy." To Hal, he said that Bernard had fired twice in the back of the head, adding, "He snapped—remember to tell that to the police if you're ever questioned. He snapped."

As the cool evening progressed, and the cocaine formed repeated white ridges on the tabletop, the conversation became overpowered by mumbled non sequiturs and difficult leaps, making it nearly impossible for the two visitors to glean any meaning from the words their host was formulating. Hal remembered Crispo suggesting a certain series of his paintings for the show, and distinctly recalled these words: "I'll never go to jail. I'll run away. I could never handle it. What I would do is I would take, I would take a handful of money, leave, and start all over, completely from scratch."

Hank remembered different, disjointed phrases. Some were about his friend's exhibit, some about Debbie Harry. Some were about the incident: "I thought it was a toy gun," and "I thought the gun wasn't loaded," and "Out of nowhere, it went off."

Then, as Hank said later, "the question was brought up about the gun, and Andrew said, 'I know where it is. It's in the airshaft at the gallery.' He said, 'I don't know how it got there.' Andrew appeared very nervous, but he's always nervous. I don't know why."

The following day, Hal Burroughs shouldered Andrew's large bag of toys and walked through the Village, throwing the magazines and the René Arlington love letters in trash bins along the way, perhaps forgetting Crispo's orders to retain the evidence. Back home, he took the police shield, which said "City of New York Police Detective Endowment Association," and placed it in a plastic cup inside his medicine cabinet. The Smith & Wesson handcuffs, presumably the same pair that had been removed from Eigil Vesti's stiffening arms immediately before he was doused with gasoline, were stashed in a disorganized kitchen drawer.

He took the remaining keepsakes in the bag of toys, and in the Pan Am bag, placed them back in the trunk of his car, and headed out of the city. On a quiet stretch of the Merritt Parkway in Connecticut, with his wife behind the wheel, Hal Burroughs tossed them out the window one by one. "You've gotta understand," he said later, "I just didn't know what else to do."

PART
V

Malignant Passions

"The fault lies with your moldy systems, your logic of two plus two equals four; the fault lies with you, Chancellors."

—ANTONIN ARTAUD,
La Révolution Surréaliste

CHAPTER

16

John LeGeros had never heard the term *S&M* before Det. Sgt. Billy Franks explained that it meant sadomasochism, which he said could involve bondage and discipline, sometimes called B&D. In the weeks following Bernard's arraignment, John read *Story of O* in an attempt to understand it.

Murray Sprung, on the other hand, made no such effort, and while preparing Bernard's defense, he felt it was more important to establish Andrew Crispo's direct role in the murder and Bernard's innocence by insanity than to make philosophical inquiries. Sadomasochism? Bondage and discipline? These were not merely repulsive activities, they were signposts of a degenerate mind. If Bernard was involved in this world, there was no question of his insanity. Sprung believed this with a stony conviction.

He arranged for the police to undertake three post-arrest interviews with Bernard, hoping something more understandable would surface.

Franks, for one, found the arrangement "highly unusual." Cops rarely get the opportunity to go back to an indicted murderer with follow-up questions. He went about the task with a studious zeal and garnered additional evidence against Bernard. With Murray Sprung's blessing, a handcuffed Bernard rode in a squad car along the Palisades Interstate

Parkway and various New Jersey side streets, indicating where certain material evidence had been deposited. He showed them the Goodwill box; he identified where a whip had been hurled through the car window, and where cans of Crisco vegetable shortening had been thrown. He hiked with them to the storm drain where, he said, "Andrew stuffed the dildo."

Although the device was not there, police later found Thomas Ruby, a light-equipment operator with the Palisades Park Commission, who plucked it from the drainage grate. "I brought it to the fellas at work," he said, blushing. "You never seen anything like that, you know." In fact, it was a monstrous thing, which required some time and energy for Ruby to successfully dislodge—gripping it, as he had, by the fist-sized synthetic testicles dangling from the end.

"The fellas," in turn, dressed the thing up—Ruby drew on a face; somebody else gave it a plaid necktie—before it was presented, scepterlike, to the boss. Police found it on top of the boss's file cabinet, from which resting place it cast a deep shadow over his desk. Stony Point authorities measured it (fourteen inches), weighed it (eight pounds), photographed it, and placed it—tie and all—in a storage cabinet, logged as evidence in the LeGeros case.

They also found the rifle, after an abortive scuba search in a tributary to the Hudson, where Bernard, according to the Billy Mayer version, said he had thrown it. With Bernard's final account, that story changed—and was later corroborated by the independent accounts of David LeGeros and Hal Burroughs. Armed with a search warrant, police officers removed the AR-7 Charter Arms survival rifle from an air-conditioner closet on the second floor of the Andrew Crispo Gallery. It was in a cardboard box, collapsed, the barrel tucked into the plastic butt. It had six live rounds in the magazine. The gun—and, indeed, the entire room—had been wiped clean of prints, leading David to believe that the frantic search of the gallery Crispo sent him on was designed to have him mark the pristine surroundings with fresh, traceable fingerprints.

Also in the gallery, the cops came up with a plastic bag of clothing, several shoes of different sizes, the MISSING poster, the René Arlington picture, and the book *La Popessa*. They found a Police Department central booking folder for Arlington, which, though they were unsure of its significance, they piled into their evidence box. Finally, on top of a wooden packing crate, they found a red file folder containing Bernard's record of the questions Stony Point police had asked him, and the answers he had proffered.

Simultaneously, a team was ransacking the Galleria apartment, where they recovered ledgers and folders relating to the gallery's financial operations. Other officers, meanwhile, searched the Twelfth Street apartment, where they found a half-dozen packed boxes, making them believe Andrew Crispo was contemplating a move. Among the things they seized were several Polaroids of unidentified naked men; six belts taken from a single cardboard box; eight slides; a shopping bag; and thirty-seven magazines. From the living room sofa, they scraped an "unknown substance" and placed it in an envelope, and another "unknown substance" was removed from the couch in the bedroom area. A pair of dark shorts with red stains was taken from an overstuffed cardboard box; a white notepad with similar red stains was removed from under clothing in a dresser drawer, where it had been stashed next to several telephone message slips for calls Bernard had made to Crispo from the Rockland County jail.

On March 27, with Murray Sprung present, Bernard again sat with authorities, this time repeating his confession with a few new variations. Eigil was not wearing his pants when he was shot, Bernard said at this time; he was clad only in the brown suede boots, the black hood, and a jockstrap. Andrew had asked Bernard where the gun was, "because this guy really wants to die," and Bernard approached Eigil Vesti, who, kneeling at the opening to the smokehouse, was holding the base of the dildo with his hands, which were cuffed behind his back. The rest of the device was buried deep in his cavity. Bernard said he threw back a long coat and produced the rifle. "I fired two shots and Vesti fell forward."

Crispo, he said, removed the dildo; Bernard unlocked the handcuffs. Crispo began unlacing the leather hood, but Bernard stopped him, saying, "Leave that alone." Both of them saw to the fire; Bernard threw the match.

At that time, according to Bernard, Andrew said, "Don't worry, I've done this before."

The interview went on for more than an hour, and Bernard supplied information that seemed unrelated to the murder. But it gave Franks an insight into the dark world Andrew Crispo had fashioned around him, a world of apparent fabrications and potentially true events—events that could have been based on a shimmer of truth but were so embroidered as to have become fantastic. Bernard did not distinguish between the probable and the improbable; he rattled on in both directions, anxious to have Franks listen if not believe. Later, Franks dictated those notes into his tape recorder:

> Bernard stated that Andrew Crispo had a friend named Tony Mordana, who is a Westchester police officer, and believes that

he knows another Westchester police officer whose first name starts with a *C*.

Bernard stated that Andrew had borrowed money—somewhere between twelve and twenty thousand dollars—from John Suchman who comes to the gallery to see Andrew and operates a tan or gold-colored Jaguar. Bernard believes that John Suchman is listed in the telephone book in Staten Island, New York, and that Andrew had agreed to buy eighty kilos of cocaine from him and that Andrew needed three hundred thousand dollars. Bernard stated that he believes that this fellow John is a Mafia guy and deals heavily in cocaine.

Bernard also advised that Andrew met many of his sexual S&M partners who he called "victims" in the Hellfire Club and in the Mineshaft, a homosexual bar on the West Side.

Bernard stated that Andrew was involved with a guy named David who is a dentist in Queens and that the dentist liked to be wrapped in plastic and whipped and that he and Andrew had told him that they would kill him. Bernard would also invite other people to watch, males in their twenties. Bernard stated that he last saw the dentist in September of Eighty-four and doesn't know what happened to him.

Bernard stated that Andrew also had a friend named Chris, no further information, who Andrew had tied up and stuck a dildo in his ass and that this fellow Chris is a sadist.

Bernard also stated that Andrew had a friend named Scott who he last saw in December of Nineteen Eighty-four at an opening at the gallery and that he may have killed Scott.

. . .

Bernard stated that Andrew is friendly with a fellow named Alan who is a driver for the Black Tie Limousine Service and that Alan is involved in coke dealing with Andrew Crispo.

Bernard stated that Andrew also did something to a guy named Paul Jeffries. Bernard advised that he was present when Paul Jeffries was at the apartment and that he was dressed as a police officer and that he had handcuffed him and that Crispo wanted Bernard to shoot him

. . .

Bernard also stated that several New York City Police Officers frequent Andrew's apartment and that they are possibly assigned to some type of plainclothes division and that they may be involved in S&M with Andrew but he has never witnessed any of them. Bernard stated that a lot of cops hang around in the Hellfire.

. . .

Bernard also stated that he and Andrew are friendly with a girl by the name of Lisa and that she was present during the first occasion where he, Bernard, engaged in this type of S&M activity. Bernard stated that a fellow by the name of Gordon and Hal Burroughs were also present and that they had handcuffed one of the guys and belittled him. Bernard stated that Andrew was very friendly with a fellow by the name of Hank, of Brooklyn, and a fellow by the name of Hal Burroughs, who lives in Manhattan, and that if Andrew was to confide in anybody, he would confide in them.

Most of Bernard's information, of course, went nowhere. There was no report of a missing dentist, for example, and no way of finding Scott—last name unknown—for whose life Bernard showed concern. John Suchman was not in the Staten Island directory, and Tony Mordana was not listed as a member of the police in any Westchester township, and in fact could not be located at all. Because Bernard could provide no names, it was impossible to trace any other police officers, from Manhattan or elsewhere, who he believed were frequenting the Twelfth Street apartment. Sergeant Franks concluded that these were just sadomasochists from the dark streets of the Village who dressed up as cops, and were able to fool Bernard. In his own experiences at the S&M clubs—he had made several nocturnal trips there himself—Franks was astonished at the number of men in uniforms, complete in every detail right down to the badges.

Alan, the twenty-one-year-old limo driver, did exist, although he offered little new information. He was the driver who took Bernard and Crispo to Southampton following the killing; his account of that trip, and the several hours following their arrival (he said he napped in a spare room), dovetailed with Bernard's. He left alone at two in the afternoon, and returned to the city, for a trip totaling $210 in billables. At the end of his interview, Alan said he was not a homosexual, and had not engaged in any "social" activity with Andrew or Bernard. (At least one coworker contradicted this, insisting "he will go either way when it comes to sex.") After a series of subsequent interviews, though, they concluded that Alan—gay or not—was not privy to any information other than what he had volunteered.

Likewise with Bernard's girlfriend Lisa. She told authorities she'd always found Crispo "dangerous," and stressed that he had exerted a detectable "control" over Bernard's mind. She confirmed being present at Bernard's first S&M encounter with his boss, which she termed "a game." But for actual inculpatory facts, she was not helpful.

With one strikeout after another, Franks was about to abandon the list of leads Bernard had given, and write off the boy's urgently recounted recollections as nothing more than a wild effort to take down his boss with him.

Then Franks found P.J., the Hellfire doorman. In an interview with Det. Joey Denise, he told a chilling story that made Bernard's tales seem less fantastic. Perhaps, the cops were forced to conclude, there was some foundation to the LeGeros opus.

P.J. had been chummy with Crispo for more than a year, having met him at the club, and said he'd often "partied" with Crispo at his apartment. On the day of the killing, he said, he had seen all of them—Bernard, Crispo, Billy Mayer, and Eigil Vesti—at the Hellfire, though at different times. "Andrew Crispo was turning everyone on to cocaine," he said, "and he and Eigil Vesti left the Hellfire Club together." A short time later, when Billy Mayer and Bernard arrived, P.J. told them Andrew had headed home. Bernard then discussed the evening's plot to "kill a guy named Freddy," in what P.J. described as an unsolicited comment. It was the first independent confirmation of Bernard's and Billy's account of that warm night in February.

P.J., who was twenty-three, tattooed, and boyish, and who, because he had no permanent address, took his telephone calls at Badlands, a cavernous bar on the corner of Christopher and West streets, had more to tell. A month before all of this, he said, he was a guest at a party (lots of coke, plenty of cute boys) at Crispo's apartment, where he first saw, and admired, the black leather bondage mask. Crispo loaned it to him, and he wore it to the Mineshaft once or twice before returning it.

A month before that, again at the apartment, he had a conversation about guns with Bernard and Arthur Smith. This conversation struck him as important.

After some prodding from Detective Denise, P.J. reluctantly discussed a sexual scene that had taken place "some time ago" at Crispo's. He was not proud of having kept it secret, he said by way of introduction. And he wasn't sure it meant anything.

Andrew Crispo had invited him up to whip a white male from Long Island, whose name he never learned. In exchange, he would receive drugs and one hundred dollars. The young man was bound and immobile. After some preliminary lashes (nothing that a person couldn't witness in the Hellfire or the Mineshaft, he said), Crispo took P.J. aside and made a proposal. He asked him to "cut the guy across the neck." "Not enough to kill the guy," P.J. told Denise. "But he wanted to make him bleed. He wanted to see him bleed."

Denise didn't know whether or not to buy the laceration angle. This, after all, was not coming from an apparently well-constructed mind. Even other people in the S&M community had harsh words about P.J., who had been eighty-sixed from a handful of Village bars for fighting with customers, managers, owners. Nonetheless, Denise had seen Eigil Vesti's remains, and he believed—as many of his coworkers now believed—that some horrible things had been done to the corpse, either before or after Eigil Vesti's final breath. "A body doesn't get that decayed in three weeks," one of the cops said, "especially not three weeks in the *winter*." By way of comparison, the body of a young black man had been found by Westchester authorities at about the same time, and the coroner put the estimated time of death at three *months* previous. "He was bloated and hard to look at," said an officer who had seen pictures of both bodies, "but he was intact! Animals, and you can ask authorities on this as I did, begin at the edges and eat in. Like when you bite into a T-Bone, where do you start? Vesti's body wasn't nibbled at the edges. It was devoured!"

In his theory, the fires were neither hot nor intense enough to have roasted the remains to the point of attracting this kind of predation. Even though Bernard LeGeros confessed to returning to the smokehouse a week later and rekindling the flames, the combined effect, especially given the windy location near the mouth of the grotto, would have scorched the body unevenly at best. Repeated slashing with a knife, he and others concluded, must have scored the flesh before it was torched. That would have caused the cooking to be accelerated, and more uniform—and more inviting to the animals that gnawed on the flesh.

Denise questioned P.J. on April 1. On April 3, a call came into the station house that would bolster the detective's suspicions. It was Rebecca Porper, the executive director of the New York City Lesbian and Gay Anti-Violence Project. She had received a call on the project's hot line from a man she declined to identify, who had a story she thought would interest the Rockland police. "He answered a pay phone at the corner of Ninth Avenue and Fourteenth Street, and was invited up to Andrew Crispo's apartment on Twelfth Street, so he went," she said in a deep, loud voice. "He said they did seven or eight grams of coke while Crispo showed him some sadomasochistic paraphernalia—he said Crispo looked as if he hadn't slept. Then Crispo put some heterosexual pornography on the VCR and said that he wanted to call up an agency and get girls up to the apartment whom he could tie up and hurt. Then he said that Crispo said he 'liked to hurt people and draw blood.' "

The call to the police took place at one o'clock, and Porper called again after six, and spoke to Sergeant Franks. She had received another call, this one from a man who was picked up by Crispo while they were both cruising Washington Street near the Mineshaft. Their first encounter, he reported to her and she reported to Stony Point, involved consensual oral sex. Two weeks later, Crispo called the man at home and invited him back. That scene was different. There were two young men there, one of whom boasted about making snuff films, movies in which an individual is actually slain before the cameras. The man left quickly.

Franks told her he was beginning to get similar reports. At four that afternoon, an unidentified caller said that in October of 1984, while walking down Bleecker near Tenth Street in the Village, he heard a ringing phone and answered it. "Said a guy invited him up to have some cocaine and beer, and he went," Franks said. "When he got there, he saw it was Andrew Crispo, who asked him to 'suck my dick,' and then he put a line of cocaine on it, and this guy said he snorted it off. So far, so good. I guess. Or whatever.

"But then the buzzer buzzes, and Crispo lets in three or four guys, younger guys who he described as tough-looking and Hispanic. Things got a little rough, he said, and he got scared and left the apartment."

"I think I talked to him, too," Rebecca Porper said. "Or maybe there's more than one."

Kenneth Gribetz's assistants at the Rockland DA's office got their share of these calls, as did prosecutors in New York City. One "informant," a marginally well-known rock-and-roll drummer who claimed to have known Crispo for two years, said that as he and Crispo passed an abandoned West Side pier near Christopher Street one time, Crispo pointed and said, "That's where I have most of my burials at sea." On another occasion, the drummer said, Andrew boasted that Bernard once killed a woman while Andrew was having sex with her. "When you're having sex with somebody and they're killed," the art dealer reportedly told the drummer, "they shit, piss, and come all at the same time when they die. And it chokes your dick."

Some callers talked about being hurt by Crispo, or having guns held to their heads, or hearing discussion of snuff films. Some said they had been invited to participate.

Stephen Saban, the nightclub correspondent for *Details* magazine, typed up his own statement and handed it over. "I attended a dinner party for Patricia Gucci given in the library of the Limelight," it said, referring to the leather-empire heir. "I sat next to gallery owner Andrew Crispo, whom I had not met prior to the party. During the dinner, he introduced himself and engaged me in conversation. One of the main topics he discussed was his interest in necrophilia (sex with the dead). He told me that he had attended clubs located in the city where patrons could observe or participate in the activity of having sexual intercourse with corpses. He did not mention any particular names of clubs or their addresses. He told me that a person in my field—nightlife writer— should experience everything that happened in New York. He suggested that I join him at one of these clubs sometime. I listened (it was a fascinating story), but did not follow up on his 'gracious' offer."

During the second post-arrest interview, Sergeant Franks put it to Bernard rather bluntly. "Listen buddy, what did you do to that body after he was shot?"

"Nothing," he said, "other than burning it, this and that. Nothing."

"Why'd you tell Billy you cut it up? He says you drank the blood. That you cut out the heart and all that."

"I just told him that. I don't know why. But it's not true, definitely not true. We set it on fire, this and that. But nothing else."

"That's not the way it looks to us. That corpse was dismembered, Bernard. The leg was amputated in mid-shin. The hand was missing. Who knows what else."

Again he denied it, and moved on without emotion to another topic he felt was more important. He stressed, for the first time, that he pulled the trigger on the AR-7 only once, leading him to believe that "Andrew may have shot Vesti a second time when my back was turned, while I was going up the hill for the gas." Either way, he added, "Andrew Crispo manipulated me, which I think makes him more responsible for the murder than I am."

Hal Burroughs agreed to talk to Franks and Investigator LiDestri, and scheduled a meeting with them at his lawyer's offices in New Jersey, a lawyer he shared with his friend Hank, who had already made a statement in the same office.

Hank's interview had taken two hours and revealed very little; because of the drugs, he said frankly, he could remember almost nothing. He spoke of his adoration for Debbie Harry, and his affinity—particularly that evening—for coke and white wine. The rest was foggier, and more jumbled, in part because the conversation had leapt so freely from an alleged killing to art shows, past and present. "Andrew described going down to the grotto, and said that Bernard took a gun from under his coat and shot the guy," he said.

Items of importance arose from the conversation nevertheless. First, that Crispo once pointed to the mammoth sculpture on the front lawn of his Southampton home, the one built by Douglas Abdell, and said to Hank, "This is my graveyard, where I bury my enemies." Second, Hank volunteered that he was currently storing dozens of files in several cardboard boxes for Crispo. It was his belief that these were tax records, as Crispo had frequently mentioned his imbroglio with the Internal Revenue Service. He agreed to hand the material over.

Finally, Hank stripped Crispo of any ability to deny knowledge of the murder weapon. "The question was brought up about the gun," he said, "and Andrew said it's in the airshaft of the gallery."

Likewise, Hal Burroughs's statement was jumbled and confusing. He told Billy Franks everything he could recall, from his first inkling that something was wrong, to his visit to the gallery, and the whispered conversation in the bathroom while the water was running when Crispo had made two karate chops to the back of his head and said, "I think Bernard killed him. I know that he killed him; I was there."

Hal tried to explain his theory of why Andrew had implied a mix-up between Eigil Vesti and René Arlington. "To make the thing just so confusing, nobody could make sense of it," he said. "To keep us focusing on René instead of on Eigil."

Hal also described the coke party later that night, and the surprise visit by Debbie Harry, and the bag of toys, and his decision to ditch the contents along the highway.

Although he believed their stories, Franks couldn't comprehend the ease with which two presentable, college-educated young men seemed to have put the whole incident out of their minds. And this made him angry. "You're telling me," he said, nearly shouting at Hal Burroughs, "you just sat there listening to this story, and it never occurred to you to *do* anything about it?"

"Exactly." Hal was shaking visibly. "I know it's hard to explain, it doesn't make any sense. But I just didn't want to have anything to do with it. And I was really pissed, you know, that he had involved me."

"And your wife felt the same way? She just dismissed it?"

"Well, she kind of said, 'That's Andrew for you.' She never liked him. She was more mad at me for getting involved, I think."

Burroughs eventually agreed to take the officers to his house, where he had stashed the handcuffs and the police badge, and to escort them to the Merritt Parkway in Connecticut to point out where the rest of the contents of the bag might be located. It was the middle of the night, so a search was out of the question. Franks marked the location, returned to Manhattan to drop off Hal, and arrived in Stony Point an hour or so before daybreak.

By mid-morning, he was back on the side of the Merritt Parkway supervising a team of Connecticut state troopers. Coke vials were recovered, along with a crushed black plastic container with traces of cocaine in it. They also retrieved a brown leather pistol holster, several cockrings, and a leather chest harness. And they recovered the nylon bag that had held them all.

It was hard for Billy Franks to celebrate the jackpot. His eyelids were bloated from a lack of sleep, and his Vantage intake had escalated to a steady three packs a day. Ten days had elapsed since Bernard's arrest, eleven since he was first detained, and Franks figured he'd never gone with such little sleep. Like Denise, LiDestri, Shae, McGowan, and Tinelli, Franks had begun each day at nine, put in a full shift at the office, and then headed for the city—knocking on doors, roaming through fashion clubs and sex clubs, grilling people on street corners and in upscale restaurants. In Rockland, he'd heard things he never would have believed before this case. In Manhattan, he'd seen things he never thought existed.

Their combined effect was not giving rise to that excitement that police officers share as an extremely complex case begins falling together. Instead, he was depressed, irritated, angry—when he finally questioned Debbie Harry, for example, he barked, "I don't give a fuck who you are, you'd better just tell me the fucking truth or I'll throw your ass in jail!" He found himself pondering the difference between "bad" sadomasochism and "good," which nonetheless struck him as sad, consensual or not. He recalled a catchy phrase used by Chuck Hammond, a spokesman for Gay Male S/M Activists, an up-front community organization well regarded by Rebecca Porper and other gay leaders. "Murder is to S&M what rape is to sex," the maxim went. It's the same motto Denise had heard from the manager of the Mineshaft.

Billy Franks was baffled by the next logical step in that equation: What, then, is S&M to sex? He had no idea. Just as he had no idea how Crispo fit into the entire dark world. Sharing breakfast with his wife as the mornings added up, he was finding it increasingly difficult to marvel, as she did, at the notoriety this case was getting and the attention it was focusing on the lead detective. A pile of video cassettes contained Franks's sound bites on the news; a stack of newspaper clippings bore his name, his authoritative musings, his dry sense of humor, pictures of his once-sparkling green eyes. He could not look at them.

* * *

Paul Jeffries, whose name had come up in one of Bernard's statements as a possible victim of an earlier torture episode, made contact with the Rockland authorities on his own. He called from a pay phone. His voice was fast and loud and desperate, driven by a long coke jag and a bubbling terror. Before telling a word of what had happened to him, he said, he would need protection. "I am not safe," he shouted.

He was invited to Rockland County, and put up in a motel near the Stony Point police station, a "guest of the state" with round-the-clock security outside his door. Although he didn't know it, he was not the only one being protected there. Billy Mayer, who was a little less frightened, was billeted in a room nearby, at the insistence of the police. And Dean Aarons was down the hall.

Aarons had been in southern Florida staying with a girlfriend when he learned about the grisly discovery on the LeGeros property from a friend who read about it in the paper and called him in the middle of the night. Assuming the authorities would consider him a suspect, he first telephoned John LeGeros (to express his sympathies), and then informed the authorities where he could be reached. They sent him a ticket and brought him back. "I had a serious drinking problem," he explained later. "I was kind of floating around the country, and I happened—by complete coincidence—to show up in New York the day this happened, or a day before, or something. And then, again by complete coincidence, I left town a day or two before they found the body. So when I heard about it, I was completely freaked out."

Back up north, he told interrogators that he didn't see much of Crispo during his three-week stay, except for a brief visit to the gallery, which was surprisingly unpopulated. "Hi, Ace," Crispo had said, "how's it going?" When told of Dean's need for a bed, Andrew suggested Bernard, but Aarons didn't see much of him, either, he explained, except for that first night.

They met up at the gallery, and went to the East Village for dinner at a funky place on Tompkins Square called Life Café. That's when Bernard made his confession: "I killed somebody," he said. "Don't you believe me?" Dean replied, "What I don't know, Bernard, I don't know. Don't tell me." All of this he volunteered to the police, adding a strange coda: "Then, after dinner, Bernard had me help him push a car in the East River. Said it belonged to a friend who wanted to make an insurance claim." (Strangely, that story proved to be true.)

The three guests of the state comprised a curious trio—one coke addict, one alcoholic, and one strange friend of Bernard's from school who, though he had been directly implicated in an early version of the confession, neither asked for an attorney nor inquired about when he could leave. The cost of the rooms, and the armed attendants, was astronomical for the township, and nobody could figure out what to do next.

Finally, it was decided that the Paul Jeffries case could be referred to Manhattan, the alleged torture and rape having occurred there. And because Billy Mayer, after two day-long interviews, had given all the information he seemed to possess, and because he'd drawn no threats after seven days in protective custody, his guard was removed and he was relocated to cheaper quarters. Taking offense, Billy Mayer called Sergeant Franks from a pay phone and announced he was "taking off."

Franks objected only halfheartedly. Money was fast becoming an issue. Overtime bills for local officers were becoming unmanageable, and some of Franks's men were donating their own time to the investigation. Officers from the county's RCBCI and state troopers were being reassigned. The window of opportunity was easing shut, and plenty of work remained.

For example, Franks's leads sheet still listed scores of people who needed to be located and interviewed. There were past employees of the gallery—Ronnie Caran, especially, among them—neighbors, doormen, maintenance workers at the Fuller Building; members of the co-op board on Twelfth Street, some of whom had already mentioned Crispo's nocturnal tide of tough-looking visitors ("Because of him, we had to change the security system," one tenant said). René Arlington had been located in Brazil—alive—and a trip there was in order (although eventually abandoned after Rio de Janeiro authorities promised to oppose it).

And the county was on the verge of incurring the heaviest expense to date. Franks had sworn out a statement to a local judge asserting that he had enough evidence to merit dispatching an excavation team to Crispo's Southampton home in search of bodies beneath the lush green lawn and the stark statue sitting in its center. It was not done lightly. Holy shit, Franks thought as he was signing it, I hope I'm not wrong. A thorough search would require coordination with local authorities, equipment rental, union wages, overtime (for day and night work), and helicopters to fly Rockland prosecutors back and forth to the site.

The judge, however, agreed with him, and a caravan of backhoes and plows was ordered to Long Island's most exclusive community.

CHAPTER
17

After his evening with Debbie Harry, after bidding farewell to Hal Burroughs and his friend Hank, after ridding himself of the bag of toys and the inculpatory materials contained therein, after talking with the cops and telephoning the LeGeroses, and meeting with David twice, Andrew Crispo rested briefly. And when morning came, he was in the office of his tax attorney, Stanley Arkin, who had assumed the tangled legal messes that Roy Cohn had abandoned. On most of the suits, he had made almost no subsequent headway, except with the IRS. A tentative deal had been worked out allowing Crispo to pay back a portion of what he'd cheated. He would plead guilty to a low-level misdemeanor and serve no jail time whatsoever.

By the tough standards of New York law circles, Arkin was a minor celebrity ("headline-grabbing," one profile called him, "a spin doctor"). In criminal matters, though, he had little experience—most having come in a single case, when client David Poindexter was accused of harboring the fugitive Angela Davis in 1971. His experience in matters of peculiar amorous proclivities, such as the one Crispo undoubtedly explained that morning, were unknown.

Arkin pulled on his trademark cowboy hat and took Andrew Crispo directly to Rockland County. There, in an audience with Kenneth Gribetz and Chief Stephen Scurti, he volunteered to have his client testify before a grand jury in exchange for complete immunity from prosecution. When that was rejected, he asserted his client's right to remain silent, which he said he would strongly encourage.

Then Arkin presented the authorities with a "hypothetical situation" that succeeded in casting a lingering doubt in their minds. "What *if* my client was actually there," he began, "and what if he had taken part in some sort of sexual ritual at that boy's house. Hypothetically, of course, what if he *did* kneel this unfortunate Norwegian down and *actually said,* '*Kill him*'? Even if these things had happened—and I am, by no means, saying that they did—my client had no way of knowing that the gun was loaded, and—again, if it happened this way—he was as shocked as anybody else that the trigger was pulled, that real bullets came out, that a young man was killed. He couldn't believe it. He was horrified." Beyond proving that Crispo actually uttered the words, New York State's "acting in concert" statute would require the D.A. to show that he had full knowledge of what would happen when he "solicited, requested, commanded, importuned, or intentionally aided" Le Geros. Otherwise, Arkin was arguing, Crispo was nothing more than a witness, and crime witnesses have no obligations or culpability under the law.

"If what Arkin said was true," said an official who was present at the meeting, "Crispo committed no crime at all. We wrestled with this; we struggled endlessly."

After the meeting, Arkin broke with his own tradition and made no comments to the press. Then, citing "an awful lot of things I've got to do," he passed off the case to fellow attorney Robert Kasanof, who told a reporter, "We feel that he is a witness at most. We will hold the district attorney and the police to strict standards in the conduct of their investigation." Pressed to comment on the presence of the weapon at the gallery, Kasanof said it was "obvious" that LeGeros had planted it there. "Even a child could see who the source of the gun was. If Crispo was guilty, he certainly would have removed it. My client could have removed it at any time since the shooting. The logical inference is that Crispo didn't know it was there."

Logical, perhaps, but not truthful.

Further deflecting the issue, Kasanof then enumerated damage he said Rockland authorities caused during their search of the gallery, which they "left in shambles." They "brutally and needlessly destroyed a price-less Louis XVI desk, a one-of-a-kind," he said, by opening the drawer with "a crowbar and a chisel." This was the prized desk that became the inaugural possession in Crispo's collection of objets d'art and masterworks and furniture valued at more than $50 million.

The defense strategy appeared to be working. Through March and into April, while the district attorney in Rockland County was publicly stating that "we know the identity of the second person" involved in the "Death Mask" slaying, he was just as regularly announcing that Andrew Crispo "is not a suspect at this time." A similar line was proclaimed on the clear afternoon when the digging beneath Crispo's Southampton lawn commenced.

Twenty police officers showed up unannounced, dragging shovels and bulldozers and dogs and a search warrant signed by the appropriate justices that cited "human remains alleged to have been disposed of on the Crispo property." It was printed in papers again the following day, when the digging continued, and again when a field across the street became the excavation site. Nothing was found in either location.

The night the digging began, Crispo was dining at a midtown restaurant with Kasanof, a Runyonesque figure with flapping jowls who spoke as though cotton filled his mouth. When his pager sounded, he returned a call to a reporter. He was asked what the police were likely to find under the statue. He asked the man to hold, and returned to his table. "What do I tell 'em?"

"Tell them there's nothing there! Tell them this is ridiculous."

"I'm happy to," he said, glowering. "But I don't want to be wrong. I have a relationship with the press."

"You won't be wrong," Crispo assured him.

Kasanof passed the information on, and repeated it with no less conviction the following day, after the heavy equipment had retreated. "They dug and they found nothing," he told *The New York Times*. "I think it must be clear now that whoever told them there would be bodies there must be lying. It must raise questions about the people who are making accusations."

Although the Stony Point authorities were certain the accusations stemmed from Crispo's own statements, the failure of the search was a public embarrassment. A Long Island police official, deflecting criticism, told reporters the orders to dig came from Rockland. The *New York Daily News* quoted a reluctant member of the search party, complaining, "We can't continue digging up all of Southampton."

The New York City authorities were simultaneously, but unknown to the press, dragging the Hudson River for bodies, also based on Crispo's alleged confessions. Unluckily, they found nothing; luckily, the failure was not trumpeted publicly.

Cornered, Rockland's Kenneth Gribetz told reporters that, despite coming up empty-handed in Long Island, his overall investigation had uncovered "new and critical" evidence that he felt sure would lead to a second arrest.

Tommy Martin, the red-haired man who had given Andrew Crispo three dollars and rushed him out of Philadelphia twenty years earlier, had been following his old friend's travails in the city papers for several days from his suburban home in West Trenton, New Jersey, which he shared with his father and brother. At first, he had chuckled seditiously, calling members of the old gang with the observation that "Andy's stories have finally caught up with him—I wonder how he's gonna get out of this one." Now an unemployed ironworker, Martin had a fanciful approach to life that had hardly changed over the years. He still talked breathlessly and rolled back his freckled face to loose peals of uninhibited laughter. And he still admired and loved Andy Crispo, taking great pleasure in watching his antics from the sideline. He made several trips a day to the newsstand for each edition of the *New York Post*.

But when Martin picked up the five-star final on March 28, the story ceased being funny. They were digging up Crispo's lawn! They were, as Martin told a friend, "trying to make him look like a mass murderer, the gay Ted Bundy!"

He called Cindy O'Shea, a criminal defense attorney working out of West Trenton. "He's in trouble, Cindy," he explained. "I just can't sit here and not help." When Andrew was eighty-sixed from Philly's gay bars, Tommy helped sneak him in; when he was being tailed by those men who were taken for FBI, Tommy helped him get out of town. It was time to intervene again.

He read her the story, which was headlined BODIES HUNTED AT ART MAN'S SOUTHAMPTON ESTATE.

"Andy was always a troublemaker," Tommy Martin explained on the phone, "and people can misunderstand that. From what I can tell, he's gotten himself in some pretty rough stuff, and not just the sex. But I know he didn't do this, Cynthia. He couldn't possibly have done this. Burying bodies in his lawn! I've had sex with this man, and I can tell you he's not like that."

He added that he'd been leaving messages for Crispo everywhere and hadn't yet reached his old friend. "I think he needs an attorney who can help make sense of this. Nobody's better at that than you, Cynthia."

At just twenty-five, Cindy O'Shea was running a successful New Jersey law practice that specialized in defending gays, although she was not gay herself. In West Trenton and the surrounding townships, she was the person you'd call if the pursuit of your sexuality had, somehow, led you into conflict with the law.

"I have two thoughts," O'Shea told Martin. "This is a friend of yours, and he's obviously in trouble. And this case sounds like it's crying out for us. We've got some research to do. When can we get together?"

That evening, they headed for the city. In the musty environs of the Hellfire, O'Shea plied the bartenders with questions while Martin worked the rooms. "Sure, I know him," one employee told her. "Terrible thing that happened, though."

He added, "You know, whatever happened, it doesn't seem like him. Like everybody else here, he'd just come to find somebody to lay. Normal stuff—at least normal for this place. I've seen him leave with plenty of guys and none of them seemed to disappear. You'd see 'em back that night, or the next, or whatever. He seemed to like the young blond ones. Had a lot of coke, too. Always had enough for everybody—I think that increased his chances with the boys."

"Have you seen him around lately?"

"Not since all of this murder stuff hit the papers. But then, I wouldn't show up either, if I were him. There's lots of people pretty angry. Cops have been all over the place."

Over the following weeks, O'Shea and Martin made continual sojourns into Crispo's world hoping to find him, hoping to help him, hoping to be a part of his tabloid life. They hung out in the lobby of the Galleria, maneuvering pointed questions into casual chatter with strangers there (who "dished him to filth," they said later); they slipped notes under the heavy doors at the gallery; they strapped a belt over O'Shea's bosom and tried, unsuccessfully, to sneak her into the all-male Mineshaft.

At Area, a hip night spot in Tribeca, they stumbled on Andy Warhol, who was sitting alone at the bar. In her delicate way, O'Shea quizzed him on Andrew Crispo, and Warhol professed to know nothing about him, though they had met several times. (The next day, according to his diary, Warhol had continued thinking about Crispo. He ran into an acquaintance, the entry said, "and I began asking him about Andrew Crispo. And then the TV cameras were around us so we didn't want them to know what we were talking about, so I began calling Crispo 'her,' and John got it right away. He said, 'I never knew her really well, I just thought she was a sleaze bag.' And John was talking about the Hellfire Club, and I'm surprised I never wound up there one night. But I can't stand the smell of those places—even the preppy Surf Club is hard to take.")

Their efforts at "investigating" the Andrew Crispo case had turned up virtually nothing, except for a deeper understanding of his after-hours downtown life—which they considered playful and erotic. And their attempts to reach the embattled art dealer had so far been fruitless, too. Early one Saturday morning (after a long night in the city), O'Shea was awakened by a call from Robert Kasanof, who loudly and angrily accused her of poaching on his client. He threatened retribution if she continued.

A week later, on April 7, Andrew Crispo called himself. He spoke briefly with her, thanking her for her concern but telling her he was quite satisfied with his current representation. Tommy Martin, who was standing by, then took the phone. Later, he recalled the conversation this way:

"Happy Easter, Andy."

"Today's Easter? I didn't even notice."

"A Catholic boy like you?"

"Well, things have been kind of rough lately."

"What the hell happened, Andrew? All that you had gone to New York for, and then this happens? How could you mess up like this?" Tommy hadn't realized until then just how angry these failures had made him.

"Well, I got a little sidetracked on cocaine, and I'm not doing that anymore. I'm doing a diet. I'm only eating fish, and this and that."

"What about this Eigil Vesti thing? What happened there?"

Crispo answered directly. He said he was there, and things got out of hand. He called it a party "that went wacky" and professed his innocence. And he added that he couldn't really talk more about it, because of Kasanof's instructions. "But I assure you," he added, "that I am not responsible for what happened up there."

He added that he had friends clipping every edition of every newspaper so he could have a "scrapbook" of the entire episode. He said the art world meant a great deal to him, and that the publicity had destroyed all of that; he was just trying to hold on to some of his professional credibility. He said his gallery was closed now. He recognized the mistakes he had made—"I played too hard"—and lamented the great toll it had taken.

"That was it," Tommy said to Cindy after recapping the conversation. "That was Andrew's Easter call to me. That's about as close as he's gotten to being religious: He was very sorry."

"Did you believe him?" Cindy asked.

"Every word."

Where Tommy Martin came from, friends stood by one another—no matter what.

One thing Det. Sgt. Billy Franks noticed as he plowed through stacks of interview notes, and address books, and Limelight invitation lists was how small the Manhattan haut monde really was. Names kept repeating:

Eigil Vesti, Crispo, Stephen AuCoin, Dallas Boesendahl, Alan Rish. People who knew Crispo also knew Eigil. But aside from P.J., the Hellfire bouncer (and a marginally reliable witness), Franks hadn't found anybody who could attest firsthand to their acquaintance.

There was a handful of people who could put Vesti and Crispo together in the same room on numerous occasions. Alan Rish, the Limelight scenemaker, had seen them both at the gallery. Boesendahl, Vesti's "intimate" and his dinner partner on his last night alive, said he was unaware of any friendship but that it would make sense. "Eigil was interested in art. I would guess he had been to the gallery."

Vesti's new roommate, the photographer Stephen AuCoin, had a dim recollection that Eigil had received phone calls from Andrew Crispo, whom AuCoin knew casually. But there was another distant memory, too. "I think Sam Collins introduced them," he said. "Maybe he'll know something."

Sergeant Franks had heard the name before. Bernard had used it when he described his first meeting with Eigil Vesti, naked and masturbating on Crispo's sofa. "He's a friend of Sam Collins's," he quoted Crispo as saying, as though there were some sort of significance to that. In Bernard's telling, it seemed to be one of the key words that had incited him to beat the victim.

It meant nothing to Franks at the time, but Bernard had given an explanation to his father, who dutifully passed it along to the officer. Sam Collins, Bernard believed, had drugged and raped him; Crispo told him so. "Bernard says he was sent to a mental home in the Midwest," John LeGeros reported. "And he says that whenever Crispo wanted to get him angry enough to take part in one of those scenes or scenarios, he'd invoke this Sam Collins. The name seems to enrage him."

And the name Sam Collins also appeared in everybody's address books, at a West Village address. His phone, though, was disconnected, with no further information given.

After learning that Collins had relatives in Ohio, Billy Franks requested a printout of drivers' license registrations for every Collins in the state. He found Sam outside Cincinnati. On the afternoon of Monday, April 15, he made telephone contact. "I refuse to cooperate," Collins replied.

"Listen, man." Franks had lost all of his casual charm. "You'd better fuckin' talk to me now or I'm gonna be on your doorstep tomorrow."

"I'm not talking to you," Collins said, "period."

Early the next morning, when Sam Collins answered his suburban door and faced down two men holding up police badges, he said, "I guess those guys in New York sent you."

"I *am* the guy from New York, buddy," Franks said humorlessly. "Let's go." He ushered the visibly shaken man downtown to the police station.

Although he was in his thirties, Sam Collins's face was drawn and leathery. It was clear to Franks that he had once been very good-looking, once vibrant and compelling. Those cheeks weren't always sunken and yellow, and something about those eyes indicated that they had lost their sparkle along some consuming journey. At the police precinct, he showed none of his previous reluctance to speak.

"Andrew and I were boyfriends in 1977—we met in Southampton," he said. "We didn't go together very long, maybe six months, and then we didn't see each other, for one reason or another, for about two years. But we stayed close after that.

"Eigil, I met sometime in the summer of 1983. Stephen AuCoin introduced me to him. He was doing *Man Alive!*, that picture book, at that point, and Eigil was working with him. His production assistant or something, but I know that he did pose for a few of the pictures. Anyway, we hit it off right away, and for a while—I think until January 1984—we were lovers. Pretty steady from the time that we met. Coincidentally, I was also seeing Stephen AuCoin during this time, I think.

"Eigil, he was one of the nicest—he was a sweetheart, really, wouldn't have hurt a fly. Liked to have a good time, really enjoyed life fully. What can I say? As bad as I was—and until I detoxed, I was pretty bad, like two *ounces* of coke a week, easy—he was always so up, and always having such a good time. We'd go to the movies, go dancing. That sort of thing, or dinner at friends' houses.

"People have sent me copies of the papers and I read about the Hellfire or the Anvil, but I never knew about any of that stuff. If he liked to go there, either he never told me about it or that kind of thing came later. Just like if he liked to get hurt. I never knew any of that, so maybe that came toward the end.

"Anyway, in the fall of 1983, there was a fund-raiser for AIDS at Lowell Nesbitt's studio downtown, and Andrew and I and one other person were the sponsors, sold the tickets—one thousand dollars apiece or something—and arranged to have one of Lowell's paintings raffled off. Eigil was my date that night, and that's where I introduced him to Andrew. They seemed to hit it off okay, I guess.

"But then later, around Christmastime, Andrew invited us both over to his apartment, for a small little gathering, and Andrew seemed to know him pretty well by that time. It seemed that way to me, anyway.

"Now, over this next year, that's when I met Bernard, who Andrew had sent over to my house, evidently, as a kind of a gift or something. I had no idea he was coming. But that's another story altogether. The last time I saw Eigil was when that book came out—*La Popessa*—by René Arlington and his father, or stepfather, or lover, or whatever he really was, at the Limelight. He wasn't my date or anything, but we talked a little, and he talked with Andrew and with René and it was all very social."

"Let me understand this," Sergeant Franks said. "You're saying that Crispo and Eigil Vesti knew each other for a year?"

"More than a year, yeah. I mean I'm not sure how well, like if they were boyfriends or not I have no idea. But they were definitely friends."

Franks silently reviewed the hypothetical scenario spelled out by Crispo's attorney—that Crispo stood by and watched, to his horror, as Bernard shot the victim. If Vesti had been a stranger, Franks thought, perhaps he could understand that Crispo did not go to authorities with information about the murder. But Vesti was no stranger. He had been a Christmas party guest! He was the lover of a friend.

How could a man watch one of his friends kill another without showing some sign of fear, anger, remorse? Could he then throw evidence out the window, and return to work, and aid in a cover-up of his friend's murder? Could he maintain a steady, unaffected appearance to everybody, right up until the day of Bernard's arrest? Could he make jokes about the killing in order to lure another friend over to a party with a rock star? This was the story for which Franks had been looking.

"Now," said Franks, "just how well did *you* know Mr. Crispo?"

"Very well. I mean, we were very close—until I moved away, which was I guess last September—we saw each other very frequently."

"Was Andrew Crispo doing much cocaine during this period?"

"As much, if not more, as I was doing. We could stay up for days partying."

"Right through till you moved?"

"Several times a week."

Franks then asked for details on Sam Collins's encounter with Bernard LeGeros, the one Bernard had called a rape.

"Nothing of the sort," Collins said. "He just showed up one afternoon—I'd met him, I think, once before. So I went into the other room, excused myself, and called Andrew, who said to just give Bernard a couple of drinks and he would do anything. I guess I was interested, a little, but when I got back to Bernard, he told me this whole story about how he wanted to be a burglar, or no—wanted *me* to be a burglar, like pretend that I had broken into my own apartment, and he was going to tie me up and whip me and handcuff me and whatever. So I laughed, you know, and told him no.

"Then, I guess, I invited him for a drink, mostly because I wanted to get him out of my house, and we went to Uncle Charlie's, this bar around the corner from where I was living. We had a drink, and I just couldn't shake him on the way back. He dragged along, and there was no way to persuade him. Then he starts disrobing, just like that! He was just a little bit too bizarre for me. He stripped naked and I —only slightly reluctantly, I admit—I got into bed with him.

"As I remember, it was very boring and awful. He didn't come—as I remember he couldn't get an erection, though he tried pretty hard—and I guess I masturbated. I remember he bit me on the neck, kind of chomped down on my neck. But nothing else happened."

Franks was busy distilling the comments onto a yellow notepad when Det. Joey Denise, who had accompanied him to Ohio and had been quiet throughout, asked about René Arlington. That whole angle of this unfolding story had baffled him. In his interviews of former gallery employees, he'd noticed that many of them spoke of the tight bond between Arlington and Crispo. And a few mentioned the trips they had made to René's stepmother's house, following his adoptive father's death. Always, the visit ended with a request to carry boxes downtown.

Collins said, "They had been seeing each other, for one. But that had stopped, and René was going with somebody named Rio. Andrew was very interested—and I was, too—in getting Jaclyn Smith to pick up the option to the book, which René thought the Wicked Stepmother was trying to block, somehow.

"On New Year's Eve, I remember that date, 1983 to 1984, Andrew called me and told me to call the doorman at Paul Murphy's building— he gave the phone number—and tell him to go outside and check for a white limo. He said, 'Don't take no for an answer.' I said I'd do it, but I asked him why. 'René's in the apartment. He's trapped; he can't get out. He's not supposed to be there, and you've got to help.' Okay. It didn't make much sense, but I made the call.

"Then a month or two later, I saw Paul Murphy's will, which I think was the most current one, the one that left Julie Murphy, who was his ex-wife, his entire estate, also assorted papers about *La Popessa*. I think this was the original, and it hadn't been filed."

"How did you see this? Who had it?"

"Andrew did. See, I don't remember the exact date, but Rio, René's friend, had moved to Brazil—he was Brazilian, and Rio was like his New York name that he adopted. Andrew had decided that Rio was getting in the way, that he was unduly influencing René. Influencing him on the movie rights. Andrew decided to get him out of the country, so we were sending him threatening letters saying 'Get out of town now.' Unsigned, of course. Cutting letters out of magazines and newspapers. And we sent brochures on Rio. Rio de Janeiro—like, 'Here's a place you might want to go.' Once, we even called up Pan Am and made a reservation for Brazil, in Rio's name, and told the clerk to call in the morning to confirm, you know, and freak him out. That sort of thing. Andrew liked to control people. And he really wanted the movie, although Jaclyn was only passingly interested. I believe that Rio got on that plane to Brazil, but I'm not sure." Collins seemed to enjoy telling the story, pleased, perhaps, in his ability to piece together the events that took place while he was in a cocaine fog.

"No," he said, "I know what it was. Instead of getting on the plane, he put all the wills and papers in a package and was sending them on the Pan Am flight to a family friend in Brazil. Rio was wanting all of this out of the country to protect René from I don't know what."

"What do you think?"

"Maybe from the Wicked Stepmother. Maybe us. They were just going to hold on to it there, and Rio wanted René to go to Brazil and hide out and get away from Andrew. And Andrew got wind of this and called the—this is what he said—he called the Brazilian ambassador, who in turn called a high official at Pan Am and had the thing held at the airport. Andrew went and got it, and I was at his house when he came back. That's when I saw the wills."

"What did he do with them?"

"Well, I think he must still have them. I know René never got them."

"What was so important about this movie?"

"That, I don't know. I guess he needed something else to obsess out on. I think he also had become intrigued with the whole Hollywood thing, with just this brief introduction."

"Debbie Harry?"

"No. He met Tony Richmond—who's Jaclyn Smith's husband—because I brought him down to look at Andrew's apartment as a possible location for a remake of *Sentimental Journey*. And so the more we started talking about *La Popessa*, the more he kept pumping me all the time about Tony and Jaclyn. And it *was* a wonderful book. As I remember, Karen Valentine and her husband had bought the rights to it, and that option was coming up, was expiring very shortly. And we were trying to pick up that option."

What Sam Collins also knew but didn't tell Denise or Franks was that the movie project was another experiment in controlling situations, manipulating people, and profiting from it. In this case, it was a large-scale exploit in which, by 1985, Crispo had been able to involve a cast of dozens—most of them unsuspecting of their own roles.

Also left unmentioned was the sudden, strangely timed death of Paul Murphy underpinning the entire mystery. While doctors considered it a natural death—a fatal heart attack—Andrew Crispo had frequently claimed a hand in it, each time altering the specifics. To Collins, he had said that his heart medicine had been replaced with a placebo. "He was making the suggestion that maybe it wasn't just a heart attack," Collins said later, "that maybe René had killed him. I really never took him seriously, because Andrew put a twist on anything. Nothing could be just black and white. Two and two make five, and he'd try like hell to get everyone in the world believing that. That was his talent. That's what he loved.

"With the old man, it was: René was afraid he was going to be left out in the cold. So he did him in. Maybe it was that he threw the medicine away. Or switched the heart medication the old man was taking. Andrew was very vague. And then, to keep René in line during all of this, he'd threaten him on occasion. You know, 'I have powerful friends,' and 'I know too much and you'd better not try to fuck me over.' Implying the Paul Murphy stuff. Implying everything else. Then, there was a time— completely unrelated—when René was arrested for something, I think there was money missing or something at the clothing shop where he worked. And Andrew took care of that. Another way to keep him in line."

That would account for the arrest folder that was recovered during the search of the Crispo Gallery, another one of the simmering questions that had baffled Franks. Crispo somehow "took care" of the arrest.

Sam Collins concluded his statement by saying, "All of this seems peculiar, I know. But it doesn't mean anything, really. It certainly doesn't mean that Andrew had anything to do with killing Eigil Vesti, which I think he would have been completely incapable of doing."

Just a week earlier, Sergeant Franks might have accepted such an assertion on face value. Then he was still operating on his assumptions that Bernard LeGeros was a highly unreliable source, and that Andrew Crispo's comments to various friends about his own criminal past were nothing more than coke-based concoctions. The fact that nothing was buried underneath his lawn seemed conclusive. The fact that only one alleged victim had come forward to lodge an official report seemed to undermine, at least legally, the allegations of the other, unnamed callers. Stanley Arkin's hypothetical assessment had still held forth: If Andrew was there, it was all a shocking mistake.

But the day before Franks flew to Ohio, he made a telephone call that swung his convictions back the other way. He entered it as item number 118 on his daily investigation report:

This officer contacted special agent Joseph Tierney, FBI, New-
burgh office, and requested he check for any arrest record
on ANDREW CRISPO. Special Agent TIERNEY advised that
CRISPO has been arrested previously and that his FBI Number
is 967972E.

The following charges have been filed against CRISPO:

1. 1964, Philadelphia, Penn., Blackmail.
2. August 26th, 1964, Miami, Fla., disorderly conduct and
wandering.
3. December 8th, 1964, Philadelphia, Penn., solicitation to
commit sodomy.
4. 9/28/75, New York City, sodomy and possession of a
weapon.

The rap sheet that supported these charges provided almost no more
information, and made no reference to how the cases were settled. The
blackmail charge, for example, gave no clue as to who had made such
allegations to the police, and Franks had no knowledge of the gay-bar
scheme, or Crispo's comments to his Philadelphia friends about getting
"lots more money" from Liberace. When Franks tried to research the
case, he found that Philadelphia's old files were virtually inaccessible.
He decided not to pursue them.

He was much more interested in the New York City case, which
seemed to foreshadow everything else that happened afterward. He
learned that Crispo had spent a single night in jail, and that the charges—
that he had brandished a weapon and raped a young man—were soon
dropped.

Years later, a person familiar with the 1975 case described the com-
plainant as a young hustler whom Crispo had brought home one Friday
night. When the police arrived Saturday morning to arrest Crispo, they
confiscated "a long kitchen knife and a wide black designer-type belt,"
both of which were considered to be the weapons used in the assault.
Crispo posted bail Sunday morning after a night in jail, and the kid
eventually dropped the charges, without citing a reason.

"Of course," said a friend of Crispo's, "we all assumed this was just
some prostitute who thought that he could get more money from Andrew
if he put on the pressure. We figured he was hustling for anything he
could get. Without question, we all accepted Andrew's version of the
events."

When Franks capped his pen and folded his yellow pad into a file
folder, he made a solemn proposition to Sam Collins. "I'd like you to

help me with something, buddy," he said. "I'm gonna ask you to call Andrew on the phone and get him to talk about this. Get him talking about Eigil Vesti. We'll put it on tape."

"Are you crazy? First, I just got out of treatment, and getting messed up in something like this—entrapment! This is definitely not what I need right now."

Franks pleaded, but Collins refused to budge. "Plus," he added, "I really wouldn't think that Andrew would be capable of something like that. Bernard, yes. But Andrew, no. If anything, it got carried away. Further than Andrew intended. Bernard's kind of a dumb schmuck. Like a puppy dog! And Andrew has such a mouth, he could spin such incredible tales."

"You believe that there's no way that one of his 'tales' could have resulted in the death of this friend of yours?"

"Maybe he has got some kind of obsession with death—I mean, he used to tell me about snuff films and bodies in his yard, and all that. But it was nothing more. It's just him."

If it had not been for the killing of Eigil Vesti, Paul Jeffries might never have come forward with his story of imprisonment, torture, and rape at the Andrew Crispo Gallery. In the panic-filled few days after he was released, he said, he ran into Crispo several times and was warned to keep the incident a secret. It was a warning he took seriously. While he was being held in the gallery, Jeffries said, he was fully convinced Crispo was prepared to kill him, or have one of his henchmen do the job. There had been talk of snuff films, mob slayings, and emotionless executions.

But then Vesti's remains were found, and the picture changed. "Eigil Vesti never told anybody anything and look what happened to him," Jeffries told a friend. "He's as dead as can be, and Crispo's still walking the streets. How do you think that makes me feel?" He contacted Rockland County authorities, and they invited him up to a guarded motel room.

But Kenneth Gribetz, deciding the case belonged in the hands of New York City law enforcement, contacted Linda Fairstein, who was in charge of the sex-crimes division of Manhattan's district attorney's office. "I'd really like you to handle this," Fairstein recalled him saying, "and it would allow us to continue beating the bushes, keep the pressure on, from down there."

She agreed, and was very supportive of Jeffries, a slight twenty-six-year-old bartender with a close-cropped beard, flushed cheekbones, and bright blue eyes. He remembered her saying, "It's not going to be an easy case to win, and it's going to be very rough on you."

As victims go, Jeffries was not an especially sympathetic one. When the pay phone rang outside the Mineshaft, on the morning of September 20, 1984, Jeffries was there to answer it. And when the anonymous caller said he was having a rough-and-tumble sex romp and cocaine fest at a nearby address, Jeffries agreed decisively. At the Twelfth Street apartment, he and Crispo shared a brief, kinky, and bizarre intimacy. And when he was invited for a more experimental encounter up at the gallery later that day, he accepted again. He was no stranger to the world of tricks and trade, and he liked his sex rough. But his idea of S&M was bound by rules and codes, the foremost one being that both parties must consent to any given act. Paul Jeffries said that he did not consent to what happened to him after he entered the gallery and met Andrew Crispo and his friends.

Sitting with Linda Fairstein for several long afternoons, and sitting again before a grand jury, Jeffries relived his ordeal. He told of the handcuffs, the snuff films, the whippings delivered to the cadence of his own cries: A-S-S-H-O-L-E. He said LeGeros pressed a pistol to his head; he said Crispo instructed, "Kill him," and LeGeros pulled the trigger, making a click; he said Crispo called it "an empty chamber," announced, "You're lucky this time," and then repeated the order to LeGeros. He told of the singing, and the urinating, and the sodomy, which Crispo had commanded at the end.

But there was a very uncomfortable coda to Paul Jeffries's story. As he was nearing the elevator on his way out of the gallery, another condition was placed on his release: Jeffries would accompany Bernard LeGeros and Andrew Crispo to dinner. He agreed—out of fear, he said—and supped leisurely at the Five Oaks restaurant on Grove Street in the Village.

It got even more complicated. When the check came, Crispo's credit card was rejected and he "borrowed" $110 from Jeffries, who subsequently called the gallery and even visited there, attempting to retrieve the money. "It was the one way I could think of to get even," he told Linda Fairstein, "because I certainly wasn't going to pay for dinner after that!"

He went on to say that the reason he hadn't come forward earlier was his belief that Andrew Crispo, through his ties to Roy Cohn, was capable of having a mob gunman exact a lasting rebuff to his testimony. Crispo had stressed this possibility, he said, during the beatings, which took place near a framed photograph of the legendary lawyer taken by Robert Mapplethorpe. "He told me if I ever told anyone about what had happened," Jeffries said, "the 'family' would reach out and 'exterminate' me." Fairstein believed him.

She met personally with Det. Sgt. Billy Franks and reviewed the results of Stony Point's investigation (which she called "top-rate"). She dispatched a New York City detective, Pat Barry, to question Bernard. On April 26, he came back with a signed statement confirming everything.

Bernard told him, "Andrew called me and said to me, 'Someone tried to break into the gallery. I want you to come over and arrest him.' When I got to the gallery, I met with Andrew. He had a set of handcuffs, a starter's pistol, and a small vial of coke." Crispo, Bernard said, instructed him to plant the drugs on Jeffries, who was in another room, and then arrest him. "So I held him against the wall and frisked him. I was brutal and rough, like cops in movies. I was abusive in language. I was extremely abusive in language as I interrogated him."

When he "found" the coke, Bernard growled, "What's this, asshole?" He pressed Jeffries against the wall savagely, elbowing him in the back. Andrew entered at that moment, and "pushed Paul's head real hard, like smacking him."

Shortly, the cab from the Bronx arrived, carrying four young men whom Crispo reportedly described as Vice Squad "fag-smashers." "They started roughing Paul up and they whipped him," Bernard continued. "During a pause in the whipping, Andrew took the gun and put it to Paul's head, the right side, and clicked it. Each time the gun clicked, Andrew said to Paul, 'You're lucky this time,' as he pulled the trigger."

Two full months after Eigil Vesti's body was found, Linda Fairstein placed a protocol call to Kenneth Gribetz in Rockland County to tell him the grand jury had handed down an indictment against Andrew Crispo and Bernard LeGeros in the Paul Jeffries case. There would be a press conference announcing it the following morning.

The Rockland DA invited himself along, but Linda Fairstein's boss, Robert Morgenthau, found the suggestion preposterous. "Absolutely not!" was his bellowed (and overheard) response. "If he wants to grandstand his own cases, let him. If he wants to pose with that so-called death mask, which was a damn piece of *evidence*, after all, well that's his business. But he's not going to make a zoo out of my case."

An associate said, "Bob couldn't imagine why the hell Gribetz thought he would belong here." Morgenthau didn't view prosecutorial work as photo opportunities or popularity contests.

Linda Fairstein reported back to Rockland: "It is a question of propriety, and of legality. He says no."

Just after dawn on May 17, Andrew Crispo surrendered himself to Linda Fairstein, in the presence of Det. Sgt. Billy Franks, and was taken off in handcuffs to central booking. In the afternoon, Robert Morgenthau held a rare press conference announcing the indictment, the arrest, and the bail. Crispo had been charged with kidnapping, unlawful imprisonment, assault, coercion, and forceable sodomy, he said, describing the incident as a kind of date rape. "The victim was in no way participating voluntarily in what occurred," he said. "This was an antigay assault."

After fingerprinting and photographing, Andrew Crispo was arraigned early in the day and released on a one-hundred-thousand-dollar bond. He told reporters, "I have nothing to hide."

Standing at his side was Robert Kasanof, who said, "This was the conduct of consenting adults. I will prove—by objective facts—that whatever happened was of a voluntary, *social* nature."

Immediately following the press conference, Linda Fairstein found that she had been "cut off" by Kenneth Gribetz and all his associates in Rockland County. Efforts to get updates on their Crispo investigation were totally rebuffed. Phone calls went unanswered. Information went unexchanged. Gribetz had erected a formidable *cordon sanitaire* around the Crispo case and around himself. "Either he's got no use for us anymore," Fairstein angrily complained to coworkers, "or his feathers were ruffled because we didn't want him at the arraignment. He's making this whole thing into a damn pissing contest."

As the months progressed, Gribetz occasionally resurrected his earlier assertions to the press of an impending arrest in the Eigil Vesti case, still not naming a suspect and still not implicating Andrew Crispo directly. In this void, Crispo issued a statement through Kasanof that slammed the innuendo campaign, which was blamed in part for causing him to shutter his gallery. "I absolutely deny the charge hinted at that I participated in a murder," the statement said. "A more professional investigation would have concluded and established that I am not guilty."

Linda Fairstein—a thirty-seven-year-old Vassar grad and Westchester native, a blond, impeccably dressed, shy-looking woman who stood, in business flats, slightly taller than Gribetz—grew increasingly impatient. She needed Rockland's help. She needed Rockland's witnesses, Rockland's evidence, Rockland's insights. That, she felt, was part of the deal. What she was handed instead was the lesser of the two cases, and she was facing the possibility of having to conduct an independent, parallel investigation.

Perhaps more disturbing than the trouble she was facing was the fact that Linda Fairstein felt Kenneth Gribetz had a moral obligation to prosecute Andrew Crispo, based on the evidence she knew the Stony Point team had accumulated in the early days of their investigation. It was that sense of moral imperative that kept Fairstein in this line of work, despite an onslaught of other offers. She never seriously considered private practice. And she had rejected countless lucrative offers from publishers to write her own story. There were nearly as many film consultancies, which she accepted only if the script suited her. (She had briefed Valerie Harper for her *Farrell for the People* television movie, which was based on Fairstein's own career.)

From fellow prosecutors, Linda Fairstein expected an extraordinary commitment. And among fellow prosecutors, she was revered as a tireless moral fighter.

"What the hell is he doing?" she once asked Sergeant Franks.

He replied, "He just doesn't want to risk a loss."

Fairstein finally confronted Gribetz herself in late summer, having cornered him at a semipublic and very crowded black-tie dinner given at the Waldorf for Governor Mario Cuomo. It was a well-known secret that Gribetz, hot off a string of high-profile convictions, had been petitioning Cuomo for a lieutenant governor's appointment. Local Democrats were also working on drafting him into a congressional bid. He seemed to be glad-handing the powerful gathering when Fairstein spotted him. Their conversation, at its most elevated moments, was overheard by many.

Gribetz's voice first rose when he said, "Don't say we're not doing anything on Crispo! We're doing plenty on Crispo."

"What are you doing, then?"

"Well, so far we don't have evidence to indict."

"Even *I* know you have enough to indict," she said quite sternly, gripping a cocktail with two hands. "You've got him on at least five federal felony charges short of the murder." She listed among them destruction of the body, obstruction of justice, and possession of the murder weapon. And she ticked off other possible charges, including reckless or negligent homicide, which would require a looser proof of mental culpability. "And I'm not convinced you can't get him on murder."

"C'mon, Linda. That would be too embarrassing. To indict on less than murder? At this point?" He laughed over her shoulder.

"Ken," she said, "there are some things that are so awful, it's your prosecutorial obligation to try them."

"Linda, Linda, Linda." Kenneth Gribetz (described by a relative as "just to the right of Genghis Khan") brooked no lectures, especially from women. "Don't give me that bullshit that we can but we're not! Don't bullshit that you did your case with promises from us. Linda"—he was shouting now—"you do your work and I'll do mine!"

CHAPTER

18

Early in the day on September 3, 1985—four weeks following Rock Hudson's shocking disclosure that he had AIDS, four weeks into the first journalistic blitzkrieg on the disease, four weeks after foreign phrases describing homosexual intercourse made their way into *Newsweek* and *Time*—a crowd of reporters muscled through the narrow doors of a courthouse in New City, New York, the Rockland County seat. They raced toward the small jury boxes that bookended the judge's bench, filling the one reserved for the press corps. A stocky man from a city tabloid jabbed a younger, thinner reporter hard in the stomach when it seemed he might have to settle for the long view from the back of the room. Three courtroom artists claimed rights to the front row and began sketching pages of graphics for their television crews, stationed right outside the door. They balanced specially designed binoculars on their noses like surgical glasses.

A very large, very timely story was at stake. It promised to be lurid and graphic and downright dirty: a strange, parallel universe of unknown sexuality involving unthinkable paraphernalia and ending in unimaginable finality. And it came at a time when, thanks to Hudson's notoriety, such things could be openly reported. Only the local Rockland paper had stuck to euphemisms such as "sexual device" while everyone else printed "dildo," without further description. If Acquired Immune Deficiency Syndrome was the season's big story, and Rock Hudson its chief photo opportunity, the trial of twenty-three-year-old Bernard John LeGeros, an apparently heterosexual youth with an irrational and violent hatred of gays, was about to become a bay window onto the world that incubated the disease.

This was not lost on David LeGeros. When singled out by the pack of reporters and approached for a comment, he might have pleaded for leniency. He might have declared his own dedication to his brother or debunked the prosecution's charges. He might even have damned the press for playing the story so luridly and unquestioningly. "My brother," he said from behind watery eyes—firmly and decisively—"is definitely not queer."

The suburbanites of Rockland County appeared somewhat less hungry than the city reporters for this event to unfold, but that didn't mean they weren't appreciating a newfound mid-eighties curiosity. At jury selection, Judge Robert Meehan told the pool of 164 prospects to buck up for testimony about "cocaine, deviant behavior, sadomasochism, and homosexuality." The field, through self-selection, narrowed only slightly; the majority remained, ready for more. To them, he announced, "If you serve on this case, when the century turns you will remember what you were doing in the early fall of 1985." That seemed just fine.

Kenneth Gribetz, a thin man with dark eyes and a slicing, nasal voice, brought more confidence and skill to his prosecution than raw experience. He was just thirty in 1974 when he was first elected district attorney— bringing with him a short resume. After a few years as an assistant prosecutor in Manhattan, where he took credit for trying radicals such as Mark Rudd and Abbie Hoffman, he became chief assistant to the Rockland DA for an equally short period. Eleven years later, when Bernard's file fell on his desk, it was only his ninth murder case.

He had won convictions in all the previous ones, and no simple adding exercise can do justice to his success on the case just closed the year before. It was in the town of Nyack, behind the Nanuet Mall, that remnants of the Weather Underground surfaced for the last time in a blaze of bullets aimed at a Brinks armored car. Two police officers and a Brinks guard died in the heist, which netted the revolutionaries $1.6 million.

Gribetz personally oversaw the investigation and prosecution of Kathy Boudin, Samuel Brown, and three other members of the clandestine radical group in a case that filled the years between 1981 and 1984. Boudin eventually took a plea and received twenty-five years to life; the rest, convicted on all counts, were sentenced to a minimum of seventy-five years each. Meanwhile, Gribetz's pinched face landed on the nation's TV sets and evening papers for three years going: *Newsweek* and *Mademoiselle* did pretrial coverage; his strategy was the focus of a "Today" show episode.

Not all the press was good. William Kunstler, representing Samuel Brown, charged the DA's office with brutality, alleging they broke his client's neck (X rays suggested the fractures were incurred after his arrest). Leonard Boudin, a noted liberal attorney, publicly denounced his daughter's Orange County jail cell as "terrible" and inhumane. Gribetz took flack for asking for, and receiving, a court order instructing defendant Nathaniel Burns to shave a beard. When he defied it, Gribetz sent in his own detectives to wrestle the man to the floor and do the job themselves. Other defendants, refusing to give up hair samples to the forensics teams, were strapped to barbers' chairs and similarly shorn.

And there was a rather public battle between Gribetz and the FBI over control of the prosecution. The FBI wanted desperately to link the prisoners with a succession of unsolved, apparently political, crimes. Nonetheless, when the first defendants to go to trial won a change of venue from Rockland to nearby Orange County, Gribetz followed—bodyguards and all. When the second trial was moved from Orange to Westchester, again he was there with his entourage. The cost to Rockland County of this prosecution war, when it was finally tabulated late in 1984, was $5.4 million; it nearly broke the banks of several townships. Legal wrangling over the bills between the municipalities, and between Rockland and other counties, wore on for years afterward.

Ken Gribetz went after the Weather Underground with such vehemence that he seemed to have spent a career waiting in shadows for these radicals. Although a Democrat, he represented the party's furthest right wing: a friend-of-Republicans Democrat, a conservative family-man Democrat who walked to shul on Fridays and had an apparently hate-laced intolerance for divergent "ideals." In the section of his memoirs on Kathy Boudin, he spelled it out himself: "From the instant I knew her identity I was determined not to prosecute an elusive radical butterfly who'd been flitting in and out of public sight and consciousness for twenty years. I was going to prosecute her and her associates as robbers and murderers." In the end, he prided himself for having rid America of this terrible scourge.

A forty-one-year-old father of three in 1985, Ken Gribetz also harbored another obsession: "unbridled sex" (responsible for "undermining the nation's moral structure," he said once). The LeGeros case, with the mounting publicity surrounding it, would become his platform to preach the perils of such activity. He was still on a roll.

His opening statements to the jury offered a cool, matter-of-fact, and emotionless recitation of events, beginning with the thwarted attack on Freddy Rothbell-Mista and ending with the second burning of the body. Bernard LeGeros would not be presented as a confused sex-angry "butterfly"; there would be no wrestling with motive or purpose or rationale. The drug culture went virtually unmentioned, and sadomasochism, bondage, and discipline—that complicated construct of slave and master, good and bad, torture and ecstasy, crime and consent—was contracted in his speech to a breezy, generic adjective: He called the killing "sadistic." "Murder for murder's sake," he explained to a reporter. Simple and horrifying.

Perhaps he felt that, by the end of this trial, a similarly permanent blow to a similarly evil "ideal" would have been struck.

When his turn came to address the ten men and two women of the jury, Murray Sprung was eager to introduce them to the dark world that he believed had seized his young client, and was willing to take off his gloves when he described it. He wanted it condemned, its denizens destroyed. Of course, that meant that Bernard would probably go down, too. But his plea to the jury was straightforward and emotional: If you decide to ship this boy away, please do not spare the "Svengali" Andrew Crispo.

He rose unsteadily from the defense table and inched toward the jurors, slapping his metal walker on the floor before each step. His eyes were small, his ears were big, and his voice was clogged with an old man's phlegm. On his chest were two Asiatic-Pacific ribbons of commendation.

"What you heard Mr. Gribetz state," he began, "was the case that the prosecution hopes to prove against Bernard LeGeros. I would say that a one-sided story was told leaving no room for the possibility of a defense. But we do have a defense. We do have our version of what happened at the time that Bernard LeGeros and Andrew Crispo were together and also what happened with Freddy Rothbell-Mista and Edo Bertoglio and others who were part of the group that frequented these places that we know are places where people are interested in S&M, B&D—outlandish sexual activities."

He barely moved as he spoke. Bernard, looking rested in an expertly tailored gray suit, wore a clear, expressionless face; he scribbled notes to himself on a legal pad.

"Now, this of course will take time and patience and an open mind to listen carefully to what is said. I am not trying to pick apart the presentation of Mr. Gribetz. But remember, you were told that what he says to you and what I say to you is not evidence. It must be proved and you must weigh both sides of the picture before you decide the fate of Bernard LeGeros.

"Now you'll hear during the course of the trial the testimony of psychiatrists, psychologists, and probably some other medical men who will testify. Some on the part of the prosecution and some on the part of the defense. That is a cornerstone of our defense. We say that Bernard LeGeros is innocent by reason of mental defect. That's the legal term." Tensing, Bernard turned his head away from the press and toward the jury, sitting in a box just a few yards away from his table.

"We will also prove that through Andrew Crispo he became a cocaine addict. Andrew Crispo, from August of 1984 to March 1985, fed himself, too, and Bernard, between three and a half and seven grams of cocaine almost daily. Andrew Crispo procured the cocaine. He bought it. He had sent on many occasions Bernard to the narcotics seller with money to purchase the cocaine. It was a daily ritual, I might almost say, for Andrew Crispo to call Bernard into his office and they would what they call *snuff* the cocaine. That became a regular part of the days that Bernard worked for Andrew Crispo.

"Now in addition—and please remember you will hear a lot of things. Mud will be splashed here and there. Bernard LeGeros is not and I repeat is not a homosexual. Andrew Crispo is an admitted homosexual and a participant in these practices that we know as S&M and B&D."

Describing the dramatis personae of Crispo's world, he said, "It is a species of mankind that we—you, decent people—would not believe possible. To have victims who were professional people to visit Andrew Crispo and willingly and happily become his slave. They would put on an apron. They would act as a maid! They would scrub the floors. They would lick the boots of Andrew Crispo. They would do things that I, if I could, blush in relating to you. . . . Think of a man in a good position acting out his part licking the boots of a master that would be Andrew Crispo. Think of that man washing the bathroom and cleaning various items left by the practice of S&M. We can't understand it. We who are normal and act so can't understand what thrills people like that receive because of their unholy acts. When we think of areas where these clubs exist—right here in New York, or parts of Greenwich Village—we have there a Sodom and Gomorrah."

"Now," he said in an apologetic, resolute conclusion, "we are going to take you through the sewers and mud and slush that this case has as its scenes."

*   *   *

Murray Sprung was handed a difficult case, to be sure, but he made it more unwinnable by permitting the post-arrest interviews, each of which had produced boxes of crucial evidence against his client. His legal experience was limited, and in the decade since his stroke, he had restricted his professional duties to handling estates and wills. He hadn't directed a criminal matter since the 1940s, when he prosecuted war criminals in Japan and the Philippines. At eighty-two, with bad hearing and a quavery gate, he hardly seemed the man for the job. "My first reaction was: 'Me? Go to court at my age in a case like this?' " He told the local paper that John LeGeros insisted, saying they'd have nobody else.

During the trial, Sprung repeatedly forgot important details, sometimes including the names of people seated on the stand. His cross-examinations of hostile witnesses amounted to little more than aimless meanderings, and many of his own witnesses only helped to bury Le-Geros, both during his own questioning and after, when Gribetz cross-examined them. Objections, when he made them, often trailed the question by several important moments, allowing the answer to be uttered, and retained by the jury. At least once, Sprung called a witness back to the stand for a line of inquiry identical to the questions he'd already answered.

His best moments came after the court adjourned, when he would hurl invective at Crispo through the press. "You bastard!" he'd call him. "You filthy scum!"

Although he succeeded in issuing a subpoena to Andrew Crispo, the judge ruled that his testimony—a promised recitation of the Fifth Amendment—should take place outside the hearing of the jury. "I'm not going to have Mr. Crispo before this jury for the theatrical effect of taking the Fifth Amendment," he said. Still, Crispo's arrival became the journalistic highlight of the case. A section of the building's second floor was roped off for Crispo's security, and a bathroom was closed to anyone but him; inside the courtroom, a section of the front-row bench was reserved for his bodyguards. Judge Meehan warned spectators that anyone making hostile remarks or gestures to Crispo would be "escorted from the courtroom."

Surrounded by guards and court officers, Crispo entered the room through a side door at 10:45 on Tuesday, September 24. He was dressed in a blue blazer, gray slacks, and a white shirt—his confirmation outfit. As he crossed the courtroom and took the stand, he did not look at Bernard LeGeros once. When he placed his right hand on a Bible, the sound of scratching pencils and flipping notebook pages rose from the press box.

For an unexplained reason, Murray Sprung's young associate was selected to do the questioning. His voice was shaky and stuttering; efforts to attain a courtroom composure were fruitless. Crispo, pale and apparently tired, looked him square in the eye, menacing, daring.

"Good morning. My name is Ken Marshall," he said between deep breaths. "I'm an attorney. You have never met me. I am, just by way of introduction, indicating to you what is occurring here. And your attorney is present to advise you, of course, if you have any questions regarding your understanding of what is occurring."

Robert Kasanof was indeed present, having positioned himself directly between Andrew Crispo and the press box, making it difficult for reporters to watch him testify and nearly impossible for the artists to sketch.

"I am Ken Marshall, attorney," he repeated, "who is assisting Mr. Sprung, who is the family attorney for Bernard LeGeros. I do practice in criminal law."

"Ask a question!" interrupted Kenneth Gribetz.

Judge Meehan seemed equally impatient, having considered the calling of this witness a circuslike ploy, a belief confirmed by the swell of press—now including reporters from as far away as Norway. For the only time in the trial, guards were posted at the door and a metal detector was erected in the hallway. Spectators, and the LeGeros family in particular, were patted down extensively as they entered. Quite sarcastically, the judge turned to Crispo and said, "He's a defense attorney," and to the defense attorney, he instructed, "Proceed."

"I would like to explain to you this situation here," the lawyer continued, apparently hoping to break through to some hidden sense of civic duty. "The situation is simply this is a criminal trial, a very serious matter in which Bernard is being accused."

"May a question be asked?" Gribetz said.

The judge said, "I won't allow this. I want this witness treated as any other witness. But based upon a letter I received from his attorney, and I don't have it here, if he turns out to be like any other witness, he will be placed before the jury. I think it goes without saying this is a criminal trial and Mr. LeGeros is on trial charged with murder. Proceed. And ask a question!"

Spectators continued piling into the back of the room; the LeGeros family sat near the door, solemn, stony faces twitching with anger.

Finally, Ken Marshall asked, "Do you have a business?"

Andrew Crispo turned to the judge and recited a prepared statement:

"I claim my rights under the Fifth and Fourteenth Amendments of the Constitution of the United States of America and under Article One of the Constitution of the State of New York not to be compelled to be a witness against myself."

Those same words were uttered five more times—after questions as innocuous as "Have you ever been in Stony Point?" and as direct as "Where were you on the evening of the twenty-second day of February?"—before the judge dismissed him, saying, "He has a perfect right."

In the lobby of the squat courthouse, forcing a strange smile for the cameras, Andrew Crispo had a bit more to say. "I think the whole affair is a tragedy. It's a tragedy for the family of Eigil Vesti and the family of Bernard LeGeros, and for myself." There was in his words a chilling distance from the events of February 22, and no hint of remorse for Eigil Vesti, the young man he had known for nearly two years.

The reporters who surrounded him did not press the point. One asked how he was holding up through this. "It's a day at a time, like a baseball game. A baseball comes in and you bat it out, and that's the way I'm going to handle it." What was it like seeing his old friend Bernard? "No feelings for or against." Where was he going after this? "I'm going to my acupuncturist to soothe my nerves."

Several feet behind Crispo, Racquel and David LeGeros stood shoulder-to-shoulder, the mother holding firmly on the arm of her son, worried he would move against this man, worried he was entertaining the same thoughts that she could barely suppress.

Sprung's defense had been an affirmative one: Bernard may have wrapped his finger around the trigger, he said, but a weak grip on the world made him not legally guilty. To prove this point, he put the parents on the stand for long stretches, where they replayed the entire LeGeros family history. His father called him an inveterate liar and referred to Bernard's "dreamy" world where myth and reality were indistinguishable. His mother described him as an "oddity." By the time he was fifteen, he believed he was possessed by a team of aliens, she explained to the jury. "One is very nice and kind and the other one would like to be violent." She spoke of his justified fear of abandonment, stemming from her own errors in motherhood. As a newborn, he was checked into a "dormitory of infants" in Yonkers, and saw his parents only on weekends; as an adolescent, she had separated him from his dogs. She believed he had found with Andrew Crispo a parental bond that he had been missing.

Murray Sprung called two psychiatrists, both of whom attested to

Bernard's troubled mind, although under ferocious cross-examination, neither called him insane. Three prosecution psychiatrists found that Bernard deliberately misled them during their exams.

But, despite promising in his opening statement that he would prove how Andrew Crispo had fanned the incident, Sprung called no witnesses who could have explained Crispo's aberrant proclivities. There were no experts on sadomasochism and nobody to describe the effects of excessive cocaine use on one's ability to reason, or on one's sexual impulses. (Observing lab monkeys, UCLA scientists found they'd forgo food and sex in favor of cocaine; observing men, Sigmund Freud noticed a "weakness of the sexual function accompanied by augmented erotic desires." Sadomasochism, a ritualized act stressing scenario over orgasm, could substitute for the now-difficult deed.)

Instead, Sprung relied upon the impressions of Billy Mayer, who first appeared during the prosecution's case. He had him describe a few dark S&M scenarios, and asked him about coke consumption on the evening of the murder. And he coaxed him into discussing the journal he'd kept, even though Gribetz had not entered it into evidence. The grotesque attributions to Bernard in Mayer's writings, Sprung must have figured, would give the jury a telescope into Bernard's disturbances. Mayer wrote that he'd regularly listened to Bernard's tales of death and dying, and had watched his collection of guns grow in the few years they had been close friends. So when LeGeros told him about the murder of Eigil Vesti, he had dismissed it out of hand, considering it "just another game" of make-believe. It took the MISSING poster, then the actual corpse, to convince him.

"I'm coming to grips with the fact that a person whom I like . . . is a psychotic murderer," he wrote. "I assume . . . that Crispo pushed him to the point of no return. And he finally slipped over into the realm of fantasy."

No doubt for the jurors it was a final nail.

Eigil Vesti's sister, Anne-Margrethe, sat silently in the unair-conditioned courtroom as the journal was read. A day earlier, she had trembled while giving testimony about being called to Stony Point to identify the skeletal remains of her brother on closed-circuit television. With the rest of her family, she carted his bones back to place them in a small grave, among a sea of white tombstones. They all agreed Eigil's marker would be black. On the day of Mayer's testimony, Anne-Margrethe Vesti appeared steadier.

"I am sure he didn't belong to the world we are facing in the courtroom," she later told reporters in a heavy Scandinavian accent. "It was just something that happened that night. It was just bad luck." Her voice grew harsh. "Andrew Crispo ought to be on trial here. In Norway, he would be on trial."

Certain important facts about Crispo were brought out during the LeGeros trial. First, that head and pubic hairs "consistent" with samples taken from Andrew Crispo were scattered about the Buckberg house (and discovered by a special police vacuum). But the only head hair taken from inside the mask that didn't belong to Eigil Vesti belonged to Bernard.

One mysterious bit of testimony suggested that Crispo gave Bernard a twelve-thousand dollar check or money order in the days following the killing; this wasn't pursued. A witness said he'd seen the mask before at the gallery, although Billy Mayer, who could have identified the dildo as belonging to Crispo, was not asked to comment on it. When Edo Bertoglio took the stand as a prosecution witness, he spoke only about Bernard's confession to him while standing near a restaurant's cigarette machine. Murray Sprung did not ask about the statements he had made to the grand jury investigating Bernard, despite the fact that Sprung had the statements in a manila file folder on the defense table. Back then, Edo Bertoglio had said that Crispo called him after he first went to the Rockland authorities, in an apparent effort to shut him up. "I know you went to the police," he was quoted as saying. "You know, you don't have to say anything. Don't worry about Bernard, he won't say a thing."

Outside the courtroom, Murray Sprung lamented, "People are losing sight of the fact that the mask belonged to Andrew Crispo, the dildo belonged to Andrew Crispo, the whips belonged to Crispo." Inside, however, he did not help to keep those notions aloft.

"I felt that it was a gross miscarriage of justice," the court reporter, Roslyn Goldstein, said. "The boy should have been entitled to a better lawyer."

Following a brief, pleading summation from Murray Sprung late on the morning of September 26, 1985, after a three-week-long trial, the jury rose and headed for their deliberation room. Judge Meehan called after them, delivering the disturbing news that Hurricane Gloria was expected to pummel the northeast coast sometime that evening. Throughout the day, he said, emergency broadcast signals were tested and tested again; radio reports had focused on the need to tape windows so dangerous glass shards wouldn't go flying. Lawn ornaments and shutters and garbage cans were ordered inside.

The judged promised that if they could reach no conclusion by late afternoon, he would not sequester them in a hotel but would allow them to be at home with their families.

Under this cloud, it took the twelve jurors—including an electrician, a civil engineer, a research scientist, a housewife, and a retired chef—just two and a half hours to reach a verdict. On a mimeographed form, the foreman put a check in the box marked "Guilty," using a blue pen.

The jury believed Gribetz, who had argued that Bernard, "in association with Andrew Crispo, intentionally planned and plotted the murder of Eigil Vesti." Perhaps they also believed him when he said, during his summation, that "the investigation into Crispo's involvement at the present time remains active and eventually, I am sure, justice will be done."

On October 17, the same judge heard arguments before deciding on Bernard's sentence. He considered Bernard uncontrite and belligerent, and called him "a brutal murderer." He gave the convicted killer an opportunity to speak, and was not convinced otherwise by the young man's statement.

"Your Honor," Bernard said, his voice steady. "I wish just to say this: I'm here before you today not because my parents have failed, but because they have succeeded, in that I did not run away to Mexico, I did not run away to Brazil. And I wish to apologize to the family of the deceased, my family, and efforts made by the law-enforcement agencies. I wish to thank them to bring this case to its close. That's all, Your Honor." Judge Meehan sentenced him to twenty-five years to life, the maximum under the law. (A subsequent appeal, alleging incompetence of counsel, was turned down by a higher court.)

More than a month later, on November 29, standing on the steps of the federal courthouse in Manhattan with tax lawyer Stanley Arkin at his side, Andrew Crispo announced that he'd just pleaded guilty to evading more than $4 million in taxes on $10 million in undeclared income. Arkin, who had previously denounced the tax case as being retaliation for his client's alleged role in the Vesti murder, had apparently talked the prosecutors down from a greater penalty. "It was a single, unwise course of action," he said now of Crispo's crime.

Crispo said, "I'm not proud of what I did."

Reporters peppered him with questions, most of which received a "No comment" from Arkin, after whispering huddles with his client. Crispo would pay back the taxes, he said, adding that his gallery was not permanently closed but in "a holding pattern" because of the Vesti case.

On January 27, 1986, Andrew Crispo was sentenced to seven years in prison, and was sent that day to a federal jail in Otisville, New York. He made no statements to the press on his way out of town. Instead, at Sotheby's and Christie's, where his breathtaking collection of prized oils and sculptures were labeled and put up for auction, he issued a written commentary—on his life, on his plight, and on his future.

"I have personally chosen all the paintings and sculptures from the gallery, and my own collection, that are included in this and earlier sales. They were chosen with quality and historical importance in mind. Each work has been a constant source of pleasure to me over the many years that I have collected them. However, as all dealers and collectors know, art ultimately belongs to everyone and eventually must circulate again. It is also my fervent hope that this auction will enable me to make a positive step toward fulfilling the promise I made of repaying my debt to the government."

Among those items sold were an oil by Edward Hopper, *Captain Upton's House*, fetching more than $2 million from a New York dealer. Another Hopper, *Hotel Window*, netted $1.32 million in a bidding war won by Malcolm Forbes. The Guggenheim Museum bought Brancusi's masterpiece, *The Muse*, directly from Crispo for an estimated $3 million, winding up with the piece that had originally been donated to them but, because of a tangle of legal suits including Crispo's, took more than ten years to make its way back.

In all of his sales, Andrew Crispo (and the IRS, and Rosenthal and Rosenthal, who were each listed as co-owners of the works) cashed in art worth nearly $20 million. A former Crispo associate said that was less than a third of Andrew Crispo's entire collection.

According to a cellmate at Otisville, Crispo was not uncomfortable there. He passed his days playing tennis and lifting weights in the jail's fitness compound, offering legal advice, and discussing art with his fellow prisoners. He developed a substantial library, and granted lending privileges to his new friends.

As 1986 progressed, he was also able to breathe relief about the Vesti matter. Gribetz had stopped his public promises of an imminent arrest. He also stopped taking calls from reporters interested in talking about it, curtly announcing, "I don't comment on open investigations."

Under New York State law, the uncorroborated testimony of a confessed accomplice can't be used as the sole evidence against a defendant—meaning that Bernard LeGeros's statements were not enough to bring Crispo to trial. But given the circumstances of this case it is extremely curious that Andrew Crispo wasn't indicted. There was heated speculation as to why not, including persistent rumors that strings were pulled—by, for example, Roy Cohn, Crispo's former attorney and long-time friend. But it is highly unlikely that Cohn—who by 1985 had his own legal problems and had already been diagnosed with AIDS, the disease that would take his mind shortly and his life soon thereafter— could have exerted that kind of influence on a high-profile criminal investigation.

A more likely scenario had the Rockland County DA simply deciding that the case against Crispo was too iffy. "It would be a *very* tough case to win," said Ed Hayes, a prominent New York lawyer who as a prosecutor tried many tough cases. Gribetz had a reputation for being ruthless and successful in the courtroom, and he also had aspirations for a grander political career. A high-profile loss would have been detrimental. Once he had LeGeros locked away, according to a former associate, he seemed satisfied to call it quits. "All he wanted was to close the case, and he believed he had."

Besides, two other sensational cases came his way in late 1985, as the dust from the LeGeros trial still hung in the air. One involved Investigator T. J. McGowan, who had played a key role in the Vesti investigation. He was charged with sexually abusing his young daughter, and was quickly sent to jail.

In the other, a New York City transit cop shot and killed his estranged wife, a city police officer, during a marital spat on a street in Piermont, New York. It was an open-and-shut case, complete with eyewitnesses and melodramatic details, and the press was at Gribetz's doorstep again.

By December of that year, Gribetz quietly called off the grand jury investigating Andrew Crispo. "There is not enough evidence to bring further indictments at this time," he said then. Three years later, he called the investigation "still open" (there is no statute of limitations for murder), but sources said no new leads had been pursued.

"Crispo became a sleeping dog," a law-enforcement official said, "and he chose not to kick it."

What was never made clear in those years was that only two people were called to give testimony as to Andrew Crispo's involvement in the killing of Eigil Vesti to any grand jury. And they were two individuals who knew virtually nothing about such involvement: Arthur Smith, Crispo's partner and next-door neighbor; and Smith's current live-in lover. Not Hal Burroughs or his friend Hank, or P.J., or Edo Bertoglio, or Billy Mayer, or Freddy Rothbell-Mista, or Steven AuCoin, or Sam Collins, the man who had introduced Crispo to Vesti in the first place. Even the cops, who provided testimony in the LeGeros grand jury, were not asked to return. These were people who, individually and collectively, had a firm idea of what evidence did exist; the grand jury members, if they actually convened, did not.

Certainly, there were problems. Some of the more promising angles of the Crispo investigation did not yield much. The "red stains" covering a white notepad and a pair of running shorts found in Crispo's apartment were of too small a quantity to be typed or "printed" with a DNA test; the "unknown substance" from the two couches, evidently semen, could not be definitively traced back to Eigil Vesti.

Then there was the fact that nobody could establish, beyond all doubt, that the sexual devices used on Vesti belonged to Crispo. "Dildos and whips are a lot like staplers," said a former Rockland assistant district attorney who was present during the gathering of evidence. "They all look alike. Who's to say where they came from?" An investigation found that as many as fifty thousand foot-and-a-half-long, stand-alone dildos were in the hands of New York–area consumers, he said. "There was a chance the case would be thrown out of court because of insufficient evidence. And if that happens, we would never be able to bring charges against Crispo again. We agonized over this."

"You can indict a ham sandwich," one official said, "but getting a verdict of guilty is a lot more difficult."

Within the DA's office there was another stumbling block: A consensus could not be formed around Andrew Crispo's alleged intent—the seed of hypothetical doubt planted by his attorney, during their single meeting with authorities, had grown out of bounds. "The question that got us hung up was whether Crispo was playing a kind of S&M game," said an assistant DA, "giving orders that he viewed only as sexual instructions, or did he actually and genuinely order an execution. That was something we had no ability to prove, and without proof you can't win a case."

A Manhattan law-enforcement official saw it differently: "Prosecutors measure their evidence in different ways, using different yardsticks. In my view, they had plenty in this case. We have a monstrous crime here, and to decide not to bring charges—that's just outrageous. Let the jury decide whether he's guilty or not."

On the matter of the death of Eigil Dag Vesti, a jury was never given such an opportunity.

CHAPTER
19

On a warm morning in June 1988, Andrew Crispo strolled into Room 948 of the Manhattan Criminal Court building, looking tanned and fit. When he spotted Darracova in a loud floral shirt in the second row of the small group of spectators, Crispo winked and gave a thumbs-up sign. Darracova, who had befriended Crispo nearly a quarter of a century earlier at the Wickersham Gallery, and who had been shunted aside once Crispo made it to the top, was now firmly back in his life, serving as his astrologist and confidant, and the one man who took in all of Crispo's public appearances.

"He looks *marvelous*," Darracova commented to the man sitting next to him. "He's thin, but not *too* thin. Not *AIDS* thin. He's never looked better." Darracova leaned closer. "You know why he's here, don't you? Petty jealousies. People trying to strip him of his dignity."

Crispo had come in through the back way, via a series of passages linking the Criminal Court building to the Manhattan House of Detention (called, simply, "The Tombs"), where he had been moved from Otisville, and on the roof of which he had developed his tan. The route had allowed him to miss Kenny Morales, a much less sanguine principal in the morning's proceedings. Now twenty-three and with a tiny criminal record of his own, Morales was pacing up and down the hallway outside, his fists jammed into his suit pockets, complaining about how "this whole thing" was a big mistake.

"This whole thing" was a nasty bit of business: Six months earlier, detectives from the Manhattan Sex Crimes squad had located Morales and charged him in the Paul Jeffries case. It was a surprise indictment for everyone concerned, coming more than three years after the alleged kidnapping, torture, and rape had taken place. It seemed that his apprehension would salvage the case.

The reason for the June appearance of Crispo and Morales (minus LeGeros, who had already pleaded guilty and made a lengthy statement to prosecutors) was to establish the pretrial parameters in the case. Crispo, still serving his tax term, was petitioning for separate trials. Kenny Morales probably didn't care much. His Legal Aid lawyer was concerned chiefly with trying to figure out some way around the written confession her client had first given to police and then grabbed away and ripped to pieces. They taped it back together, and it became part of the public record. "The man was whipped," Morales wrote, and "pissed on by Andrew. . . . I also hit the man with a whip." In a separate interview with the detectives, who showed up unannounced at the fifth-floor walk-up apartment in the South Bronx where he lived with his mother, Morales said that the handcuffed victim was forced to kiss his boots.

Bernard LeGeros was there, he said, and so were three graffiti artists, also from the South Bronx—Dax, Zeal, and The Leak. Morales was known to them as "Ken 007." For his labors, Morales said, Crispo paid him $150. The others took cocaine instead of cash. And he added something that prosecutors found very important, something that confirmed Paul Jeffries's story directly. "At the end," Kenny Morales recalled, "the guy thanked Crispo for not killing him. . . . He was scared."

That's why there had been so much pressure on Morales. According to Nina Epstein, his lawyer, the detectives who visited Morales first begged him to testify against Crispo. He refused but agreed to write down his account—thinking the police would then leave him alone. He signed his name "Ken 007." Immediately, though, he panicked. "This could get me in trouble," he told the detectives. He shredded his one-page statement into thirty-five pieces.

The officers left his apartment with most of the scraps and, after a month of fruitless pressure on him, the authorities indicted Morales. Prosecutors immediately began an effort to plead him down—from felony kidnapping to a low-level assault—in exchange for testimony against Crispo. "They're offering him a misdemeanor," Epstein said then. "They want him bad." She encouraged her client to keep quiet.

If the case hadn't dragged on for so long, they might never have found Kenny Morales at all. The delays came from both sides. Linda Fairstein had become enmeshed as the lead prosecutor in the "Yuppie Murder" trial of Robert Chambers, accused of strangling Jennifer Levin during "rough sex" in Central Park. She passed Paul Jeffries down to two junior assistants, Joel Seidemann and Bill Hansen, who struck a kind of Ratzo Rizzo/Midnight Cowboy image behind their oversized courtroom table.

Robert Kasanof, Andrew Crispo's lawyer, also busied himself elsewhere as a member of the bloated defense team that had recently won an acquittal for Raymond Donovan, the Reagan administration labor secretary charged with fraud and grand larceny. With plenty to gain by distancing Crispo's Manhattan case from the raucous coverage of the Eigil Vesti killing in Rockland, Kasanof had requested or acceded to the majority of the postponements that brought them into 1988.

Once his attorney arrived, Morales marched into the courtroom and sat down at the defense table next to Crispo. They were elbow-to-elbow but did not speak. Then Judge Jeffrey Atlas came in, and after some formalities, he handed down an important ruling: Their cases would proceed separately, beginning with Crispo's. Most significantly, it meant that Kenny Morales's two confessions, key pieces of evidence against him, would not be read to a jury considering Crispo's guilt. It also meant that Crispo's jury would never see Morales—moody and savage-looking, despite his double-breasted, unvented suit—who otherwise might have remained at Crispo's side like a time bomb.

The unfortunate effect, from the DA's perspective, was that they were back at square one in their case against Crispo. It would be the word of Paul Jeffries, a clean-cut, cocaine-using sadomasochist, against a prominent, better-dressed, softer-spoken citizen. By law, no juror would learn of Crispo's criminal status; he would not have to prove his side of the story, just disprove enough of Jeffries's account to create a reasonable doubt.

Bernard LeGeros, now a resident of the Clinton Correctional Facility in upstate New York, would also make an appearance in the trial. But cross-examination could easily reveal that he was a convicted murderer, a strange, tough-talking former associate of the defendant with his own axes to grind. Besides, he had a deal with the prosecutors: In exchange for "truthful" testimony, they would not seek a maximum sentence for his own confessed role in the case. Juries view deals with suspicion.

Crispo wasn't expected to testify, and there were hints that the defense would call no witnesses. Kasanof's comments, then, would become the only representation of Andrew Crispo's perspective on the charges, and in the hallway outside Room 948, he churned the press with heavy oars.

"There is no crime here," he said that summer afternoon. "What we have is a case of mutual sexual eccentricities. It was a sexual game of ice hockey, no more or less. Not my cup of tea, exactly—not innocent, but not criminal in any way. As Prince Edward said, 'I don't care what you do as long as it doesn't scare the horses.'"

Kasanof's Andrew Crispo—out of the public eye since 1986—was a gentle, sensitive, misunderstood victim of circumstances, a casualty of his own successes who wanted only to return to private life. He was a latter-day Oscar Wilde whose sexual escapades, in a civilized world, should have remained his own business. After an earlier appeal, Crispo's seven-year tax sentence had been rolled back to just five. "Once this trial is over," Kasanof said, "he could be eligible for a halfway house or another remedy to his confinement. He's ready to put all this behind him and resume his productive life."

Reporters found Robert Kasanof to be an immensely agreeable source for the story, particularly in comparison to the sullenness of Joel Seidemann, whose policy of never granting interviews kept him outside the dubious give-and-take relationship that his opponent was enjoying. Kasanof's exaggerated dramatics, his jowly old–New York irreverence, quick wit, and natural patter with the press (all of whom were years younger than he) helped win allies. "Walk with me," he would say to one reporter or another, embarking on an exclusive stroll through the ninth-floor corridors to "leak" various aspects of his defense.

For the most part, these were not experienced court reporters, or they would have been stationed at one of the more flashy courtroom dramas already in progress. The fall of 1988 had a bumper crop of hot trials, led by Bess Myerson, the former Miss America and former make-believe girlfriend of Mayor Ed Koch, charged with bribing the judge hearing her boyfriend's divorce case. Next in importance was Joel Steinberg, who, with common-law wife Hedda Nussbaum, had been charged in the murder of a girl they had illegally adopted.

Robert Kasanof used his power over the press in a devious way. He launched a campaign against the alleged victim, stressing that "this is his ultimate degradation, his ultimate fantasy—don't you see? Standing up before the court and the press and humiliating himself? He loves this." He intimated that Jeffries was a drug dealer, that he was "a game player," a gold digger, a fraud. "He was looking for a job! He thought more would come of their liaison, and now he's mad."

Kasanof complained frequently that Paul Jeffries's true identity was not publicly known (for thirty-five years, the press and the courts had agreed informally to protect the identities of sex-crime victims). Especially when squinting into television lights, Kasanof spat out Jeffries's real name as often as possible, making it difficult to glean a pithy sound bite from him without breaking tradition. Long before the jury was seated in mid-September, almost every paper and television news report had given up trying, and, following Kasanof's lead, they shattered the trust.

Jurors and the public were not the primary target of this pretrial hallway strategy. Paul Jeffries, who had been relocated to Montreal by New York City police, was. And the message Kasanof hoped would reach him there was how ugly this was going to get. To at least one reporter, Kasanof strongly suggested Jeffries had been suffering from AIDS (this was never printed), while telling another there was a chance he wouldn't show for the trial (this was).

It didn't end there. Late the year before, Paul Jeffries had begun furtively calling his friends from pay phones in Quebec. "Crispo's got people following me," he breathlessly told Karl, his former New York roommate. He told another friend that they were "perched outside his window, taking pictures of him when he came and left." He moved out of his new apartment, quit his job, and went underground. Only a handful of close friends—and Linda Fairstein—knew how to find him.

He told Joel Seidemann, the ADA, that two police officers came to his door one night with a summons for his arrest on an old marijuana charge, one that had been settled long ago. At their sides were two private detectives, hired by Crispo. Although the legal mix-up was straightened out later that evening, Jeffries said, the detectives did not go away. They followed him everywhere. (Kasanof later admitted sending detectives to Montreal but denied the harassment charge.)

Bernard was reporting similar, though less traceable, pressure as the trial approached. Mark Weinstein, his new attorney, said Bernard was experiencing "some sort of harassment" that he believed came from Crispo. "He found himself in a holding pen with Crispo at the courthouse," where he had recently been moved, the lawyer said, despite the existence of a separation order instructing court officers to keep them apart. And Weinstein said that his client was roughed up on several occasions. During one of the incidents, Weinstein said, "Bernard was issued a very pointed threat. 'You could be hurt very easily,' he was told." Prison officers confirmed that Bernard had lodged a number of complaints alleging beatings at the hands of prison guards. A Bureau of Corrections official said that in one of the complaints Bernard gave badge numbers for his alleged assailants, but the numbers did not correspond to current employees. "He may have been beaten," the official said, "but we just don't know by whom."

Andrew Crispo, it seemed, was not going to play by the rules, even here.

Jury selection took six days and precluded anybody who appeared antigay—and there were many. A Jehovah's Witness said he "followed the instructions of the Tribe" in matters sexual; another said, "I am very unbending and intolerant with homosexuality." More than one hundred people were excused, including the two who were openly gay, one of them because he exhibited an excellent recollection of the Vesti murder. "Contaminated," Kasanof said. "His recollection might poison the rest of the jury."

Judge Atlas agreed. For his part, he wanted nothing to do with the Rockland matter. "I'm as much interested in gossip as anybody else," he said, "but this trial is not about Eigil Vesti, as much as some people would like it to be."

In part because of this cautiousness, Atlas rejected the prosecutor's desire to call Hal Burroughs as a witness. Seidemann said Burroughs could testify about similar acts, and would say what happened to the gun that was held to Paul Jeffries's head. "He disposed of it," Seidemann pleaded. "He was asked by Mr. Crispo to dispose of several items, including a starter's pistol, holster, shield, and some whips. It's alleged that the pistol was the one involved in the instant case." Atlas said no.

Filling the jury box for the first time on the morning of September 27, 1988, all twelve members appeared smart and comfortable. Most were college-educated; most were white. They ranged in age from early twenties to early seventies. Sitting on the edge of their chairs, they seemed embarrassed to look directly at Andrew Crispo, who sat childlike in his confirmation outfit—a large blue Armani blazer and baggy gray pants—studying them unflinchingly from the defense table. His eyes were clear, cool, and mahogany-colored, as they had been in his youth. He appeared much younger than his forty-four years. The only hint of his more slovenly appearance "before" was worn on his nostrils: Slashing red and blue veins were evident even from the second row of the courtroom.

Judge Atlas, a young and very casual man, was the first to address the jurors. His aviator-shaped glasses, open robe, and maroon and white striped shirt seemed to put them at ease. When a point needed emphasis, he waved a thin plastic swizzle stick (explaining, "Not too many of us use a gavel anymore"). "The accused in this case is named Andrew Crispo," he said. "He is accused, by an indictment, of several crimes. They include, in the first count, the crime of kidnapping in the second degree.

In New York County, on or about September 20, 1984, it is claimed that the accused kidnapped a person known to the grand jury. That Andrew Crispo abducted this person.

"There's another charge of unlawful imprisonment in the third degree, and a third, of assault in the second degree . . . with intent to cause physical injury to this individual, known to the grand jury, by means of a dangerous instrument, to wit a whip.

"It goes on to charge another count of the same, then the fifth charge, the crime of coercion in the first degree . . . held and induced another person to engage in a certain act that the person had a right not to do.

"Finally, the defendant is accused of the crime of sodomy in the first degree . . . a claim that Andrew Crispo committed this crime, that he engaged in deviant sexual intercourse *by forceable compulsion.*"

As Atlas spoke, stressing key words, breezily uttering others, a television camera stationed in a far corner of the room focused on Andrew Crispo's face, almost completely covered by his hand. The large doors in the back squeaked open, and Linda Fairstein, the lead Sex Crimes prosecutor, entered quietly and filed into a bench seat behind the reporters.

"This case," Atlas continued, "as I'm sure you may be guessing, will necessarily involve an explicit discussion of this claimed sexual conduct. I believe you will hear testimony concerning homosexuality, oral sex, and claims concerning sadomasochistic actvity between adult males. By sadomasochism, I mean an act where one person, for the purpose of enhancing sexual enjoyment, inflicts pain and suffering, physically or mentally, on another person who, in turn, derives a sexual pleasure from the act. This activity is said to include but is not limited to the use of several instruments, including whips, chains, handcuffs, and similar devices. . . . Under certain circumstances, the restraint of another person, or the striking of another person, or even the sodomizing of another person, *under some circumstances*, may not be against the law."

Kasanof's law partner, Mary Shannon, had been resting one hand on Crispo's forearm during the judge's introductory cautionary words. Now she turned to her client and, smiling, brushed invisible lint off his lapel. Looking back toward the judge, she allowed her hand to linger casually, safely, over her client's shoulder. A moment later, she stroked her fingers down his suit coat and parked them, once again, near his cuff. For the duration of the trial, her soft hand would only seldom leave that spot; its presence there told the jury that this was not a dangerous man.

Just before lunch on September 27, 1988, Paul Jeffries took the witness stand following brief opening statements from Joel Seidemann and Robert

Kasanof. He seemed small and skinny, and his gray suit—wrinkled from the suitcase he'd brought from Montreal—bunched up at his shoulders. His blue-checkered tie was reflected off his eyes, which were bright enough to be seen from all over the large courtroom.

Seidemann addressed him delicately, as though he were too frail or too wounded to go over the material once more; his replies were delivered in a soft voice, occasionally interrupted by whimpering, and then silence. Several times, Jeffries asked for a recess, to pull himself together.

His testimony continued after lunch, and into the next day, when Mary Shannon began a cross examination with all the personality of a dominatrix. "Sir," she barked, "is it not true that you told Mr. Crispo that you get the biggest thrill of your life having your life in somebody's hands?" She stood square in front of him, one arm cocked behind her back crisply.

"What I said was—"

"Sir! Answer my question, sir!"

"No."

"Isn't it true, sir, that you enjoy being fist fucked?"

"No," he said.

"You have *never* been fist fucked?"

"To the best of my knowledge, I have attempted to be on two or three occasions, but it didn't work for me."

"But you wanted it? Answer the question."

"Yes. Yes, I did."

She drilled him on his finances, established that the Canadian had allowed his student visa to expire, had falsified a Social Security number in order to continue working, had developed a cocaine habit which he couldn't afford.

"You were hoping to meet people who could help you advance your career, is that right?"

"No, ma'am."

"You had no interest whatsoever, sir, in hoping to get assistance from Mr. Crispo in the art world, is that right?"

"No. I mean yes."

"Sir. At that time, you thought that Mr. Crispo would be a fruitful source of cocaine, didn't you?"

"That's not correct."

"Sir. At that time you believed that Mr. Crispo could help you through your time of financial need, is that not true?"

Jeffries began barking his replies to Shannon's questions in the same tone she was using, no longer whispering demurely. Once, he called her "sir," in the same militarized tone with which she had addressed him. It made his earlier testimony under direct examination seem theatrical, rehearsed; now he appeared to possess a combative personality.

Through the next day, and into a third day, she marched back and forth in front of him, plying him with questions which he was now shouting down as "lies" and "fabrications" and "total untruths." Shannon suggested that the two men didn't meet over the telephone, but had socialized a week earlier at the Mineshaft; that Jeffries had even visited the gallery previous to the alleged incident; that when Crispo finally gave him a check for $110, it was with the understanding that Jeffries would buy him cocaine; that three months later Jeffries left a message at the gallery saying, "Let's keep in touch." She offered no proof for these allegations; she just hurled the charges at Jeffries and let the jury watch him wrestle them to the ground.

Finally, she attacked the issue of Jeffries's delay in reporting the crime. "Sir," she said, "when you left the Five Oaks, you didn't stop a police officer, did you?"

"No," he said quietly.

"So you never went to any law-enforcement official in September 1984, did you?"

"No."

"Or October. Did you?"

With each month she rattled off, he answered in the negative, fidgeting in the witness stand. He had been instructed by Judge Atlas that he could not mention the Eigil Vesti case, could not tell the jury why he came forward when he did, could not "smuggle in the Rockland matter," as Kasanof put it. In this informational void, then, Shannon was free to plant in the jury a different impression: She made it appear as though he had expected more from their initial liaison, and when nothing more materialized, he felt spurned—and pressed these outrageous charges. She asked him 647 questions in all, not one of which was about the alleged crimes of September 20, 1984.

Bernard John LeGeros took the stand on September 30, at eleven in the morning. Now twenty-six, he had lost his boyish slenderness and his face and neck were thick and stiff. Under his left eye, a small scar had appeared. Though he wore a new navy suit and a soft maroon tie, he seemed taut, dangerous. When he spoke, he became everybody's idea of a convict.

About his initial telephone conversation with Jeffries, who told him to "Go fuck yourself," he told the jury: "I said, 'Do you know who the fuck you're talking to?' And I told Andrew, 'I'm going to kick the shit out of

that piece of shit.' " About accosting Jeffries in the gallery's waiting room
later that day, he said: "I told him if he didn't shut up I'd put his head
through the fucking wall—those were my exact words." When asked if
he had ever had sexual relations with Andrew Crispo, he threw himself
backward in the witness chair. "*Hell* no," he said, then looked over at
his old friend with repulsion.

It was nearly impossible to imagine that Bernard John LeGeros and
Andrew John Crispo—the soft-faced, childlike man sitting speechlessly
beside Mary Shannon—had anything in common. Except for the fact
that his statements to the court echoed Paul Jeffries's comments directly,
they seemed otherwise unbelievable. When he said Jeffries "seemed like
he was in pain," it was difficult to imagine that Crispo might have enjoyed
that. It was easier, as Robert Kasanof himself suggested, to picture Bernard LeGeros as "a galloping liar" who was "circling over the carcass of
his fabrications."

The trial resumed on October 4, the following Tuesday, and the prose-
cution filled the week with police witnesses, a doorman from the Fuller
Building, and a thwarted attempt to call a psychologist to testify on the
Stockholm Syndrome—that strange penchant of a hostage to identify
with those holding him prisoner. And at 11:59 on Friday morning, Joel
Seidemann stood and announced: "Your Honor, The prosecution rests."
At noon, Robert Kasanof rose and cleared his throat. "The defense rests,"
he said without calling a single witness.

On Tuesday, October 11, 1988, at 10:45 A.M., Kasanof began his
summation to the jury, poking holes in the case, arbitrarily bouncing
from one witness to another, and back, underscoring "contradictions"
and "the bills of goods." He called Jeffries "the Blanche Dubois" of
cocaine addicts and "the Mimi Sheraton of sadomasochism"; of Jeffries's
conversations with LeGeros, he said: "Two cinema verité critics having
tea." Kasanof concluded on an incredulous note. "And at the end of a
perhaps peculiar social event, this festival, he says, 'I'll go for dinner,
but I'm not paying for it.' You decide."

Joel Seidemann's turn came at 1:35 P.M., and he began with an acknowledgment that his oratory skills were no match for Kasanof's. "If
eloquence were evidence," he said, "Mr. Crispo would be sitting pretty
at this moment." He spoke for over an hour, and at 3:15 Tuesday afternoon, Atlas began a two-hour lecture defining the law, defining sadomasochism and sodomy, and sent the jury to deliberate shortly before six.

On Wednesday, October 12—the first full day of deliberation—a me-
lée broke out in the jury room and produced shouting so loud it could

be heard in the hallway outside. According to two notes passed out by the jury forewoman, Ara Derderian—juror number five—had been playing an ungentlemanly role in the proceedings. There was no question about the allegiances of Derderian, a sixty-one-year-old, wide-bellied architect who wore pink-lens aviator glasses low on his shiny nose. Each morning, after sinking into his seat in the jury box, he had actually winked at Andrew Crispo, who responded with a smile and a raised hand. As testimony was spoken from the bench, their eyes frequently met—without expression—and for several steely, unblinking minutes, the room became tense with their silent communiques, as though a crackling fiber had linked them. Each evening, on his way out the back door, juror number five had flipped a slight wave over his shoulder.

Judge Atlas summoned the jury back to the courtroom to upbraid them. "I'm asking you—no, I'm *directing* you—to go back to the jury room and discuss this case in a rational and civilized way. This is a rational and civilized process; there will be no personalizing of these differences."

On Thursday, he received another note from the forewoman, this one pleading for intervention. "We, the jury, request that something drastic be done regarding the outbursts of juror number five," the note said. "One juror has approached me because she is afraid of physical harm, and judging (if I may) by the altercation yesterday, she may have reason to feel afraid. There has been another exchange this morning leaving me uncomfortable about continuing deliberations with this juror. The problems we've had all along are building and unfortunately are affecting the deliberations of the other jurors. We also question his impartiality in light of these events." Again, the judge lectured the entire jury and sent them back.

Deliberations resumed without incident on Friday, and by Saturday afternoon another note came out, this one asking for permission to attend church services the following day. Atlas made arrangements and announced the court would not resume until noon Sunday.

At five after three on Sunday afternoon, the forewoman sent out a note announcing a partial verdict had been reached, and at 4:50, after heated conferences with the attorneys, Atlas agreed to accept their verdict on all but the charge of unlawful imprisonment, a charge on which he accepted that they were "hopelessly divided." Crispo was asked to stand at the defense table, and the forewoman—a stern, slim, fashionable woman in her late thirties who had sat through testimony with her chin pinched between the thumb and index finger of her left hand—spoke in a deep, angry voice. She pronounced Andrew Crispo not guilty of kidnapping, assault, coercion, and sodomy.

Crispo didn't move for a moment, except to slacken his jaw almost imperceptibly. He then nodded to the judge, turned and spoke in the direction of Ara Derderian. "Thank you," he said, the only words anyone in the courtroom would hear him utter.

The DA's office immediately announced they would not seek a new trial on the remaining charge.

In an angry rebuttal to the jury and the judge, Paul Jeffries issued his own statement through a spokesman. He called Atlas's rulings from the bench "subtly biased" and designed to swing the verdict toward Crispo. "The jury couldn't know that I was speaking for scores of other men, the victims of Andrew Crispo," Jeffries said.

He had returned to Montreal following his testimony with the belief that his ordeal was over. What he found, however, was that the local paper had received a photograph of him through anonymous channels—identical to a picture that Kasanof had entered into evidence in the Manhattan case—and ran it alongside a story about the trial. His real name had been featured prominently. Once again, he packed his bags. This time, he fled to Vancouver, British Columbia, as far away from Montreal as a Canadian could go.

Only one New Yorker knew how to reach him. Bill Elverman, a playwright, had been keeping Jeffries abreast of developments from a pay phone in the court building. When the verdict was read, Elverman let loose a deep grunt, as though he'd been thrown to the ground. It was the only noise in the room.

After a brief call to Vancouver, Elverman stood in the dirty hallway outside the courtroom facing television cameras, the transcribed statement quavering violently in his large hands. "I was speaking for scores of other men, the victims of Andrew Crispo," Elverman read. "Of course, I couldn't speak for Eigil Vesti. It was too late for that. I thank God that I'm alive."

His comments were cut short by a frantic press charge for the elevators, reporters racing toward the cool garage beneath the Criminal Court building, hoping to catch the jurors as they left. There, one stopped to speak to reporters while the others pushed past him, into the street and back to their lives. On their way, each of them fired an angry glance at Ara Derderian, who strolled out to the sidewalk behind 111 Centre Street, smiling with exhaustion.

"We simply didn't find the witnesses credible," he said. "Not LeGeros, not Jeffries." Explaining, he added, "There was a master-slave relationship that had been established between Jeffries and Crispo. Jeffries did not protect himself by saying there was a limit." He said three jurors had been holding out for conviction on the last count. "You just couldn't shake them of that."

Pressed to discuss the outburst in the deliberation room, he called it a "personality conflict" that, he insisted, had been settled. Asked about his winking and smiling at Crispo, he brightened and explained it this way: "I have had the occasion to be the subject of somebody accusing me of out-and-out lies, too."

EPILOGUE

For orchestrating the Paul Jeffries evening, for paying people to beat and humiliate him, for importuning his friend Hal Burroughs to scatter the relevant contents of his bag of toys along a Connecticut highway, Andrew Crispo received no additional time in prison. He quietly served out the remainder of his tax sentence. His two codefendants were not so lucky.

Later that year, Bernard LeGeros had four additional years tagged onto his life term for his role in imprisoning and beating Paul Jeffries. On a sweltering day the following summer, Kenny Morales withdrew his not-guilty plea and admitted to having beaten Paul Jeffries in an incident that, he acknowledged, lacked any semblance of consent. He apologized. He was sentenced to several months in prison, which in real time (given early parole and "good time" accumulations) amounted to a little over five weeks.

A month later, in early July 1989, Andrew Crispo was released from federal prison after serving three and a half years of his sentence. The event went unnoticed in the media, and Crispo returned to his life with Arthur Smith at the West Twelfth Street property they shared.

As a welcome-home gift, Smith had redecorated Crispo's beloved Southampton estate and stuffed it full of his favorite possessions: Arman's

Pouring Blue, Hockney's *Une Autre Piscine à Minuit*, works by Ilya Bolotowsky, Thomas H. Hinckley, and Robert Motherwell. Over the varnished teak tub in the varnished teak bathroom, he hung Fernando Botero's famed *Hommage à Bonnard*, a painting by the artist whose penchant for lissome young women was nearly as notorious as Crispo's affinity for narrow-hipped boys. Esoteric, eccentric, enigmatic Andrew Crispo would, undoubtedly, enjoy the joke.

And a very public joke it was. Smith had the two-story white stucco home photographed and written up in a six-page spread in *Architectural Digest*, in the July issue—just in time for his friend's release.

It is not known whether Andrew Crispo had an opportunity to visit the house, and the millions in artwork displayed there, during his first two weeks as a free man. The house was believed to have been unoccupied on July 22, a pristine, blue Saturday afternoon that drew scores of Southampton neighbors to their country homes. News anchorman Chuck Scarborough, for example, had spent the morning stretched out just beyond the thick hemlock hedge that separated his property from Crispo's; his wife, Anne Ford Uzielli, entertained the two children indoors. Finance wizard Felix Rohatyn was at his Southampton home, as was Frances Lear, the publisher, and Alfred Taubman, the chairman of Sotheby's fine-art auction house.

A cloud or two skipped above the high summer sky, hopscotching the gusty breezes that puffed off the ocean a block away.

If Scarborough smelled the gas, the significance didn't register. The afternoon was full of sweet, fleeting vacation scents: charcoal fires, salt air, lotions, trimmed lawns and bushes, and spices. If this had been a younger or more common community, the whoops of children might have also floated through the crystalline air. Except for the splashing of ocean waves and the intimate whistle of wind through each neighbor's ears, there was silence. The explosion came with no other warning.

It rumbled first beneath a concrete patio near the sunken pool, and spread instantly below the entire stucco structure. The blast was raw, unheralded, immediate. It sent the flat roof tilting and twirling overhead and into the wind. It blew the hemlocks flat over, giving the flash and the roar a clean, unfiltered channel in every direction. A second explosion, and a third, staged a decibel competition with the collapsing walls, bursting windows, rocketing bricks, tiles, statues, the roof returning to earth.

In an instant, the two-story house was leveled. Over the next several minutes, large pieces of debris showered down on nearby roofs and distant ones. Police found artifacts from the wood-paneled library a half a mile away.

Chuck Scarborough and his wife were in their second-floor bedroom when the roof headed their way, casting an immense shadow over their estate. Long before they could gather in their first breaths, the fire took off. Great erect tongues of flame penetrated the summer sky with a wailing intensity. They drew pulsing arches fifty feet tall—sizzling, lashing, retreating, and thrusting upward again. Stringy black cables of smoke shot like fireworks in every direction, carrying the acrid smells of flaming oil paintings, antiques, and lacquered walls, accounting for the sticky richness of the pollutant. A twisted column of it darkened the air in all directions, visible even to downtown merchants several miles away.

Not more than two minutes had passed before the entire stucco house, piled densely upon itself, was engulfed in a crackling, imperial white-orange ball. The crab apple tree that had stood in the circular drive burst into flames. Green leaves of a dogwood tree near Gloria Vanderbilt's property curled up like caterpillars, broke loose, and launched themselves upward on dark ripples of soot. Fires crawled about on the sodded lawn where years earlier police had searched for bodies. They raced beneath the Douglas Abdell sculpture and hopped at the roots of the surrounding shrubbery. Cinders leapt the bushes toward the street, toward the town, toward the city, screaming horrible, pounding epitaphs.

Chuck Scarborough bolted around his home to check for damage, to count the broken windows. He glanced in a mirror to assess his wounds, and then shouldered a small video camera. It was a newsman's reflex. The footage he captured, in the minutes before the fire fighters arrived, showed how complete and violent the damage had been. When breezes cut a sight path through the blackness, they revealed that only a single two-story chimney remained stiffly erect. The rest, in a heartbeat, was gone.

Like the other hallmark incidents that embody Andrew Crispo's life, the explosion on Gin Lane was rife with speculation. Some people wanted to believe he set the blaze himself as part of an insurance scam. Others wanted to call it private revenge against a man who had skirted any legal accountability for the Eigil Vesti slaying.

A corrections officer who had met Crispo during his incarceration suggested another explanation. "He talked too much," he told an acquaintance, "made enemies." Former Crispo associates believed the "enemies" included certain high-level members of the Gambino crime family, imprisoned at the Manhattan House of Detention at roughly the same time Crispo was there awaiting his trial in the Paul Jeffries case.

The Long Island Lighting Company, for its part, said a gas leak under a solid concrete patio was the source, and labeled it an accident. In the weeks following the incident, Andrew Crispo blamed LILCO, and Robert Kasanof told reporters the artwork was underinsured—he placed its value at nearly $2 million, and said the insurance policy was for a fraction of that. In addition, police estimated the house's value at near a million and a half.

A few months later, Kasanof was quietly removed from the case. Crispo's new attorney said the works were worth more than $6 million. In legal papers filed against the utility company, he said the house had a market value of $3.5 million. They sued for $10 million, according to the attorney, to keep similar tragedies from befalling other LILCO customers. "There but for the grace of God go their houses," the lawyer said.

A longtime associate of Crispo's, and a frequent visitor to the Southampton house, could not entertain the theory that Crispo had done this himself. "That was his favorite possession," said the friend, "his dream house, his fantasy house. It was the only thing he owned outright, without Arthur Smith. It was his private possession. Losing that house and all those paintings inside," he said, "was the worst thing that could ever have happened to Andrew. Worse than going to jail, worse than losing his gallery or his friends. Total devastation."

But the friend, citing the impeccable timing of the destruction, was equally adamant in his support of the revenge theory. "When that house exploded, it was a punishment greater than anything he might have gotten in the Vesti case. It was justice. If somebody caused this, they knew Andrew very, very well."

Finding the truth behind whatever touched off the explosion, in the end, was a quest with which only the utility company concerned itself. Andrew Crispo's friends and enemies, casual acquaintances and sexual partners and slaves have all received signs from the incident that crystallized their impressions of the man: victim, or villain, or mob informant, or cursed.

Perhaps Andrew Crispo enjoyed the mystery in this turn of events, just as he had fanned the enigmas of his youth. It resonated, literally, with the maxim Ronnie Caran had offered a dozen years before, and Crispo had embraced: "Make sure there's lots of smoke and flames. Otherwise, nobody will notice that you were here at all."

After all, a bursting home in the middle of one of the country's most exclusive enclaves was an exciting announcement that another phase of Andrew Crispo's life was behind him, and a new one lay ahead. He was back from exile.

I N D E X